WRITING AND IDENTITY

D1615129

STUDIES IN WRITTEN LANGUAGE AND LITERACY

AIM AND SCOPE

The aim of this series is to advance insight into the multifaceted character of written language, with special emphasis on its uses in different social and cultural settings. It combines interest in sociolinguistic and psycholinguistic accounts of the acquisition and transmission of literacy. The series focusses on descriptive and theoretical reports in areas such as language codification, cognitive models of written language use, written language acquisition in children and adults, the development and implementation of literacy campaigns, and literacy as a social marker relating to gender, ethnicity, and class. The series is intended to be multi-disciplinary, combining insights from linguistics, psychology, sociology, education, anthropology, and philosophy.

Volume 5

Roz Ivanič
Writing and Identity

WRITING AND IDENTITY

THE DISCOURSAL CONSTRUCTION OF IDENTITY IN ACADEMIC WRITING

ROZ IVANIČ
Lancaster University

JOHN BENJAMINS PUBLISHING COMPANY
AMSTERDAM/PHILADELPHIA

TM The paper used in this publication meets the minimum requirements of American National Standard for Information Sciences — Permanence of Paper for Printed Library Materials, ANSI Z39.48-1984.

Library of Congress Cataloging-in-Publication Data

Ivanič, Roz.
  Writing and identity : the discoursal construction of identity in academic writing / Roz Ivanič
    p.   cm. -- (Studies in written language and literacy, ISSN 0929-7324 ; v. 5)
  Includes bibliographical references (p.) and index.
    1. English language--Rhetoric--Study and teaching--Psychological aspects. 2. English language--Rhetoric--Study and teaching--Great Britain. 3. Academic writing--Study and teaching--Psychological aspects. 4. Discourse analysis--Psychological aspects. 5. English language--Discourse analysis. 6. English language--Written English. 7. Identity (Psychology) I. Title. II. Series.
PE1404.I9   1997
808'.04207--dc21   97-23076
ISBN 90 272 1797 1 (Eur.) / 1-55619-322-X (US) (Hb; alk. paper)   CIP
ISBN 90 272 1798 X (Eur.) / 1-55619-323-8 (US) (Pb; alk. paper)

John Benjamins Publishing Co. • P.O.Box 75577 • 1070 AN Amsterdam • The Netherlands
John Benjamins North America • P.O.Box 27519 • Philadelphia PA 19118-0519 • USA

For my family:

John and Eve Sutton,
Murray, Molly and Annabel Sutton,
and
Milan, Tim and Suzanna Ivanič

Contents

List of Figures

Acknowledgments

I am particularly grateful to the people who have been most closely involved with the book: David Barton — the Ph.D. supervisor, colleague and friend who has supported me immeasurably throughout the research and writing; Romy Clark and Mary Lea — colleagues in the field of academic literacy who took the time to give me detailed and valuable feedback on a draft version of the whole book; and Brian Street — the series editor who not only gave meticulous and inspiring editor's feedback, but also gave me the encouragement to produce this book.

I thank all the students, colleagues and friends who have encouraged me, discussed ideas and given me insights which have contributed to work in progress on this book. Thanks especially to the members of the Teaching of Writing Group, who must have become thoroughly bored with the topic of writer identity, and members of the Literacy Research Group: discussions in those groups have been particularly valuable to me. Thanks also to my co-researchers, most of whom have also become friends: you have been a constant source of inspiration and, as I explain frequently, have provided the majority of insights on which this book is based.

Thanks to individual friends and colleagues have done special things for me at particular times:

– to Tim Johns, the person who first inspired me to study linguistics, whose standards as a linguist and educator I am constantly trying to emulate;
– to Meriel Bloor, Kathy Doncaster, Norman Fairclough, Mary Hamilton, Greg Myers, Rachel Rimmershaw, Al Thomson and Sue Weldon for reading and responding to drafts of different sections for me: your second opinions were enormously helpful;
– to Benita Cruickshank, Andrew (Disk Doctor) Littlejohn and Wilma Shaw for being true friends with their practical advice and moral support;

–   to Dick Allwright, for all his words of wisdom about academic writing, but particularly for the ones which I have pinned above my screen, which I needed to heed over and over again while writing this book:

If you have a problem, share it with your reader.

With all these people's help, what, one may ask, is the identity of the writer?

Above all, I thank my family for all their support, patience, encouragement and practical help over the six years of research and writing this book, and always.

* * * * *

I am grateful to Sarah Padmore and the Research and Practise in Adult Literacy group for permission to reproduce on the front cover and on page 8; to Biff Products for permission to reproduce the Biff cartoon on page 87; to Addison Wesley Longman Ltd. for permission to reproduce Figures 2.1 and 5.2; and Verso for permission to reproduce the extract on page 194.

To cheer you up before you start reading

One day while I was working on this book my daughter Suzanna, who was aged seven at the time, came and looked at what I was writing, and said:

Suzanna   Mummy, why do you keep on writing the word 'discourses' ?
Roz   Erm ...
Suzanna   Anyway, when I read it I thought it said 'dinosaurs'.

CHAPTER 1

Introduction

Me and you

Who am I as I write this book? I am not a neutral, objective scribe conveying the objective results of my research impersonally in my writing. I am bringing to it a variety of commitments based on my interests, values and beliefs which are built up from my own history as a white English woman aged 51 from a middle class family, as an adult educator in multi-ethnic, central London in the 1970s and 80s, as a wife and mother, as someone who only seriously engaged with the academic community in my late thirties, now a lecturer in a department of linguistics, teaching and researching in the field of language, literacy and education. I am a writer with a multiple social identity, tracing a path between competing ideologies and their associated discourses. I have an idea of the sort of person I want to appear in the pages of this book: responsible, imaginative, insightful, rigorous, committed to making my research relevant to adults who return to study. At any rate that is the sort of person I think I want to be as a member of the academic discourse community. I would want to appear responsible, imaginative, insightful, rigorous and committed in most of my social roles, but not all. For example, I'm not sure how important it is to me in my role as a mother to be rigorous. There are also parts of my identity as a mother which I don't think I portray in my academic writing, such as being loving.

Who are you, the reader? This is a difficult question for a writer to answer, as you will see in detail in Chapters 6 and 8. I am picturing you as someone who has a professional interest in writing: probably a teacher of writing, perhaps someone who is doing research about writing, maybe not very familiar with linguistics — probably more familiar with one of the other social sciences. I don't know your nationality, which language(s) you speak, or anything about your cultural background and experience. What can I take for granted that you know about, so I only need to allude to it in my writing?

What do you need me to spell out in detail because it is not entirely familiar to you? What are your positions on issues which come up in this book? Which positions on contentious issues can I assume you will agree with, and which will I need to support with persuasive argument? What would you consider irrelevant, tedious, or too basic for me to be writing about in this book? What, if anything, do you know and think about me, before you start reading? In the light of all this, how are you going to react to the identity that I am constructing for myself as a write? Will we get along well together, or will I alienate you? The answer to these questions will be different for each of you reading this book.

I haven't read any other book which begins in this way. It is your first impression of me as a writer, so it is important. The reason I have dared to use such an unconventional opening is that all these questions about my identity as a writer, about you as readers and about the impression you will form of me are the topic of this book: I can justify this introduction on the grounds that I am trying to introduce you to my topic in a vivid way. But I would go further than that: I am doing explicitly here what is usually left implicit or, at best, relegated to the edges of the book itself. Readers try to figure out who is speaking to them, even though they often have to do this by detective work: reading the texts around the text, and, less consciously, searching for the writer's identity in the writing itself. You may have already scoured the Library of Congress Cataloguing Data for my age, checked the bibliography for my academic standing and may already be trying to get a *feel* for me from my choice of words, sentence structure, and numerous other discoursal cues. Working on this topic has convinced me that, although dilemmas about self-representation in relation to readers are rarely made explicit, they are at the heart of most acts of writing. The social struggles in which the self is implicated through the act of writing are the topic of this book, and they affect the way I am writing it.

Introducing the topic: the fine art analogy

The complexity of the relationship between writing and identity is thrown into sharp focus by comparing writing with fine art. Writing is in many ways different from visual art, so the analogy does not completely hold, but the very places where the two do not quite map onto each other reveal many fascinating issues of identity.

The identity of an artist, and the extent to which s/he is drawing on the work of other artists are million-dollar questions in the world of fine art. If a painting is by a well-known artist its value is immensely high. If it is a fake, it is relatively worthless. If dealers mistakenly identified it in either direction, they would lose their reputations and their money. If it was in fact a fake, the forger would stand to gain enormously if not found out, and to lose all if found out. But what of the picture? Is it beautiful anyway?

These issues of attribution, copying, faking, forgery, and values in fine art are laid wonderfully bare in the autobiography of a celebrated forger: Eric Hebborn (1991). Hebborn saw himself as working within the tradition of the old masters: a member of his academy *par excellence*, accepting its values, subject matter and tried and tested forms of representation. He greatly admired the classical work, and produced paintings and drawings in the style of well-known artists and 'schools'. However, when he signed these with his own name, he did not have much market success. Therefore he started to sell them without a signature, or deliberately put some mark on them which falsely attributed them to someone with a reputation. Dealers were taken in, or entered the deception because they knew that buyers would be taken in. Hebborn contends that his drawings and paintings are as beautiful as they are beautiful, whoever produced them. He claims that the buyers, who erroneously attribute value to the name of the artist instead of to the product itself, are as much to blame as he is.

Writing an academic essay raises similar issues. Writers have to decide when to attribute a word or an idea to another writer, and when not, just as Hebborn had to decide whether to mark his work as his own or the work of the artist or 'school' he had followed. Writers have to recognize that they are involved in a process of self-attribution: forging their own allegiances to particular traditions and sets of values by their language choices, just as Hebborn did in his signed work. Writing is forging in the sense of welding together elements which have benchmarks of their own, and it is often also forging in the pejorative sense of masking the identity of the originator.

The sin of plagiarism in academic writing is on the surface the opposite of the sin of forgery in art. In plagiarism the sin is to use the words and ideas of another and claim them as your own by failing to attribute them to their original author. In forgery the sin is to attribute your own work to an established expert. However, I suggest that the underlying issues are the same. In both worlds there is an erroneous view that value resides in originality. Neither world recognizes the way in which any member is drawing on the common stock of subject-matters, techniques and forms of representation in the traditions of its community. The only way an apprentice member of a community can learn to become a full member is by copying, adapting and synthesizing from the work of other members. This was well recognized in the world of fine art in the Renaissance, where the majority of paintings and sculptures were 'school of': made by apprentices, honourably copying both content and form from their masters. In academic writing today this would be thought to be most dishonourable, and the writing would be considered valueless. This can be partly explained by the difference between writing and visual art in the way content is related to form. But these differences are not so clear cut as they may seem, since every work of art or piece of writing is the product of its social context: of the multiple traditions on which it is drawing as well as the socio-economic relations among the participants in its production.

In writing as in painting one might well ask who is who. Which provenance can be attributed to which words and ideas? What can be attributed to the author, what to the reader, and what to the community? Is copying from another writer a positive act, a way of showing agreement and allegiance? A way of taking to yourself the values, ideas and discourses of your discipline? Or is it a sin comparable to forgery, known as plagiarism? Is 'intertextuality' (as defined in Chapter 2) really just an extension of plagiarism? When do the words writers write count as their own words? What difference do formal marks of attribution such as inverted commas make? What are the ways in which writers show themselves to be members of a community yet at the same time preserve other aspects of their identity? In what ways do writers intentionally position readers into attributing identities to them which are valued but deceptive? Which parts of all this are conscious and which subconscious? These are the sorts of questions I am addressing in this book.

The visual art analogy is particularly striking, because the value of the artist's 'own work' is translated into vast sums of money. Issues of identity and ownership in writing are usually less fraught with financial implications, but they are none the less crucial and interesting. These issues are the subject of this book, particularly as they manifest themselves in the writing of mature students in institutions of higher education in Britain. In the next section I explain my reasons for choosing this particular research site.

The academic writing of mature students as a research focus

My interest in the topic of writing and identity did not originate from theoretical concerns; it arose as a practical issue in my work as an adult literacy tutor with mature students. Here I explain what I mean by 'mature students', and why their academic writing is a particularly interesting site for the study of writing and identity.

In Britain it is possible for adults to return to study later in life: in the 1980s and early 1990s a student who entered higher education over the age of 25 was deemed to be 'mature', and eligible for a special grant (the eligible age has recently changed). Many mature students have obtained regular qualifications for entering higher education at school, and have just delayed taking up their opportunities. Even these people often find academic life in general, and its literacy demands in particular, alienating. The values, beliefs and literacy practices they have developed outside education affect the way they view and undertake academic writing assignments. Others did not obtain regular qualifications at school, and may have left school without even the basic qualifications, even with limited literacy. Many have, at some time in their lives, been labelled 'illiterate', but they have proved that this label is not for ever, and that its public connotation of 'unintelligent' is mistaken. Proving this is not easy. Almost everything is still stacked against these students, especially the second group. Traditional undergraduates have experienced a steady, gradual apprenticeship in the language of education over a period of 14 years full-time schooling between the ages of 4 and 18. Even the best Adult Basic Education provision in the world could not substitute for this. Only their own amazing strength and persistence, along with the wisdom of a few enlightened members of staff in higher education, carry them through.

As Candlin (in his preface to Fairclough 1989) writes:

> we should address our talents as explorers and explainers to those texts which evidence crucial moments in discourse where participants may be placed at social risk during communication, suffering disadvantage in consequence of the inequalities of communication. (viii–ix)

I suggest that mature students engaged in academic assignments provide a prime example of such "crucial moments in discourse". They have not had a smooth, uninterrupted path through the education system like regular undergraduates, so what is demanded of them is unlikely to 'come naturally'. Returning to study represents a turning-point in their lives, when other adult commitments and experiences — other social worlds — are juxtaposed with the academic world. In such circumstances they are caught up in conflicting social pressures when writing. Whatever aspect of writing we are interested in is therefore likely to be thrown into sharp focus by studying these writers.

Most of my professional life has been spent working with such students. As the coordinator of the Language Support Unit at Kingsway College in London for 11 years, as instructor in developmental education at San Joaquin Delta College, Stockton, California for a year, and as someone involved in the various developments in the U.K. national adult literacy campaign since 1974, I see the purpose of my professional life — my vocation — as contributing to work which helps adults develop the literacies they need to fulfil new aims in their lives. Now as a member of the Literacy Research Group at Lancaster University my main aim is to do research which will serve the same ends. My reason for focusing on writing rather than any other aspect of their studying processes is that students themselves perceive writing as their main stumbling-block.

The mature students I worked with often said things about their writing which struck me as issues of identity. I had previously worked with three mature students as co-researchers to explore issues of writer identity in their academic writing and we as a group have written about them collaboratively (Ivanič and Simpson 1988, 1992; Ivanič and Roach 1990, Roach 1990, Karach and Roach 1994). In addition two of my colleagues in the Teaching of Writing Group at Lancaster University, Romy Clark and Rachel Rimmershaw, have been studying academic writing collaboratively with their students and discovering that identity seems to be a crucial aspect of writing for them too (Clark, Constantinou, Cottey and Yeoh 1990, Benson, Rimmershaw and others 1994, Elleray and Rimmershaw 1995).

It may well be as a consequence of working with mature students that I became interested in identity rather than other aspects of writing: when working with mature students, multiple and conflicting identity in writing is hard to ignore. But it is not an issue only for them: the reason for focusing on them in this research is that they provide clear and often startling instances of something which in my view is crucial, if not apparent, in all writing.

Researchers who have interviewed these students often mention how issues of identity are involved in this experience of returning to study. Moss, for example, interviewed eight women about their experience of *Fresh Start/Return to Study* courses at one London educational institution. She writes:

> The traditions of teaching and learning in H.E. [Higher Education] are often markedly different from those of school, or adult or further education. Study here is a relatively isolated and self-directing process: students are encouraged in 'independent' learning and thought. At the same time, I would suggest, HE has unvoiced traditions, expectations and values that all new students must learn — a culture of academic institutions. This combination may put enormous demands on women who have not been in full-time education for 15–20 years ....In these circumstances it is not surprising that women felt unsure of themselves, and that they often found their first term, if not year, stressful. "It was like going into a different life" as Clare put it — a world of different values and expectations that they had to learn to judge. (Moss 1987: 46)

Hockey (1987) conducted unstructured in-depth interviews with 16 mature students at Lancaster University. One of his conclusions concerned

> the great difficulty mature students have in establishing a confident and positive self-image. For, despite having gained a university place, their academic identity often remains contested, threatened and insecure .... Confidence and a new educational identity are hard won in the face of considerable difficulties. (26)

Gardener (1992) points out how these students experience a connection between their use of language and their sense of identity. She sums this up:

> We do change our speech — we can, as one student put it, fit in anywhere. There's strain attached to it, though, and the strain is caused by feeling pretentious and false. (81)

I am particularly focusing on the way in which writing academic assignments causes people to "change their speech", to take on particular identities, and how they feel about it.

These studies establish that entering higher education as a mature student is associated with change, difficulty, crises of confidence, conflicts of identity, feelings of strangeness, the need to discover the rules of an unfamiliar world. Roach (1990) crystallizes this in her article about her own experience, entitled "Marathon":

> When I entered into academia it made me feel as if I was expected to run the London marathon whilst 10 stone overweight....
>
> I had no formal qualifications but was accepted into university because of my experience gained via the 'university of life' (the real world, day to day living ....). Although I was pleased about being accepted into the 'higher

echelons' of education — I found that gaining a place at university did not necessarily mean that everything was going to be plain sailing.

....

I hope that these metaphors will make sense to students who are entering into study. ..... Such metaphors were developed out of my experience of trying to accommodate myself within the academic community.

Academia has made me feel

Like a puppet on strings,

Like an Alien from   Like a junk food   Like a working class
another planet,   addict in a vegetarian   person trying to talk
                          conference,   'posh' on the phone.

(Roach 1990:5, illustrations by Sarah Padmore)

These quotations show how mature students feel that the onus is on them to change in order to identify themselves with the institutions they are entering. But as new populations of students from diverse backgrounds participate in higher education, should not the institutions themselves respond to these differences? These new populations present a challenge to the dominant values, practices and discourses of the institution of higher education, as Karach suggests in an article entitled "The politics of dislocation" (1992). She interviewed five women mature students and described how

> Mature women undergraduates bring to higher education a wealth of valuable, diverse and common experiences, knowledge and skills from which we all can share and learn. That is, knowledge and skills we have gained from our experiences of work, political activities, motherhood, our multicultural and class backgrounds, our diverse sexualities, friendships and special interests — to name just a few. These experiences constitute dimensions of who we are. Together they form our identities, consciousnesses — our whole living beings — and influence us in how we relate to other beings, nature and society. Yet in general, in ... conventional ... courses, we find our knowledge continues to be devalued in higher education, and excluded from the shallow academic definition of what constitutes worthy knowledge. (309)

Interviews and personal accounts such as these testify to the way mature students feel alienated and devalued within the institution of higher education. Their identities are threatened, and they respond either by attempting to accommodate to the established values and practices of the context they are entering, or — more radically — by questioning and challenging the dominant values and practices, and recognizing the possibility of change. Such painful and sometimes desperate personal accounts place an urgent responsibility on the academic community to provide adequate theoretical understandings of 'identity'. There is a need for theory which can be of practical use in making sense of experience: "theory as liberatory practice" (hooks 1994, Chapter 5), forming the basis for engaging in struggle for alternatives to dominant practices and discourses.

The central part of this book is based on research in which eight mature students and I worked as co-researchers to explore the issues of identity arising in their own writing, with the aim of producing understandings which would be of value both to them and to others. I introduce my co-researchers and discuss the way we conducted the research in the Introduction to Part Two (Chapter 5). However, I frequently mention them from here onwards, because insights I have gained from working with them interact with the theoretical issues I discuss in the rest of this introduction, and in Part One of the book.

Ways of talking about 'identity'

Researchers from different disciplines are not agreed about distinctions between terms like 'self', 'person', 'role', 'ethos', 'persona', 'position', 'positioning', 'subject position', 'subject', 'subjectivity', 'identity', and the plurals of many of these words. I examine some of these distinctions in more detail further on in this book, but just to give an idea of what is involved, here is an overview. A distinction between 'self' and 'person' is used in anthropology (see Besnier 1991, 1995, Street 1993a): 'self' refers to aspects of identity associated with an individual's feelings (or 'affect'), and 'person' refers to aspects of identity associated with a socially defined role (see Chapter 3 for discussion of this distinction). The term 'role' is often considered to be simplistic, suggesting stereotyped behaviour. The term 'ethos' is used by Fairclough (1992a) as a general way of referring to a person's identity in terms of world view and social practices. But Cherry (1988) makes a distinction between 'ethos' and 'persona', based on his understanding of the original usage by Aristotle and Cicero (see Chapter 4 for Cherry's definitions). The words 'person', 'role', and 'persona' seem to me to be referring to the public, institutionally defined aspect of identity; the words 'self', 'identity' and 'ethos' to the more private aspect. While these distinctions have an intuitive appeal, they are in danger of suggesting a separation of some essential, private self from social context: a separation I reject in this book.

The terms 'subject', 'subject position' and 'positioning' are used by people drawing on the work of social theorists such as Althusser and Foucault to emphasize the way in which people's identities are affected (if not determined) by the discourses and social practices in which they participate. I find the singular term 'subject position' somewhat misleading, since it suggests one, unitary position to which an individual is subject, rather than a variety of dimensions on which a person might be positioned simultaneously. The terms 'subjectivity', 'subjectivities' and 'positionings' and my own term 'possibilities for self-hood' avoid this trap to some extent, carrying the connotation that identity is socially constructed and that people are not free to take on any identity they choose, but adding a sense of multiplicity, hybridity and fluidity. These words suggest both that the socially available resources for the construction of identity are multiple, and that an individual's identity is a complex of interweaving positionings.

The term 'identity' is useful, because it is the everyday word for people's sense of who they are, but it doesn't automatically carry with it the connotations of social construction and constraint which are foregrounded by the terms 'subject' and 'subjectivity'. It is also a misleadingly singular word. The plural word 'identities' is sometimes better, because it captures the idea of people identifying simultaneously with a variety of social groups. One or more of these identities may be foregrounded at different times; they are sometimes contradictory, sometimes interrelated: people's diverse identities constitute the richness and the dilemmas of their sense of self. However, talking of a person's 'identities' can make the person sound disconcertingly fragmented. The term 'multiple identity' might avoid this to some extent, but also suggests the opposite problem: a comfortable coherence among identities, which is not true to most people's experience.

In spite of its limitations, I am using the word 'identity' as a general-purpose word to refer to the topic of this book, and draw finer distinctions when they seem useful. I intend the word 'identity' to signify the plurality, fluidity and complexity I have mentioned here, without always having to put it in the plural or add the word 'multiple'. The noun 'identity' sometimes seems too abstract for talking about specific people and their self-representa-tions, so I often use the word 'self' for this purpose.

Perhaps more important than subtle distinctions between nouns in the semantic field of 'identity' is a different type of distinction: between nouns and verbs. While the noun 'identity' has the disadvantage of suggesting a fixed condition, the verb 'identify' refers to a process. In this book I use the verb 'identify' and its nominalization 'identification' to focus on the processes whereby individuals align themselves with groups, communities, and/or sets of interests, values, beliefs and practices. This process of identifying with socially available possibilities for self-hood links individual social action to larger processes of social change (see also Fairclough 1996, Laclau 1994). I also frequently use the verb 'positioned' to mean something like 'made to seem to be a certain type of person', or 'given a particular identity, or aspect of identity'. I intend it to capture the tension between the freedom people have to identify with particular subject positions through their selection among discoursal resources, and the socially determined restrictions on those choices.

Ways of thinking about 'identity'

The social-scientific debate about the nature of social identity is concerned with the way it is constructed socio-culturally, discoursally, and through the mechanisms of social interaction. In this section I deliberately overturn the chronology of theory and research on identity by discussing the social constructionist paradigm first and Goffman's social-interactionist theory of self-representation second. This is because I do not want to present the social constructionist theory as either replacing or building on the social interactionist theory. Rather, I want to espouse the social constructionist theory as all-embracing, and then propose that the social interactionist theory makes a contribution within it.

Social constructionist views of identity

The social constructionist view is that

> entities we normally call reality, knowledge, thought, facts, texts, selves, and so on are constructs generated by communities of like-minded peers. Social construction understands reality, knowledge, thought, facts, texts, selves, and so on as community generated and community maintained linguistic entities — or, more broadly speaking, symbolic entities — that define or "constitute" the communities that generate them (Bruffee 1986: 774).

People who take a social constructionist view of identity reject the idea that any type of identity — political, sexual, emotional — is solely the product of individuals' minds and intentions, and believe that it is the result of affiliation to particular beliefs and possibilities which are available to them in their social context (see, for example, contributors to Gergen and Davis 1985, John Turner 1991, Gergen 1991, Burkitt 1991). So if people entering higher education experience an 'identity crisis', it is not because of any inadequacy in themselves, but because of a mismatch between the social contexts which have constructed their identities in the past and the new social context which they are entering. However, this formulation still suggests that the only possible way of participating in the activities of a community is by taking on its values and practices: is by becoming one of those "like-minded peers".

But identity is not socially *determined* but socially *constructed*. This means that the possibilities for the self are not fixed, but open to contestation and change. Parker (1989) warns against understanding the social construction of identity in an uncritical way. He concludes:

> We need to ask how the self is implicated moment by moment, through the medium of discourse, in power (68).

I would add that a corollary of *power* is *struggle*: "the self is implicated moment by moment" not only *in power* but also *in power struggle*. Foucault warned against too deterministic a view of the effect of power on the subject. He recognized the crucial role of the individual in what he called 'the technology of self'. In a seminar just before his death, he said:

> Perhaps I've insisted too much on the technology of domination and power. I am more and more interested in the interaction between oneself and others and in the technologies of individual domination, the history of how an individual acts upon himself [*Foucault's generic pronoun*], in the technology of self. (1988: 19.)

This does not seem to me to run contrary to Foucault's earlier work in which he put more emphasis on the 'technologies of power, which determine the conduct of individuals and submit them to certain regimes of domination, an objectivizing of the subject' (same place: 18). Rather, his last work restores a balance. In my conceptualization of writer identity, I am interested in the sense writers have of competing 'technologies of power', and of their 'technologies of the self' in establishing a position among them.

A critical view of the social construction of identity not only recognizes the powerful influence of dominant ideologies in controlling and constraining people's sense of themselves, but also recognizes the possibility of struggle for alternative definitions. For individuals alone contestation of damaging constructions of their identities may well be doomed to failure, but struggle as a member of an oppressed group has the potential for producing change, as political action during the late 1980s, most notably in South Africa, has shown. Without this possibility of contesting dominant constructions of reality and, as part of reality, our social identities, the prospect for humanity would be extremely bleak. These issues of power and power struggle are relevant to all aspects of the social construction of identity, among which language, literacy and writing exist alongside other forms of social action and semiosis.

In institutions of higher education certain ways of being are privileged by being supported by more powerful groups within the institution, but they are not monolithic, as I argue in Chapter 10 of this book. There already exist alternative ways of being, and the established possibilities for self-hood are being resisted and contested. This critical view of subjectivity can help mature students to respond positively to the 'identity crisis' in which they find themselves, and reinterpret it as a position from which to engage in movements within the institution of higher education for contesting dominant constructions of the self. In the final chapter of the book I discuss further how theory relates to action for mature students facing the writing demands of higher education, and the practical implications of a critical view of identity for all of us who write. In the rest of this section I summarize some specific aspects of the social construction of identity which have been pointed out by different theorists in a range of social sciences.

Social identity theory (Tajfel 1982) and social categorization theory (John Turner 1985, 1991, Chapter 6)) focus on the way in which people identify themselves in relation to social groups, categories, or stereotypes. (A summary of these theories and recent contributions to them are presented in Abrams and Hogg, 1990). This is particularly relevant to the study of mature students. They are at a critical time in their lives, ostensibly re-categorizing themselves as adults-with-higher-education, having for many years been, among other things, adults-without-higher-education. In addition, they have already identified themselves with social groups outside higher education — probably more fully than many regular undergraduates. In this study I view writing as both evidence of these processes and an act which contributes to them.

However, individuals do not define themselves entirely in terms of group membership(s). They also have a sense of themselves as defined by their difference from others they encounter (for discussion of this issue see especially Connolly 1991, and contributions to Rutherford 1990). Connolly, focusing on the nature of political identity, argues that identity only establishes itself in relation to difference: that in order to talk of identity at all it is necessary for there to be other identities, other affiliations which are being rejected. Connolly points out that the adoption of one identity and rejection of others is in itself a political act, involving a power struggle (as I discussed above). Similarity, boundaries and difference between social groups play an important role in the process of establishing an identity. (See also Hogg and McGarty 1990, Hart, Maloney and Damon 1987 and Kreitler and Kreitler 1987.) The question of similarity, boundaries and difference is a fraught one for mature students. They feel themselves 'the same as' other members of the academic community, but also have strong ties with other groups from whom the academic community might seem to be differentiating itself. The boundary which might help to establish their identity is not at all clear: even as they engage in 'boundary work' to identify themselves with the community they are entering, they feel untrue to themselves. The writing of an academic essay is a particularly powerful instance of such boundary work. In Chapter 8 I quote detailed testimony of how academic writing involves mature student writers in problematic processes of identification with and differentiation from others, both making and breaking boundaries.

Several theorists point out the multiplicity of socially constructed identities. Parker (1989) questions the notion of a unitary self and commends Harre's (1979) "notion of a multiplicity of social selves clustered around any single biological individual" (Parker 1989: 67). As I discussed in the previous section, people find this idea disconcerting. But perhaps it is even more disconcerting to be trying to find a singular self within a host of contradictions. Better to recognize the multiplicity, and see that it is a positive, dynamic aspect of our identity. Mature students are likely to be juggling multiple, often conflicting identities in their writing, as I illustrate in Chapters 6, 8 and 10.

Baumeister (1986) focused on the fact that issues of identity are defined by their historical context. He traced the relationship between self and society through history, and pointed out that the cultural conditions of twentieth century western society affect the way in which people see themselves.

> Modern self-definition requires choice, achievement, and frequent redefinition of self; medieval self-definition did not. The historical movement toward the more complex and difficult self-definition processes is a major reason for identity being a problem. (151)

> Changing social conditions have made it more difficult to meet identity's defining criteria with the major components society offers. Destabilization and trivialization have undermined the extent to which social identity is continuous across time and is different in important ways from the identities of others. (247)

Giddens (1991) points out that the diversity of socially available options for the self is a characteristic of what he calls "the late modern age":

> In the settings of what I call 'high' modernity or 'late' modernity — our present-day world — the self, like the broader institutional contexts in which it exists, has to be reflexively made. Yet this task has to be accomplished amid a puzzling diversity of options and possibilities. (3)

and

> In the post-traditional order of modernity, and against the backdrop of new forms of mediated experience, self-identity becomes a reflexively organized endeavour. The reflexive project of the self, which consists in the sustaining of coherent, yet continuously revised, biographical narratives, takes place in the context of multiple choice. (5)

The value of these observations for the study of identity in relation to the academic writing of mature students is that they draw attention to the social conditions of modern times which support the whole practice of returning to study. In late twentieth century Britain people don't look down their noses at changes in employment, domestic arrangements, aspirations, and interests the way they might have done 100 years ago. This change in attitudes means that mechanisms exist for people to move into new contexts which will necessitate renegotiating their identities.

Giddens' claim that "[t]he reflexive project of the self ... consists in the sustaining of coherent, yet continuously revised, biographical narratives" is a powerful way of conceptualizing continuity and change in a person's identity over time. It locates identity in events and experience, rather than reifying it as a quality or attribute. Further, the self consists not of a person's life-history, but of the *interpretation* they are currently putting on their life history. The self is in this way doubly socially constructed: both by the socially constrained nature of the life experience itself, and by the social shaping of the interpretation. I suggest that writing makes a particularly tangible contribution to 'the reflexive project of the self', with a three-way interplay between the writer's life-experience, their sense of self, and the reality they are constructing through their writing. I develop this connection between writers' "biographical narratives" and their writing in Chapter 7 of the book.

Several of the articles in Honess and Yardley (1987) also emphasize the changes in identity across a lifespan. The articles focus on the role of critical periods (such as adolescence: Gecas and Mortimer 1987), critical events and moments (such as childbirth: Rossan 1987). In this study I view the experience of entering higher education later in life as one of these critical experiences which foregrounds change in identity. In his study of perceived change of self among adults, Handel (1987: 331) concludes that people have a sense of four different selves: a present self, a retrospective self, a desired self, and a prospective self. This is a useful way of thinking about identity at moments of flux such as engaging in higher education as a mature student. I discuss the interplay between these different selves and the way they manifest themselves in writing in Part Two: in Chapters 7 and 8 I discuss the relationship between the discoursally constructed present self, and retrospective, desired and prospective selves; Chapters 9 and 10 are about the way in which the 'present self' is constructed in discourse.

In spite of the fact that identities are not fixed, individuals have a sense of unity and continuity about their identity. Slugoski and Ginsburg (1989) write

... the question is one of accounting for the *experience* of continuity over time and the *sense* of unity despite diversity in conceptions of oneself. (same page)

However, they argue that this sense of unity and continuity, and of having a choice as to personal identity, is in itself socially constructed by the very language used by psychologists and in everyday life. In Chapter 8, I show how the mature students I worked with talked about 'the real me' as a psychological reality, however much it is dismissed by social theory.

Identity, discourse and literacy

Recently social scientists have turned their attention to the concept of 'discourse' as the mediating mechanism in the social construction of identity. This is particularly relevant to the topic of this book: the relationship between writing and identity. In this section I mention briefly the approach social psychologists have taken to discourse and identity, as a backdrop for the detailed discussion of more linguistic approaches in Chapter 2. I then distinguish between a 'discourse' perspective and a 'literacy' perspective, in anticipation of Chapter 3.

The term 'discourse' is used as shorthand for a complex concept, and is used in many different ways by different people, usually but not always involving the use of language, often including far more than language. As I understand it, *discourse*, as an abstract noun with no plural, means something like 'producing and receiving culturally recognized, ideologically shaped representations of reality'. The term refers more to the **process** of representing reality than to the product, but encompasses both. I'll try the definition out on part of the first sentence of this section. 'Discourse is the mediating mechanism in the social construction of identity' means that the way in which people take on particular identities is by producing and receiving culturally recognized, ideologically shaped representations of reality. I think it works.

The term can also be used as a count noun *a discourse:* this means something like 'a culturally recognized way of representing a particular aspect of reality from a particular ideological perspective'. I think this definition works for the way Shotter and Gergen use the term *a discourse* below. These definitions purposely do not specify any particular medium of representation. The term *discourse* usually refers to representation through language, the physical form of which is a spoken or written 'text'. But many people like to extend the term 'discourse' to include representation through visual, bodily and other media, using the word 'language' metaphorically to include 'visual language' and the word 'text' to mean 'a representation in any medium'. Some people also extend the term *discourse* to include all the social practices associated with a particular set of values, beliefs and power relations. In this book I stick to a relatively narrow definition of discourse as involving verbal language.

All the contributors to Shotter and Gergen (1989) emphasize the fact that discourses are the site in which identity is manifested. Shotter and Gergen (1989) explain that the articles they edited

> share a concern with the issues of textuality, with the construction of identity and with cultural critique. They are concerned with the way in which personal identities are formed, constrained and delimited within ongoing relationships.... The primary medium within which identities are created and have their currency is not just linguistic but textual: persons are largely ascribed their identities according to the manner of their embedding within a discourse — in their own or in the discourse of others. (ix)

Together the articles in this volume show that 'the self', should not be conceived of as something to be studied in isolation, but as something which manifests itself in discourse. They emphasize the need to focus right down to the 'text' in order to see how identity manifests itself in discourse. However, social psychologists are not linguists, and they do not demonstrate in detail how this happens. I agree with Fairclough (1992b) that cross-disciplinary theory and research on the way in which discourse functions in society needs more sophisticated linguistic and intertextual analysis to show more precisely *how* discourse constructs identity. One of the aims of this book is to apply the sort of analysis that Fairclough recommends to the academic writing of mature students, thereby making a specifically linguistic contribution to thinking in the social sciences about discourse and identity. In Chapter 2 I describe in detail what is involved in linguistic and intertextual analysis, and in Chapters 6, 9 and 10 I use this form of analysis to show how specific linguistic features of academic writing construct identities for the writers.

Foucault used the term 'discourse(s)' very broadly to refer to the "technologies" by which powerful ideologies position subjects, and he also talked specifically about his new interest in "the role of reading and writing in constituting the self" (Rabinow and Dreyfus 1983: 62, quoted in Martin, Gutman and Hutton 1988), although he never developed this interest. It seems to me that talking about "reading and writing" implies a rather different perspective from talking about 'discourse'. The expression 'discourse' focuses on language and other media of representation, with other social practices as an optional or subsidiary extra, whereas the expression 'reading and writing' focuses on *literacies*: the culturally shaped practices surrounding the use of written language among which what might be called 'linguistic practices' are a subset. Taking a 'discourse' perspective on research on writing and identity draws on methodologies from linguistics; taking a 'literacy' perspective draws on methodologies from anthropology. In this book I do mainly take a 'discourse' perspective, focusing on the way language constructs identity in the process of writing, but I discuss how the literacy practices associated with writing relate to identity in Chapter 3, and integrate this perspective into Chapters 6 and 8.

The role of social interaction: Goffman 1959

In the previous two sections, I have presented a critical view of the relationship between identity and social conventions and practices, recognizing the role of power in this relationship, and the possibility of collective struggle to redefine the possibilities for self-hood. I have referred to the processes of identification through boundary work between 'the self' and 'the other', and outlined some of the characteristics of identity as multiple, historically situated, negotiable, and changing over the lifespan. Finally I have referred to the role of 'discourse(s)' and 'literacies' in constituting identities, providing an introduction to more detailed discussion in the next two chapters. These ideas must form the overarching framework for thinking about identity, because they emphasize the way in which the macro-socio-cultural environment supports particular identities, and they dismiss the idea that 'who we are' is just a matter of individual biological and cognitive traits. But people ARE agents in the construction of their own identities: they send messages to each other about these socially ratified ways of being, and thereby reproduce or challenge them in the micro-social environment of every-day encounters. These very real, situated processes of identification are, in my view, an important component of a theory of the social construction of identity, and it is possible to supply this component from Goffman's work on self-representation.

Goffman's theory of self-presentation was developed on the basis of his fieldwork on social behaviour in the Shetland Isles. He was interested in social action in its broadest sense, including such things as slight inclinations of the head, timing of appearances in a room, arrangement of furniture and ornaments: there are a wide range of means of conveying meaning which do not necessarily involve language at all. His claim is that such forms of social action convey information about people, that the people producing and receiving these messages may do so consciously or subconsciously, and that the messages can be manipulated. In this section I first discuss the dramaturgical metaphor he uses and then discuss ways in which his theory can be placed within the framework for thinking about identity outlined in the previous two sections.

Throughout *The presentation of self in everyday life* (1969, first published in 1959), Goffman uses an extended metaphor of everyday behaviour as a theatrical performance. Dramaturgical metaphors for human action are open to criticism on two grounds. Firstly, dramaturgical metaphors suggest that 'actors' — that is, individuals — are in charge of their own situation, which is contrary to a social constructionist view of human action; secondly, dramaturgical metaphors have backgrounded tensions and conflicts inherent in social action, focusing on the smooth, 'on-stage' performance. Billig (1987: especially 12–17) draws attention particularly to this second limitation, but he also suggests that an extension of the theatrical metaphor to include backstage disagreements would actually capture the tensions and conflicts in which he is interested very well. He points out that

> psychologists will be unable to give due attention to argumentation so long as they employ theoretical frameworks which subtract the argumentative aspects from human activities. (1987: 30)

In making use of Goffman's work, I take account of these criticisms. Firstly, I am attempting to place Goffman's contribution within the framework of social constructionist accounts — specifically, to claim that his insights about social interaction show how social construction operates in real people's day-to-day lives. Secondly, I suggest that it is precisely because of the 'backstage' tensions and conflicts to which Billig draws our attention that a social constructionist view of identity needs to include reference to the way an individual constructs an impression of self from the available, usually conflicting, resources. Further, it is important to recognize the workings of power and patterns of privileging within these 'backstage tensions'. These issues concerning the institutional and cultural possibilities for, and constraints on self-hood are thrown into sharp relief by considering what happens when a person is actually engaged in an act of self-representation.

In his early work Goffman distinguishes between two aspects of the person in this dramaturgical metaphor: the *performer*, and the *character*. He describes the individual as both:

> a *performer*, a harried fabricator of impressions involved in the all-too-human task of staging a performance;

and

> a *character*, a figure, typically a fine one, whose spirit, strength, and other sterling qualities the performance was designed to evoke. (1969: 222)

These are rather colourful, exaggerated definitions, and taking them literally would lead, in my view, to a misrepresentation of social behaviour as overly conscious of strategic performances and effects. Taken as a metaphor, however, they capture the emotionally fraught, usually subconscious nature of self-representation. In this book I am specifically concerned with the *writer-as-performer*'s task of creating a *writer-as-character*: negotiating among alternative possible ways of being positioned by those discourses s/he has available.

The terms *performer* and *character* are the forerunners Goffman's later terms *animator, author* and *principal* (Goffman 1981: 143–145). He suggested these terms to distinguish three aspects of identity in relation specifically to language production. In spite of the fact that the later terms are language-specific, I prefer the earlier terms *performer* and *character,* for three reasons. Firstly, the consistent dramaturgical metaphor makes the earlier terms easier to understand. Secondly, the term *performer* is more flexible, not limited to the mechanical aspects of language production which are implied by the term *animator,* nor to the composing process which is referred to by the term *author.* Goffman in this later work was interested in distinguishing between three aspects of language production in order to argue that they can, in principal, be undertaken by different individuals, whereas I am concerned with the nature of self-presentation by a single writer. For my purpose, Goffman's distinction between *animator* and *author* is not so useful as being able to refer to this 'creator' of writing by a single term. Thirdly, I want to use the terms 'self-as-author', 'authorial presence' and 'authority' in ways which span both the *performer* and the *character* aspect of identity, as I discuss in the next section. This usage does not map directly onto Goffman's term *author.*

Goffman uses his dramaturgical metaphor to emphasize the fact that the *character* this *performer* creates is not identical to the person creating it. Goffman writes:

> A status, a position, a social place is not a material thing, to be possessed and then displayed; it is a pattern of appropriate conduct, coherent, embellished, and well articulated. Performed with ease or clumsiness, awareness or not, guile or good faith, it is none the less something that must be enacted and portrayed, something that must be realized. (1969: 65–66)

In this extract Goffman is suggesting that identity — "a status, a position, a social place" is an abstract set of conventions rather than an intrinsic characteristic of an individual. This identity only comes into existence when "portrayed". This seems to me to make the connection between the abstract, 'macro' picture of socially and discoursally available subject positions and the more concrete 'micro' picture of the identities of real people going about their daily lives. Goffman is talking about the role of actual people in donning — and thereby reproducing — socio-culturally constructed identities.

Goffman does not pay any attention to the institutional practices, values and beliefs which support these 'patterns of appropriate conduct', nor to the power-related issue of who gets to portray which identities, but he was not unaware of the effect of the wider social context. He wrote:

> When an individual presents himself [*Goffman's generic pronoun*] before others, his performance will tend to incorporate and exemplify the officially accredited values of the society ...[it will be] an expressive rejuvenation and reaffirmation of the moral values of the community. (same book: 31).

This seems to me to be too a monolithic view of community, and a deterministic, normative view of the effect of social forces, which is only part of the picture. Not all writers want to, or are willing to 'reaffirm the moral values' of the academic discourse community. Some do accommodate to these values, but others resist and/or challenge them, as I discuss in Chapter 8.

Goffman has been criticized for reducing self-presentation to a set of guiles and deceptions under the control of the individual, rather than recognizing that the self is socially constructed. *The presentation of self in everyday life* reads a bit like an actor's handbook. His explanation of the mechanisms of self-presentation deal weakly with the macro-social dimension. It does not foreground the question of social conventions and norms, nor does it pay any attention to contestation and struggle over which conventions are privileged, and which stigmatized. Yet Goffman provides a detailed account of how identity is constructed in the micro-social contexts of interpersonal encounters, which is missing from other accounts.

It seems to me that the social constructionist view of identity needs to address the issue of how individuals react to the alternatives available to them — what Billig calls 'argumentation' (see above). Social constructionist accounts do not pay any attention to what Goffman calls "the performer", yet the processes of social construction need real people to realize them. It is essential to theorize the role of 'the individual' precisely because of the existence of alternatives in the context of culture: this would be irrelevant only if writers were really 'written', or 'socially constructed' by a single, dominant discourse over which they had no control at all. Individuals are constrained in their selection of discourses by those to which they have access, and by the patterns of privileging which exist among them, but this does not dry up the alternatives altogether. I think Goffman's work provides a productive metaphor to enrich our understanding of the local mechanisms by which the social construction of identity takes place, giving an insight into the sorts of subconscious selections among culturally available possibilities for self-hood that particular individuals make when confronted by particular others in particular social settings. I see the social constructionist and social interactionist perspectives on identity as interdependent, and I develop this view in the rest of this book.

In Chapter 4 I provide further detail about those aspects of Goffman's work on self-presentation which can be applied to the way students portray themselves in academic writing, and comment on how this is the same as or different from self-presentation in other forms of social action. In the same chapter I also draw on Goffman's *performer/character* distinction to show how a focus on the process of writing — associated with the *writer-as-performer* — has led writing theorists and researchers to overlook the *writer-as-character*. In Chapters 6 and 8 I discuss in detail my co-researchers' conscious and subconscious motives, and the processes of trying to control the impressions they were conveying, using Goffman's approach and demonstrating its persistent value despite contemporary critiques.

Four aspects of 'writer identity'

When people talk about identity in relation to writing, they may be referring to one or more of four things. These can be summarized as:

aspects of the identity of an actual writer writing a particular text	*abstract, prototypical identities available in the socio-cultural context of writing*
AUTOBIOGRAPHICAL SELF	
DISCOURSAL SELF	POSSIBILITIES FOR SELF-HOOD
SELF AS AUTHOR	

I suggest that there are three ways of thinking about the identity of a person in the act of writing, which I am calling the writer's 'autobiographical self', the 'discoursal self' which the writer constructs in the act of writing, and the 'self as author', referring to a writer's relative authoritativeness. These three 'selves' are all socially constructed and socially constructing in that they are shaped by and shape the more abstract 'possibilities for self-hood' which exist in the writer's socio-cultural context. As I will be showing in the rest of the book, these aspects of writer identity are not hermetically sealed from one another but interrelate in a number of ways. I have used the word 'self' in these four terms for the sake of consistency, and to keep the focus on the particular, but I also use the expressions 'autobiographical identity' and 'discoursal identity', especially when discussing these aspects of writer identity more generally.

Of the three aspects of the identity of actual writers, 'autobiographical self' and 'discoursal self' map fairly directly onto Goffman's *performer/character* distinction, but 'self as author' is something different, not entirely synonymous with what Goffman calls the *author*. Each aspect of writer identity raises its own research questions which generate their own methodologies. In the following sections I explain what I mean by each of these, identify research questions and methodologies associated with them, and discuss how they relate to one another. (See also Ivanič 1995 or Clark and Ivanič 1997, Chapter 6, for further discussion of these four aspects of writer identity.)

Autobiographical self

This is the identity which people bring with them to any act of writing, shaped as it is by their prior social and discoursal history. The term 'autobiographical self' emphasizes the fact that this aspect of identity is associated with a writer's sense of their roots, of where they are coming from, and that this identity they bring with them to writing is itself socially constructed and constantly changing as a consequence of their developing life-history: it is not some fixed, essential 'real self'. The term also captures the idea that it is not only the events in people's lives, but also their way of representing these experiences to themselves which constitutes their current way of being. This aspect of writer identity is the closest of the three to what Bourdieu (1977) calls 'habitus': a person's disposition to behave in certain ways. In terms of Goffman's distinction, this is the identity of the *writer-as-performer:* the person who sets about the process of producing the text. It is the 'self' which produces a self-portrait, rather than the 'self' which is portrayed.

It is difficult to make categorical statements about the nature of a writer's autobiographical self, since it may be below the level of consciousness. But this aspect of writer identity can be researched through life-history techniques, designed to address questions such as:

a.   *What aspects of people's lives might have led them to write in the way that they do?*
b.   *How has their access to discourses and associated positionings been socially enabled or constrained?*
c.   *More generally, how does autobiographical identity shape writing?*

The autobiographical aspect of writer identity is the focus of Chapter 7 of this book, in which I theorize and exemplify the identity my co-researchers brought to writing specific academic assignments. I have also written collaboratively with two of them about the relationship between their past experience and a particular piece of academic writing (Ivanič, Aitchison, and Weldon 1996).

Discoursal self

A writer's 'discoursal self' is the impression — often multiple, sometimes contradictory — which they consciously or unconsciously conveys of themself in a particular written text. I have called this aspect of identity 'discoursal' because it is constructed through the discourse characteristics of a text, which relate to values, beliefs and power relations in the social context in which they were written. In terms of Goffman's distinction, this is the *writer-as-character:* the identity which the *writer-as-performer* portrays. It is fleeting, insofar that it is tied to a particular text, yet it may leave a relatively permanent impression of the writer on whoever reads the writing. It is concerned with the writer's 'voice' in the sense of the way they want to sound, rather than in the sense of the stance they are taking.

Research on discoursal identity needs to address several related questions, including:

a.   *What are the discourse characteristics of particular pieces of writing?*
b.   *What are the social and ideological consequences of these characteristics for the writers' identities?*
c.   *What characteristics of the social interaction surrounding these texts led the writers to position themselves in these ways?*

d.   *More generally, what processes are involved in the construction of a discoursal self, and what influences shape discoursal identities?*

Addressing question (a) involves linguistic and intertextual analysis as recommended in Fairclough (1992a and b) (see Chapter 2 for further explanation of these). Addressing question (b) involves making connections between research on socially available possibilities for self-hood (see below) and the discourse characteristics identified in (a). Addressing question (c) involves extensive interviewing of discourse participants, particularly the writers, about how they wanted to appear in their writing, and why.

The only other study which has concerned itself with this aspect of writer identity is Cherry (1988), which I discuss in Chapter 4. The writer's discoursal self is the main focus of this book: Chapter 2 provides the theoretical framework for analyzing the discoursal construction of identity in this sense; Chapter 8 is about how and why my co-researchers came to portray themselves in the way that they did; Chapters 9 and 10 present the nature and diversity of the discoursal selves constructed in their writing.

Self as author

The 'self as author' is a relative concept: writers see themselves to a greater or lesser extent as authors, and present themselves to a greater or lesser extent as authors. This aspect of writer identity concerns the writer's 'voice' in the sense of the writer's position, opinions and beliefs: a different sense of 'voice' from the one associated with the discoursal self. The self as author is particularly significant when discussing academic writing, since writers differ considerably in how far they claim authority as the source of the content of the text, and in how far they establish an authorial presence in their writing. Some attribute all the ideas in their writing to other authorities, effacing themselves completely; others take up a strong authorial stance. Some do this by presenting the content of their writing as objective truth, some do it by taking responsibility for their authorship. Considering the self as author provides a different perspective on writer identity from the other two, but it is not entirely separate from them. The self as author is likely to be to a considerable extent a product of a writer's autobiographical self: the writer's life-history may or may not have generated ideas to express, and may or may not have engendered in the writer enough of a sense of self-worth to write with authority, to establish an authorial presence. The self as author is also an aspect of the discoursal self: one characteristic of a writer's discoursal self which can be discoursally constructed is authoritativeness.

Authoritativeness in academic writing has already received considerable attention from other researchers, which I summarize in Chapter 4. This research uses textual analysis to address questions such as

a.   *How do people establish authority for the content of their writing?*
b.   *To what extent do they present themselves or others as authoritative?*

While I do not devote a chapter of Part Two to this aspect of writer identity exclusively, it is part of what the writers bring with them to the act of writing (Chapters 6 and 7), and also part of the identity they portray through their linguistic choices. I discuss the discoursal construction of authoritativeness in my co-researchers' writing in Chapter 10. The self as author is also at stake whenever I am talking about the writers' choices of content (for example, in Chapter 8), which is as salient in the discoursal construction of identity as choices of form.

Possibilities for self-hood in the socio-cultural and institutional context

The three aspects of writer identity which I have discussed so far are all concerned with actual people writing actual texts. The fourth meaning of 'writer identity' is concerned with prototypical possibilities for self-hood which are available to writers in the social context of writing: 'social' identities in the sense that they do not just belong to particular individuals. In any institutional context there will be several socially available possibilities for self-hood: several ways of doing the same thing. Of these some will be privileged over others, in the sense that the institution accords them more status. As social constructionist theorists have convincingly argued, possibilities for self-hood and the patterns of privileging among them shape and constrain actual people writing actual texts. These possibilities for self-hood do not exist in a vacuum, but are themselves shaped by individual acts of writing in which people take on particular discoursal identities.

As I mentioned earlier, the term 'subject positions' is in common use for talking about these socially available possibilities for self-hood, but I often find the term limiting because it suggests unitary, coherent social identities. On the whole I prefer the terms 'positionings', and 'possibilities for self-hood' because they allow for social identity being multi-faceted. In my view several types of socially available resources for the construction of identity operate simultaneously: it is not just a question of occupying one subject position or another, but rather of being multiply positioned by drawing on possibilities for self-hood on several dimensions. For example, the academic context might support several disciplinary identities, several roles in the academic community, several gender identities, several political identities. Talking about 'subject positions' suggests off-the-peg combinations from these sets of alternatives; talking about 'possibilities for self-hood' seems to allow each dimension to operate independently.

On the other hand, however, the term 'possibilities for self-hood' suggests a rather cosy, over-optimistic picture of unlimited alternatives, whereas the term 'subject positions' does draw attention to the way in which possibilities for self-hood are socially constrained. I therefore use both terms depending on the meaning I want to foreground.

One of the ways of occupying a subject position is by writing. Social, cultural and institutional possibilities for self-hood shape all three aspects of the identity of 'actual' writers. A writer's 'autobiographical self' develops in the context of socially constrained access to possibilities for self-hood. This means that different individuals will feel able to identify with different subject positions according to their social group memberships. Writers construct a 'discoursal self' not out of an infinite range of possibilities, but out of the possibilities for self-hood which are supported by the socio-cultural and institutional context in which they are writing. The constraints and possibilities open to the particular writer interact with the constraints on and possibilities for self-hood which are opened up by a particular occasion for writing. Possibilities for self-hood also socially construct the self as author: there are conventions for whether and how to establish authorial presence which differ from one type of writing to another, and from one social context to another. These conventions influence whether and how actual writers establish themselves as authors in their writing.

But the relationship between the identity of individual writers and the socially available possibilities for self-hood available to them is two-way. Clashes between writers' autobiographical identities and institutionally supported subject positions have the potential to contribute to changing the possibilities for self-hood available in the future. Every time a writer constructs a discoursal self which draws on less privileged possibilities for self-hood they are, like a drop in the ocean, infinitesimally redefining the possibilities for self-hood which will, in turn, be available to future writers. This is a process which would be doomed to failure if people acted only as individuals: the discoursal identity of one individual will not do much to shape the possibilities for self-hood available to future generations. But challenging the status quo is rarely an isolated act: it is more a question of individuals aligning themselves with the less privileged subject positions of existing, but less powerful, social groups. Acting — in this case, writing — as a member of a social group is what contributes to change.

Research on possibilities for self-hood complements research on the three aspects of the identity of actual writers, addressing questions such as:

a.   *What possibilities for self-hood, in terms of relations of power, interests, values and beliefs are inscribed in the practices, genres and discourses which are supported by particular socio-cultural and institutional contexts?*
b.   *What are the patterns of privileging among available possibilities for self-hood?*
c.   *In what ways are possibilities for self-hood and patterns of privileging among them changing over time?*

These questions are addressed by social scientists both theoretically and through detailed ethnographic studies of particular institutional contexts. This sort of research is particularly important for answering question (b) under the heading 'Discoursal Self', since a writer's discoursal self in any particular piece of writing is constituted by their adoption of a particular configuration of possibilities for self-hood which position them in terms of relations of power, interests, values and beliefs.

Concluding comments on these four aspects of writer identity

The three aspects of the identity of an actual writer change, perhaps quite radically, from one act of writing to the next. A writer's autobiographical self is constantly evolving over time. A writer may construct a quite different discoursal self from one text to another, depending partly on autobiographical changes and partly on the different demands of different occasions for writing. A writer may be relatively authoritative in one text, and relatively unauthoritative in another. However, the socially available possibilities for self-hood change much more slowly over time.

By drawing distinctions among these four aspects of writer identity I am raising the crucial question: What do people mean when they talk about 'my identity' when they write? The answer is not straightforward. The autobiographical self is perhaps the closest thing to what people mean by 'my identity' since this is unique to each individual, but it cannot necessarily be traced in their writing. The only aspect of a writer's identity for which there is evidence in the writing is a discoursal self — perhaps unique to that particular piece of writing. Yet writers do not always own the discoursal self in their writing, as I will discuss in Chapter 8, so this cannot be interpreted as 'the writer's identity'. Writers are often said to 'have an identity' when they establish a strong authorial presence in their writing, but that only refers to the self as author of the content of the writing, and does not include the autobiographical self which the writer brought to the act of writing nor the discoursal self constructed by it. Finally, none of these aspects of identity can be thought of as the unique property of an individual writer, since they are instantiations and recombinations of possibilities for self-hood which are available in the wider social context in which they are writing.

In this section I have introduced four meanings of 'writer identity' — three of which distinguish among aspects of the identity of actual writers, and the fourth refers to the prototypical possibilities for self-hood available in the social and institutional context of writing. Of the three aspects of the identity of actual writers I have distinguished, this book focuses on the discoursal self, since this is less well theorized and researched than the autobiographical self or self as author, but this does not mean disregarding the others, as they are related to the discoursal self in the ways I have explained here.

Linguistic choices and my own identity as a writer

Ending this chapter as I began it, in this section I am giving some examples of how my own identity is bound up in the linguistic choices I make as I am writing this book.

I am using 's/he' for singular generic reference in subject position, as I like the way it captures singularity along with reference to both genders. Until recently I have been using 'her' as an anti-sexist gesture for the object and possessive. However, I no longer feel strongly committed to the radical, feminist project of doing this to make up for the years of 'him' and 'his'. My current approach to this issue is to challenge the grammatical convention that such pronouns and determiners must remain in the singular form. I am therefore using 'them', 'themself' and 'their' as gender-free singular object and possessive forms, a linguistic practice I should like to see becoming commonplace through the processes of struggle and consequent language change. I may be giving all sorts of impressions of myself by this choice, ranging from failing to join the anti-sexist lobby to being uneducated.

I use the spelling '-ize' rather than '-ise' for suffixes, because it is closer to the way they sound. I think that this spelling is easier for people with spelling difficulties to learn, and I'd like to see it adopted as the standard form in Britain. I expect to be viewed as a bit eccentric for doing this, and I am happy to be conveying this impression of myself.

I have not used Latin expressions like 'sic' and 'ibid', replacing them instead by English equivalents. It seems to me to be an outdated and exclusive practice to use Latin in this way, and I want to contribute to change in academic discourse in this respect.

I have avoided the use of the future tense for what I have placed further on in the book, because it establishes a pretence that I actually wrote it in the order in which it finally appears. I've used the present tense where many would use the future. I think this makes me sound a little more authoritative than I feel, partly because it is not established practice, and you are likely to be struck by its oddness.

In some places, particularly towards the end of sections, I allow myself to use slightly more allusive and/or metaphorical language, leaving a bit more to the reader's imagination than is common in academic language: I think this makes for slightly more interesting reading, and also conveys the commitment I feel towards some of the issues I am writing about. I hope it balances the impression I may be giving of myself elsewhere of being pedantic and impersonal.

On the whole I have tried to be as direct as possible, using 'I' wherever I am responsible for an action, a mental or verbal process. I am doing all I can to choose language which presents knowledge as subjective, and created by everyday inquiry, and so identifying myself with that view of knowledge. I have been casual wherever possible, trying to avoid using formal language just for the sake of it. I hope that positions me as someone committed to plain speaking, not unnecessarily exclusive. On the other hand, I sometimes use quite specific terminology, particularly from Halliday's (1994) functional grammar, as a shorthand for concepts which are explained in detail elsewhere. I am positioning myself as someone who is familiar with this descriptive framework, and I am positioning you, the readers, as people who are familiar with, and/or interested in it.

An overview of the book

This book is about the ways in which writing intersects with identity. Although it explores various aspects of this relationship, it presents one overarching argument:

Writing is an act of identity in which people align themselves with socio-culturally shaped possibilities for self-hood, playing their part in reproducing or challenging dominant practices and discourses, and the values, beliefs and interests which they embody.

There are several interconnected elements to this argument which I attempt to summarize here.

- What people do conveys a message about their identity. An important type of action which constructs identity is discourse, and a particular type of discourse is writing.
- Writing is a particularly salient form of social action for the negotiation of identities, because written text is deliberate, potentially permanent and used as evidence for many social purposes (such as judging academic achievement).
- Negotiating a 'discoursal self' is an integral part of the writing process: there is no such thing as 'impersonal writing'.
- Writers create an impression of themselves — a discoursal self — through the discourse choices they make as they write, which align them with socially available subject positions.
- The relations of power, interests, values, beliefs and practices in institutional settings enable and constrain people's possibilities for self-hood as they write.
- Some discourses are more powerful, and/or more highly valued than others, and people are under pressure to participate in them through adopting them in their writing.
- In spite of these powerful shaping social forces, individual writers participate in the construction of their discoursal identities through selection (mainly subconscious) among the subject positions they feel socially mandated, willing, or daring enough, to occupy.
- Writers bring an 'autobiographical self' to an act of writing. This is shaped by their life-histories and the social groups with which they identify. Different social groups have differential access to the subject positions inscribed in discourses. In this way, writers' autobiographical selves are very varied, and do not have equal social status.
- A writer's autobiographical self influences the discoursal self they construct for themselves in a specific piece of writing, and leads them to own or disown aspects of it.

- When people enter what is for them a new social context such as higher education, they are likely to find that its discourses and practices support identities which differ from those they bring with them.
- Both writers' sense of themselves (autobiographical self), and the impression which they convey of themselves in writing (discoursal self) is normally multiple and subject to change over time.
- Every time people write, they reaffirm or contest the patterns of privileging among subject positions which are sustained by the relations of power in the institution within which they are writing.
- The reader-writer relationship is a crucial element in all this: the discoursal self which writers construct will depend on how they weigh their readers up, and their power relationship with them.
- The effect of writers' alignments on the community as a whole will depend on 'uptake' by readers.
- Writers can accommodate to or resist the pressure to conform to readers' expectations.

I approach this argument in two ways. In Part One, I expand on the argument I have presented here, linking it to published theory and research, elaborating and refining it. I examine the relationship between writing and identity from three theoretical perspectives: linguistic theory (Chapter 2), literacy theory (Chapter 3), and theory and research on academic writing (Chapter 4). In Chapters 2 and 3 I consider how the positions and issues in these fields of research relate to academic writing in particular, and often illustrate points by reference to academic writing. I do not bring in specific examples from the writing of my co-researchers, but I do occasionally refer to them and their experience of academic writing. Our work together is the source of many of the insights and positions which I present in Part One, and I indicate some of the ways in which they have contributed as my account unfolds.

Part Two contains five chapters about specific aspects of the discoursal construction of writer identity, each of which can be read independently of the rest of the book. Part Two is the core of the book, bringing the theory in Part One down to earth, discussing writing and identity in relation to particular people writing particular texts. It is based on the research my eight co-researchers and I carried out on the relationship between writing and identity in their academic writing. I first explain briefly how we conducted the research (Chapter 5), and then give 'the whole picture' in the form of a case study of one person, Rachel Dean, writing one essay (Chapter 6), including detailed discussion of extracts from her writing. In the following four chapters I take up particular aspects of the relationship between writing and identity in more detail, with textual examples and quotations from all eight of my co-researchers. In Chapter 7 I discuss the way in which aspects of academic writing have origins in different experiences and encounters in the writers' life histories. In Chapter 8 I focus on issues of ownership, accommodation and resistance to conventions for the presentation of self, and the influence of the reader-writer relationship on the discoursal construction of identity. Next I analyse the discoursal characteristics of the essays themselves, using some of the concepts and tools for analysis introduced in Chapter 2. In Chapter 9 I focus on the linguistic characteristics which the essays have in common, identifying the values, beliefs and interests embodied in the dominant discourse of higher education. In Chapter 10 I focus on diversity both within and between essays, showing the range of alternative possibilities for self-hood available within the discourses of higher education.

In the Conclusion I return to the issue raised in this chapter of the relationship between theory and practice. I develop the claim that particular ways of thinking about writing and identity can be of use, even have a liberatory power, for all of us as we write and help students to write in institutional settings. I suggest ways in which ideas in the rest of the book can be drawn upon in courses which address the writing demands of higher education. I suggest that research of the sort reported in Part Two of the book enables us to see what otherwise remains hidden beneath the surface of students' writing, revealing the complexity of the decision-making which they face, and the subtlety of their reasons for writing as they do.

There are several ways in which you might want to approach reading this book, other than from beginning to end. One way might be to start with the case-study, Chapter 6. This brings the issues of writing and identity to life, and reads almost like a story: you can use it as an introduction to issues you might want to pursue in other chapters. Chapters 6, 9 and 10 are more linguistically oriented than others, and may be the main interest of readers with a back-ground in linguistics. However, I have tried to explain my analytic techniques as I go along in those chapters, in such a way that readers from other disciplines can understand them. Teachers of writing might want to go straight to Chapter 11, and then work backwards into Parts One and Two.

PART ONE

Theoretical approaches to writing and identity

CHAPTER 2

Discourse and identity

Introduction

In this chapter I move from general issues of identity to the more specific issue of the discoursal construction of writer identity. Identity is attracting increasing attention in linguistic theory. Halliday's view of language, as developed since the mid-seventies, mentions identity as one of the aspects of social life which is bound into grammar. More recently Fairclough, Wertsch and others taking up the ideas of Bakhtin and Vygotsky have fine-tuned our understanding of the relationships between language and identity.

Before considering these contributions I need to address the thorny issue of how to use the terms 'language' and 'discourse'. The term 'discourse' is good because it foregrounds the concern with social issues in the study of language. It is a term used by social scientists working in many different fields who recognize the role of language in social processes, but who may not be as interested as linguists in the specifics of the text. I have chosen the title 'Discourse and Identity' for this chapter, in order to keep strong the connections between what I am writing about here and the broader, sociological views of identity I outlined in Chapter 1. By contrast, the term 'language' seems rather narrow. However, there are good reasons for using it. The main one is that socially-oriented linguists want to reclaim a socially situated, discoursal scope of reference for the terms 'language' and 'linguistics'. In other words, we do not want to leave the word 'language' available to be used in contrast to 'discourse', as if 'language' can exist, or be studied separately from its social context. An advantage of using the word 'language' is that it foregrounds the linguistic aspects of discourse, which can become obscured by the broader scope of the term 'discourse'. For these reasons I use both the terms 'language' and 'discourse' to refer to language-in-its-social-context. I also use the related adjectives 'linguistic' and 'discoursal' and adverbs 'linguistically' and 'discoursally' to refer to the whole, socially situated acts represented by Figure 2.1.

I reserve the term 'text' for referring to the physical manifestations of discourse: in this study of writing, this means the marks on the page. When using the terms 'text', 'textual' and 'textually' I am foregrounding the role of *form* in discoursal/linguistic processes and practices as a whole.

The focus on speaker identity in sociolinguistics

Although the discoursal construction of writer identity is only beginning to interest writing researchers, the relationship between language and identity has always been on the agenda in sociolinguistics which is concerned with the way in which linguistic variation is geographically and socially determined. I mention this work briefly in order to point out the similarity between my project and theirs. Sociolinguists such as Labov (1963) in Martha's Vineyard, a small island of the East coast of the United States, Milroy (1980) in Belfast, and Gumperz and Cook-Gumperz (1982) in studies of different ethnic groups have demonstrated the strength of people's desire to identify with some social groups, and to disassociate themselves from others, and the way in which this desire to identify determines their phonetic, syntactic and lexical choices in language. They have shown how individuals can be consistent or ambivalent in their identification, and how that consistency or ambivalence manifests itself in language. They have also shown how people's allegiances and therefore language choices change over time, sometimes abruptly, sometimes gradually.

Most of this research has concentrated on the phonological dimension of spoken language. But the underlying idea that language is a means of expressing social identity applies to all aspects of the language system. That same strong desire to identify manifests itself in choices in written language, including choices beyond sentence boundaries. I see the full range of written discourse choices as part of writers' social categorization processes, just as much as phonetic and other choices are part of speakers' social categorization processes. In the next two sections I outline linguistic theory which is more broadly conceived than traditional sociolinguistics in several respects. Firstly, it does not restrict itself to spoken language. Secondly, it is concerned with syntactic, lexical and whole-text aspects of language patterning, not just phonological patterning. Thirdly, it is concerned with linguistic differences associated with different social activities and ideologies, not just differences associated with ethnicity, geographical location, social class, or gender.

Halliday

The view of language I use as my starting point is Halliday's "language in a social-semiotic perspective" (Halliday 1978, 1994; Halliday and Hasan 1989). The word "semiotic" in Halliday's work conveys two principles which seem to me to be important. Firstly, language is only one of many sign systems which convey meaning: it is part of a much larger network of symbolic systems which can, in principle, all be drawn on to convey meanings, although in fact some are preferred over others for particular purposes in particular cultural settings.

Secondly, language is integrally bound up with meaning, and all linguistic choices can be linked to the meaning they convey. There is no such thing as meaning in a text independent of the form in which it is worded. Halliday's *"Functional Grammar"* (1994) demonstrates that lexico-syntactic forms can be explained in terms of their function in conveying meaning. The distinction between form and content breaks down further when discussing language choices beyond clause level, because decisions concerning what sorts of things to write about, what counts as grounds for a claim, what to include and what not to include are all determined by discourse conventions just as much as decisions concerning how to write it. Every discoursal decision positions the writer doubly: as a thinker of such things and as a user of such words and structures. In practical terms, using this view of language as an analytical tool, it is not possible to discuss the content a writer wants to convey separately from discussing the linguistic forms in which s/he conveys it.

The extension of the term "semiotic" to "social-semiotic" conveys a third principle which is central to any discussion of the relationship between language and identity. The meaning that is conveyed by language is not free-standing, open to each individual to construct at will. Meaning is dependent on social context in two ways, which Halliday calls "the context of situation" and "the context of culture". Explaining what he means by the context of situation, Halliday says that meaning (and the linguistic choices which follow from it) is dependent on the actual, immediate situation in which it is used, with particular, unique interlocutors engaged in particular, unique activities:

> words...get their meaning from activities in which they are embedded, which again are social activities with social agencies and goals. (Halliday and Hasan 1989: 5)

Explaining what he means by "the context of culture", Halliday says that meaning (and the linguistic choices which follow from it) is also dependent on the way in which language has been used in the past: only certain meanings are possible because of socio-historical constraints. The language system itself has been socio-culturally constructed. Halliday himself does not discuss the nature of these socio-historical constraints in any detail. This aspect of the view of language with which I am working is more fully worked out by Fairclough and others, as I discuss in the next section.

Within this broad conceptualization of language as a social semiotic, Halliday proposes that language simultaneously performs three macro-functions. Two of these represent two types of meaning which are conveyed simultaneously in language. "Ideational meaning" is Halliday's term for the ideas, content, subject-matter, story conveyed by language. "Interpersonal meaning" is Halliday's term for the effect of the speaker/writer on the hearer/listener — "expressing the self and influencing others". Halliday and Hasan (1976, 1989) say that, in addition to conveying two types of meaning, language also simultaneously performs a third macro-function: the "textual function" of making the meanings hang together.

Halliday refers in passing to the expression of "identity" as part of the interpersonal function of language, but he does not pay much attention to it. In my view social identity is not just a part of interpersonal meaning but has three dimensions to it, corresponding to the three macro-functions of language. I am suggesting that social identity consists firstly of a person's set of values and beliefs about reality, and these affect the ideational meaning which they convey through language. Social identity consists secondly of a person's sense of their relative status in relation to others with whom they are communicating, and this affects the interpersonal meaning which they convey through language. A third component of social identity is a person's orientation to language use, and this will affect the way they construct their message. Looked at from the other direction, the ideational, interpersonal and "textual" meanings conveyed by language all contribute towards constructing the participants' identities. The way in which language constructs and conveys all three aspects of social identity for writers is the focus of this book.

Halliday uses these three macro-functions as the framework for the grammar which he presents in the *Introduction to Functional Grammar* (1994). This description provides a powerful analytical tool by which linguists can link the syntax of a text to the meanings it is conveying. I will be explaining some of these techniques when I use them for analysis of specific examples of students' writing in Chapters 6, 9 and 10.

Fairclough: a social view of language

A framework for integrating a description of language with a description of its context of production is provided by Fairclough (1989, 1992a and 1995). In Figure 2.1 I have reproduced Fairclough's diagrammatic representation of this framework as he presented it in *Language and Power* (1989), adding arrows of my own.

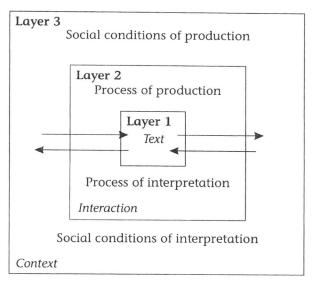

Figure 2.1   Discourse as text, interaction and context (adapted from Fairclough 1989: 25)

One advantage of this diagram is that it illustrates graphically how words themselves are embedded in the processes and social forces which produce them. Fairclough shows how a text (written or spoken) is inextricable from the processes of production and interpretation which create it, and that these processes are in turn inextricable from the various local, institutional and socio-historical conditions within which the participants are situated.

Fairclough (1992a) says that "text" represents two types of content: "social reality", and "social relations and social identities". "Social reality" corresponds to what Halliday calls "ideational meaning". "Social relations and social identities" are what Halliday calls "interpersonal meaning", although in his account of interpersonal meaning Halliday focuses mainly on "social relations". Fairclough does not deal with what Halliday calls the "textual" function of language.

The middle layer of Fairclough's diagram represents the processes of production and interpretation of texts. This refers to the mental, social and physical processes, practices and procedures involved in creating the text. People are located in this layer, thinking and doing things in the process of producing and interpreting texts. This layer of the diagram includes the role of social interaction in discourse: Goffman's theory of self-representation (which I introduced in the last chapter, and will discuss further in Chapter 4) can be seen as an elaboration of some of the processes represented by this layer. Related specifically to the production process of writing, this layer connects the wider social context to the words on the page through the head of the writer. It represents the writer's mental struggles which lead, among other things, to particular identities being written into a text.

A major feature of Fairclough's diagram (Figure 2.1) is the outer layer, the social context which shapes discourse production, discourse interpretation and the characteristics of the text itself. This is the "context of culture" which Halliday mentioned but did not expand upon in any detail. As Street (1993c) says, 'culture' is not a thing but a verb: the constant interaction of competing systems of values, beliefs, practices, norms, conventions and relations of power which have been shaped by the socio-political history of a nation or an institution in the interests of privileged members of it. There is a strong pressure in any cultural context to conform to dominant values, beliefs and practices, as they appear to be the means of achieving social, and often financial, gain, although they usually reinforce the status and serve the interests of the privileged few. However, the systems of values, practices and beliefs, and the patterns of privileging among them are not fixed, but open to contestation and change.

The context of culture for any social act consists of a set of 'contexts' embedded in each other: the context of the whole world at a particular moment in history (what is called 'global culture'), of a whole hemisphere ('Western culture'), of a nation ('British culture'), of an institution ('university culture') and of smaller units which define themselves by difference from others ('Lancaster Linguistics Department culture').

Fairclough, Kress, Bakhtin, and others have contributed towards our understanding of the way in which values, beliefs and practices in contexts of culture constrain what can be said in a particular instance of language use, and of the role of language in maintaining and contesting values, beliefs and practices within particular contexts of culture. A single instance of language use draws on conventions which embody particular values, beliefs and practices in the context of culture. The single instance of language use thereby minutely contributes to reinforcing those values, beliefs and practices, and opposing others. This is how Bakhtin summarizes it:

> language has been completely taken over, shot through with intentions and accents. For any individual consciousness living in it, language is not an abstract system of normative forms but rather a concrete heteroglot conception of the world. All words have a "taste" of a profession, a genre, a tendency, a party, a particular work, a particular person, a generation, an age group, the day and hour. Each word tastes of the context and contexts in which it has lived its socially charged life; all words and forms are populated by intentions.
> ...
> Language is not a neutral medium that passes freely and easily into the private property of the speaker's intentions; it is populated, overpopulated —with the intentions of others. (Bakhtin 1981: 273–274)

Halliday (1988, 1989, 1993) contributes to this view the point that it is not only the words but also the grammatical structures in which they are carried which "taste of contexts".

The arrows which I have added to Fairclough's diagram represent the way in which language is both shaped by and a shaper of social context. The inward-pointing arrows represent the way in which the cultural context with its competing values and ideologies and its shifting relations of power affect texts indirectly 'through the heads' of participants in specific linguistic interactions. Fairclough uses the term "members' resources" to refer to what is in the heads of participants as they produce or interpret texts. He says that members' resources include "their knowledge of language, representations of the natural and social world they inhabit, values, beliefs, assumptions, and so on" (1989: 24). It is through members' resources that the context of culture is brought into the context of situation. The outward-pointing arrows represent the way in which every linguistic act contributes to the future life of the competing ideologies in the cultural context, by reproducing or opposing them, in this way participating in the ongoing process of social change.

Another way in which this diagram seems to me to be a useful representation of discourse is that the 'text' box is relatively small in relation to the socio-cognitive and socio-cultural dimensions of language. Fairclough proposes that linguistic description and explanation should take account of all these elements. This connects to the thorny issue of whether to use the term 'language' or the term 'discourse' to refer to the whole of what is represented in this diagram. For the reasons I gave in the introduction to this chapter I use both the terms 'language' and 'discourse' to refer to the whole set of objects, relations, processes, practices, ideologies and patterns of privileging among them represented by Figure 2.1, depending on what I want to foreground.

Fairclough's major contribution to the discussion of discourse and identity is that he places the construction of identity in the context of fluctuating cultural and institutional values. All his samples in *Discourse and Social Change* (1992a) are of spoken discourse, but what he says applies to written discourse too:

> ... discourse contributes to processes of cultural change, in which the social identities or 'selves' associated with specific domains and institutions are redefined and reconstituted. (137).
>
> most if not all analytically separable dimensions of discourse have some implications, direct or indirect, for the construction of the self (167)

and

> When one emphasizes construction, the identity function of language begins to assume great importance, because the ways in which societies categorize and build identities for their members is a fundamental aspect of how they work, how power relations are imposed and exercised, how societies are reproduced and changed. (168)

In conclusion, Fairclough shows how language is socially constructed and probably the most powerful of all semiotic media for the social construction of reality. His diagram relates social construction to social interaction, it relates texts to other texts, and it provides a framework for relating discourse to identity, as I will explain in more detail in the rest of this chapter. In my opinion this view of language, combined with the analytical tool of Halliday's Functional Grammar, is the most powerful tool for the study of language in context, and hence for understanding the relationship between language and identity.

The heterogeneity of discourse

A consequence of Halliday's and Fairclough's view of language as consisting of text, interaction and context is the idea that language varies according to context. Halliday dealt with this through the concept of 'register', proposing that each set of regularly occurring contextual characteristics predicts a particular 'register': a set of textual realizations. But this is too static and deterministic a view of the relationship between language and context. Fairclough emphasizes that it is important not to take a typological approach to language variety (1988, 1992c) arguing that there is not a fixed one-to-one relationship between context and language, and any attempt to make a typology or prescribe appropriate use is misleading:

> the matching of language to context is characterized by indeterminacy, heterogeneity and struggle (1992c: 42)

Indeterminacy, heterogeneity and struggle mean that any text is constructed out of discourse conventions which have diverse origins, as suggested by Bakhtin in the extract quoted above. This critical genre theory of variety eschews typologies, and is therefore at odds with both Halliday's idea of a predictable register, and with more normative versions of genre theory such as Swales (1990) and Martin (1989).

On the one hand it is important to recognize the "indeterminacy, heterogeneity and struggle view" of language variety, in order not to suggest that certain discourse characteristics are correct, or that discourses are static, and to avoid the prescriptivism which comes from such a view. On the other hand if we take this caution too far it is impossible to talk about the idea of people drawing on discourse conventions at all. I try to take a middle position, not claiming that certain characteristics are discourse-specific in any fixed way, but suggesting that particular discourse characteristics *are* shaped by the current interests, values, beliefs and practices of particular social groups, and so position the writers as participating in these interests, values, beliefs and practices. This means that, when a writer words something in a particular way, by a particular choice of words and structures, they are aligning themselves with others who use such words and structures, and hence making a statement of identity about themselves. In Chapters 6 and 10 I show how the mature student writers with whom I was working aligned themselves to particular disciplinary views of the world, to particular ideologies of knowledge-making, and to particular views about their role in the institution by writing in particular ways.

One aspect of heterogeneity is that, according to Fairclough (1992a and c), Kress (1989) and Kress and Threadgold (1988), any text is drawing on conventions of both 'genre' and 'discourse'. This distinction is not made by Halliday, Bakhtin, or other theorists, but is one which I have found useful in this study. Conventions of *'genre'* are those which are dependent on the social situation in which language is used, and the social purpose for which the language is being used in this situation: the 'interpersonal' elements in that situation. In contrast, conventions of *'discourse'* are not dependent on the purpose and the social situation, but more on what is being spoken or written about: the 'ideational' elements.

Any piece of language might be categorized as primarily belonging to a particular genre (for example poem genre, or newspaper editorial genre), and can be shown to have characteristics of a particular discourse (for example, 'anti-war discourse' or 'natural science discourse'). So a single discourse can be found in several different genres. In the same way, a single genre (for example, undergraduate essay genre) also provides the container for a wide variety of discourses (for example, philosophy discourse, natural science discourse). In some cases, however, a particular genre will be expected to be used for talking/writing about particular content, in other words, it will be associated with a particular discourse. For example, the prototypical sermon genre is often associated with the discourse of the Christian religion. In attempting to give simple examples, I am beginning to fall into the trap of assuming simple, one-to-one fits between texts and single genres or discourses. Critical genre theory warns against this, pointing out that actual texts are usually drawing heterogeneously on conventions of more than one genre, and more than one discourse. For example, I have recently been involved in petitioning for a piece of intellectual work in the genre of a novel to be accepted as an undergraduate dissertation.

This distinction between 'genre' and 'discourse' is useful for a theory of writer identity, since they foreground different aspects of identity. Genres are shaped by institutionally defined purposes, roles, and the social relationships associated with them, such as 'student' — subordinate to tutor, applicant — subordinate to admissions tutor; administrator — sometimes wielding power over academic staff, sometimes subject to their power. So the conventions of genres make available certain roles and role relationships, which people may conform to, or they may resist. Discourses, by contrast, are shaped by subject-matters and ideologies such as history, skiing, a feminist perspective, a commitment to disabled people's rights. By making particular discourse choices, writers are aligning themselves with particular interests (in terms of subject-matter) and ideologies. In recognizing the way in which writing constructs identities it is important to keep both these aspects of identity in mind.

However, the terms 'genre' and 'discourse' can be confusing. Particularly, as I have already said, 'discourse' is a useful term to refer to the whole interrelated language act represented by Fairclough's diagram, as well as for the more specific aspect of language described above: with a perspective on content. I do use the term 'discourse' in both senses, and try to make it clear when I am using it in the more restricted sense I have just described, in contrast to genre. The term 'genre' is also used much more broadly by many theorists, but I avoid this usage in this book. I also use the term 'discourse types', following Fairclough 1989, when I need a catch-all term to refer to linguistic conventions which does not distinguish between 'discourse' and 'genre'.

Intertextuality and identity

Social construction of identity requires 'building materials'. The materials are socially determined, and individuals draw on them, in socially constrained ways, in the process of 'construction'. As many theorists argue, the most important of these 'building materials' is language. In this section I first use Fairclough's (1992a) definition and elaboration of the concept of intertextuality, focusing on those aspects which are particularly relevant to writing and identity. I then introduce Bakhtin's terminology for writing about intertextuality, showing how it maps on to Fairclough's and others' terms.

The distinction between 'actual intertextuality' and 'interdiscursivity'

Fairclough (1992a) uses the term "intertextuality" (first coined by Kristeva in 1966 — see Kristeva 1986), as a very general term to refer to all the ways in which a specific text relates to other texts in any way. It is an extremely broad term, which he subdivides into "manifest intertextuality" and "interdiscursivity".

"Manifest intertextuality" is his term for parts of texts which can be traced to an actual source in another text. It includes discourse representation in the forms of quotation, paraphrase and copying, but also other ways of incorporating, responding to, or anticipating other texts or utterances, such as irony and presupposition (Fairclough 1992a: 104 and 118–123). Manifest intertextuality is an optional characteristic of texts: in principle it is possible to find texts with none at all. In my view "manifest intertextuality" is a misleading term, as it suggests that the source texts are always clearly visible in the new text. This type of intertextuality *is* often explicitly signalled, especially in many written genres where quotation marks serve this purpose, but it is not *always* signalled. Since I make a distinction between signalled and unsignalled forms of intertextuality later in the book, I do not use the term "manifest intertextuality" at all, but replace it with 'actual intertextuality'. This term seems to me to capture the idea that it is an *actual* text that is being drawn upon, rather than an abstract text *type*, as described below. Actual intertextuality is relevant to writer identity in two ways. Firstly, writers in academic contexts (such as those described in Part Two of this book) have to position themselves in relation to the highly valued convention in academic writing of quoting from authoritative sources. They have to ask themselves the question: am I the sort of person who quotes others? and if so, how? I take up this issue and the interesting questions it raises in Chapter 10. Secondly, writers are sometimes echoing the actual voices of people they have met and identified with, thereby aligning themselves with those very people rather than with an abstract social position. I discuss this in more detail in the next section and give examples in Chapter 7.

"Interdiscursivity" is Fairclough's term for "intertextual relations to conventions" (104). The key difference here is that the echo in the new text is not of another specific text, but of a recognizable, abstract text *type*, or set of conventions: a pattern or template of language use, rather than a sample of it. The linguistic phenomena which Fairclough lists as such patterns are: genres, discourses, styles and activity types (103 and 125–130). Fairclough's term "interdiscursivity" is useful because it is based on the word 'discourse': it means the way these abstract text types or sets of conventions — 'discourse types' — are being drawn on. A further distinction can be made between the process of drawing on conventions of discourse, and the process of drawing on conventions of genre: some call this 'intergenericity'. However, it is usually simpler to use the term 'interdiscursivity', as I use 'discourse types', to refer to both discourses and genres. Interdiscursivity is not an optional characteristic of texts: all samples of language in use can be identified as drawing on such conventions in some way or other. Interdiscursivity is not so often explicitly signalled as actual intertextuality, but it is sometimes, as some of the examples I give in Chapter 7 show.

Building on the understanding that a person's identity is constructed by the language s/he uses, interdiscursivity is a central concept for a theory of language and identity. It explains how people come to be making particular discoursal choices. They are drawing *interdiscursively* on the discourse types they have available to them. This repertoire of possibilities for self-hood is the connection between a person's past and their future. The idea of interdiscursivity therefore underpins the whole of this book, and particularly the analyses in Chapters 9 and 10.

Summing up the key distinction between the two types of intertextuality, Fairclough writes:

> Manifest intertextuality is the case where specific other texts are overtly drawn upon within a text, whereas interdiscursivity is a matter of how a discourse type is constituted through a combination of elements of orders of discourse. (1992a: 117–118)

This distinction is extremely important to understand, but I want to raise a word of caution. How can analysts tell if they are looking at a sample of actual intertextuality, or of interdiscursivity? Actual intertextuality may be obvious enough in public texts: political speeches, literary texts, media discourse, for example. The original speakers and their actual words are likely to be part of public knowledge. In private, personal texts, however, actual intertextuality is less likely to be recognized, unless the analyst knows the speaker/writer's discourse history intimately. What may look to the analyst like interdiscursivity may have, probably does have, actual text supporting it of which the analyst and probably the person themselves is unaware. I am introducing this point here in anticipation of my discussion of Vygotsky in the next section, and of the origins of writers' discoursally constructed identities in Chapter 7.

Bakhtin's ways of writing about intertextuality

Bakhtin does not use the term "intertextuality", but talks about the same phenomenon in more metaphorical ways which map onto Fairclough's and Kress's terminology. According to Bakhtin's broad approach to language study (or "translinguistics", as he calls it), all the language choices in any "concrete utterance" are "double-voiced", that is, intertextual in some way, whether or not they are signalled in any way as belonging to others. The idea that any instance of language is "double-voiced" means that, in addition to the writer's own, unique role in shaping the discourse, it is "interanimated" by what Bakhtin calls "social languages and speech genres": in Kress's terms "discourses" and "genres"; in Fairclough's terms "discourse types"; in Wertsch's (1991) terms "voice types". The crucial words in these terms are "social" and "type", meaning that these are abstract "voices", existing in the context of culture, rather than concrete utterances. This is the same distinction as Gee (1990) attempts to bring out between the abstract and the concrete by using capital letters for social Discourses and small letters for actual, specific discourses.

Bakhtin also uses the term "ventriloquation", meaning providing the mouthpiece for language which is not your own. When language users make discourse choices they "ventriloquate" both particular voices they have encountered in the past (actual intertextuality), and more abstract voice types (interdiscursivity). This refers both to content — what gets talked about, and to lexico-grammatical characteristics. Finally, Bakhtin refers to "dialogic over-tones" emanating from the way in which each concrete utterance is "popu-lated — overpopulated — with the intentions of others" (1981: 294), or "interanimated" by other voices. The unifying idea behind Bakhtin's terms "multivoicedness", "othervoicedness", "doublevoicedness", "hybridization", and "ventriloquation" seems to me to be similar to what Fairclough calls interdis-cursivity, although in Bakhtin's way of putting it there is more emphasis on individual encounters as the way in which people gain access to discourses.

> When each member of a collective of speakers takes possession of a word, it is not a neutral word of language, free from the aspirations and valuations of others, uninhabited by foreign voices. No, he [*translator's generic pronoun*] receives the word from the voice of another, and the word is filled with that voice. The word arrives in his context from another context saturated with other people's interpretations. His own thought finds the word already inhabited. (Bakhtin 1973: 167)

I find that Bakhtin's terms (as found in the translations of Bakhtin 1973, 1981, 1986, and Voloshinov 1973, and Wertsch's 1991 application of them) supple-ment the "intertextuality" discourse, providing an extremely expressive repertoire for discussing the issues in this chapter. One of the advantages of Bakhtin's rich vocabulary for intertextuality is that it makes all parts of speech available: nouns, verbs, adjectives and adverbs; Fairclough's way of talking about intertextuality has no verbs. Another advantage of Bakhtin's expressions is that they range across all aspects of the phenomenon, providing ways of talking about the source texts, the process of drawing on them and the characteristics of the new texts. Some ways with words I have adopted from him are — as they appear in the translations of his work — voice(s), multi-voiced(ness), othervoiced(ness), doublevoiced(ness), reinvoice(d), populate(d) with, interanimate(d) (ion), ventriloquate(d) (ion), dialogic (al) (ism), over-tones, reaccentuate (ion). Bakhtin seems to use these expressions for all types of intertextuality, often blurring the distinction between actual intertextuality and interdiscursivity as he does so — sometimes usefully, sometimes annoyingly.

The social origins of the mind: Wertsch 1991

As I discussed above, Fairclough (1992a) proposes that the discoursal construction of 'self' is a crucial mechanism in processes of social reproduction and change, and he uses the concept of intertextuality to explain how this works. However, he does not concern himself with change over time for the individuals involved in these processes: his theory of language does not have a theory of language acquisition built into it. In my view, the most satisfactory theory to supply this dimension is Vygotsky's, as interpreted by Wertsch.

Wertsch's book *"Voices of the mind: a sociocultural approach to mediated action"* (1991) connects social construction both to language and to a theory of intellectual growth. This helps me to link Fairclough's, Kress's and Bakhtin's observations about the socio-cultural nature of language with Vygotsky's theories of the individual's discoursal history and psychological development. Wertsch summarizes Vygotsky's main claim about intellectual development as:

higher mental functioning in the individual derives from social life (19)

Vygotsky explained acquisition and development in terms of "intermental" and "intramental" functioning. He claimed that whatever an individual becomes able to do independently (that is, by functioning of their own mind — intramentally) is a result of social experiences with other humans (that is, as a result of the interaction between their own mind and that of others — intermentally).

This is relevant to the study of writer identity because it explains how writers reach the intramental condition which determines what they produce on paper. It doesn't seem to be stretching Vygotsky's terminology too far to suggest that most intermental encounters are sources of actual intertextuality, in the sense I have introduced the term above. That is, when two individuals interact, an intermental encounter takes place. The encounter contains seeds of cognitive growth for one or both participants. Discourse(s) are used, some of which may be new to one or both participants. In future performance, each individual may draw on the experience of that encounter, having taken to themselves, internalized, made "intramental" some of its seeds for cognitive growth, including its discourse type(s). This seems to be what Wertsch is suggesting, using different terminology.

Bakhtin (1986) also writes about the role of actual voices, belonging to real people we have encountered, in our mental growth, and in building the unique, personal repertoire of discourse types on which we draw each time we use language afresh.

> One can say that any word exists for the speaker in three aspects: as a neutral word of a language, belonging to nobody; as an *other's* word, which belongs to another person and is filled with echoes of the other's utterance; and, finally, as *my* word, for, since I am dealing with it in a particular situation, with a particular speech plan, it is already imbued with my expression. (88)

> The unique speech experience of each individual is shaped and developed in continuous and constant interaction with others' individual utterances. This experience can be characterized to some degree as the process of *assimilation* — more or less creative — of others' words (and not the words of a language). (89)

> Our thought itself — philosophical, scientific, and artistic — is born and shaped in the process of interaction and struggle with others' thought, and this cannot but be reflected in the forms that verbally express our thought as well. (92)

The discourses writers have available for writing have been acquired through specific encounters with them in actual (spoken and written) texts in their past experience. These intermental/intertextual encounters have provided the "scaffolding" (a Vygotskyan term) for acquiring the discoursal repertoire available to them at the moment of writing.

In summarizing this view I have been careful not to talk in terms of unilinear development. Vygotsky was writing about progression from lower to higher mental functioning because he was interested in young children's development, but I would rather see the development of intramental resources in terms of an ever-widening repertoire of functions, without assuming a hierarchy among them. In terms of this study, it is important not to think simplistically about 'the acquisition of academic discourse'. There is no such single-tracked process: it's not a smooth progression towards possession. People change their preferences as their life experiences and values change, moving in and out of discourses according to particular demands of particular occasions for writing and particular readers. It would be wrong to see the heterogeneous discoursal choices in this data as marking transition: a single path from one, less powerful, less efficient, inferior discourse to another, more powerful and efficient, superior one. The situation is much more complicated. Certainly there are some discourse choices which are less well received by those with power to award grades: they are less privileged, in Wertsch's terms. By the dominant conventions of the institution, some discourses are judged more 'appropriate' than others. However, many would contest that these are in fact necessary for superior intellectual activity (see, for example, Fairclough 1992c). Mature student writers are not altogether committed to a single path of acquiring these 'appropriate' discourses. Most of them, while partly desiring these statusful discourses and believing in their power, are also resistant to them in some way — a resistance brought out and intensified by the research process, as can be seen in Chapter 8. Discourses other than academic discourse are not so obviously ranked according to status, and therefore the issues of hierarchy and transition are not always relevant when choosing among them.

While rejecting the idea of a simple progression from lower-order to higher order mental functioning, I do espouse Vygotsky's central idea that the development of "intramental" resources "derives from social life". I understand the resources writers bring to writing as having their origins in previous "intermental encounters", and in Chapter 7 I show how "voice types" which the eight writers employ in their academic essays originate in particular voices associated with intermental encounters in their past experience.

Wertsch connects Vygotsky's social view of cognitive development to the idea of intertextuality, using the concepts of a "toolkit", "an array of mediational means" and "mediated action" to refer to the repertoire of discoursal resources which people have at their disposal.

> A toolkit approach allows group and contextual differences in mediated action to be understood in terms of the array of mediational means to which people have access and the patterns of choice they manifest in selecting a particular means for a particular occasion. (Wertsch 1991: 94)

Wertsch does not problematize the way in which "the patterns of choice people manifest in selecting a particular means for a particular occasion" are socially constrained. The "array of mediational means to which people have access" is not the same for everyone: this access is unequally distributed, and dependent on people's social circumstances such as education, employment opportunities and interpersonal networks. This means that some people's "toolkit" will be bigger, and/or contain more statusful "tools" than others.

The so-called "patterns of choice" are also constrained by the fact that some mediational means (specifically, discourse types) have higher status in particular contexts for particular purposes than others, and are therefore the default choices. Wertsch introduces the concept of "privileging" to describe the difference in status accorded to particular mediational means within the array in any particular cultural setting. He writes:

> I shall address the issue of the organization of mediational means in a dominance hierarchy in terms of the notion of "privileging". Privileging refers to the fact that one mediational means, such as a social language, is viewed as being more appropriate or efficacious than others in a particular sociocultural setting. (Wertsch, 1991: 124)

I prefer his terms "privileged" and "privileging" to the terms "dominant" or "domination" because they focus on the processes of raising the status of one mediational means over another, rather than on a static state of affairs. They retain the sense that there were human agents responsible for the process of making something dominant. These patterns of choice are not fixed but fluctuate under the influence of social change.

Finally, I think it is important to examine what it means to say that a writer makes "a selection" within an array of discourse types. Expressions like 'selection', 'options', 'language choices' are dangerously misleading. They imply firstly that a particular writer is able to choose freely among alternatives, secondly that the choice is something which resides in the individual will, and thirdly that it is conscious. I want to imply none of these things, but I do believe that the writers' *unconscious* act of selection from alternatives is an important component in the discoursal construction of identity — constrained by social factors, and highly influenced (though not determined) by socio-historically situated conventions as it is. Both the very idea of selection and the possibilities for selection are socially constructed. I use the word 'choices', and ask the reader to understand it, as a simplifying metaphor for what are in fact fleeting, subtle, complex subconscious processes which are socially con-strained and not under the full control of the individual.

In this book the "mediated action" I'm interested in is writing an essay. The "tools" in the "array of mediational means" I'm interested in are those provided by human language. These include both spoken and written dis-course types; both what Bakhtin calls "social languages" (what Kress and Fairclough call "discourses") and what Bakhtin calls "speech genres" (what Kress and Fairclough call "genres"). They include both "referentially semantic content" (i.e. what gets talked about), and lexico-grammatical characteristics (i.e. how it is worded — Wertsch, Chapter 6). The cultural contexts which sustain this particular array of mediational means, and the patterns of privileg-ing among them, are the institutions of higher education in Britain. I suggest that the set of mediational means to which an individual writer has access, along with their socially constrained patterns of choice within that array, is what makes each writer's writing unique: the individual stamp, which is often simplistically called the writer's 'own voice'. I prefer to refer to this as the writer's 'owned voice': the writer's choices, from among many competing socially available discourses, of ones s/he is willing to be identified with.

Conclusion

In this chapter I have explained what I mean by the discoursal construction of writer identity, drawing on Halliday's view of language, on Fairclough's theories of discourse, intertextuality and identity, and on Wertsch's integration of Vygotsky's and Bakhtin's work. I have drawn a picture of writers positioning themselves by the discourse types they draw upon. They are constrained in this by the limited array of discourse types to which they have access, and by the patterns of privileging among discourse types in the context in which they are writing. This understanding of the discoursal construction of writer identity underpins the analysis of specific cases in Part Two of the book. However, I have been talking about the discoursal construction of writer identity as if it depended entirely on the intersection of the writer's history of intermental encounters, and the discourse conventions in the social context. Literacy studies, research on academic writing and Goffman's insights into social interaction also contribute to a theory of writer identity, and I discuss these in Chapters 3 and 4.

CHAPTER 3

Literacy and identity

Introduction

Literacy involves language. The issues discussed in Chapter 2 therefore apply in totality to literacy. However, literacy has recently been the focus of interest within many disciplines in addition to linguistics: anthropology, sociology, education, and psychology. Many studies of literacy are interdisciplinary, and bring insights beyond those contributed by linguists, often integrating the perspectives I have dealt with in Chapter 1 with those in Chapter 2. In this chapter I give an overview of the contribution made by literacy research to the study of writer identity. First, however, I discuss various aspects of the definition of 'literacy', and how it relates to language.

'Literacy' is both *less*, and *more* than 'language'. It is less, in the sense that language is a superordinate term, encompassing both spoken and written language, while literacy makes written language its focus. It is more, in the sense that 'literacy' is a different sort of word from 'language' and refers to more than the language itself. In terms of Fairclough's diagram (Figure 2.1) 'literacy' focuses on the middle layer rather than the inner box. Literacy theorists and anthropologists investigating literacy in a wide range of settings have paid far more attention than linguists to the physical, mental and social practices and processes in which written language is embedded, because they are not so concerned with the written text itself. Their work fleshes out and extends what I have said so far about the middle layer of Fairclough's diagram. In fact, by making social activity rather than a text their central focus they lead me to suggest a possible adaptation to Fairclough's diagram (see below).

The word 'literacy' is used in two different ways.

Meaning (a)

In everyday use, the word 'literacy' means '*the ability to use written language*'. The everyday expression 'literacy campaigns', for example, means 'campaigns to develop *the ability to use written language'*. Literacy in this meaning has an opposite, 'illiteracy', which is used by some to mean 'inability to use written language'. This brings out an important difference between the terms 'language' and 'literacy': there is no equivalent opposite of the word 'language', in theoretical or everyday usage. The existence of the negative word 'illiteracy' draws attention to the fact that 'literacy' in meaning (a) is concerned with people's use of a semiotic system, rather than with the semiotic system itself.

Meaning (b)

Literacy theorists often also use the word without the emphasis on 'ability to', to mean *'(way(s) of) using written language'*. For example, when Klassen writes "literacy changes from place to place" (1991: 40), he doesn't mean *'ability to use written language* changes from place to place'. Rather, he means *'ways of using written language* change from place to place'.

Gee (1990) goes to great pains to make the distinction between these two meanings clear. He systematically uses the term 'discourse(s)' in place of 'literacy (ies)' in sense (b), reserving the term 'literacy' only for sense (a): "mastery, or fluent control over .... a discourse" (153). These two distinct yet overlapping meanings of the word 'literacy' are important in understanding recent literacy theory, and I am concerned with both in this book.

Gee considers it "rather pedantic" (153) to distinguish discourses which involve print from those which do not. Recently several researchers have moved in the same direction, concerning themselves with the whole process of semiosis (see, for example, Hodge and Kress 1988), with the similarities and differences between visual and linguistic representation of meaning (as in Kress and van Leeuwen 1996), and with more broadly conceived literacies such as 'media literacy' (see, for example, the book edited by Graddol and Boyd-Barrett 1994). Meaning (a) has been used metaphorically to mean 'ability to understand and/or use' a whole variety of things, in expressions such as 'read a film', 'computer literacy' or 'political literacy' (see Barton, 1994: 13 and 187). This is, in my view, an interesting development which breaks through unproductive dichotomies to recognize similarities and more broadly applicable generalizations. However, I think it remains useful to make more specialized studies of particular semiotic systems such as written language. Written language is still — although maybe not in perpetuity — a particularly important semiotic system, since it is one which has a gatekeeping function in many social contexts, and the inability to use it according to particular, privileged conventions affects many people's life chances. My specific focus in this book is on academic writing, and I therefore I use the term 'literacy' to refer specifically to uses of written language, in spite of what Gee says.

In the next section I compare spoken and written language in terms of their relationship to context as a precursor to discussing the social approach to literacy, and the place of writer identity within it.

Literacy is embedded in social context

Until recently it has been assumed that there is a great divide between spoken language and written language (Ong 1982, Olson 1977). Spoken language has been characterized as 'involved', that is, affecting and affected by the social relations of the interlocutors (Chafe 1982, Tannen 1985), context-dependent; written language by contrast has been characterized as detached, decontextualized, autonomous. This view has been challenged, especially by Street (1984, 1995) who claims that literacy is not autonomous but 'ideological', that is, shaped by the values and practices of the culture in which it is embedded.

One of the features of the 'great divide' position is that those who hold it equate spoken language with face-to-face encounters and written language with communication which is separated in time and space. In fact the varieties of spoken and written language cannot be neatly separated in this way. In addition it seems to me that these polarized positions arise from different characterizations of context, as summarized in Figure 3.1. I have discussed this in detail elsewhere (Ivanič 1994a, Clark and Ivanič 1997, Chapter 3).

The idea that literacy is decontextualized is consistent with an extremely simplistic view of context. When context is thought of just in terms of physical surroundings and the physical presence of individuals, then there is an important difference between face-to-face encounters (that is, most spoken language) and communication which is separated in time and space (that is, most written language). Most 'spoken language' does make use of this physical presence, whereas most 'written language' has to compensate for the fact that the interlocutors are separated in time and space, and do not share a physical setting. To take an example from academic writing, a student is working in his bedroom, surrounded by books, lecture notes, and perhaps transcripts of some interviews. He is very interested in the topic he is studying and keen to make the connections between what he has read and the data he has collected. He has to write about it, but he doesn't know what the tutor who will read his essay will be interested in, what she will value, what she will need explaining,

Aspect of context	Effect on face-to-face encounters	Effect on communication which is separated in time and space
Context of Situation		
(i) Physical situation	Interlocutors can refer to shared physical setting and monitor each other's reactions	Interlocutors cannot refer to shared physical setting and cannot monitor each other's reactions
(ii) Specific purposes and interpersonal relationships	Affect both spoken and written language	
Context of Culture Competing systems of values, beliefs and practices in the cultural context	Shape and constrain both spoken and written language	

Figure 3.1   The effects of different aspects of context on spoken and written language

what she will need justifying. Several weeks later, a tutor reads the essay the student has written in her office, with piles of other essays beside her, and a computer screen showing lecture notes for her next lecture. She finds the topic of the assignment boring, as it is no longer in the forefront of her research. If the tutor and student were able to meet together to talk about the topic in the same space they could use the resources around them as part of their discussion, and the student could figure out what to say from the tutor's on-going reactions. In writing, however, the student has to write his sources into his essay, and anticipate the tutor's reactions as best he can. It seems to me important to recognize this difference between face-to-face communication in a shared context and communication in which writing and reading take place in contexts which are physically separated from each other. This difference is especially salient for such prototypical written language as academic writing, since it is what causes some of the difficulties people face with writing. At the same time, however, it is important to recognize other aspects of social context which apply equally to both spoken and written language.

A slightly richer characterization of the actual, concrete context in which individuals are communicating includes not only physical presence and surroundings, but also people's social purposes and social relationships (Context of Situation (ii) in Figure 3.1). When context is understood in this way, 'written language' is embedded in social context just as much as 'spoken language' is. Literacy (in the sense of 'using written language') serves some specific social purpose: it is used in order to respond to some particular life demand, not practised for its own sake. Literacy involves communication between individuals who have a certain social relationship with one another. Written language is imbued with purpose and interpersonal relationships in just the same way as spoken language is. For example, the academic essay described above is embedded in a particular social context which consists of a particular course in a particular department, a particular assignment set by a particular tutor, due on a particular date, and the essay is part of a developing social relationship between the student and the tutor who is going to read it.

A third interpretation of 'context' is what Halliday calls 'context of culture', and what Fairclough calls 'institutional' and 'societal' context, as described in Chapter 2: the more abstract, but ultimately most powerful aspects of the context of literacy: the competing conventions, norms and practices of the culture, institution(s) and society. Spoken and written language are equally affected by context in this respect. Each decision a language user makes will be drawing more or less conventionally, more or less creatively, on these norms. This is the characterization of context which supports Street's claim that literacy is not autonomous, but ideological. The essay described above, for example, was written in the early 1990s in a department of sociology in a university in Britain. In this cultural context the dominant set of conventions for writing sociology essays included writing in rather long sentences, using many abstractions throughout the essay, and not mentioning personal experience. There were other, less dominant sets of conventions too, such as one in which the presentation, discussion and analysis of personal experience was valued. However, this cultural context did not support the practice of asserting views as to what is morally right or wrong as part of a sociology essay: a practice which might be valued in academic contexts in other cultures, or in other types of writing. This is a very schematic example, but enough to show, I hope, what I mean by the more abstract 'context of culture'. Context in this characterization is in a constant state of flux, continuously being re-shaped by social processes of alignment with some conventions and contestation of others. Both spoken and written language are enmeshed in these social processes: both are heavily 'contextualized' in this sense of 'context'.

In this study I am viewing academic writing as just as much embedded in social context as any form of language use. Recognizing the contextualized and ideological nature of literacy is what leads me to concern myself with identity as a crucial factor in academic writing. However, I am also recognizing that written language *is* different from spoken language insofar that speaking usually takes place in a single physical context, whereas the writing takes place in a different physical context from the reading. This explains why people who are used to making meaning in face-to-face interaction may encounter considerable difficulties when academic writing requires them to communicate without the immediate presence of their interlocutor.

The ecology of literacy

Thinking about literacy in sense (b), as 'ways of using written language', has led to a focus on physical and social activity: the way in which the on-going mêlée of social life gives rise to the use of written language. Reading and writing are not undertaken for their own sake but in order to fulfil social goals. Barton (1994) uses the metaphor 'the ecology of literacy' to add detail to this idea. This metaphor conveys vividly the idea that recognizable acts of reading and writing have come to be the way they are because of the social needs and purposes they have evolved to serve. The metaphor of 'the ecology of literacy' also conveys the idea that a large number of interrelated social factors support the survival of particular acts of reading and writing, just as, for example, a large number of interrelated physical factors support the survival of a particular species of newt. Acts of reading and writing all have their own 'ecological niche', and these cultural settings are extremely diverse. The metaphor implies that research should uncover social explanations not only for the linguistic nature of written texts, but also for the variety of literate behaviour, and for the way in which various types of written language fit into different social contexts. Barton and Hamilton (forthcoming) and the books edited by Street (1993b) and Hamilton, Barton and Ivanič (1994) provide examples of this type of research.

This view of literacy is totally opposed to one which treats written language in isolation. With an ecological view of literacy, grapheme-to-phoneme correspondences cannot possibly provide an adequate account of written language. Literacy is not just about texts but also about actions around texts. Even psychologically-based aspects of literate behaviour — comprehension strategies and writing processes — are only a small part of the whole picture. This is particularly important for its pedagogical implications. Activities which learners undertake as part of the formal teaching of literacy are all too often divorced from context and purpose, as if reading and writing were autonomous. An ecological view of literacy suggests that experiencing the need for literacy in context is an essential element in its acquisition.

Central to an ecological view of literacy is the idea of literacy events. The term 'literacy event' has been coined (see Heath 1983, Barton 1991, 1994, Chapter 3) for social occasions which involve written language in some way. Thinking in terms of literacy events produces some useful insights. Firstly, written language is intertwined with spoken language in many ways. For example, ideas are talked through before and during writing. Secondly, (written) language can be relatively central to or relatively peripheral to the action. For example, written language is central to an occasion when someone sits in the library and reads an article, but less central to a shopping expedition. Thirdly, an event can involve one or many texts. For example, in writing an assignment for a course, there is the evolving written essay, there are notes being written, other notes being read, books and articles being consulted. Fourthly, texts can participate in one or many events — either in sequence, as when someone writes a letter, someone reads it, and then shows it to or talks about it to someone else, or independently, as when thousands of people read the same article in a newspaper. Fifthly, many literacy events can be broken down into sub-events. For example, the literacy event of finding out some information in a library involves many sub-events, such as visiting the inquiry desk, consulting the catalogue, scanning the rows of books, surveying selected books, reading a small number of pages in more detail. Studying academic literacy includes paying attention to the constellation of literacy events in which people engage when producing an academic essay.

Making literacy events the focus of attention suggests a variation on Fairclough's diagram along the lines of Figure 3.2.

To maintain comparability with Fairclough's diagram, there is still a text at the centre. The 'text' box in Figure 3.2 draws attention to the way in which written texts employ both verbal and visual modes of representation and communication. Even if a text consists entirely of words it still has visual characteristics: the size, font and layout of the words, which in themselves convey meaning. However, the main focus of interest is not a text but an event, and the people and actions which constitute it. The event includes 'interaction' — the middle layer of Fairclough's diagram, the physical activities which surround the use of written language, and the immediate social context. A literacy event may involve several texts; this observation foregrounds the fact that language may only be peripheral to the total event, and recognizes

Values, beliefs, interests and power relations

Practices and discourse types

Event

Text

Figure 3.2   Literacy in context (developed from Fairclough 1989, page 25)

the interplay between texts, both spoken and written — a different perspective on 'intertextuality'. This representation matches Fairclough's diagram in that the outer layers represent the social context. This consists, firstly, of the conventions on which people are drawing in the literacy event: practices, the conventions for behaviour (as discussed below), and discourse types, the conventions for language use, as discussed in Chapter 2. The outer layer of the diagram represents those aspects of the socio-cultural context which shape practices and discourse types: the configuration of values, beliefs, interests and power relations.

The value of an ecological view of literacy for a theory of writer identity is that it brings onto the agenda the way in which people's identity is implicated in and constructed by their literate activities as well as their linguistic choices. Halliday and Fairclough make an important step forward by emphasizing that language cannot be studied without also paying attention to social action. Literacy theorists go further (as long as they don't lose sight of textual characteristics) by saying that language is only a part of the whole scene, not centre stage. But literacy events are not the whole story, either: in terms of the diagram, it is essential to attend also to the outer layers. By focusing on literacy events literacy theorists raise the question:

"What is it that is generalizable from one event to another, similar event?"

And they answer:

"Not only discourse types, but also literacy practices."

Literacy practices

The activities and behaviour associated with the written text(s) reflect the values, patterns of privileging, and purposes in the social context. Literacy practices are the culturally shaped ways in which literacy serves social ends. In this section I first discuss what the term 'literacy practices' refers to, and then consider what it means to say that they are 'culturally shaped'.

Literacy (in the sense of 'ability to use written language') is not a technology made up of a set of transferable cognitive skills, but a constellation of practices which differ from one social setting to another. (See Scribner and Cole 1981, Heath 1983, Street 1984, 1993a, 1994, 1995, Barton 1991, 1994, Barton and Hamilton 1998, and Baynham 1995, for the development of the notion of 'literacy practices'.) 'Practices' is a much broader and more powerful term than 'skills'. Social practices are ways of acting in and responding to life situations, and literacy practices are a subset of these. Some people's social practices in response to some life situations include literacy ('using written language'): those social practices are their 'literacy practices'.

As I discussed when putting forward a social view of language in Chapter 2, social practices are not universal: they differ from one social context to another, and social groups differ from each other in which practices they will employ in the same context. One aspect of a group's or a person's social practices is the role of literacy in them. For example, in British culture, many people consider that the appropriate response to another person's bereavement is to send a written card or letter of condolence. A visit would be considered intrusive, unless you are a very intimate friend. But in Tanzanian culture, a written condolence would be considered disrespectful. To take another example, in Czech academic culture, written answers are not part of the examination system; in British academic culture, they are.

It is not only the decision to use literacy but also the way in which it is used which is culturally shaped: imbued with the values, beliefs and power relations which exist in the cultural context. However, as Street has argued (1993c, 1994), there is not a simple, one-to-one relationship between literacy practices and culture. Values, beliefs and power relations are in a constant process of contestation and change. Indeed, cultures themselves are not hermetically sealed, but interact with other cultures, defining their own values and beliefs in relation to others. As a result, a variety of literacy practices may co-exist in any cultural setting, so that one person may engage in a particular literacy event in a different way from someone else within the same culture. This is not to say, however, that there is an undifferentiated, limitless range of possibilities: in most cultural contexts there are dominant values and beliefs, including beliefs about people's relative status, which privilege some literacy practices over others (to use Wertsch's term, see Chapter 2). For example, the literacy practice of publishing in academic journals is more highly valued in the academic community of the mid-1990s than publishing in newsletters and magazines designed for teachers. Academics who devote their time to writing in the highly valued publications gain status in the academic community, whereas those who spend time writing for the other publications do not. By engaging in the privileged literacy practices people reinforce and reproduce the dominant values, beliefs and structures of a culture, and they align themselves with those values, beliefs and interests. In the case of this example, they perpetuate the divide between academic theory and research, and practical application of the ideas generated by academic work. Yet this pattern of privileging has no natural logic to it: it is constructed and supported by the interests of people with power in academic institutions at this particular socio-historical moment. This is, above all, what leads Street to insist on using the word 'ideological' in relation to literacy practices (1993a, 1994, 1995).

This idea of aligning oneself with particular values, beliefs and interests through social practices, including literacy practices, concerns the interface between 'culture' and 'identity'. An individual's personal constellation of practices (differing from event to event) will draw, possibly in a unique way, on the practices which are common in the culture(s) with which they are familiar. Individuals rarely draw on a single set of practices. Most individuals, particularly in a society such as Britain, have variable access to, and partial membership of, a range of cultures. They select, usually subconsciously, from among the practices associated with those cultures, thereby engaging in heterogeneous practices of their own which simultaneously reaffirm some cultures and deny others. For example, I see myself as a member both of the culture of the academic institution in which I work, and of the Adult Literacy network of which I still see myself a part. I therefore engage in literacy practices from both cultures, writing for both types of publication mentioned above, and often mixing the discourses drawn from these two cultures within the same piece of writing. My identity is heterogeneous, and this affects my literacy practices, including my discourse choices.

It is important to recognize the distinction between the actual, observable practices of individuals, and the abstract, theoretical idea of the practices which are the norm for a cultural group. Gee neatly makes a similar distinction by using the term 'discourse' with a small 'd' for the individual use, and 'Discourse' with a capital 'D' for the abstract norms. It would be possible to adopt a similar convention, using 'practice(s)' for what individuals do, and 'Practice(s)' for the abstract idea of the prototypical ways of doing things which people draw on. However, making this sort of distinction has two disadvantages. Firstly, it suggests that 'Discourses' and 'Practices' are given, fixed entities, whereas I prefer to think of them as in constant flux as a result of everyday use. Secondly, the two are also closely interrelated in the way I have just suggested: an individual only knows about the 'Practices' of a social group by observing the 'practices' of individual members of it. In this way the distinction between the real and the abstract breaks down. I therefore find Gee's terms a little too rigid, and I use the terms 'discourses' and 'practices' ambiguously: purposely ambiguously.

Literacy practices are a person's or group's responses to a particular life demand which involves written language in some way. Some literacy practices are event-specific, such as writing a cover-sheet when handing in a piece of coursework, and are employed in instances of the same event, but not in a variety of events. Some literacy practices are employed in more than one type of event, such as skimming a text to get the gist of it. Literacy practices include not only mental processes and strategies, but also decisions such as whether to employ written language at all, which types of writing reading and writing to engage in, discourse choices, feelings and attitudes, and practical, physical activities and procedures associated with written language. Literacy practices of all these types are both shaped by and shapers of people's identity: acquiring certain literacy practices involves becoming a certain type of person.

The notion of literacy practices is particularly relevant to the study of identity in academic writing. Mature students are adults who are changing their identity: attempting to take up membership of the academic community which is an addition to, possibly at odds with, other aspects of their identity. They will be encountering literacy practices which belong to people with social identities different from theirs. In order to take on these new aspects to their identities, they need to engage in these practices; in order to engage in these practices they need to be people of this sort. It is a vicious circle, fraught with conflicts of identity. Most mature students are outsiders to the literacies they have to control in order to be successful in higher education. My study attempts to show how they are dealing with their mixed desire for and resistance to insider status, how far they are being "colonized" as Gee puts it, or "appropriated" as Bartholomae (1985: 135) puts it, and their response to this.

Multiplicity

As a consequence of thinking of literacy being embedded in social context, current literacy theorists have challenged the idea of a singular 'literacy', that is, a monolithic ability to use written language. They prefer to talk in terms of 'literacies', that is, ways of using written language which differ according to social context. In any culture there are multiple, jostling literacies, which individuals draw upon heterogeneously, and which vie for social recognition. 'Literacies' in British culture include 'academic literacy', 'bureaucratic literacy', and literacies associated with different workplaces and aspects of home and community life. Recognizing a multiplicity of 'literacies' is a big step forward from thinking about 'literacy' as a single, unified ability.

It is sometimes also useful to discuss multiplicity in terms of finer-grained distinctions. A difficulty with the term 'literacies' is that there are no clear criteria for cutting off one literacy from another. The term is sometimes too all-embracing, trying to capture both the plurality of contexts in which literacy can be embedded, and the plurality of ways of using literacy in those contexts. As Street has argued (1994 and elsewhere), it is perhaps necessary to think not only of differences between institutional contexts in which literacy is used, but also of a multiplicity of literacy *events* and of literacy *practices* in these contexts. This allows us to talk about the different types of plurality separately, and to theorize the fluidity of practices and events across contexts. Academic literacy consists of a multiplicity of more or less context-specific literacy events, and a multiplicity of practices available for participating in those events. In terms of writer identity, a person has a multiple identity as a writer *both* as a consequence of participating in a variety of culturally shaped literacy events *and* as a consequence of employing a variety of culturally shaped practices in those events.

Developing and extending literacies

The every-day meaning of the term 'literacy' is 'the ability to use written language' (meaning (a) in the introduction to this chapter). Literacy theorists almost always concern themselves with how people develop and extend this ability, in addition to describing and accounting for the nature of different ways of using written language (meaning (b)). There are many implications of the view of literacy I have outlined here for an understanding of how people develop and extend their repertoire of literacies, including:

- ability to use written language is not a single skill;
- literacy cannot be measured on a single scale;
- literacies can be developed and extended in the same way as languages, by participating in social activities which require their use;
- entering a new cultural context will involve a new phase of literacy development;
- developing and extending the ability to use written language never ends: people are always increasing the repertoire of literacy events with which they are familiar, and changing their literacy practices.

Developing and extending literacies is not a simple matter of 'learning' or 'acquisition'. The term 'learning' implies that particular activities need to be designed for the purpose of developing and extending literacies, whereas a social view of literacy suggests that literacies are best developed and extended in the context of use. The term 'acquisition' implies that there is a pre-ordained 'thing' to be acquired, and suggests that there can be some end-point by which someone has completed the process of acquisition. This does not accord with a social view of literacy, in which literacies are bound up with use and meaning-making. Developing and extending literacies involves rather the creative re-production of socially available practices and discourses for new purposes as they arise in people's lives. Kress (1996) argues that each individual creates these resources anew for themselves out of those to which they have been exposed, rather than simply 'acquiring' them.

All these issues in relation to developing and extending literacies are relevant to people entering higher education. It is not a question of whether students are literate or illiterate, as the media often suggest. Rather, this new experience is going to require people to extend their repertoire of literacy practices: to build and adapt existing ones and to engage in new ones. What distinguishes students is not whether they are or are not literate, but the characteristics of the repertoire of resources they bring with them to the task.

Becoming more literate is in itself an issue of identity. People who feel more at home with spoken language as a way of communicating may have ambivalent feelings about the identities supported by written language. On the one hand, these are likely to be prestigious identities, and so it is in people's interests to develop and extend their literacies. On the other hand, they may be alien identities, and this will get in the way of engaging in the literate practices which support them. For some of my co-researchers, becoming a student entailed taking on the identity of a person who reads and writes, an identity about which some felt more positive than others.

People who have grown up using spoken language for all their communicative needs often find written language extremely unattractive, because it is stripped of those phonetic and prosodic markers of linguistic variety which would locate them ethnically, socially, or geographically. This was brought home to me by Joe Flanagan, one of the founder members of Pecket Well College, a self-help adult basic education residential college in Hebden Bridge, Yorkshire. He once said: 'What I don't like about writing is that people don't know I'm Irish.' For someone who thinks this way, there is little incentive to engage in written discourses.

There are two ways of thinking about developing and extending literacy which are often seen as contradicting each other. One is that literacy is a less natural form of language use than speaking, and therefore people need special conditions in order to acquire it. Gee (1990) puts forward this view, using the terminology I introduced earlier. He talks in terms of 'primary discourses' and 'secondary discourses', primary discourse being the way of using language a child acquires in its first few years of life, and secondary discourses (including those involving the written word) being all those developed later in life. The danger of this view is that it is liable to be interpreted to mean that 'secondary discourses' are not developed at home, and need to be taught in a different way from 'primary discourses'.

The idea of literacy developing differently from and later than spoken language is contradicted by work on emergent literacy with very young children, which suggests that children begin to develop familiarity with using written language extremely early (see the arguments in Barton 1994). These studies show that children develop written language in exactly the same way as they have developed spoken language, and that the two processes go on alongside each other in literate homes, not sequentially. However, there is a certain psychological reality for many people in the idea that the discourse of everyday conversation is more immediate, closer to their sense of themselves than any discourses (spoken or written) or practices which they consciously undertake to acquire, particularly relatively exclusive discourses such as academic discourse. As I discussed under the heading 'Written language is embedded in social context', there is a simple definition of context which does distinguish spoken language from written, and this is the aspect of spoken language which makes it closer to some people's sense of themselves. In Part Two of this book I show how some of my co-researchers identified more closely with linguistic features of their essays that are more like spoken conversation than written composition. In this respect Gee's distinction between primary and secondary discourses is relevant to the question of how writers are positioned by their writing.

Literacy practices, written language and the construction of identity

The main contribution of literacy theorists to the study of writer identity is a greater understanding of the way in which the use of written language is connected to other aspects of social life. In this section I pursue the connections between linguistic theory and analysis, and this more anthropologically-oriented approach.

Besnier (1989, 1990, 1991, 1995) studied the uses of literacy on Nuku-laelae Atoll, a group of Polynesian islands inhabited by 350 people. He made two useful observations about the relationship between literacy practices, written language and identity. First, he made the distinction between person-hood and self-hood which I mentioned in Chapter 1, section 1.4. Person-hood is the aspect of identity which is associated with someone's social role in the community as leader, as postperson, as farmer, as preacher. Self-hood is the aspect of identity which is associated with someone's private life and personality traits. Both these are socially constructed, and both affect a person's literacy practices. This connects to Besnier's second contribution: that different forms of literacy foreground different aspects of identity, and that these can be tracked to specific discoursal choices in written language. Particularly, he

observed that, on Nukulaelae Atoll, writing a sermon foregrounds the 'person'
of the preacher, and backgrounds private aspects of self (Besnier 1990, 1991).
By contrast, writing letters — a vigorous and pervasive literacy practice on
Nukulaelae Atoll — foregrounds the private 'self' of the writer, and is a vehicle
for the expression of affect which is a highly valued of quality of 'self' in this
culture. Besnier (1989) identified a range of linguistic features which encoded
the expression of strong interpersonal feelings in the corpus of letters he
studied. This is important for literacy theory because it shows that the expression of feeling and interpersonal involvement is not specific to the use of
spoken language, but can be found in either written or spoken language,
depending on culture-specific practices.

By starting from the culture rather than the language, but pursuing his
observations right down to the linguistic features, Besnier provides important
insights about writer identity. Firstly, he shows how participating in a particular literacy practice in a particular culture simultaneously positions writers and
dictates their linguistic choices. Secondly he points out that a culture contains
both (a) social roles for people — their 'person-hood' — with associated
particular literacy practices and linguistic choices, and (b) a set of highly
valued personal qualities which people should display in appropriate places,
such as in letters — their 'self-hood'.

Gee (1990) neatly connected practices to linguistic choices by insisting
that the word 'Discourse' encompasses both. Here are some of his definitions:

> What is important is not language, and surely not grammar, but *saying
> (writing)-doing-being-valuing-believing combinations.* These combinations I will
> refer to as 'Discourses', with a capital D. (142)

> Discourses are ways of being in the world, or forms of life which integrate
> words, acts, values, beliefs, attitudes, social identities, as well as gestures,
> glances, body positions and clothes. (142)

> A Discourse is a sort of 'identity kit' which comes complete with the appropri-
> ate costume and instructions on how to act, talk, and often write, so as to take
> on a particular social role that others will recognize. (142)

> A *Discourse* is a socially accepted association among ways of using language,
> of thinking, feeling, believing, valuing and of acting that can be used to
> identify oneself as a member of a socially meaningful group. (143)

Through these definitions Gee captures the relationship between literacy
practices, linguistic choices, ideologies and identities, breaking down the
distinction between the outer two layers of Figure 3.2.

It is not easy for a person to control the relationship between literacy and identity. As Gee writes:

> ... someone cannot engage in a Discourse in a less than fluent manner. You are either in it or you're not. Discourses are connected with displays of identity — failing to display an identity fully is tantamount to announcing you do not have that identity — at best you are a pretender or a beginner.
>
> ... colonized students control (and accept values in) the Discourse just enough to keep signalling that others in the Discourse are their 'betters' and to become complicit with their own subordination. Thus...you are an *insider*, *colonized*, or an *outsider*.....Functional literacy is another term for the literacy of the colonized. (155)

This is particularly relevant to the people who are the focus of Part Two of this book. As I document through detailed examples in Chapter 8, most of them feel, for various reasons, that they are not '*in*' academic discourse. They aspire to this discourse but are, to a greater or lesser extent, colonized by it, and therefore occupy subordinate roles within it. However, the situation is not so simple as Gee makes out in several ways, as the examples in Part Two show. Firstly, people's motivations, aspirations and feelings are very varied. Secondly, some of them pretend quite successfully. Thirdly, a person who is colonized by or an outsider to one Discourse may be an insider to others: people have multiple identities, different aspects of which are foregrounded in different situations and at different times in their lives. Fourthly, Discourses — literacy practices and the written language embedded in them — are not monolithic but leak into one another, as I argue in Chapter 10.

Conclusion to this chapter

In this chapter I have discussed similarities and differences between writing and speaking which are relevant to the study of academic writing. I have explained how literacy theorists have widened the lens on writing, sharing the view of language I outlined in Chapter 2, but filling out parts of the picture which linguists merely mention in passing. I have drawn out the implications of these positions for writer identity, portraying 'identity' as constructed by the practices associated with writing as well as the linguistic choices writers make.

CHAPTER 4

Issues of identity in academic writing

Introduction

Academic writing is one type of literacy, and is the specific focus of this book. It has been the object of study for a very different group of researchers from those I have mentioned so far. Most of the study of academic writing has been carried out by those who also teach it, or have been teachers of it. The majority of these are basing their theory and research on the *Freshman Composition* classes which are obligatory in North American universities and colleges and higher education systems around the world which have adopted this system. European universities do not have the same requirement for university students to take a writing class, and consequently there has been less research in Europe in this field. But interest in academic writing is growing, certainly in Britain, as exemplified by the work of Andrews, Mitchell and Costello on argument and rhetoric (see, for example, Andrews 1989, 1995, Mitchell 1994a, Costello and Mitchell 1995). My own interest in this field arises from being involved with adults who return to study after many years outside the education system, and experience academic writing for their coursework as something of an identity crisis.

As a result of their origins as writing teachers, many researchers in this field have focused on student writing, either in composition classes or in the rest of the university. Some of these researchers have understandably concerned themselves with ways of facilitating students' socialization into 'proper' academic practices, without taking a critical view of these practices. They have nevertheless produced some interesting insights about issues of identity in academic writing.

In addition to research on student writing, there is also the specific research field of the Sociology of Scientific Knowledge which is interested in the way in which professional academics work, and their writing practices form part of this interest. The theory and research I discuss in this chapter comes from both these two traditions.

The issues I discuss in this chapter all contribute to building a picture of how identity is implicated in academic writing. I have been selective, since there is too much theory and research on academic writing to include it all. I had three criteria for this selection. Firstly, I am focusing on the constitution of identity for students writing *in a higher education setting*. Some of the theory and research I refer to is about writing in general, and writing in compulsory education, but I am drawing on only those studies which contribute to understanding writing within higher education. I will include some references to the Sociology of Scientific Knowledge, but only where they seem directly relevant to understanding student writing. Secondly, I am focusing on *people writing in their first language* (although occasionally I shall refer to studies where the author was interested primarily in people writing in their second language). Thirdly, I am focusing on *writing in subject areas,* sometimes called 'writing across the curriculum', rather than writing in composition classes or study skills classes. Although I hope this book will be of interest to educators, it is not about pedagogy: I will not be referring to the literature on methods of teaching writing.

In this chapter I distinguish between those who treat academic literacy as a fixed set of practices to which students need to be initiated, and those who take a more critical view, recognizing that such practices are socially constructed and consequently open to contestation and change. I first discuss the recent shift in the study of academic writing to a 'social view' of writing, relating the more wide-ranging issues I discussed in Chapter 1 specifically to academic writing. I then discuss some specific concepts arising within a social view of academic writing which have a bearing on the study of writer identity: the notion of 'discourse community'; the particular issues of intertextuality, imitation and plagiarism in academic writing; questions of authority and authorial stance; the distinction made by Cherry between *ethos* and *persona* in academic writing; ending with critical views of academic writing and the idea of accommodation and resistance to conventions. I discuss why it might be that writer identity has not been a focus of writing research and show how it seems to be lurking in the wings of theory and research on other aspects of academic writing. Finally I discuss how Goffman's theory of self-presentation can be applied to academic writing.

A social approach to the study of academic writing

Here I explain the development of a social view of writing and in the following sections some aspects of this view which are relate specifically to developing a theory of writer identity.

Bizzell (1986) and Faigley (1986) point out the trend towards a social view of academic writing in theory and research in North America. Faigley (1986) identifies four lines of research which contribute to a social view of writing: poststructuralist theories of writing, the sociology of science, ethnography, and Marxism. Bizzell identifies two other influences: literacy theory and an interest in writing- across-the-curriculum. Bizzell relates these recent developments in composition theory to trends in other disciplines: "questions are being raised about any theory of language that claims to transcend social contexts." (1986: 38). I particularly like this way of putting it, because it suggests that a social view of writing is more down to earth, less abstract than the cognitivist attempts to define literacy and its attributes in some general or universal way.

Many composition theorists have been working towards a more comprehensive theory of writing to integrate cognitive and social approaches, for example, Faigley (1986), Rose (1988), Flower (1989, 1994), Greene (1990), Nystrand (1989). So what does it mean to pay attention to social contexts for writing? There are differences in approach to what 'social context' means. Nystrand (1990) compares and contrasts social constructionist and social interactionist approaches to discourse, focusing on the key contrast between constructionist interest in the norms of discourse communities and the interactionist interest in "the give-and-take of real-time, situated discourse" (10), in terms of the relationships between writers and readers. These are the two approaches I discussed in Chapter 1, and they map on to Halliday's distinction between context of culture (social construction) and context of situation (social interaction), discussed in Chapter 2. Nystrand argues in favour of a social-interactionist approach to the study of writing, maybe because he is focusing on the effect of the reader on writing. However, in studying writer identity, it seems to me to be important to pay attention to both types of social context: the immediate interaction between real individuals, and the norms of the cultures in which they are operating, as I have discussed extensively in previous chapters. In the following sections I explain particular ideas within a social view of writing which seem relevant to my focus on writer identity.

The idea of 'academic discourse communities'

The term 'academic discourse community' is now common in discussions about the nature of academic writing in North America, and some version of this concept is essential to a social view of writing. Publications which focus on the notion of 'discourse community' are Brodkey (1987) Freed and Broadhead (1987), Bizzell (1989), Cooper (1989), Harris (1989), Nystrand (1990), Swales (1990, Chapter 2).

Harris (1989) points out that the notion of 'discourse community' is a blend of the more abstract 'interpretive community' used by Fish (1980) and the more concrete 'speech community' used by sociolinguists such as Hymes (1974). The distinction between these is rather like Nystrand's distinction between a social constructionist approach to discourse and a social-interactionist approach. The abstract element in the term 'discourse community' relates to the context of culture, the socio-historically produced norms and conventions of a particular group of people who define themselves by, among other things, their discourse practices. This more abstract element seems to be uppermost in the way most people use the term, especially when they use it in the singular. This may be particularly true in talking about contexts in which written language plays an important role, including the 'academic discourse community', at least in the U.S. and the U.K., though less so in many other European countries. When people interact with each other mainly through written language, their sense of 'community' may seem to be held together by abstract norms and conventions, rather than the identities, values and practices of real individuals. Nystrand, for example, associates the term 'discourse community' entirely with a social constructionist approach to discourse.

However, as Harris puts it,

> Most theorists who use the term seem to want to keep something of the tangible and specific reference of 'speech community' — to suggest, that is, that there really are 'academic discourse communities' out there, real groupings of writers and readers, that we can help 'initiate' our students into.
> (1989: 15 — *note Harris's scare quotes on the word 'initiate'*)

This seems to give the term a place in Nystrand's social-interactionist approach to discourse too, and is associated with the more concrete use of the term in the plural: specific academic discourse communi*ties*. If we cut an idea like 'discourse community' off from real individuals, it may be possible to theorize about, but it becomes difficult to research. Another practical issue is that it also becomes difficult to challenge community norms and conventions unless we see them residing in some way in individual heads. It seems to me to be useful to keep hold of both the cultural and the local way of thinking about academic discourse communities.

Swales (1990: 24–27) proposed six defining characteristics of a discourse community which do seem to take account of the abstract with the concrete. I quote them in full, and then discuss the strengths and weaknesses of this definition.

1. A discourse community has a broadly agreed set of common public goals.
2. A discourse community has mechanisms of intercommunication among its members.
3. A discourse community uses its participatory mechanisms primarily to provide information and feedback.
4. A discourse community utilizes and hence possesses one or more genres in the communicative furtherance of its aims.
5. In addition to owning genres, a discourse community has acquired some specific lexis.
6. A discourse community has a threshold level of members with a suitable degree of relevant content and discoursal expertise.

This definition adds two important details to other conceptions of 'discourse community'. First, Swales identifies specific activities in which discourse community members engage (2 and 3). This brings literacy practices into the definition, rather than the rather narrower textual focus of many definitions. Second, he specifically mentions the discoursal characteristics of discourse communities (4 and 5). This makes the link with the rest of his own work on genre and that of Australian genre theorists such as Martin (1989) — but bringing with it the danger of a normative view of genre, which I discussed in Chapter 2 of this book. At the end of the chapter Swales acknowledges Harris's criticism of his view that it is "oddly free of the many tensions, discontinuities and conflicts in the sorts of talk and writing that go on everyday in the classrooms and departments of an actual university." (Harris 1989: 14). Another limitation of Swales' definition is that he rather uncritically suggests that what holds members of a community together is "a broadly agreed set of common public goals". This suggests a rather monolithic idea of a discourse community, disregarding what Harris calls the "effects of broader social forces ... involving power but not always consent", which support the discourse practices of statusful communities. Swales himself has more recently pointed out these dangers in the whole idea of 'discourse community' (1993).

These tensions, discontinuities and conflicts also characterize the boundaries between discourse communities. Is there such a thing as an overarching 'academic discourse community' which can be marked off from other discourse communities? Do the different departments of a university constitute different discourse communities? In working with the notion of 'discourse communities' it is important to recognize that they are not monolithic but "can, over a period of time, lose as well as gain consensus" (Swales 1990: 32), can merge, overlap and split along new lines.

The term 'discourse community', as Harris explains, has developed mainly in order to explain group norms and conventions in relation to written discourse. I don't imagine anyone using the term would want to claim that they are talking/writing entirely about written discourse, but in fact little mention is made of the spoken discourse in academic discourse communities, nor of the interplay between spoken and written. It seems important to make it explicit that in academic communities there are both spoken and written discourse practices, and a complex interplay between spoken and written discourse. The roles of spoken and written discourse vary considerably from culture to culture, the written playing a bigger role in academic institutions in the U.S. and the U.K., the oral in academic institutions in many other European countries.

A question which is suggested by literacy theory, but does not seem to have been addressed in the discussion of academic discourse communities is whether there is any distinction between the idea of 'a community' and the idea of 'a discourse community' The literacy theorists I mentioned in Chapter 3 emphasize the point that literacy is embedded in its social context. This means that it is necessary to recognize the interests, values and practices which hold people together and see how discourse emerges from those, rather than starting by looking at discourse. Discourse practices are an important type of social practice that defines and constitutes a community, but not the only one. This seems to me to be rather a different way of thinking, focusing on the broader concept of 'community', with spoken and written discourse practices both shaped by and shaping it. So do we need the term 'discourse community' at all? The term draws attention to the fact that discourse is one important social mechanism at work in communities. On the other hand, the term distracts attention from other, equally important social mechanisms which interact with discourse. I will continue to use the term 'discourse community', since discourse is what I am writing about, but I intend it to mean 'community in which spoken and written discourse is one element among others': that is, a weak rather than a strong version of the term.

The term 'discourse community' can be used for very large social groups or for very small social groups. It is possible to talk about 'the academic discourse community' in general, specific disciplinary discourse communities, and possibly also micro-discourse communities such as a particular tutorial group in a particular department. The middle of this continuum has attracted considerable attention from researchers. Recognizing that each academic community will have its own, socially constructed norms and conventions for writing led many scholars in the 80s to study writing in particular disciplinary communities: biology — Myers (1989, 1990), physics — Bazerman (1981, 1988), English — Brodkey (1987), social sciences — Faigley and Hansen (1985), Hansen (1988), chemical engineering — Herrington (1985), behaviour in organizations — Currie (1990, 1991), economics — Dudley-Evans and Henderson (eds.) 1990, various — Maimon et al. (1981), Jolliffe (ed.) (1988), Swales (1990), Berkenkotter and Huckin (1995). (See Chapter 10 for further discussion of this work.) Much of this work on writing informs and is informed by the Sociology of Scientific Knowledge (e.g. Gilbert and Mulkay 1984 and Latour and Woolgar 1979). In addition there are genre theorists working in Australia who have been identifying the linguistic characteristics of writing within different school discourse communities: primary versus secondary education in general — Martin (1989), geography and history in secondary education — Eggins, Martin and Wignell (1987).

There is an unspoken assumption that research in this field is aiming to produce a definitive description of each discourse community. Surely such a resource would be very convenient for educators and researchers: educators could use such a description to teach apprentices the conventions, and researchers like me could match particular data against it. However, teachers and researchers should treat such findings with caution for the reasons I have already mentioned. This approach suggests that learners simply have to be initiated into a fixed set of discourse conventions in order to gain access to a discourse community. The most important objection to this is that norms and conventions, however powerful, are not static, and are not universal. These studies identify characteristics of discourse communities which are specific to a particular, local context at a particular time, and not necessarily generalizable to others. Such an approach takes an uncritical view of the status quo, treating the conventions as if they were natural — the product of common sense, rather than natural*ized* — the product of relations of power. Secondly, there is a lot in common across different academic discourse communities which often gets lost in this taxonomic approach. Thirdly, most of the studies focus on the writing of established experts in the community. What they find out about the writing practices of the experts may not apply directly to apprentices in the same community who have a different status and role. Fourthly, those working in this tradition often assume that students can become members of academic discourse communities by direct teaching of such conventions — an assumption which I would challenge. In my view the value of studies of disciplinary discourse communities is not that they produce a taxonomy of their characteristics; but that they uncover in increasing degrees of subtlety and sophistication the social processes at work in such communities.

What I gain from these studies is a rich picture of what it means to be a member of an academic discourse community. Academic discourse communities are constituted by a range of values, assumptions and practices. Individuals have to negotiate an identity within the range of possibilities for self-hood which are supported or at least tolerated by a community and inscribed in that community's communicative practices. Discourse community members, of varying affiliations in relation to the values, assumptions and practices, are also locked in complex interpersonal relationships, characterized by differences in status and power (see especially Myers, 1985, 1989 for insights into this). The writers I am studying are attempting to establish their identity within such communities, at the same time bringing with them complex identities from their social life outside the academic community.

Other scholars have focused on the experience of students who present a challenge to the expectations and norms of academic discourse communities, particularly those labelled 'remedial' or 'basic writers'. The titles of some of their articles and books give a flavour of this work: *Narrowing the mind and the page: remedial writers and cognitive reductionism* (Rose 1988) *Lives on the Boundary* (Rose 1989) *Dark shadows: the fate of writers at the bottom* (Haswell 1988). These studies develop the position originally staked by Shaughnessy in 1977 that, just because these students are not familiar with academic discourse, they are not cognitively deficient. Haswell brings evidence to show "complexity at the bottom" (same place: 310). Rose (1988) summarizes his argument in this way:

> Human cognition — even at its most stymied, bungling moments — is rich and varied. (297)

Rose (1989) tells how he himself started his education on the boundary and, as he says, "managed to get redefined". He describes his uneven progress, lurching between his old identity as an educational failure, and his new identity as someone with academic potential. Just as his own "life on the boundary" was temporary, he believes that most people can cross the boundary too, once they meet teachers who recognize that disadvantage is constructed by the system, not a characteristic of people.

Finally, several writers, particularly Cooper (1989) and Bizzell (1989 and 1992), point out that it is important to take a critical view of the notion of discourse communities. Having recognized that social practices such as discourse define social groups, it is easy to be led into the trap of accepting the status quo, that is, if members of a certain discourse community do certain things, it is necessary to do those things in order to be a member. As The Progressive Literacy Group in Vancouver (1986) put it, the language of statusful communities "leaves you out and sucks you in" (11). If teachers accept this uncritically it can lead to courses which attempt to teach students the discourse of the statusful community — the academic community — they wish to enter: to a new form of prescriptivism. A critical view of discourse communities brings to the fore the power relations, the struggles, and the possibility of change within and among them. For these reasons I prefer to use the term 'discourse community' in the way Bizzell suggests:

> Healthy discourse communities, like healthy human beings, are also a mass of contradictions.... We should accustom ourselves to dealing with contradictions, instead of seeking a theory that appears to abrogate them. (Bizzell 1987: 18–19, quoted in Harris 1989: 20.)

The notion of discourse communities is particularly relevant to the study of writer identity, because each individual takes on an identity in relation to the communities they come into contact with. Discourse communities are the 'social' element in the expression 'the social construction of identity': a person's identity is constructed by their membership of, their identification with, the values and practices of one or more communities. One of the ways in which people identify with a community is through the intertextual process of adopting its discourse, which I discuss next.

Intertextuality, plagiarism, imitation and identity in academic writing

I discussed the concept of intertextuality in detail in Chapter 2. There has been some theory and research which applies this concept specifically to the learning of academic writing. Faigley (1986) explains the place of intertextuality in a social view of writing:

> Thus a social view of writing moves beyond the expressivist contention that the individual discovers the self through language and beyond the cognitivist position that an individual constructs reality through language. In a social view, any effort to write about the self or reality always comes in relation to previous texts. (536).

Faigley's term "in relation to previous texts" is a good working definition of intertextuality. Porter (1986) connects intertextuality specifically to discourse communities, seeing the task of teaching writing as helping students to acquire the discourses of the communities they wish to enter. He recommends that writing teachers recognize that their students are reproducing other texts in their own as they attempt to write what will be acceptable in the community, and develop their pedagogy around this view of writing.

Ritchie (1989) uses Bakhtin's theory of language to study the writers in a writing workshop, one of the composition courses in a North American university. She presents two case studies "to illustrate the polyphonic texture of workshops" and "the struggle to construct a voice of their own from the counterpoint of voices in the various cultures surrounding them" (154). She writes that

> The personal, educational, and linguistic histories students bring to our classrooms contribute to the rich texture of possibilities for writing, thinking, and for negotiating personal identity. They also contribute to the confusion and anxiety many students experience (157),

and that

> students and their writing contribute to the linguistic, political, psychological, and social richness of the classroom, creating what Charles Schuster, describing Bakhtin's view of language, calls "a rich stew of implications, saturated with other accents, tones, idioms, meanings, voices, influences, intentions" (587). (Ritchie 1989: 159).

She thus draws attention to the fact that student writers are not only drawing intertextually on the discourses of the community they are entering, but also on the discourses they bring with them.

Recchio (1991), trying specifically to apply Bakhtin's ideas about inter-textuality to student compositions, recommends that

> As readers of student writing, we can approach our students' texts with an eye toward locating the multiple competing and/or interanimating discourses manifest in each. (447).

He illustrates how this can be done by showing, in one student paper, the interplay of "four distinct modes of discourse" (449). He ends by suggesting that making this sort of analysis explicit might help "the writer to begin to find her own voice" (453).

My view of writer identity starts with the same assumptions as Ritchie's and Recchio's: that the student writer's 'own' discourse is not something totally original, but a "rich stew" of the discourses with which s/he is familiar. Although their theoretical starting-point and methodology are similar to mine, my study is different in that I am studying the "rich stew" in writing across the curriculum, rather than in writing produced for composition teachers.

Brooke (1988) distinguishes between imitation and "identity modelling". While the whole idea of 'modelling' sounds rather uncritical and mechanistic, Brooke's article is a useful contribution in that it focuses attention on the writer rather than the product or the process of writing. In the context of a study of students developing literary rather than academic discourse, Brooke writes:

> when a student (or any writer) successfully learns something about writing by imitation, it is by imitating another *person*, and not a text or process. Writers learn to write by imitating other writers, by trying to act like writers they respect. The forms, texts, processes are in themselves less important as models to be imitated than the personalities, or identities, of the writers who produce them. (23)

He shows that there are ways of modelling identity which do not require taking on the identity of another writer wholesale, but adapting it in individual ways. He concludes that the teaching of writing should be, above all, helping students to take on an identity as a person who writes:

> Composition teaching works, in the modern sense, when it effectively models an identity for students which students come to accept. It works when part of their identity becomes a writer's identity, when they come to see that being a writer in their own way is a valid and exciting way of acting in the world. (40)

Bartholomae, while not using the term 'intertextuality', nor referring to Bakhtin, is referring to the same phenomenon when writing about the way in which student writers have to "invent the university":

> The student has to appropriate (or be appropriated by) a specialized discourse, and he [*Bartholomae's generic pronoun*] has to do this as though he were easily and comfortably at one with his audience, as though he were a member of the academy or an historian or an anthropologist or an economist; he has to invent the university by mimicking its language while finding some compromise between idiosyncrasy, a personal history, on the one hand, and the requirements of convention, the history of a discipline, on the other. He must speak our language. Or he must dare to speak it to carry off the bluff, since speaking and writing will most certainly be required long before the skill is 'learned'. (Bartholomae 1985: 134)

This is an intuitively appealing explanation for why students write as they do, pointing out that students have to adopt a voice which they do not yet own. However, Bartholomae treats the "requirements of convention" as if they were incontestable, and does not explore the possibility of students bringing alternative discourses to the academy which might eventually have an effect on its conventions. In the rest of this book I explore what this "compromise between idiosyncrasy, a personal history, on the one hand, and the requirements of convention, the history of a discipline, on the other" means not only for my co-researchers, but also for the institution of higher education.

Through studies such as these it is becoming increasingly recognized that learner writers (like all writers) are not so much learning to be creative as learning to use discourses which already exist — creatively. Intertextuality contributes to a theory of writer identity in two ways. A writer's identity is not individual and new, but constituted by the discourses s/he adopts. On the other hand, a writer's identity is determined not completely by other discourses, but rather by the unique way in which she draws on and combines them.

Scollon (1994, 1995) and others (Stein 1986, Sterling 1991 Pennycook 1993), and 'Biff' in the cartoon opposite (Figure 4.1), have drawn attention to the fact that there is a fine line between 'intertextuality' and 'plagiarism'. They have questioned the simplistic view of plagiarism as stealing someone else's ideas and wordings, recognizing that there is no such thing as originality in discourse: writing can only be a redeployment of available resources for meaning-making. Scollon (1995) draws on a number of concepts in discourse analysis to tease apart the concept of 'author' in ways which throw into

Figure 4.1   The Biff cartoon about plagiarism (from Biff, *September 1993)*

question the whole idea of private ownership of discourse. Scollon and Pennycook, both working in Hong Kong, have further pointed out that putting a high premium on originality and authorship is ideologically and culturally loaded, and Scollon has shown how these values are neither historically nor culturally constant. The discoursal construction of writer identity is at the heart of these issues: in Part Two of this book I show how writers have drawn in subtle and complex ways on discourses to which they have had access, and how the line between 'plagiarism' and taking on the voices of the academic discourse community is hard to maintain.

Authority and authorial presence in academic writing

Bartholomae presents intertextuality not only in terms of taking on the words of others, but also taking on the roles of others. He writes:

> To speak with authority [student writers] have to speak not only in another's voice but through another's code; and they not only have to do this, they have to speak in the voice and through the codes of those of us with power and wisdom; and they not only have to do this, they have to do it before they know what they are doing. (156)

and

> Their initial progress will be marked by their abilities to take on the role of privilege, by their abilities to establish authority. (162)

He is making the point that a writer, when writing with the discourses of a community, takes on the identity of a member of that community. In the case of writing within the university, that is the identity of a person with authority. This is a crucial insight, because the one thing that characterizes most of the writers I worked with was a sense of *inferiority*, a lack of confidence in themselves, a sense of powerlessness, a view of themselves as people without knowledge, and hence without authority. For some, this was the legacy of a working-class background. For others, it was associated with age or gender; for all, it was associated with previous failure in the education system and an uncertainty as to whether they had the right to be members of the academic community at all. On the other hand, there are some who bring authority of different types into the academic institution from different domains, such as business, local politics or parenthood: authority which often goes unrecognized by the academic community. I take these issues up with examples in Chapter 10.

As I mentioned in Chapter 1, there has been a substantial body of research on the specific issue of the establishment of authority in academic writing. Spivey (1990) summed up the project of this line of research:

> Another important factor ... is the writer's own sense of authority in writing the piece. ... How is the writer's position in the discourse community for whom he or she is writing related to the appropriation of source material and the generation of content? (281)

Theory and research related to this issue includes studies of writing from sources (for example, Nelson and Hayes 1988, Flower and others 1990, Campbell 1990), the use of reporting verbs (Thompson and Ye 1990), the idea of "entering the conversation" (Bazerman 1980, 1981, Rose, 1989, Chapter 3), a focus on the issues of authority and authorship (Greene 1991, Scollon 1994), a focus on paraphrasing (Arrington 1988), the idea of 'novelty' or 'designing to be new' (Kaufer and Geisler 1989, Berkenkotter and Huckin, 1995, Chapter 3), and the concept of authorship in collaborative writing (Ede and Lunsford 1990). This is an extremely important and interesting field of research and scholarship: the self as author; one of the four aspects of writer identity which I mentioned in Chapter 1. However, it has already received considerable attention in recent years, and is therefore not the main focus of this book.

The distinction between ethos and persona in self-presentation: Cherry 1988

Cherry (1988) is, as far as I am aware, the only writer on the topic of academic writing who has specifically addressed the issue of self-representation in academic writing, and I therefore discuss his work in detail.

He reviews contributions to this topic from rhetorical theory and literary critical theory. He points out that self-portrayal is interrelated with other facets of the rhetorical situation. He examines the meaning of the two terms commonly used in rhetorical theory for self-representation: *ethos* and *persona*. These terms seem to me to make a similar distinction to the one made by Besnier which I discussed in Chapter 3, *ethos* being associated with 'self-hood', and *persona* being associated with 'person-hood'.

He explains that Aristotle's term *ethos* is used by rhetorical theorists, and that the word entails a

> focus on credibility, on the speaker's securing the trust and respect of an audience by representing him- or herself in the speech as knowledgeable, intelligent, competent, and concerned for the welfare of the audience. (256)

I understand from this and other parts of Cherry's article that *ethos* means the personal characteristics which a reader might attribute to a writer on the basis of evidence in the text. They might include, as I suggested in my introduction, being warm, loving, caring, sincere, reliable, astute, along with a full range of possible qualities. Some of these will be more highly valued in some social contexts than others. Presumably, writers always attempt to represent themselves as having what count as 'good' qualities in the eyes of a particular socio-cultural group. This applies even when a person wants to set themselves up in opposition to dominant values: they want to seem to be a 'good' radical. The fact that *ethos* is always associated with a value judgement is one of the things which distinguishes it from *persona*.

Cherry sums up the distinction between the two terms:

> *ethos* refers to a set of characteristics that, if attributed to a writer on the basis
> of textual evidence, will enhance the writer's credibility. Persona, on the other
> hand, ... provides a way of describing the roles authors create for themselves
> in written discourse given their representation of audience, subject matter,
> and other elements of context. (268-9)

I understand from this and other parts of Cherry's article that *persona* means the social role(s) which a writer adopts while producing a particular piece of writing. This could include such roles as a student of philosophy, a Black activist, an apprentice social worker. A writer might adopt several *personae* either simultaneously or in different parts of the text, and the examples I present in Chapters 6 and 10 provide evidence for this plurality.

In the examples he presents, Cherry also shows how *ethos* and *persona* overlap and interact in complex ways. A particular *persona* is often associated with particular personal qualities (*ethos*). On the other hand, some personal qualities (*ethos*) are independent of social role, and can be textually represented within a range of social roles. Cherry does not use the concept of discourse community, nor the idea of context of culture, but it seems to me that these help to clarify the relationship between *ethos* and *persona* and help to make the distinction more useful. The term *persona* seems to me to be useful for describing a particular social role, such as 'mother', or membership of a particular community, such as English literature student. The term *ethos* seems to me to be useful for describing the sorts of values which are associated with a particular role, or held by members of a particular community, particularly values as regards what counts as a good member of that community. The context of culture determines these values. It is therefore the *ethos* associated with a particular *persona* which is open to contestation and change, in the sense described in Chapter 2. Throughout Part Two I will be suggesting that discourse types are shaped by the values of a community, including the sorts of personal qualities (*ethos*) that it values.

Cherry concludes that it is important to recognize these two different dimensions of self-representation in writing:

> It is only by discriminating among different dimensions of self-portrayal that we can be sensitive to how these dimensions interact with one another. When we approach self-representation starting with *ethos,* we assume a real author and look for the transformations the author will undergo as a result of appearing in print. When we begin with persona, we assume a degree of artifice or transformation and search for the real author. From either perspective, maintaining a distinction between *ethos* and persona can sharpen both rhetorical and literary criticism by giving us a means of differentiating and describing the multiple selves we project into written discourse and the changes in self-representation that might occur within a single written text. (268)

This summary shows that Cherry equates *ethos* with 'the real author', which I would contest. It seems to me that *ethos* can be discoursally constructed just as much as *persona* is, and that neither are necessarily the 'real self' of the writer — if such a thing exists.

Cherry's distinction between *ethos* and *persona* and his emphasis on the interrelationship between self-representation and other aspects of the 'rhetorical context', as he calls it, make a useful contribution to a view of writer identity. However, he does not incorporate in it any understanding of the way in which writers' identity is constructed by the norms and conventions of the community within which they are writing, as discussed earlier in this chapter. I make use of the distinction between *ethos* and *persona* as two aspects of identity within the broader framework of the discoursal construction of writer identity, but I treat *ethos* as discoursally constructed just as much as *persona*.

Critical approaches to academic discourse

Bizzell (1982, see also 1992) argues that we need to take a critical view of the "cognition, convention and certainty" associated with academic discourse communities. In this early article she doesn't go so far as to say that teachers should be encouraging students to challenge the conventions, but she does encourage students and teachers to examine conventions critically together.

In a later article (Bizzell 1986) she reviews the trend in composition studies towards taking account of the way social context shapes writing. She contrasts what Rorty (1979) calls a "foundationalist" with an "anti-foundationalist" view of social context in academic writing.

> an anti-foundationalist understanding of discourse would see the student's way of thinking and interacting with the world, the student's very self, as fundamentally altered by participation in any new discourse. (43)

A social approach to the study of writing for Bizzell also involves "get(ting) at the larger political implications of who gets to learn and use complex kinds of writing." (1989: 225). She describes her type of social approach to writing as "cultural criticism", which foregrounds ideologies that might not only be taken for granted but also actively suppressed from the consciousness of people acting on them' (same page).

Chase (1988) contributes to this more critical view by applying Giroux's terms *accommodation, opposition,* and *resistance* to student writing.

> Briefly, *accommodation* is the process by which students learn to accept conventions without necessarily questioning how these conventions privilege some forms of knowledge at the expense of others. *Opposition* is a category that refers to student behaviour which runs against the grain and interrupts what we usually think of as the normal progression of learning. In the case of discourse conventions, opposition refers to instances in which students fail for one reason or another to learn the patterns and conventions of a particular discourse community and fail to engage in behaviour that would enable them to learn those conventions. ... *Resistance*, on the other hand, ... is a behavior that actively works against the dominant ideology. ... It refers to a student's refusal to learn in those cases in which the refusal grows out of a larger sense of the individual's relationship to liberation. (14–15)

Chase uses these definitions to describe the differing approaches to academic writing of three student writers. I have found this framework extremely useful, and drew on it for an earlier study of identity in academic writing (Ivanič and Roach 1990). However, I now find that it presupposes too monolithic a view of academic discourse, as I argue in Chapters 8 and 10 of this book. I no longer see it as just a question of accommodating to or resisting academic discourse as a whole. Rather, writers align themselves with one or more of the discoursal possibilities for self-hood which are available within the academic community, thereby contributing to reproduction or change in the patterns of privileging among those discourses in the whole order of academic discourse (see Fairclough 1992a for the concept of an 'order of discourse'). Resistance consists of alignment with — perhaps even 'accommodation to' — less privileged discourses, rather than wholesale dismissal of one discourse and creation of another.

Chase ends by exhorting teachers to

> encourage students to affirm and analyse their own experiences and histories, not without question, but as starting points for connecting with the wider culture and society ... [and to] exercise the courage to act in the interests of improving the quality of human life. (21–22).

The point is that resistance is not resistance for its own sake. It is motivated by a commitment to represent the world in a way which accords with the writer's values, by a refusal to be colonized by the privileged world views and discourses of privileged others, and by a desire to open up membership of the academic discourse community. This critical approach to issues of identity in academic writing has been endorsed and taken in new directions in the 90s by those concerned with gender equality (for example, Haswell and Haswell 1995) and with African American subject positioning (for example, Jones Royster 1996).

This more critical stance towards writing conventions is also articulated by Kress (1994, originally published in 1982), and in relation to bureaucratic literacy by The Progressive Literacy Group (1986). It has been developed in relation to the learning and teaching of academic writing in settings other than North America by a group of us associated with Lancaster University: Clark, Constantinou, Cottey and Yeoh (1990), Ivanič and Roach (1990), Ivanič and Simpson (1992b), Janks and Ivanič (1992), Clark and Ivanič (1997).

This idea of accommodation, opposition and resistance to conventions is closely linked with writer identity. Writers position themselves by the stance they take towards privileged conventions. Writers who take a resistant stance towards privileged conventions are making a strong statement of an alternative identity, and are also, in Cherry's terms, demonstrating the personal quality (*ethos*) of non-conformism.

Reasons why writer identity has not been a focus of recent research

In the trends I have discussed so far in the chapter, the discoursal construction of writer identity is implicated but not foregrounded. Only in Cherry's article is there a specific focus on this issue. Yet writers are so important to writing. Writer identity is, surely, a central concern for any theory of writing in two senses: what writers bring to the act of writing, and how they construct their identities through the act of writing itself. Why has there not been more attention paid to these specific issues? I suggest two reasons. Firstly, writer identity is an aspect of a social view of writing, rather than the 'process approach' which has dominated research on academic writing until recently. Secondly, research has recently focused on the role of the reader in shaping writing, and treated the role of the writer as unproblematic.

'Process' versus 'social' approaches to the study of writing

In the 1970s and early 1980s there was a change of focus in writing research and writing pedagogy from the product of writing to the process of writing. Theorists about writing and learning to write (for example Murray 1978, Graves 1983), psychologists (for example Flower and Hayes 1980, Hayes and Flower 1980, Matsuhashi 1982), educational researchers focusing on writing in higher education (for example, Hounsell 1984a and b) and practitioner-researchers (for example Emig 1971) wrote about the importance of under-standing how writers produce their texts. This led to a change in pedagogical focus from what an ideal piece of writing should be like to the composing processes involved in writing. Researchers and teachers were concentrating on the writer, but on what the writer is *doing*, not on what s/he is *being*. I have tried to represent this distinction diagrammatically in the contrast between Figures 4.2 and 4.3, using Goffman's distinction between *performer* and *character* which I explained in Chapter 1 to make the distinction between 'writer-as-performer' and 'writer-as-character' in Figure 4.3. In the eternal triangle between writer, reader and content, the writer was thought of in terms of what s/he does and what she means (Figure 4.2), without any consideration of who s/he is and/or how s/he appears as a social being in the text (Figure 4.3). (These figures are drawn from the perspective of the writer; including a satisfactory representation of the reading process would further complicate Figure 4.3)

In Figure 4.2, the 'process' view of writing, the text is thought to consist of 'subject matter' which the writer represents and the reader interprets. In Figure 4.3, the 'social' view of writing, the text is thought to consist not only of 'subject matter' but also of the writer's portrayal of themselves, the reader, their relationship, the writer's commitment to the ideational content, and their

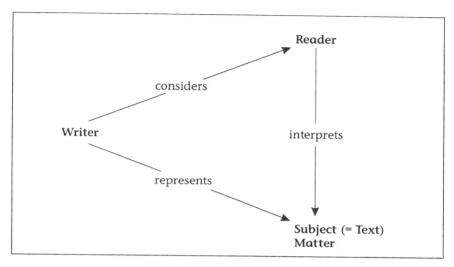

Figure 4.2   A 'process' view of writer and reader as doing something

assessment of the reader's knowledge and beliefs. In Figure 4.2 the writer and reader exist only as interlocutors: producers and interpreters of content. In Figure 4.3 they are still interlocutors (in Goffman's terms *writer-as-performer* and *reader-as-performer*), but they are also participants who are constructed by the text which they are engaged in producing and interpreting (*writer-as-character* and *reader-as-character*). This seems to me to be a crucial distinction which was overlooked in the enthusiasm for putting process rather than product at the centre of attention.

One of the principles of the 'process approach' to writing was that, through the composing process, writers could, and should, 'find their own voice'. An excellent overview of published exhortations for writers to find their 'voice', and for teachers to help them to do so, is given by Hashimoto (1987) in his critique: "*Voice as juice: Some reservations about evangelic composition*". 'Voice' sounds like writer identity, but the way it was conceived by its proponents in the 80s was associated with simplistic, romantic ideas of the creative individual. The idea was, in essence, that writers have ideas, and particularly ways of talking which are in some way their own, unsullied by the models of correct writing which were presented in prescriptive, product-oriented approaches to the teaching of writing. So the process approach to the study and teaching of writing concentrated on what the writer does, and on helping

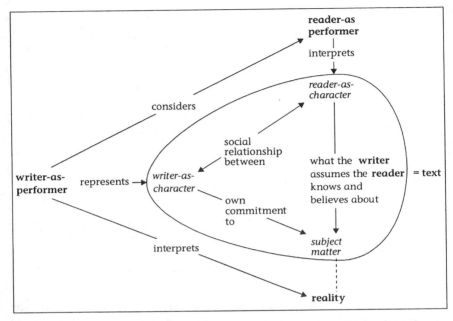

Figure 4.3   *A 'social' view of writer and reader as both doing something and being represented in the text*

writers express their 'own ideas' and find their 'own language'.

However, during the 1980s many people recognized that the focus on process was too narrow, assuming that there is a generalizable process, independent of context, and that decisions about writing emanate primarily from writers' goals and purposes. The emphasis on process has since the late 1980s been dismissed as a-social, as conceiving of writing as something which happens independent of its social context. It has been pointed out that writing is not an individual act of discovery and creation, but an act embedded in social context, as I have argued earlier in this chapter. As a result of these insights writing researchers rejected a purely cognitive conceptualization of the writing process, in which the writer, her meanings, intentions and 'voice' were central to the shaping of written discourse. A focus on the writer's voice in teaching or research became unfashionable, because it seemed to be a notion associated with the decontextualized view of writing. Those espousing a 'social' view of writing and literacy now attack the idea of 'voice' in the sense of the writer's 'real self' speaking out, seeing it as incompatible with the social constructionist view of reality. Post-structuralist theories of writing take this to the other extreme, understanding the social and discoursal construction of identity to entail 'the death of the author', and the conflicts of identity which real writers experience are overlooked along the way.

In reacting against a cognitive view of writing, and denying the existence of a writer's 'voice', I think that these theorists lost sight of other aspects of the writer which are extremely important to a social view of writing. That is, by attacking the simplistic view of the writer represented in my Figure 4.2, they overlooked issues concerning the writer-as-character as represented in my Figure 4.3. The idea of writers conveying, intentionally and unintentionally, an impression of themselves through their writing is not incompatible with a social constructionist view of writing, but complements it, as I argued in Chapter 1.

Theorists who are taking up the ideas of Vygotsky and Bakhtin, such as Fairclough, Barton and Wertsch (discussed in the previous two chapters) do not focus specifically on writing or academic writing, but they do pay attention to the producers of language and they way in which their identity is discoursally shaped. Paradoxically, the word 'voice' is being used again, taken from translations of Bakhtin, but to mean something very different from what the 'evangelists' (as Hashimoto called them) meant. 'Voice' in this new way of thinking is multiply ambiguous, meaning a socially shaped discourse which a speaker can draw upon, and/or an actual voice in the speaker's individual history, and/or the current speaker's unique combination of these resources, as I discussed in Chapter 2. In this book I am arguing for a revival of interest in the writer, set within a social view of writing, taking further the ideas I reviewed in the first half of this chapter, and viewing the writer's voice as discoursally constructed in the ways I presented in Chapter 2.

The recent focus on the reader at the expense of writer

Another reason why writer identity has not received much attention from writing theorists and researchers is that they have been pre-occupied with the effect of the reader. Researchers concerned with the writing process have tried to identify components of the writing process, and those concerned with the social context of writing have tried to identify elements of context which affect writing. From both perspectives an aspect of the process/context which has been the topic of a great deal of writing research is the reader. In this research the writer is unproblematically treated as the person who makes decisions about what to write in the light of their conception of the reader. In spite of the considerable body of published theory and research about the way in which the writer conceptualizes the reader in the writing process (for example, Ede (1984), Roth (1987), Kirsch and Roen (1990) Nystrand (1982, 1986) writing researchers have not concerned themselves with the way writers conceptualize and represent *themselves*, as Cherry (1988) points out:

> Although numerous studies have begun to explore the complexity of audience representation, no corresponding literature on self-representation has yet emerged. (252)

The lack of attention to the writer's identity seems again to be caused by viewing the writer as *doing* the writing, but not also as *being* an aspect of the context represented in the text.

Reader identity has also been the focus of attention at the expense of writer identity in another line of research which seems relevant to my study: research on how participants are positioned by text. Although theoretical accounts of subject positioning such as Fairclough (1989, 1992a) say that it applies to both producers and interpreters of discourse, in practice subject positioning has been studied mainly from the point of view of readers/hearers/interpreters being positioned, interpellated by producers of discourse who appear to be relatively powerful in the local and institutional contexts in which the texts are produced. For example, Kress (1989) shows how readers are positioned by the language of the magazine *Seventeen* and by geography textbooks. It is not surprising that critical linguists should pay more attention to the way in which readers, rather than writers, are positioned, since public texts are the objects of most critical discourse analysis. In these the writer is often more powerful than the reader, and the reader is more apparently the social subject in need of emancipation. However, I am looking at subject-positioning from another angle (though not entirely new: see Kress 1994: 11): that of how relatively powerless writers are positioned by readers who are their assessors.

Applying Goffman's theory of self-presentation to academic writing

So far in this chapter I have, as in previous chapters, emphasized the importance of taking a social constructionist approach to the relationship between writing and identity. But social construction of identity can only happen during social interaction in a specific context of situation. In this final section of Part One, I return to Goffman's social interactionist account of self-representation, first introduced in Chapter 1, to complement the more social constructionist views of academic writing discussed so far.

As I argued in Chapter 1, I think Goffman provides a productive metaphor to enrich our understanding of the local mechanisms by which identity is constructed in the micro-social contexts of interpersonal encounters. He claims that people employ complex strategies to manipulate the impression they convey of themselves. He has been criticized for suggesting that identity is a question of conscious strategic behaviour on the part of an individual. Taken as a *metaphor* for *sub-conscious* behaviour, however, this describes vividly the dilemmas writers face in self-representation through writing.

Goffman was interested in "the minute social system of face-to-face interaction" (1969: 11). Although writing is not face-to-face, it certainly is interaction, in which "the minute social system" consists of the writer(s) and the reader(s). The expected receivers of language (hearers and readers) influence the choices people make from their array of mediational means. The "toolkit" (as discussed in Chapter 2) is drawn upon selectively according to people's assessment of what the receiver(s) will value, and how much they care about the reader's opinion of them. In terms of written communication, writers' discoursal choices — and hence, self-representation — will be constrained partly by the discourses to which they have had access and partly by what they anticipate will create a good impression in the mind of the readers, especially if the readers exert any power over the writer, as they do over students writing academic assignments. In this section I suggest how particular aspects of Goffman's theory of self-representation can be applied to academic writing.

Goffman was interested mainly in impression management in institutions, and a large part of his theory is about the way in which individuals present themselves as members of teams. One of the difficulties of much academic writing is exactly that of *not* being a member of a team. In academic writing a student is expected to manage alone the impression that will be received, although several of them may actually engage in various collaborative practices 'behind the scenes'.

Goffman is concerned with the physical nature of interaction, and most of his examples refer to such things as furniture layout, clothing, lowering of eyes, which he calls "front". These characteristics of setting and physical appearance are not apparent in academic texts, which contributes to the false impression that writing is decontextualized. In spite of these superficial differences, it seems to me that writing shares many characteristics with face-to-face interaction, as I argued in Chapter 3. The encounter between performer and audience may be removed in time and space, but it is still an encounter: a dialogue in which the performer must assess the likely response of the audience and decide accordingly what impression to convey of self and how to convey it. When Goffman's theory is applied to writing, the physical details have the power of a metaphor, illuminating aspects of writing which are not so apparent when it is described literally. For example, the "furniture" associated with an academic essay might be seen as the paper, the folder. The "clothing" might be seen as the choice of handwriting or typing, and the choice of ink or typeface.

Goffman distinguishes between the intentional expression that an individual *gives* and the unintentional

> expression that he *(Goffman's generic pronoun) gives off,* [which].....involves a wide range of action that others can treat as symptomatic of the actor, the expectation being that the action was performed for reasons other than the information conveyed in this way. (1969: 2)

I understand "intentional expressions of ... self" to be what people actually say about themselves in such statements as 'I am the sort of person who .... ', for example in answering questions on forms, and the way I wrote the first paragraph of this book. These are extremely rare in academic writing: part of the myth that it is 'impersonal'. "Unintentional expressions" of identity, however, pervade all human action. This is one of my reasons for claiming that no writing is ever 'impersonal': whether writers like it or not, they are "giving off" an impression of themselves through their social action of *writing*, from the large-scale action of being involved in an act of writing of any sort, through the many social, cognitive and physical practices they engage in in order to do it, to the moment-by-moment linguistic choices they make in constructing their written message.

Goffman points out that individuals have little control over the expression that they "give off", and that this is likely to be what others use to form their opinion (6). In academic essays the only evidence available to tutors who will read them of the characteristics of the writers may be the discourse choices they have made. As I argue throughout this book, writers are usually unaware that they are "giving off" an impression of themselves in this way.

Goffman is particularly interested in the fact that the character a person projects is what counts in any situation, and that what that person may or may not be, behind the mask, is irrelevant. He writes:

> when an individual projects a definition of the situation and thereby makes
> an implicit or explicit claim to be a person of a particular kind, he automati-
> cally exerts a moral demand upon the others, obliging them to value and treat
> him in the manner that persons of his kind have a right to expect. He also
> implicitly forgoes all claims to be things he does not appear to be and hence
> forgoes the treatment that would be appropriate for such individuals.
> (same book: 11–12)

This is particularly telling when applied to academic writing. As I have already
mentioned, a piece of writing may be the only evidence a tutor has of the
writer. Most of you reading this book will have had the experience of making
a judgement of a person on the basis of their academic writing, for example
during the 'blind' marking of exams. However much we try to be 'impersonal'
about it, the quality of the work, the choice of topic, what is written about it,
and the discourses adopted in the course of writing: all these convey to us an
impression of the writer, whether we are conscious of it or not.

　Goffman also says that a person

> may not completely believe that he deserves the valuation of self which he
> asks for, or that the impression of reality he fosters is valid. (same book: 18).

This presupposes that the valuation of self is positive. It applies to academic
writing in many cases: writers may be conforming to what appear to be the
values of their readers and obtaining good marks without really believing that
they live up to these assessments, as Bartholomae (1985) says (see above).
However, in academic writing there is a negative interpretation to this observation too. People who have difficulty with writing, such as Rachel in my study,
have a sense that their writing is failing to convey a true impression of their
qualities. Rachel sees herself as a fully-fledged member of the academic
community in the sense that she shares its values of rigorous and critical
enquiry. However, she does not engage in the writing practices and does not
control the discourses which will convince a reader that she has these qualities. Rachel feels strongly that she deserves a different valuation, and could
show her qualities through means other than writing, but in the academic
community *writing* is the dominant form of social action for giving evidence
of our selves (see Chapter 6 for further discussion).

　Goffman discusses how people can be relatively sincere or relatively
cynical about their performances:

> While we can expect to find natural movement back and forth between
> cynicism and sincerity, still we must not rule out the kind of transitional
> point that can be sustained on the strength of a little self-illusion. We find

> that the individual may attempt to induce the audience to judge him and the
> situation in a particular way, and he may seek this judgement as an ultimate
> end in itself. (same book: 18)

Although this extract, too, assumes that people are fully in control of the
forms of social action at their disposal, it describes particularly well the way in
which student writers attempt to create a good impression in their writing,
combining the best of intentions with a little judicious deception. In Chapter
8 I focus on this distinction between sincerity and cynicism (or deception) in
self-representation, linking it to my co-researchers' sense of owning and
disowning discourse.

Later, however, Goffman warns of the ultimate consequences of too much
calculated impression management:

> to the degree that the individual maintains a show before others that he
> himself does not believe, he can come to experience a special kind of alien-
> ation from self and a special kind of wariness of others. (same book: 209)

Some of the student writers I interviewed mentioned this "alienation from
self", and I give examples in Chapter 8.

The complex task facing the performer is to make their character (*ethos*,
in Cherry's terms) seem like that of a good person — but who is to define what
counts as good? The performer does not fabricate the character in a vacuum,
but in the socio-cultural context in which they live. This context includes
system(s) of values and beliefs defining the qualities which its members might
seek to portray and thereby claim for themselves. Goffman rather assumes in
his account that all participants in a situation will have a common and
relatively clearly-defined view as to what counts as 'a good person' — something which might be relatively true in a small, close community like the
Shetland Isles. However, in the very different socio-cultural context of an
academic community the values and beliefs which define what might count as
'a good person' are heterogeneous and mainly implicit, as the detailed
examples in Chapter 10 illustrate.

Students writing academic essays have to constantly bear in mind the
interpretive practices of the reader. The reader's values and beliefs may not be
the same as the writer's. Writers construct an image of themselves in the light
of their estimates of their expected reader(s) interpretive practices, and of the
various power asymmetries between them. Writers-as-performers do their very
best to make that image one which is in their best interests, but may not
succeed. In spite of their best efforts to anticipate the values, beliefs and
interpretive practices of the reader(s), they may end up creating a character

who does not make a good impression on the reader.

Goffman details both the "defensive practices" employed by performers to ensure that the impression they intend to convey of themselves is not sullied (1969: 12 and 187–201), and the "protective practices", or "tact" employed by those interacting with them to help them manage their performances (same book: 12 and 201–209). He characterizes self-presentation as a precarious matter, with traps at every turn:

> Given the fragility and the required expressive coherence of the reality that is dramatized by a performance, there are usually facts which, if attention is drawn to them during the performance, would discredit, disrupt, or make useless the impression that the performance fosters. (same book: 123)

This sounds as if the impression a person wishes to give off is homogeneous, whereas intended and unintended impressions are probably heterogeneous, usually because of the performer's ambivalence about self. However, this observation does not detract from the power of Goffman's main point here: that whatever impression of self the performer intends to convey can be inadvertently subverted by some unconscious behaviour. This seems to be very true of academic writing: tutors can sometimes see through student writers' attempts to appear scholarly. Going a step further, however, some student writers are so skilled at not allowing any traces of their impression-fostering tactics to show that their tutors are convinced.

Goffman's concept of "protective practices" is interesting when applied to the act of writing. Writing has the special characteristic of being relatively permanent. Whereas many other social acts are fleeting, and open to a range of interpretations, writing is there 'in black and white' — often literally. It leaves a trace which cannot be denied, and is often used as evidence. Whereas people may, as Goffman says, employ co-operative practices to protect the face of others, overlooking or putting a kind interpretation on any negative impression they may have created through their actions, I suggest that readers are less likely to be so generous in their reaction to impressions writers create of themselves in their writing. And I think this is especially true of academic assignments. In the current climate of higher education, academic life is unremittingly competitive and discriminatory, in the sense of needing to discriminate among students by giving them different grades, and ultimately dividing them into different degree classes. In such a setting, "protective practices" or "tact" on the part of tutors is probably rare. I think it is common for tutors to approach the task of reading students' work with a sense that it is their duty to notice what they regard as inadequacies, however unconscious that sense may be. Tutors reading essays do not, on the whole, help students to give a good impression of themselves by overlooking slips in their "performance". Thinking about "protective practices" in relation to academic writing reveals that this is an area in which members of the academic community would do well to be much more critically aware of their practices (as discussed further in Chapters 8 and 11).

Goffman recognizes that social identities are not hermetically sealed, but leak into each other:

> When an individual does move into a new position in society and obtains a new part to perform, he is not likely to be told in full detail how to conduct himself, nor will the facts of his new situation press sufficiently on him from the start to determine his conduct without his giving further thought to it. Ordinarily he will be given only a few cues, hints and stage directions, and it will be assumed that he already has in his repertoire a large number of bits and pieces of performances that will be required in the new setting.(63)

What Goffman says here about learning to take on a new social identity (*persona*, in Cherry's terms) seems directly relevant to the experience of adults taking on their new role as students. They will not be given precise instructions on how to play this role, specifically, on how to produce the written "performances" known as 'assignments'. They will have to piece together what they know about writing from other roles — knowledge which will not necessarily be adequate to the situation. In Chapter 7 I give detailed examples of how my co-researchers built on their existing repertoires of writing practices and discourse types in order to fulfil the writing requirements of their new roles as members of the academic community.

In this section I have discussed how some aspects of Goffman's theory of self-presentation can be applied specifically to academic writing. My understanding of the discoursal construction of writer identity (as summarized at the end of Chapter 1) incorporates both a social constructionist and a social interactionist perspective: I am claiming that writing is an act of identity in which both discourse-as-carrier-of-social-values and discourse-as-social-interaction play a part.

This account of the discoursal construction of identity raises an interesting question: where does a person's identity reside, and at what moment is it 'constructed'? To simplify, I will discuss this in relation specifically to writer identity, although the question is relevant to all aspects of social identity. Is a writer's identity

a.   the outcome of previous experiences, so that people's 'identity' is a part of themselves, whether or not it is expressed in any future act?

or is it

b.   the way they position themselves in an act of writing, by drawing on particular discourse types, whether or not the writing is read?

or is it

c.   the impression received of them by a reader?

Which of these three actually counts as a writer's identity is, perhaps, an academic question: in my view all three of these elements are important to an understanding of writing and identity. But they are not at all the same thing, and they are interrelated in various ways. In terms of the four aspects of writer identity Iproposed at the end of Chapter 1, (a) is the 'Autorbiographical Self'. But which is the 'Discoursal Self' — (b) or (c)? As I discussed in Chapter 2, (b) is dependent on (a). However, (b) will be to some extent a selection from and distortion of (a). Yet there can be no evidence for (a), other than (b), and the writer's own account of their sense of self. Further, (b) is a definition of identity divorced from the relentless onward motion of social life: (c) is the only version of identity which really counts in a person's unfolding personal history. In this book I focus on (b), and through it, indirectly on (a). I do not have the data for detailed discussion of (c), but recommend it as a focus for future research.

Conclusion to this chapter and to Part One

In the Introduction and Part One, each chapter has narrowed the perspective on identity. In Chapter 1, I introduced ways of thinking about social identity in general. In Chapter 2, I narrowed my focus to the way discourse constructs identity, and introduced the theoretical framework for the analyses of writing in Part Two. In Chapter 3, I discussed relationships between identity and literacy: both a narrower and a broader concept than 'discourse'. In this chapter I have focused specifically on student writers in academic contexts, and the ways in which their identities are inscribed in writing practices. I have discussed aspects of theory and research on academic writing which have a bearing on identity, and introduced concepts which provide the grounding for the research-based chapters in Part Two.

Much of the theory and research on academic literacy takes an uncritical view of its norms and conventions as unitary and monolithic, but in this chapter I have been focusing on issues of identity which, in my view, contribute to a more dynamic way of understanding academic literacies as multiple, shifting and open to contestation and change. I have been emphasizing the dangers of thinking about entering the academic discourse community as a process of initiation into powerful discourses, and suggesting instead that there is always tension and struggle at the interface between the institution and its members. Students bring into institutions of higher education multiple practices and possibilities for self-hood, all of which have the potential to challenge the status quo. The act of writing a particular assignment is a social interaction in which all these issues are brought into play. In Part Two I draw on the concepts and approaches which I have introduced here to examine the tensions between the institution and the self which eight mature students experienced as they wrote particular academic assignments.

PART TWO

The discoursal construction of identity in academic writing

An investigation with eight mature students

CHAPTER 5

Introduction to Part Two

The scope of Part Two

Chapters 6–10 are the core of the book, bringing alive the theoretical perspectives introduced in Part One. These chapters are about Rachel, John, Angela, Frances, Sarah, Justin, Donna and Valerie and the issues of identity which arise in academic essays they wrote during their second or third years at university, documenting the discoursal choices they made, the origins of these choices, and the dilemmas they faced as they wrote these essays. Each of the chapters in Part Two makes a specific contribution to the overarching argument that writing is an act of identity in which writers align themselves with interests (in both senses), values, beliefs, practices and power relations through their discourse choices (see the end of Chapter 1 for a more detailed outline of this argument). This part of the book also provides the basis for arguing, in Chapter 11, that academic literacy is not a neutral, unproblematic skill which students simply have to acquire, but a multiple, complex and contested set of social practices which should be given more explicit and critical attention by all members of the academic community.

I focus on the discoursal construction of writer identity, drawing mainly on the theoretical perspectives I outlined in Chapter 2 and bringing in the other perspectives outlined in Part One wherever they seem relevant. I am aware that this is a slightly biased approach, with texts rather than practices centre-stage (see the discussion of Figure 3.1 in Chapter 3). However, I believe that the study of textual detail can produce insights into academic literacy which might otherwise remain hidden, and I hope that my approach will help to reclaim a place for linguistic analysis alongside other disciplinary approaches in the multi-disciplinary field of literacy studies.

In this chapter I explain how the research for Chapters 6–10 was conducted, I introduce you to my co-researchers and the contexts in which they were writing, and give an overview of Chapters 6–10, and of how they relate to one another.

The co-researcher relationship

This research was 'collaborative research', and the people I interviewed about their writing were 'co-researchers' rather than as 'subjects', 'informants' or 'students'. Collaborative research is a form of research which minimizes the distinction between 'researcher' and 'researched', in which all participants work together as co-researchers. Co-researchers may not all have the same goals for the research process: goals can include some form of personal or political action as a result of the findings, as well as generalization and publication.

In my approach to research I was trying to reflect my understanding of academic literacy: that it is not a question of a set of conventions and practices which people are relatively successful or unsuccessful in acquiring. Rather, there are many alternatives to the dominant conventions, and possibilities for contesting them. The aim of this research was to find out about the alternatives people bring with them from their experiences outside the institution of higher education, and to understand from their own point of view the dilemmas they face, and the nature of the pressure exerted on them to conform. By the very act of examining these matters collaboratively as a 'teacher-and-student team' we were rejecting a simple 'acculturation' view of academic literacy and affirming the possibility of subverting the dominant conventions.

The difference between 'teaching' and 'research' is a subtle, but crucial one. In 'teaching' I, as tutor, would be suggesting how they, as learners, could improve their writing. In 'research' we were discussing why they wrote what they did, how it differed from other writing, and what they wanted to do about it. Instead of talking about how I thought the writing should be done, they often gave good reasons for keeping it the way it was. In 'teaching' I would be the knower, the tutor, the teacher. In 'research' we were joint investigators, each bringing different insights to the problem at hand. There were, inevitably, inequalities between us: my status as a member of university staff was a complicating factor. However, I believe that by the time we engaged in the work on which this book draws, the effect of that was considerably reduced. In my view by turning tuition into research we were putting into practice two fundamental principles of Adult Basic Education: maintaining symmetry if not equality among adults, and empowering both learners and tutors.

Although all my co-researchers except one had signalled that they had difficulty with writing, our relationship was not, at any rate at the time of this research, a teacher-student relationship. Two of the relationships — those with John and Frances, began in tutor-tutee roles. In those cases we gradually turned our 'tuition' sessions into 'research sessions' — what I have called elsewhere 'Research which grows out of learning' (Hamilton, Ivanič and Barton 1992). In three other relationships, those with Rachel, Justin and Sarah, there seemed to me to be a sub-plot of 'tuition' which surfaced from time to time. Although our initial contact in each of these cases was explicitly for research purposes, these three people from time to time acknowledged that our meetings had a dual function. Sarah once said that one of the benefits to her of our meetings was having a tame member of university staff to consult. Rachel from time to time asked my advice about work-in-progress and used my skills to proofread and type for her. Justin viewed our meetings throughout as what he termed 'a symbiotic relationship' which would lead to him getting his assignments completed and me getting data for my research. However, the main interview about the particular assignment I used as the focus for this project was in each case entirely a 'research' session, rather than a 'tuition' session.

My co-researchers

All my co-researchers were mature students, and they were all in the first generation of their families to enter higher education. My only criteria for selection were that they should be over 25 years of age, that English was not a second or foreign language for any of them, and that they had experienced some sort of difficulty with academic writing. I met them all through contacts in the related fields of study skills, effective learning programmes, return to study, fresh horizons, academic support programmes, and adult basic education. All of them (apart from Angela) had done something at some stage in the course of returning to study which signalled that they would like help with writing, or that they were not entirely confident about their writing. I had no other criteria for selection. This means that my eight co-researchers are extremely different on many dimensions. These are summarized in Figure 5.1. (? indicates that I did not know their sexuality). Some of them wanted their own names to be used, others preferred pseudonyms.

The dry facts in this table are extremely inadequate as portraits of the people the book is about, but they make it possible to compare the eight people in terms of some of the factors which are relevant to the social

Characteristics	John	Rachel	Angela	Frances	Justin	Sarah	Donna	Valerie
Gender	M	F	F	F	M	F	F	F
Race	White	White	White	White	White	White	Black	Black
Age	28	29	35	54	35	43	26	33
Current sexuality	homo-sexual	homo-sexual	homo-sexual	hetero-sexual	hetero-sexual	hetero-sexual	? sexual	hetero-
Number of children	0	0	1	2	0	2	0	1
Left school without qualifications	✓	✓			✓			✓
Identified self as working class	✓	✓	✓					✓
Course for which they were writing	Medical Ethics	Social Work	Independent Studies: *Mature women undergraduates*	Anthropology	Aesthetics	Environ-mental Ethics	Independent Studies: *Black women in Western society*	Communication Studies

Figure 5.1 Some characteristics of my eight co-researchers at the time when they wrote the essays

construction of their identities. I bring in other details of their lives as they relate to the issues I am discussing in Chapters 6–10: as you read on you will get to know these eight people well. Chapter 6 provides a more detailed description of Rachel to show how these bare facts fill out into the complexity of one real life, but it would take up too much space to give more detailed descriptions of everyone (see also Ivanič 1995 or Clark and Ivanič 1997, Chapter 6 for a more detailed description of Sarah). I am writing for and about them here, but hope to publish some of their own accounts of their lives and experiences of academic writing (see Ivanič, Aitchison and Weldon 1996 for the first of these).

One thing this table does show is that it would be wrong to consider these eight people as a group. They all share the same "critical life event and experience, ... a psychological transition, milestone or turning point" (adapted from Handel 1987: 334): that is, returning to study after 8 or more years of adult life outside full-time education. But in all other respects they are eight separate case studies. I can make generalizations about the nature of writer identity at such a critical moment, but I cannot make generalizations about the nature of the group, nor of subsections of it. Although it is tempting to draw conclusions about the relationship between some of the outcomes of this study and some of the characteristics in this table, the numbers are too small. I use these characteristics as the basis for some speculations and hypotheses, but not for drawing conclusions.

The data collected for each co-researcher

One complete academic essay

The essays are all coursework assignments, in most cases from the second year of my co-researchers' university programmes of study. I chose to study their writing at a time when they had already been exposed to a certain amount of acculturation into the academic community in the hopes that they would have a lot to say about what they felt was required of them, how they had found this out, and differences from one assignment to another.

The courses are all different from each other, but are all within or related to the constellation known as 'social sciences'. The way in which the assignments were set up also differed from one essay to another. Angela and Donna, who wrote these essays as part of an Independent Studies course, were free to select their own topic to write about in consultation with a supervisor. Rachel had no choice of assignment. All the others had a choice between two or more topics offered by their course tutor. I mention other details about how the writing was assigned and supported in relevant places in Chapters 6, 7 and 8.

The criterion for selecting this essay was that it should be one which interested the writer, and/or that s/he was pleased with it. In most cases these essays were written entirely 'naturalistically' in the sense that the writers did not know at the time of writing that the essay would become the object of research. This is not quite true for Justin, Frances and Sarah, who knew at the time of writing the essays that I would be wanting to discuss with them *something*, but we had not already decided that it would be this particular essay. However, this is a still good deal more naturalistic than if they had been writing the essay specifically for research purposes, or as part of a study skills programme. The essays vary in length from 1,750 words to 4,500 words. They were very different from each other, but to give you an idea of the sort of writing I am discussing, Rachel's essay is reproduced in its original form, with line numbers added and reduced to 50% of its original size, at the end of Chapter 6.

I should explain my reason for using the term 'essay', rather than using the more common term 'assignment' for what my co-researchers wrote. There are various places where I want to distinguish the written text from the task that was set and the whole process of completing that task, including, but not limited to the writing of the text itself. I therefore decided to reserve the term 'assignment' for the whole task, and use the term 'essay' to refer to the written outcome of that assignment. This limited way of using the two terms appeals to me linguistically: the agent of the verb 'assign' in the word 'assignment' is the tutor; the agent of the verb 'essay' (meaning 'try') is the writer. My interest is in the writers' attempts to put ideas into words; not in the tutors' process of setting a task. However, the term 'essay' also refers to a specific genre: the presentation and discussion of a topic, including a position on the topic and justification for it. The pieces of writing were not all 'essays' in this sense, although most of them had some of these characteristics.

One retrospective discussion about their discourse choices in this essay

We tape-recorded a discussion about the chosen essay as soon as possible after it was written. In some cases we had also discussed it during the drafting stage, but the main discussion was the one based on the final version. In some cases this was before the essay was assessed by the subject tutor, in some cases (Valerie, Donna, John, Angela) after. This collaborative analysis was often spread over two or three meetings, and in many cases supplemented by further questions and answers over the phone or on subsequent meetings, usually prompted by my analysis. When our main discussion was before assessment, we had additional discussions, varying in length, after assessment. I do not assume that such analyses by writers provide any ultimate truth about their intentions, but I think they give useful insights into the dilemmas, if only the retrospective dilemmas, which writers experience.

We discussed how my co-researchers had approached this particular assignment, their practices and processes while engaged in it, and their feelings about it. Focusing on the essay itself, we attempted to identify the voices in the text: explicit quotation, scare quotes, words which seemed to be 'coming from somewhere', and what my co-researchers felt was their 'own voice'. My main aim was to find examples of what I called 'interdiscursivity' in Chapter 2.

These tape-recorded discussions show just how insightful people can be once prompted to reflect on their writing. However interesting and complex the writing process may appear in theory, the observations of writers them-selves are even more interesting and reveal even greater complexity. The insights contained in extracts from these discussions throughout Part Two are proof of the value of listening to student writers' own perceptions. This value needs to be recognized not only as a research methodology but also as a pedagogic practice: rather than assuming that we know what students need to be taught about academic literacy we would do well to listen to what they have to say about their experiences and about the demands and dilemmas they face.

One or more discussions about their literacy history and current literacy practices

I tape recorded a conversation with each co-researcher about the role of literacy in their lives, past and present. In most cases this discussion preceded the discourse-based work. It was a way of getting to know my co-researchers in preparation for the detailed study of their writing. These discussions were in most cases loosely chronological, tracing my co-researchers' lives from birth to the present day. They were about their family, friends, school experiences, memories of literacy at home, learning to read and write, reasons for not continuing with their education straight from school, work, families and interests since leaving school, the decision to return to study, experience of access to and entry into higher education, and feelings about their present experiences. They were also about their literacy practices in general and their views on various aspects of higher education and the place of writing in it. These discussions provide a rich picture of my co-researchers, 'where they are coming from' in all its meanings, and of the shaping of their identities as writers.

Observation and accumulated knowledge of my co-researchers' lives

This complements and enriches the information provided by the discussions described above. It provides additional insights into my co-researchers' problems, interests, affiliations, commitments, values and practices. I believed that knowing these intimate details would help me to see aspects of them-selves played out in their discoursal choices. I visited all my co-researchers in their homes. These visits varied enormously. At one extreme was Justin's rather reluctant agreement to my visiting him in his bed-sit on a single occasion. At the other extreme was my relationship with Rachel, with whom I have spent whole days at a time, working together on our joint projects of learning and researching, as often in her home as in mine.

Interviews with the tutors who assessed some of their essays

I could not interview Valerie's tutor, as he was not available, nor Donna's tutor, because Donna was unwilling for her to be approached. I had been Angela's tutor myself, so I am able to contribute my own responses directly. Justin interviewed his own tutor; I interviewed John's, Sarah's and Rachel's tutors personally, and Frances's by phone. These interviews were quite short, and took place as soon as possible after the tutors had read the essays. I asked them to explain why they had given the grade they did, to give any further responses they could to the essay, and particularly to comment on what the essay contributed to their impression of the writer.

Critical Language Awareness as a research methodology

The discussions between my co-researchers and me constituted a critical language awareness-raising exercise, in the sense of 'Critical Language Awareness (C.L.A.)' which colleagues and I have described elsewhere — (see Clark, Fairclough, Ivanič and Martin-Jones 1990 and 1991, Ivanič 1990, Clark and Ivanič 1991, Ivanič and Moss 1991, Fairclough 1992d). C.L.A. takes the view of language outlined in Chapter 2, treating language not as a 'rich tapestry' of neutral varieties, but as a site of struggle. In educational settings C.L.A. aims to show learners how language positions them: how their language choices are shaped by conventions and construct their identities. C.L.A. is intended not only to raise learners' consciousness about language and social context, but also to help them gain control over their own roles in discourse, and find ways of challenging positions with which they may not wish to identify.

In our article "Consciousness-raising about the writing process" Romy Clark and I suggest that C.L.A. can simultaneously be a research tool, proposing that there is an interrelationship between awareness, action and research. Figure 5.2 summarizes this relationship.

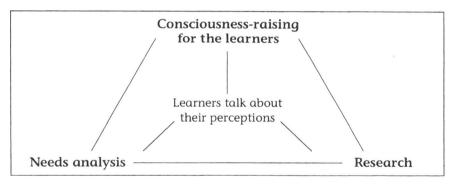

Figure 5.2   Potential aims of consciousness-raising activities
(Reproduced from Clark and Ivanič 1991: 183.)

In our discussions my co-researchers and I jointly engaged in the interrelated processes of consciousness-raising, needs analysis and research, as suggested in Figure 5.2. I brought the insights of a linguist; my co-researchers brought their knowledge of their own writing situations and discoursal choices. This consciousness-raising was 'critical' in the sense that we were focusing on how the writers felt positioned or constructed by the task and the linguistic choices they were making. We were identifying places where the writers felt compromised by the demands and expectations they perceived to be made on them by the academic community in the persons of those who would be assessing the essay. We also discussed what they had done or would like to do to resist these compromises. In some cases this critical language awareness-raising led to action. For example, in the writing she did during and immediately after this interview Sarah became progressively more resistant to academic discourse conventions which she felt were positioning her into a particular view of knowledge. C.L.A. as a research methodology can result in an increased understanding for everyone involved: rich insights for research as well as greater control for us all over writing events we are engaged in.

Integrating analysis of texts with analysis of interviews about texts

The data I collected included written texts, transcripts of discussions and notes made as a result of observation. The issue for analysis was not only how to deal with each of these types of data, but also how to integrate them. As I explained in Chapter 2, I draw mainly on Halliday's and Fairclough's techniques for the analysis of texts. Here I mention issues to do with linguistic analysis in general, and issues to do with using linguistic analysis to complement interview and observation data analysis, and vice versa.

I found that approaches to linguistic analysis which count features across whole texts were unsatisfactory for two reasons.

a.   I am interested in the ways in which the texts set up multiple subject-positions for their writers, by being composed of two or more discourses, juxtaposed or intertwined. Therefore differences from one part of a text to another and boundaries between discourses are more interesting than global features or global comparisons from one text to another.

b.   To understand the discourse characteristics of a text it is often necessary to go to considerable degrees of delicacy. For example, number of modalizations may not be so interesting as what sorts of things are modalized; number of material process verbs is too crude a category for the reasons outlined above: the analysis only gets interesting when you see what sorts of actors they have. Therefore detailed analysis of samples may be more revealing than global counts of broader categories.

Although I tried global counts of linguistic features, I abandoned most of them in favour of more local types of analysis.

I also found it unsatisfactory to isolate particular sections of text. It would be more convenient and neat as an analytic procedure to focus, for example, just on the introductions, as Swales (1981, 1984 and since then) has done. But in order to spread my net for issues of identity as wide as possible, I decided that I needed to undertake the more complex task of looking at the whole text.

The chapters of Part Two integrate the various types of data in different ways. Chapter 6 takes a single writer as its starting point, bringing together in one place what she said about her literacy history, analysis of extracts from her essay and of what she said about writing it. For the discussion of origins in Chapter 7 my starting point was what my co-researchers said in the interviews about the origins of particular parts of their writing. In my discussion of these I made connections with what I knew about their literacy history and literacy practices. Chapter 8 is based on categories and understandings which I derived from the interviews. In these two chapters (7 and 8) I use extracts from the essays to locate discussion of particular issues, but I do not engage in further linguistic analysis of these extracts. For the study of the discourse characteristics of the texts themselves (in Chapters 9 and 10) my starting-point was the linguistic data. However, even in these chapters the interview data played an important supporting role in a) motivating what sorts of discourse types I chose to comment on, b) helping me identify parts of the texts which were particularly interesting from the point of view of the discoursal construction of identity, c) providing commentary on the way particular discourse types position their users in particular ways.

In the discourse-based interviews my co-researchers had identified parts of their writing which were particularly interesting or troublesome for them, and those for which they could identify a particular source. I initially focused my attention on these parts for detailed linguistic analysis. Often they identified discourse types which I may not have noticed alone. We may also have missed some others, but the fact that these extracts had been picked out by my co-researchers made them significant anyway.

However, I did not limit my attention to parts of the text which my co-researchers had picked out in our interviews. Rather, I used what they had said as a lead into the texts, helping me to know what else to turn my linguist's eyes on. So, for example, in Chapter 10, I focused on discoursal characteristics which distinguished discourse types of different subjects and courses. The issue of differences between ways with words on different courses had been raised by my co-researchers, and they had pointed out some instances; I then went on to look for others.

Finally, I drew on my knowledge of the institution of higher education in Britain, and on my understandings of my co-researchers' experiences, interests, affiliations, values, beliefs and practices to take the crucial extra step of suggesting how the various discourse types in the essays positioned their users. Without this knowledge, Chapters 9 and 10 would have been a series of linguistic descriptions which would mean little more in terms of writer identity than 's/he has become the sort of person who uses these words and structures.' With the benefit of my 'insider knowledge' it is possible to suggest what sorts of values, beliefs and social relations these words construct for their users.

Data presentation conventions

Conventions for presenting extracts from essays

Each extract is numbered sequentially in the text of Part Two and cross-referenced to the complete essays. For example, the first extract in Chapter 9 is labelled 'Extract 9.1: John — *Medical Ethics* (lines 205–214)' to indicate that it is the first extract discussed in Chapter 9, that it is from lines 205–214 of John's essay, and that the essay was for a course entitled 'Medical Ethics'. The only essay which is reproduced in full in the book is Rachel's, but anyone interested in seeing the complete originals can contact me.

All text from the essays appears in a *slanted sans serif type* (like this). As far as possible I have reproduced spelling, punctuation and capitalization as in the original. However, in places where I discuss individual words from an extract in more detail I usually use conventional spelling in order to make the intended meaning clear. I have not used quotation marks for any extracts, even when embedded in my own text, as quotation marks in the original are sometimes the topic for discussion.

Conventions for presenting extracts from interviews

– Extracts from the interviews are in the same typeface as the text, as they are not just colourful illustrations of the argument, but should be read as contributions to the content of the chapter.
– Extracts from the interviews always start with the name of the speaker. Where it is necessary to reproduce dialogue, I appear as 'Roz'.

- The words of the interview are in serif typeface, but when words from the writing are mentioned, they are in *slanted sans serif*, like the extracts from the essays.
- I have attempted to make the parts quoted as relevant and easy to read as possible. I have therefore not transcribed hesitations and false starts, unless they seem to contribute to the meaning. Where conventional punctuation (commas, question marks) will make the quotation easier to follow, I have used them.
- Anyone interested in consulting the interview transcriptions can contact me.

Here is a key to the symbols used in presenting these quotations:

..	indicates final intonation and/or a pause in places where the syntax of the quotation does not lend itself to conventional punctuation.
(...)	indicates that a part of the interview which is not relevant to the point under discussion is omitted. If it is only a few words omitted, the quotation carries on immediately after the (...). If a substantial portion is omitted, the (...) is on an otherwise blank line.
(.?.)	indicates that a part of the interview which is indecipherable is omitted.
(?word/s)	indicates that I am not quite sure if this is the word spoken.
[word/s]	adds words or replaces a proform with words to complete the sense.
(*word/s*)	explains who or what is being referred to.

The organization of Part Two

This part of the book begins with a case-study: the story of Rachel Dean, her experience of leaving school without qualifications and then returning to study at the age of 26. I show how the complex, ambivalent self which Rachel brings to the act of writing is the product of her social opportunities and of the allegiances she has formed. At the end of the third year of her four-year course in Social Administration she was given an assignment to write a *Family Case Study* based on her placement in a Social Work office. I discuss the wording of her essay, the discourses and practices she is drawing on as she writes it, and how they position her. I end this chapter with a discussion of the way in which she attempted to position herself in the light of her anticipation of the values and beliefs of the people who would be reading her essay. Chapter 6 is an introduction to the topics which are the focus of the next four chapters, integrating them around the experience and writing of a single person.

Chapters 7–10 each address a particular aspect of the discoursal construction of writer identity. These chapters are slightly more impersonal than Chapter 7, having abstract topics as their chapter headings, rather than a person's name. They move beyond the theory which was presented in Part One, each making its own contribution to a comprehensive understanding of the discoursal construction of identity in academic writing.

Chapters 7 and 8 form a pair in that they document what my co-researchers said about factors which influenced how they portrayed themselves in their writing. In Chapter 7 **The origins of discoursal identity in writers' experience** I discuss the way in which the resources on which writers draw are themselves socially and discoursally constructed by their life experiences. In Chapter 8 **The sense of self and the role of the reader in the discoursal construction of writer identity** I consider these choices from the point of view of social interaction: the way in which writers select (consciously or unconsciously) among the discourses on which they are drawing according to their allegiances and sense of the discoursal self they want to convey, and the influence of their readers. There is a loose chronology underlying the organization of Chapters 7 and 8. Chapter 7 is concerned with what writers bring with them from the past to the act of writing; the first part of Chapter 8 is concerned with the self which is discoursally constructed at the moment of writing; the second part of Chapter 8 is concerned with the way in which writers anticipate a future moment when readers construct an impression of them on the basis of their writing.

Chapters 9 and 10 form a pair in that they both contain linguistic analysis of the characteristics of the writing itself. In these chapters I discuss the sorts of impressions the writers were conveying of themselves through their discourse choices, and consider the values, beliefs, practices, and patterns of privileging among them which shape the discourse types on which the writers were drawing. In Chapter 9 **The discoursal construction of academic community membership** I focus on what makes all the pieces of writing instances of 'academic writing', and how this positions all the writers as members of the academic community. In Chapter 10 **Multiple possibilities for self-hood in the academic discourse community** I focus on the discoursal variety within and between these eight pieces of writing, and I discuss the multiple and varied ways in which this positions the writers. Insofar that these chapters are based on extracts from my co-researchers' writing, they are about these writers' identity at the moment of writing itself, but they are also about the socially available discoursal resources for the construction of identity (the 'possibilities for self-hood' as I called them in Chapter 1) which transcend the chronology of any individual piece of writing.

The combination of linguistic analysis and insights from the writers themselves in Part Two elaborates on and clothes in detail the central argument of the book as introduced in Chapter 1. Through the practices and discourses which writers draw on as they write they identify with socially available possibilities for self-hood and thereby contribute to maintenance or change in the configuration of possibilities for self-hood available to other writers in the future. In this way writing is an important site for the processes of identification which are the mechanisms of social change. In the conclusion I then revisit the main theoretical issues I raised in Part One, briefly indicate how the chapters in Part Two have contributed to them, and suggest some implications of this research for pedagogic practice in higher education.

CHAPTER 6

Rachel Dean

A case study of writing and identity

Rachel's story

Rachel was born and brought up in a South Lancashire town. Other members of Rachel's family did not read much. At the beginning of primary school she had the impression that she had learnt to read and had seen herself as a successful reader. However, one year when she returned to school after the summer holidays she was treated in such a way that she realized that she was not defined as a successful reader by the school. It is as if she had the identity of 'person-who-is-able-to-read' taken away from her. From then onwards and through secondary school she was treated as a 'remedial reader'. She began to have difficulty with reading and was barred from certain educational routes such as learning a foreign language. This caused her much frustration. She tried to resist being defined as someone who was not ready take up educational opportunities, but without success. But she never totally lost the sense of 'being a reader', of

Rachel: knowing I can do it even though I can't get to it.

Rachel had been expected to leave school at the earliest possible leaving age — 16 — in order to start work, and she did. No-one else in her family had continued in education beyond the minimum leaving age, and no-one at the school encouraged her to stay on. She left with no formal qualifications. However, before she left school she had already decided that she intended to return to study as a mature student. She knew she would be able to get a grant for full-time study after the age of 25 and never lost sight of her intention to do so. She worked for ten years in low-paid manual, tourist, catering and caring jobs.

Rachel did not have any of the standard qualifications for a university place. She had taken two 'O' Levels in Further Education: Sociology and English, and got low grades for them. She applied to university at the age of 26 on the basis of having taken a Fresh Start course at an Adult Education college: one day a week for two years. This course had given her some practice in academic reading and writing. She bought a textbook consisting of short readings of extracts from seminal publications in the Social Sciences, and read some of it at her own pace. She also wrote three essays as part of the course-work, with a lot of help from her tutors. She got a place on a four-year course leading to a double qualification: B.A. in Social Sciences and C.Q.S.W. (Certificate as a Qualified Social Worker) at a major university. This was a course which recruited a larger than usual number of mature students, offering places on the basis of experience in the field in lieu of academic qualifications. Rachel impressed the admissions tutors so much at interview that they didn't ask her about reading and writing. They seem to have assumed that someone with her intelligence, as demonstrated by the way she talked, would be able to cope with the demands of a degree.

Rachel saw social work far more as a way in to higher education than as a goal at the end of it. The C.Q.S.W. would tie together her past experience, but her long-term goal for herself was not to be a social worker. She was resistant to it because of the way she felt she had been cornered into it in the past: colonized into a low-paid, low-status, female profession. She chose this combined course as a way out of social work as a career. She hoped the degree would give her the opportunity to explore other options and that she would be able to use it as a passport to another course or a different area of work. On the other hand, she had no idealistic notions that the degree would give her the world. Being realistic, she knew she might need to work as a social worker again in the future, and the C.Q.S.W. might at least mean she would be better paid than in the past.

Rachel was much more interested in feminist issues and theory associated with the women's movement than in social work. Apart from one history book, the only books she bought for herself in the first three years at university were about feminism. However, Rachel didn't identify herself as a feminist unreservedly.

Rachel: I don't buy wholesale all the interpretations of 'feminist'.

Rachel did not view herself as a prospective social worker, although she was an extremely committed student. In her first three years she took every opportunity to choose courses which were not directly related to social work, courses such as 'Women in Society'.

Rachel: My degree wasn't Social Work, more Independent Studies and Sociology. I avoided Social Work. I thought I didn't really want to be a social worker. I didn't really know many people on my course. It's changed a bit [in Year 4], because my friends have graduated.

However, six out of nine of her Part II courses were compulsory Social Work courses. This forced her to spend much of her time in the role of Social Work student, even though she did not identify with this positioning.

Rachel was a leading member of three women's groups at the university: the Women's Group, the Feminist Reading Group, and the Lesbian Society. She was actively involved in many areas of the women's liberation movement. She had a strong sense of identity as a lesbian, but felt that the pressures of living in a heterosexist and homophobic world forced her to hide this identity. She felt it was not safe to reveal her sexual identity, particularly when it might affect her employment prospects, and this led to conflicts of identity for her. When talking about her experience as a youth worker, she said:

Rachel: I don't do mainstream youth work, but when I'm applying for jobs I have to say that I do. I say I work with girls and young women which is true, but I just don't say that it's actually lesbian youth work.

She also felt that most of the academic books she read did not relate to her as a lesbian, that they excluded her, and that few tutors at university would value her particular perspective.

Rachel saw the experience of being a mature woman student as very different from being a regular undergraduate. Her life revolved around getting assignments done. She did not feel in a position to choose how to spend free time: it had to be spent 'catching up on twelve years of your life'. Her only social activities were associated with the women's groups. She saw those as part of 'the survival tactic of creating an environment in which you gain support'. Although she enjoyed those activities for their own sake, they were also essential to her in her major endeavour of surviving academically. I noticed something at her house which is evidence of the amount of effort Rachel had to put into writing her assignments. On the main door leading from the living room to the stairs she had stuck a post-it with 'You can do it' written on it. She said that she had to keep convincing herself.

Rachel said that she never writes two assignments the same way. Her study and writing practices are constantly changing over time, depending on several factors. For example, how many people are living in her house affects how much space she has available. What her social life is like at the time affects whether she is carrying her work around with her or mainly doing it at home. What equipment and stationery she has available makes different practices available to her. A good example of this is that, at the time of writing the assignment we discussed, Rachel did not use post-its for notes. However, when she was writing another essay on a similar topic, she had most of her notes on post-its, stuck to her bookcase and her radiator. This was because she had a free supply of them from her third practical social work placement, and found a way to make good use of them.

At university her image of herself as a reader was contradictory: she saw herself as a reader but also as someone who couldn't read. She saw herself as a reader in the sense that she was interested in what was in the books, and still knew she would eventually be able to grapple with the text. On the other hand she also knew she couldn't read fast enough to be the reader she wanted to be. She said:

Rachel: It was that pressure that disabled me to read. I have to put all my energies into strategies to get round it.

Rachel's assignment

Rachel wrote the assignment which I discuss in this chapter at the age of 29, in the first term of her fourth year in university. At the time when we discussed it she had handed in the assignment and was working on others. It was later assessed and graded by her tutor and I then interviewed her tutor about her response to it.

The assignment was set before the students started their second professional placement (as part of the C.Q.S.W.) Rachel's placement was in an N.S.P.C.C. (National Society for the Prevention of Cruelty to Children) office. They were told that they would be required to write a case study drawn from that placement. They could either write a case history of one of the cases they worked on, or they could analyse a particular interview with a client in detail. Rachel decided to do the case history because she felt it would give her the opportunity to get to grips with social work theory in general, choosing according to her own agenda of what was worth her while to spend time on.

Rachel: [It was] more important to do than the essay on interview techniques: to look at a case and see what it involved.

The word limit was 2,500 words, which did not daunt Rachel. She said:

Rachel: 2,500 compared to 4,000 seemed peanuts, whereas looking back to first year 2,000 would have been like mega. You can hardly get going before you've ended.

Rachel's literacy practices associated with this assignment

At the time she wrote this she only had her own room to work in. This meant sitting at a very small desk without space to spread out papers or books. There was a bookshelf above the desk, but Rachel had very few books on it. In fact she spent a lot of time at her friend's house, sometimes for company, and sometimes baby-sitting. She carried her work there in a folder and opened it whenever there was an opportunity. She also carried this folder to the university and occasionally worked from it in the library. However, she did not use the time in the library to consult extra books, just to get on with drafting the essay.

Rachel found settling down to work on an assignment at home extremely difficult. If there was writing to do, she would automatically look for a distraction. She would suddenly become aware how dirty and untidy her house was, and find herself hoovering and washing the dishes much more assiduously than usual, only to recognize that this was all part of the avoidance strategy.

Rachel did not do any preparatory reading for this assignment. She felt that she knew the theoretical issues which she had to incorporate in the essay. She took one book out of the library — 'Social Work Practice: an Introduction' (Coulshed, 1988) — which she knew was a 'very good reference work' from a previous course and from revising for her third year exams. As she did not identify with the role of 'social work student', she did not want to spend a lot of time reading books about social work methodology.

The entire work on this assignment was spread over a long period.

Rachel: That's what I came up with and I spent lots of sleepless nights
           thinking about it.

All the time she was on her placement, Rachel knew that she would be writing
about Ms A., so she was thinking simultaneously about what to do on the case
and what she would be writing about it.

Rachel: Cos I'd been thinking about it a lot, so I thought it would just
           flow, the story.

Rachel also took a lot of trouble over the drafting process, in some places
redrafting 'so many times!'. The writing took a long time and a lot of effort, in
spite of the fact that she had thought it would 'just flow, the story'.

Rachel: I'm (...) running and then I get near the end and I just feel too
           tired to properly give it the same as I've given the beginning and
           I just go back on what I know even though it's what I believe and
           it's just kind of like: 'Oh I just want to end this,' not like: 'I'll just
           put this in.' It's still painful at the end just struggling on.

Rachel made six pages of plans and rough notes of various types, and wrote a
complete rough draft in addition to the neat version. The rough draft shows
evidence of a great deal of effort and thought, with an extra bit blutacked on
in one place, several parts, ranging in length from a paragraph to a word,
crossed out and/or rewritten. Sometimes she wrote in single spacing, sometimes in double. Both the rough notes and the draft are written with several
different writing implements: three different colours of biro and pencil. These
do not seem to be used in a systematic way. For example, red is used on the
rough notes, for some parts of the first draft, and for corrections. She used
three different types of paper: blank, wide feint and narrow feint. She usually
buys narrow feint to save money: narrower lines mean more writing for less
money; the other types of paper were given to her by friends when she hadn't
any with her. Rachel pointed out the analogy between the way she uses paper
and the way she uses language: borrowed or given paper, like borrowed or
given words, like borrowed or given clothes: borrowed or given identity. I
suggest that these writing practices are also an expression of the conflict of
identity Rachel experiences over academic writing. Partly she wants to do it
well: she wants to be in control of this aspect of her life. She is willing to put
considerable time and effort into assignments. But partly she resists the
identity of being a writer: she feels it doesn't 'fit' with her sense of her self.

Consequently she has not adopted a systematic approach to writing academic essays, and seems to be 'starting from scratch' each time she approaches a new assignment.

Although Rachel is strongly committed to collaboration as a form of knowledge-making in the university, she also needed to prove to herself that she could do something entirely independently. She wrote this assignment almost entirely alone, without collaboration or support from her friends as she had had for many previous assignments. However, she added some underlining as a result of her friend reading the essay over after it was finished.

As these details of Rachel's literacy practices show, an unexpectedly wide range of factors determine what ends up in the written text. Rachel's particular configuration of practices and feelings are created by the person she is, and determine what she writes as much as the nature of the task itself and the influence of the readers.

Rachel's essay *Family Case Study*: an overview

Rachel's essay is reproduced in its original form in the appendix to this chapter. Now would be a good time for you to read it in its entirety to judge for yourself what sort of impression Rachel conveys of herself through this piece of writing. Figure 6.1 gives a brief outline of the development of the essay to act as a backdrop to the detailed discussion in the rest of this chapter. In the next section I show how the linguistic characteristics of essay construct a multiple, sometimes contradictory discoursal self for Rachel. In the following section I examine the way in which these aspects of identity are sometimes juxtaposed, sometimes interwoven as Rachel switches from one discourse or genre to another, or embeds one in another. I then discuss Rachel's ambivalence about the discoursal self she presents here: the way in which she owned some aspects of it and disowned others. I end the chapter by discussing how this discoursal self is shaped by the way in which Rachel anticipated the reactions of her readers and responded to the patterns of privileging among discourses in her social context.

This sort of study of the discoursal heterogeneity of students' writing brings into the open the complexity and sophistication of their writing processes and of the decisions they are making. By revealing the care and attention which often lie behind what might at first be dismissed as inadequate written products, I am throwing into question the sorts of quality

lines	section
1– 24	Background information about the case of Ms A.
25– 47	Rachel's first meeting with Ms A.
48–133	Rachel's plan for handling this case, with theoretical justification for the decisions based on Social Work theory
134–158	What happened after Ms A did not turn up for her fourth meeting with Rachel
158–162	Rachel's analysis of what had happened in terms of Social Work theory
163–181	Rachel's reflections on her choice of how to handle the case, and on the subsequent events
182–196	What Ms A said during Rachel's last visit to her, and Rachel's interpretation of it
197–219	Rachel's radical feminist perspective on the case

Figure 6.1   Outline of Rachel's essay: **Family Case Study**

judgments which are often made by tutors in the assessment process. No tutor is ever going to conduct in-depth research about each assignment they assess, but I hope that this analysis of one such assignment will give an indication of the sorts of things that might be going on in many others.

Rachel's multiple positioning in this essay

In this section I show how Rachel moves between at least seven different subject-positions in her essay *Family Case Study* — some major, some minor; some of which she identifies with, some of which she feels ambivalent about, and some of which she rejects. Of these, her positioning as an apprentice social-worker is in itself multi-faceted. I show how these identities manifest themselves in specific discoursal choices. (For this analysis I originally used Halliday's Functional Grammar (1994) as my main analytical tool. However, wherever possible I have avoided the technical terminology of this analytical approach in order to make the analysis accessible to readers who are not familiar with Halliday's framework.) I also discuss how far this discoursal self matches the autobiographical self I have mapped above, and identify the origins of some of these discourses in Rachel's personal experience.

Rachel's identity as an apprentice social worker

The course Rachel was following is different from other academic courses in that it has a practical, work-related aim, leading to a practical qualification. The assignment was set up in such a way as to encourage the interplay between academic and workplace discourse types: something with many inherent pitfalls for the writers. Were they supposed to be taking on the *persona* of an apprentice social worker, or of an academic student of social work? The answer seems to be that they were required to maintain both these identities simultaneously, switching between them strategically — a writing task demanding considerable skill. In this section I analyse five extracts from her essay in detail (lines 1–2, lines 3–24, lines 25–51, lines 77–81, and lines 217–219), to show how she positioned herself as a social worker, and as an apprentice social worker through drawing on different discourses and genres of professional social work. I am suggesting that the discoursal elements which I focus on in these sections construct a workplace identity rather than an identity associated with the academic community.

Writing social work case notes
Rachel establishes an apprentice social work identity at the very beginning of the essay. She does not start with a conventional academic introduction, outlining the structure of the paper, but with the following sentence:

Extract 6.1 (a) (lines 1–2)

> I worked with family C during my Second placement with a Child Protection Agency.

This contrasts with the way she started at least one other essay in the same year:

Extract 6.1 (b)

> I will first outline what is currently known about HIV/AIDS.

However, the choice of how to begin the essay was not just a difference between the nature of the assignments. The student who got the highest mark for the 'placement' essay followed the academic convention of outlining the content of the essay in her opening:

Extract 6.1 (c)

> The introduction to this essay will take the form of a brief outline of the referal taken in respect of the case study I intend to look at. From then it will then be possible to examine the social work practice undertaken, the theory involved in this and the outcome of the intervention and how this might have differed if other options had been explored.

Rachel, by choosing NOT to introduce her essay in this way, identified herself as not taking an academic approach to the assignment. She started with '*I worked*' — identifying herself as a student social worker by referring to her own past action. This first person, past tense verb is not typical of the discourse of social scientific essays, except possibly for the reporting of anthropological fieldwork.

Rachel and I identified lines 2–24 as having the discoursal characteristics of professional social work case notes, interwoven from line 15 onwards with a more informal narrative. Of this section she said

Rachel: The first bit is quite kind of clinical isn't it — like *two referrals made, prior to my involvement*, it's kind of professional

What Rachel calls 'clinical' is represented by several linguistic features, particularly prevalent between lines 2 and 22. Although this section presents background information about events in the life of a family, it starts with a grammar of nouns and states rather than human agents and actions. First, there is a heading and list format for the *Family composition*. This is very much as it might appear in case notes at the Agency.

Secondly, between lines 13 and 17 Rachel uses three nouns without determiners (i.e. words such as 'a', 'the', 'his', 'her'), underlined below.

Extract 6.2 (lines 12–17)

> this was an none accidental injury (NAI) caused by _mother's cohab_ during an incident of domestic violence aimed initially at Ms A. The second referral N reported to _teacher_ that there was increased violence in the home, caused again by _cohab._

This is a characteristic of note form rather than connected written discourse. She writes *cohab* again without a determiner in line 41, so this note form associated with case notes was not restricted to the opening section.

Thirdly, Rachel uses words and formulaic expressions which characterize discourse of the Social Work profession (itself a hybrid discourse, drawing on medical, legal and psychological discourses): *referals* (line 7), *prior to my involvement* (line 8), *none accidental injury (NAI)* (line 13), *incident of domestic violence* (line 14), *verbally threatened* (line 18). Discussing the most obviously technical of these *none accidental injury (NAI)*, Rachel told me that it is a semi-legal term, and that the acronym would be used in the courts and among social workers without needing to be explained. By using the acronym Rachel was identifying herself with that professional community, but she was also identifying herself as a writer of an academic essay by including the full version of the term, as is the convention for academic writing. I see this as a sophisticated embedding of a feature of academic discourse into the report-writing conventions of the social work profession.

Fourthly, there is a focus on causes, with the words *because*, (line 10), *caused* (line 13, line 20) and *causing* (line 19). This is a discoursal element associated with states rather than events and actions: a function of the social worker report is to present a case as a current state of affairs, rather than just relating the events which happened.

Fifthly, there are two long nominal groups, one extremely long and complex, with multiple embedding:

Extract 6.3 (lines 12–15)

> *an none accidental injury[caused by mothers cohab[during an incident [of domestic violence [aimed initially at Ms A]]]]*

This syntax reifies actions, turning them into objects (*injury, incident, violence*), classifies them within the discourse of professional social work, and turns them into a single participant in the syntax. In so doing, Rachel is making herself one with those for whom such events are the taken-for-granted, day-to-day material of their professional life.

Sixthly, there are few human participants as grammatical subjects, and few actions in this section. The only clause with a human grammatical subject before line 15 is *because the eldest son N had got a large bruise on the inside of his right arm*. This is a subordinate clause, reporting a state rather than an action, and it further creates distance from the human individuals and their actions by classifying N as *the eldest son*. After line 15, two main clauses have human agents, as the rigid case notes grammar breaks down. The sentence:

Extract 6.4 (lines 15–17)

> The second referal N reported to teacher that there was increased
> violence in the home, caused again by cohab.

begins with a pattern established before, the nominalization *referal* as the first
head noun of the sentence. However, it is not developed in the same way as
The first referal had been, with a verb such as *was made* next. It seems that
Rachel was attempting to maintain a grammar in which nominalizations such
as *referal* are the major grammatical participants, but gave it up. The actual
events with human agents were uppermost in her mind and subverted the
conventional grammar of clinical reports. She abandoned the grammar of her
sentence starter, and restarted with N, a human agent, as grammatical subject.
However, she remained in the discourse of social work reports in that the
clause represents a verbal process: N *reported that* rather than an action. Even
though N. is the grammatical subject of the clause, he is talking, not doing
something. This is the grammatical realization of a moral dilemma for the
writer who wants to write about the human subjects and actions she was
concerned with, but is constrained by the conventions of social work discourse, which objectifies actions and removes or depersonalizes human subjects.

The next sentence contains the first action with a human actor as main
clause: *the cohab had verbally threatened* (line 18), but the distance of the
social work report is preserved in the past perfect tense.

The discourse characteristics of social work case notes reappear in the
grammar of the opening of the next sentence:

Extract 6.5 (lines 20–22)

> This had caused N on one occasion to escape from an upstairs bed-
> room window jumping 30 ft to safty.

The use of discoursal *This* (that is, the word 'this' referring to a prior portion
of discourse: to a process rather than to a thing) as the subject of a clause of
causation in the past perfect tense seems to me to belong more to the discourse of reporting states than to a narrative account of events or actions.
These three sentences (lines 15–22) contain a mix of expository and narrative
grammar, constituting a transition between the grammar of states with which
the essay begins, and the grammar of happenings which erupts at line 22:

Extract 6.6 (lines 22–24)

> N then ran through the town in the early hours of the morning to
> contact his natural father.

Here is an action with a human agent and a verb in the simple past: the grammar of narrative, not of exposition. The actual events on which the case notes are based, but which are conventionally nominalized or embedded in the grammar, surface here.

This constellation of grammatical characteristics with which the essay begins position Rachel as a professional social worker, writing case notes. Rachel said she had learnt to write like this from reading case studies and also from the sheet she had to fill in when taking phone referrals on her placement. She had a clear idea of what the discourse characteristics of this writing are:

Rachel: They want to know the facts — they don't want you to be like describing ... so that was stripping it to the bare bones: they want to know the crucial, the crux of it.

She felt herself relatively consciously creating a *persona* as the efficient matter-of-fact social worker which she knew her course and this assignment required of her and which she knew her readers expected her to be. However, as I have suggested, the discourse she had acquired as part of her literacy practices as an apprentice social worker gave way to a much more familiar and pervasive grammar of narrative.

Writing social work visit reports
The discourse characteristics in lines 25–51 seem also to position Rachel as a social worker, including both elements which position her as an established professional and others which identify her as an apprentice. Some of these characteristics are similar to the previous section, maintaining a 'social worker discourse' associated with the values and practices of social work as a pro-fession, reifying the activities of social workers and their clients, pinning them down and classifying them as entities with which the social work profession is accustomed to deal. For example, the words underlined in extract 6.7 are part of the grammar of 'being' rather than 'doing':

Extract 6.7 (lines 27–28)

My role at this point was to observe.

This reifies and normalizes the apprentice social worker's activities, and makes them part of an unquestionable state of affairs.

There is a preponderance of lexis in the semantic field of verbal processes: referal (line 29), wanted to talk to us (line 34), confirmed (lines 36, 43), checking out and information (line 42), telephone number (line 46) rang, *asking* (line 47). This is the lexical realization of a key function of social work: to make contacts and establish information. There is also other lexis which I suggest is either specific to, or common in professional social work discourse: *role, supervising officer* (line 27) and *child protection officer* (lines 28–29).

In these respects this section is similar to the previous section, but other grammatical features distinguish it. The main difference is that in this section there are also many clauses describing actions, such as *visited, had left,* and human agents as grammatical subjects — *I, The child protection officer, we, Ms A, the cohab. -.* These are often in Theme position: at the beginning of a clause or sentence, making them the point of departure for the message. Many of the verbs are in the simple past tense: *visited, dealt, were asked, wanted, confirmed, became, left, rang.* These are characteristic of reporting events — what I earlier called 'the grammar of narrative' — rather than states of affairs. The participants and processes are, however, mainly events associated with the social workers' visit, rather than with the lives of the family concerned, in contrast to extract 6.6. I suggest that these characteristics are associated with the social work visit report genre rather than the social work case notes genre.

The discourse of social work visit reports may also account for two clauses which begin with expressions of time:

Extract 6.8 (lines 29–30)

On being let into the home by Ms A,...

Extract 6.9 (lines 41–43)

On checking out whether information given by the school was true (Ms A confirmed it was)...

It seems to me that putting these expressions at the beginning of sentences — that is, in the position normally reserved for 'given information' — depends to some extent on assumptions about social work practice which a member of that community might share with other members. Certainly it is recoverable from the text that they would be let into the home: line 26 introduces the fact that they visited the home. But this seems to depend to some extent on an expectation that social workers are let into clients' homes. However, there are no other indications in the text that social workers as a matter of procedure check out the information given by a school. I suggest that, by putting this element at the beginning of the sentence where one would expect 'given information', Rachel is identifying with a community who know, and treat as given, the sorts of things social workers do on home visits.

The verbs in both sections are categorical: that is, with no modal elements such as 'might', 'could' or 'perhaps'. This gives both sections the discoursal function of presenting fact, and so conforms to the conventions for social work discourse identified above. There is one modalized clause expressing likelihood:

Extract 6.10 (lines 40–41)

> Otherwise she stood a good chance of loosing N if cohab stayed.

This clause seems at first sight to be the words of the writer, in which case the uncertainty is uncharacteristic of the position she has otherwise set up for herself in this section of presenting factually what happened and the information they established. Rachel may be expressing her own uncertainty as an apprentice social work professional as to the consequences of Ms A.'s cohab. staying. However, this clause follows on from ones presenting what Ms A. confirmed (lines 37–38), so Rachel may also partly be reporting Ms A.'s expressed uncertainty as to whether she would lose N. if her cohab. stayed. There is also one clause of obligation:

Extract 6.11 (lines 49–50)

> I was to befriend, support and build confidence with Ms A with a view to protecting her children in the long term.

The modal verb *was to* positions Rachel firmly as an apprentice: the obligation is coming from a superior.

This analysis leads me to conclude that this section is still part of the discourse of the professional social work community. However it differs from the previous section in that it is characteristic of a visit report rather than case notes. Rachel is still positioning herself discoursally as a professional social worker, although particular details of content (lines 26–29 and lines 48–49), and the modality and modulation discussed above construct her as an apprentice too.

Other aspects of the professional social worker identity
There are three further sections in which Rachel positions herself discoursally as a social worker in slightly different ways from those already discussed.

Extract 6.12 (lines 77–81)

> I felt that this would served three perhaps*
> (* *perhaps* is a misspelling for *purposes*)
> (i)   To get Ms A and the twins out of the home.

(ii)   Give all three people the opportunity to mix in a different envi-
           ronment.
(iii)   A way of monitoring the home situation.

Rachel said that this section takes the format of particular forms provided by
the N.S.P.C.C., on which social workers have to record their aims, objectives
and plans of work. There are four noticeable characteristics of it:

a.   the list format using *(i)*, *(ii)* and *(iii)*
b.   the syntax and lexis associated with purpose: served three perhaps, To
     get.., give ... the opportunity to, A way of monitoring,
c.   the formulaic collocations associated with social work aims: mix in a
     different environment, monitoring the home situation.
d.   the people and circumstances concerned in the case — Ms A and the
     twins, all three people, the home situation. These are the people who
     are affected by processes rather than the actors who are in control of
     them.

This is a third professional social work genre to add to case notes and visit
reports. Through it Rachel positions herself firmly as a professional social
worker, taking on the activity of defining purposes for people, and taking
control over their lives. The important point for this chapter is that it is has
different discoursal characteristics from other sections of her essay, or indeed
anyone else's. It is also interesting that as a linguist I could see it had particular
generic characteristics, but in order to identify its genre I had either to be an
insider to the particular social work community in which Rachel worked, or to
ask her. This shows that thorough discourse analysis is impossible without
consulting participants for contextual detail.

At line 127, Rachel uses an expression she had invented herself, and puts
it in inverted commas:

Extract 6.13 (line 127–129)

These 'goal aimed tasks' were arrived at by me as a worker actively
listening to what Ms A had been saying during our 1 hr long sessions.

She says about this:

Rachel: I'm aware that I've got goals that are set, so by putting them in
            quotes it's like they should know where I'm coming from

The expression 'goal aimed tasks' positions her squarely within the professional social work community: she is hoping her readers will identify her as the sort of person who has tasks with clear goals and aims. However, it is not clear to the reader what the function of the inverted commas is. Rachel said that 'goal aimed tasks' is not quoted *verbatim* from anywhere, and by using the inverted commas she did not intend to distance herself from the expression, although she didn't identify with it whole-heartedly. Rachel said that she was using the inverted commas to indicate that she was creating her own linguistic package for what she had been writing about before. She said about it:

Rachel: It's another way of saying goals and aims but that didn't fit there so I put goal-aimed tasks and then put those (*the inverted commas*) in to say — you know what I mean — I should hope most social workers know they've got a goal. So by saying 'goal aimed tasks' I'm just like putting a bow around it...it's taking that language on board I suppose.

Here Rachel is saying 'This is mine, but it's me playing a role.' She recognized that goals, aims and tasks are the sorts of things social workers talk about. People in social work will recognize her as one of them by talking about such matters. By inventing this expression she was identifying herself with the role of social worker — a role about which she is ambivalent, but said at this point that she was willing to accept. So she owns the process of inventing, but not the discourse which is the raw material for the invention.

This example shows that even when a writer coins an expression of her own, it is still double-voiced. It is saturated in currently available discourses, even though it is at the same time her own, uniquely creative contribution to discourse. It also shows that writers can use inverted commas to signal *ownership* of this sort: a signification which a reader or analyst might not be able to distinguish from signalling *distance*. Another example of the same thing is the expression 'cohab-free', which I discuss later.

Rachel's identity as an apprentice social worker also seems to be shaping her discourse choices in the word *Personally* (line 197), which I discuss in the section on 'Rachel as a person with a heart' below. The final extract I want to mention in terms of positioning as a social worker is the very end of the essay: the last sentence in extract 6.14.

Extract 6.14 (lines 213–219: i.e. the end)

> *How I am going to do this is a much more difficult question to answer. Particularly as the role of the social worker is so bound with perpetuating the institutions mentioned previously. However it is a challenge to which I hope to succeed.*

Rachel pointed out that her motivation for ending the essay in this way was to do with the impression she thought she should convey as an apprentice social worker.

Rachel: I felt like I'm supposed to come up with an answer now, and try to be positive, rather than doom and gloom

In her view, social workers are supposed to be optimistic, and have solutions to problems. She does not herself hold these aims and attitudes, as I discuss in the section on 'Rachel's identity as an academic feminist' below, but she felt it was an impression of herself that she should be fostering in the eyes of her readers in the Social Work community.

To summarize this discussion of workplace discourses and identities in Rachel's essay, I am suggesting that Rachel felt that it was required of her in this assignment to construct herself as an apprentice social worker. She did this by drawing on at least three professional social work genres, using the discourse of the professional social work community within these genres, using the word *Personally* to give the impression of being a person with feelings (an aspect of *ethos*), and expressing aims and attitudes consistent with the identity of a social worker.

Origins of some of Rachel's discourse in workplace literacy practices
When I asked Rachel where she had picked up the 'language' of the social work profession, she said:

Rachel: Yeah, loads of case studies I read .. and when I was doing duty on the phone you had to fill in the sheet afterwards — that's what you would do .. headings to fill in in front of you .. so that's kind of learnt .. not just from the N.S.P.C.C. .. so a bit of reading .. and the way I've learnt it.

This is an example of the way in which specific literacy practices lead to specific ways of wording. Talking about extract 6.12, she said:

Rachel: I got this from my supervisor saying 'what's the purpose?', 'What are the aims?' They've got sheets where they fill in aims, objectives and work and they evaluate it and if it hasn't got so many ticks you're out. That is something I've learnt in the way I think.

Literacy practices at the office where she had done her placement were acting as a scaffolding for her writing. She was drawing on the format, structure, and lexico-syntactic characteristics of two record sheets: the one to record telephone referrals, and the 'internal evaluation sheet' for recording aims and objectives. Both these record sheets were also associated with spoken interaction: the telephone referral sheet provided the structure for answering phone calls in the office; Rachel's supervisor asked the questions which were on the evaluation sheet. These actual intermental and intertextual encounters are the origin of the discursive resources on which Rachel was drawing in her writing, which positioned her as a professional social worker. What Rachel said about talk around the social work office record sheets shows how written discourse characteristics are often interwoven with some form of talking as well.

Rachel's identity as a member of the academic community

As I pointed out in the previous section, Rachel does not begin this essay in a way that identifies it unequivocally as academic discourse. Most of the extracts I have discussed so far could be identified as professional writing, although they actually appeared in a document which was to be handed in to an academic tutor. In other parts of the essay, however, the university context for the writing prevails. Rachel draws on certain pervasive discourse conventions associated with the institution of higher education, which I discuss in detail in Chapter 9. However, Rachel's identity as a member of the academic community is by no means uniform: she participated in the discourses of two very different disciplinary configurations: Applied Social Science and Women's Studies, as I show in this section.

Student members of the academic community are, on the whole, receivers of knowledge rather than contributors to it. As I show in Chapter 10, some students do take on a relatively authoritative role, but Rachel did not. I identified several ways in which she positioned herself more as a 'receiver' of knowledge than as a 'contributor' to it. Firstly, while she did refer to her experience in that her topic was a social work case study in which she was involved, she did not refer to her own experience as grounds for any of her theoretical discussion. Secondly, any assertions she put forward were backed by appeals to authority rather than her own argumentation (see, for example, extracts 6.18 and 6.19 below). She assumed that her task was to show her familiarity with already existing theory, rather than to critically examine or contribute to it. Thirdly the concluding sentence (extract 6. 14 above) expresses aims which are not consistent with the academic projects of writers making a contribution to knowledge. Rachel states that she hopes to succeed in a challenge in her future role as social worker. While academic articles could in principle end with 'hopes' for improvements in the future, the detail would be subtly different: the improvements would be likely to concern society or perhaps the research community, rather than the performance of the writer. These specific discourse characteristics are associated with the social purposes of student essays, positioning Rachel firmly as a student member of the academic community.

Rachel's identity as an Applied Social Science student
Rachel identified several parts of her essay which she felt positioned her as what is known as 'a Social Work student': that is, a member of the Department of Applied Social Science at her university — the department which is responsible for the courses associated with the award of the C.Q.S.W. These parts were lines 48–75, 96–122, 158–162, 165–196, 217–219, and occasionally in between these sections.

The main characteristic of these sections is that in them she uses a particular set of theoretical constructs and methodologies to analyse and justify her social work practice on her placement. These constructs and methodologies constitute a specific set of lexical items and collocations:

> *crisis, crisis intervention, task centred work, tak(ing) into account the person's own view of the problem, a sense of powerlessness, isolation, identified need, the negotiation process, set(ting) the ground rules, agendas, prioritiz(ing), potential for change, goal aimed tasks, actively listening, working within the framework of task centred approach, calling on counselling skills, change in intervention, child protection model, medical (model), controlled by medication, assessment of intervention, treatment model, fear and threat of violence, loneliness, overdependence, repercussions, challenge.*

In two places social work methodologies appear as actors in idiomatic expressions, using the categorical present tense for expressing a timeless truth.

Extract 6.15 (lines 65–67)

> As task centred work takes into account the person's own view of the problem and ideas for change,

Extract 6.16 (lines 96–98)

> The negotiation process that comes into play in the first session often sets the ground rules,

This syntax seems characteristic of social work theorizing, and different from some other disciplines, such as anthropology, where categorical present might be eschewed in favour of past tense narrative or greater modalization of generalizations. I am suggesting that the lexis and syntax of these sections positions Rachel discoursally as an Applied Social Science course member: someone familiar with these constructs and methodologies, and participating in the practice of applying them to particular cases.

Rachel recognized that a lot of her terminology originated in books on social work theory which she had encountered second hand. She pointed to words she used between lines 83 and 100:

Set of extracts 6.17

> a verbally agreed contract,

> we discussed whether ... Ms A. chose

> the negotiation process that comes into play often sets the ground rules

She said that these extracts relate to whole books on the subjects of contracts, client choice and negotiation, which she had read about in secondary sources, or heard about in lectures, but hadn't bothered to chase up and put in her bibliography. What to write about, the lexis and possibly some of the syntax originated in the titles and references to these books. So her discoursal positioning as a student of social work theory was mediated by her indirect encounters with these books.

Between lines 48 and 133 Rachel was interspersing an account of the decisions she made on the case with theoretical justification for them, drawn from Applied Social Science theory: shifting between a discoursally constructed identity as a professional/apprentice social worker and an identity as a student. Extract 6.18 exemplifies this.

Extract 6.18 (lines 103–109)

> Both of us coming to the session with different adgendas ment that we
> had to prioritize where we were to begin. (Adair 1976) Ms A's wanted
> help with coping with being on her own with the children. I had to
> work towards preventing the children from being involved in further
> acts of violence.
> I had in mind the view expressed by Coulshed that
>   "focused help given at the right time is as effective as long term
>   service" (ibid: 59.)
> And as a change in the family had occured, than the potential for
> change must be present. (Davis. M. 1985.)

The clause structure is typically academic, as I show by analyzing the first three sentences in Chapter 9. Yet many of the clauses and embedded clauses have human participants engaged in physical and verbal processes — part of the professional social worker discourse I described earlier. The way in which Rachel incorporates her references to the course texts seems particularly disjointed — evidence of the discomfort she felt with the Applied Social Science student identity. In academic writing, references are usually appended to sentences which contain theoretical points of view or arguments. Rachel's references to Adair and Davies are, by contrast, appended to sentences which describe decisions and actions with human participants. The quotation from Coulshed is introduced in a very unconventional way:

> I had in mind the view expressed by Coulshed that

This academic assignment required Rachel to engage in the academic literacy practice of writing about how her decisions were grounded in standard theory. Instead, she wrote that she was engaging in those practices mentally at the time as she was actually making the decisions. Presumably this is exactly what the course was training Rachel and her fellow students to do, yet to write it like this in an academic assignment appears gauche and contrived. (I should add that Rachel admitted that she did *not* actually think of Coulshed at the time!)

This last example shows Rachel participating very uncomfortably in the academic discourse of the Applied Social Science department. Yet there was another academic discourse with which she identified wholeheartedly.

Rachel's identity as an academic feminist

Rachel felt that she introduced a completely different aspect of her self in the last two paragraphs of her essay. I quote them here in full, although I have already discussed part of the final paragraph above, as extract 6.14.

Extract 6.19 (lines 197–217) — the end of the essay

> Personnely Ms As 'problems' and sence of powerlessness was part of a wider social problem. That of 'compulsory heterosexual relationships(Rich A 1981), the institution of marriage, the family, motherhood and unequal social relations. All of which I think social workers take for granted as being so 'natural'. The most I could do as a worker, to aleviate the problems of women like Ms A. (was) to place great emphasis on the importance of keeping open those links with her female friends; to offer help, support and provision of information which will aid women to value their lives more. As opposed to comparing their lives and seeing themselves in relation to men.
>
> How I am going to do this is a much more difficult question to answer. Particularly as the role of the social worker is so bound with perpetuating the institutions mentioned previously. However it is a challenge to which I hope to succeed.

Rachel thought that this final part of her essay identified her with a feminist position which challenges the dominant ideology which privileges heterosexuality over homosexuality. She felt that in these two final paragraphs she was taking on a *persona* which belonged to a Women's Studies course for which she had written an essay entitled *Is the technological control of reproduction a solution to sexual inequality*:

Rachel: I just wondered whether you recognized some of this, kind of ideas.
             (...)
             This is basically the same stuff as in the technology essay

She does this mainly by citing Adrienne Rich and taking on her discourse. She shows that she is quoting Rich by opening quotation marks at 'compulsory heterosexual relationships, but she never closes the quotation marks, presumably a slip, but to me the missing/'/ is symbolic of the leakage between Rich's and Rachel's voice.

    I suggest that Rachel's non-standard punctuation in this section is communicatively significant. There are four places (underlined) where she

uses a full-stop where the grammar requires some form of non-final punctuation. On the one hand, she is in full swing here: she is writing in syntax
consisting of well-formed, complex subordination and coordination. On the
other hand, she is crowding into this syntax ideas which are extremely dear to
her heart: each subordinate clause is rich with the interpretations of Ms A's
situation in which Rachel really believes. The result is that she gives each
subordinate clause the status of a full sentence, in order to demand of the
readers the time and attention she feels it deserves.

Take, for example, the non-finite clause: *As opposed to comparing their
lives and seeing themselves in relation to men.* It seems to me that the
unconventional punctuation draws attention to the fact that this alternative is
the naturalized view of what women should do, and something quite apart
from what Rachel is recommending. As Rachel was saying this in her head, she
would have given it a complete intonation pattern of its own: this is what led
her to punctuate it as a separate sentence. The punctuation gives more
communicative significance to this clause, which would otherwise have
assumed low prominence in the information structure of the sentence.

Rachel said that she was happy with the impression she felt she had
created of herself here as a feminist, committed to a non-dominant view of
sexuality. She said:

Rachel: I think it's because I think that everything ends in the wider social
            context so I just take that kind of .. that you've got to incorporate
            that, because I don't believe in it's pathological.
            (...)
            I felt like this is me, this bit, but I'm playing a game in the sense
            that I can only put it in at the end, I can't put it in all the way
            through.
            (...)
            Even though this is what I believe in it's .. I've just kind of stuck a
            big stick in the end and said 'I'm here'.

She is claiming that 'this is me ... I'm here', as if it were some sort of 'real self'.
I understand this to mean that Rachel identified herself fully with this *persona;*
that she owned the representation of herself which this part of the text
displays; that it was written sincerely, with no pretence, as opposed to the
'game' into which the essay genre as a whole enrols her. Had she not been
constrained by her assumptions about one of the readers, she might have
started her essay with this paragraph and conveyed this *persona* more consist-

ently (I discuss the influence of Rachel's multiple readership on her presentation of self further at the end of the chapter). Rachel sees this as a compromise in that she feels she is expressing her own perspective in language she identifies with, but she has had to bow to her idea of what the readers expect by only writing a small amount on this topic and putting it at the end of the essay. She felt that putting this paragraph at the end of her essay somewhat diluted her 'true' identity as someone with a non-dominant view of sexuality, but was better than leaving it out altogether.

Overall Rachel felt that this section reflects her ambivalence about what identity she should be projecting in this essay, in the light of what she knows about her readers. The identity which she owns, that of an academic who makes a radical feminist analysis of social conditions, is up-played and down-played at the same time. It's here, but it's at the end. It is in subordinate or embedded positions in clause and sentence structure (as in the examples just discussed), yet punctuated to receive more prominence. In summary, I suggest that in this extract Rachel is participating in feminist discourses, and so positioning herself as a feminist. This is the only part of her essay in which she does this, although her discomfort with other parts of the essay — her apparent carelessness and disfluency with other discourses — perhaps indirectly positions her as opposing them, and hence more at one with herself in this discourse.

Rachel the person

In terms of theoretical distinctions between different aspects of identity which I introduced in Part I, the aspects of Rachel's identity I have discussed so far have been, I think, largely concerned with what Cherry calls *persona*, with social roles, with more public aspects of identity, with 'person-hood' in Besnier's terms. In the next two sections I give an insight into aspects of Rachel's identity which I think are more concerned with what Cherry calls *ethos*, with personality traits, with more private aspects of identity, with 'self-hood' in Besnier's terms.

Rachel's identity as a 'person with a heart'

Rachel began the penultimate paragraph of her essay with the word personally because she wanted to express her own personal commitment to the view in the rest of the paragraph. She distinguished this from the use of I think elsewhere in the essay:

Rachel: It's kind of, you know like *personally* she really does have feelings,
            so if you write *personally* it comes from you, rather than *I think*.
            It's very patronizing to write *I think* when you're talking about
            someone's life. If I make it *personally* it's like this person has got a
            heart after all.

Rachel seemed to be distinguishing between a relatively neutral, 'thinking'
stance, and the more committed, 'feeling' stance of a 'person who has got a
heart'. For her the word *personally* positioned her as a person committed both
to helping Ms A (the social worker in her), and to the feminist perspective on
social problems which she presents in the rest of the paragraph. The word
'*personally*' is a rare attempt at the expression of what Besnier calls 'affect'
(1989).

     Rachel felt that the word *personally* constructed her in a particular way,
but does this actually amount to positioning? Is she positioned by selecting
the word, or only when a reader interprets it as conveying a particular impression? I do not know how her tutor, Chris, reacted to this choice, but I guess
that she did not pick up the subtle distinction which Rachel herself was
making.

Rachel as a 'right-on person'
I have already discussed Rachel's use of quotation marks for an expression
which she knows to resound with connotations. Here is a second example of
the same thing.

Extract 6.20 (lines 185–187)

     However, during those few weeks when she was 'cohab-free' Ms A
     had been struck by a greater fear; lonliness.

I am able to suggest how the expression 'cohab-free' positions Rachel as a
result of having talked to her about her intentions in using it. Rachel used
quotation marks to signal that the expression 'cohab-free' was coined by her.
They mean something like 'as one might call it, using a currently fashionable
way of expressing things'. This is, I think, what Bakhtin means by 'other-
voiced'. The suffix -*free* shows her to be familiar with various recently coined
expressions associated with green issues such as 'sugar-free', 'cfc-free', but the
quotation-marks position her as questioning the simple solutions such
expressions suggest. Of this, Rachel said:

Rachel: It goes with the mood, doesn't it? It's the green kind of every-
            thing's ozone-friendly, CFC-free or whatever .. so I thought this
            woman would be better off .. more green if she was cohab-free,
            even if it reads as if .. (.?.)
Roz: Did you make it up?
Rachel: Yes. It was part of my I suppose humour really. I suppose theories
            that come up for solving people's problems are like trends, aren't
            they? Like green issues have been around for donkeys' years but
            now they're trendy .. so is being cohab-free: we just can't push the
            message.

Rachel is saying 'this is mine, and it's partly me'. She was juxtaposing the term
cohab from Social Work discourse with the *-free* suffix from Green discourse
in order to express concisely and exactly what she was recommending.
However, this also conveys messages about Rachel herself: she is not taking
social-work practice or Green politics entirely seriously: she is casting doubt on
the current trends. On the other hand she is also identifying with the position
represented by the term *cohab-free*, wanting to 'push the message' that
women would be better off if they weren't so dependent on male partners. It
is as if she is lexicalizing in order to promote an ideology: something not
usually associated with a student role. It seems to me that many contradictory
processes of identification were going on simultaneously as Rachel invented
this term, used it, and put it in inverted commas.

Rachel's identity as a person with a sense of humour and as an entertainer
This section is about the impression Rachel wants to give of herself as a writer.
In terms of Halliday's macro-functions of language, it seems to me that it is
more to do with how she positions herself textually, although this cannot be
neatly disentangled from ideational and interpersonal positioning. Here is an
extract from her essay which draws on conventions more closely associated
with creative writing, story-telling and journalism than with academic writing.

Extract 6.21 (lines 134–139 and line 182)

> On our fourth session Ms A did not turn up. What was I to do? [Not
> wanting to seem like an over enthusiast student] I found it best to wait
> — This was difficult for me as all I could do was think of the worst (that
> the cohab had violently returned!)
>
> On my last visit ...

Rachel talked about the question in extract 6.21 as a way of building up suspense for the reader: making it like a detective story. She had a sense that, as in a detective story, the story she was telling was supposed to come to a satisfactory conclusion in the end — although her view of social life is that it is not as neat and simple as such fictitious stories.

Rachel: It's very much like a story, isn't it?
            (...)
            It's telling a story in some ways (...) a couple of lines made me feel like we're on a journey, like the detective thing. I felt like that was too short and that I didn't come up with an answer, and I felt like I'm supposed to come up with an answer now.

She also saw this section as casual and jokey:

Rachel: This is me being casual .. in my casual outfit.
            (...)
            A joke about being enthusiastic social workers. Like 'the cohab had violently returned' — just a joke: story stuff.

In both extracts 6.20 and 6.21 Rachel is trying to breathe a bit of light-hearted life into her writing. It is as if she were acting out voices of others, with and without quotation marks, in the expressions 'cohab-free', *over enthusiast student* and *had violently returned*. In addition to having its serious meaning,'cohab-free' is a humorous play on an expression like 'cfc-free', aimed at making the reader laugh as well as conveying particular messages about Ms A, and about Rachel's ideological position. The bracketed clause [*Not wanting to seem like an over enthusiast student*] is making fun of herself, imagining a criticism that someone might level against her. By using the vivid descriptive adverb *violently* in a marked position between *had* and *returned*, Rachel is taking on the identity of someone who can write a lively description, more like a sensational journalist or fiction-writer than like a social worker or academic. However, by using the exclamation mark after it she is showing that she is aware that there is something different about her wording here.

Jostling voices in Rachel's writing

Work-place discoursal and generic characteristics constitute most of the essay, interspersed with academic discoursal and generic characteristics, and with snatches of others along the way. Here are two examples which illustrate vividly the way in which these discourse types interanimate each other.

Extract 6.22 Rachel (lines 182–187)

> On my last visit Ms A admitted to me that she was better off without her cohab. as the fear and threat of violence was reduced. However, during those few weeks when she was 'cohab-free' Ms A had been struck with a greater fear, lonliness.

I have already discussed the use of the term 'cohab-free' in this extract. In addition to the issues of identity associated with that word, there are many other voices in this slightly longer extract. It begins in the discourse of social work reporting, with human participants and a verbal process. The clause *as the fear and threat of violence was reduced*, however, is very different in its lexico-syntactic characteristics. This clause is headed by three nominalizations: *fear, threat* and *violence*, abstracting from the actual feelings and experiences of the human individual involved. It is not at all clear who, or what *'reduced'* these emotions. This second clause uses the grammar of the academic social work community, to abstract from the individual human participants and experiential processes with which the sentence began. In the second sentence the interanimation of discourses is not even set apart by a clause boundary. The sentence begins as it might have been reported by Ms A. with the grammar of human actions (*Ms A. admitted*) set in real time (*On my last visit*), but it ends with two nominalizations of her emotions in apposition to each other (*a greater fear, lonliness*): nominalized as if by Rachel's process of intellectualizing them.

An important feature which contributes to this slippage from one discourse to another is the ambivalence over boundary maintenance between Ms A's voice and Rachel's voice in the whole extract. It begins with *Ms A admitted to me that*, giving the impression that some, if not all, of what follows is indirectly reporting Ms A's words. However, the parts which contain the nominalizations are Rachel's appropriation and revoicing of what Ms A. said. It is worth quoting my interview with Rachel at length on this point, as what she says is so revealing.

Rachel: I suppose the end bit is me, and this bit here as well.. *On my last visit* .. I wrote this so many times — *she admitted to me she had been better off without the cohab* .. so that's being honest in what she said .. *as the fear and threat of violence had been*

reduced .. I suppose I'm just still describing there aren't I?
(...)
That's like describing and then I go into the story.. so some of the story's descriptive and some of it's just describing.

Roz: I don't know what you mean.

Rachel: Sometimes I'm just telling a story and in my storytelling I'm describing things .. and then other things it's not like the story plot, it's just, like, I'm describing .. I know I shouldn't differentiate it between the whole story, which this is .. It's like plots within plots, like stories within stories, isn't it? .. and some of the story is me and some of it is like normal describing, descriptive words.

Roz: For example?

Rachel: Like this bit here *On our last visit Ms A admitted to me that she had been better off without her cohab* .. I am describing what she said. And then it's like .. she's describing that to me, and my interpretation is *as the fear and threat of violence was reduced* .. she didn't say that to me .. she just said 'he's not knocking me about any more'.. I interpreted that in this kind of language .. because really I should have quoted her and said 'because he is not knocking me about any more'. That would have said the violence had been reduced. But I'm taking over, because it's my story, to say that.

And then *However, during these weeks when she was 'cohab free'* — this is humour trying to come in here — *she was struck with a greater fear, loneliness.* I think that's underlined too cos it's just one word: I could go on to describe how she felt and it would mean loneliness, but basically the woman was lonely.

Roz: Did she actually say that or is it your interpretation then?

Rachel: I think she said it. She didn't say 'I am lonely' .. or did she? She was saying I am lonely and bring in kids off the street to talk to .. so she did say she was lonely, yeah. (...)
So can you see what I mean by that's describing and then that goes back to my story and I'm describing the story? .. Are all these stories descriptive? Are they?

Roz: It's a stretchy sort of word.

There are parts of what Rachel says here which seem to me to pinpoint exactly what Bakhtin/Voloshinov mean by multivoicedness. Rachel had a meeting with Ms A. This was an everyday conversation between two people, which included discourse such as 'he's not knocking me about any more' and 'I'm lonely'. Rachel then reported this meeting: both the speech event which took place *she admitted to me that*, and what she talked about, as she would in a visit report. But she also 'interpreted that in this kind of language ... taking over, because it's my story, to say that': she ventriloquated academic discourse and imposed it on Ms A.'s words, thereby taking control in some way of Ms A's experience. This complexly heterogeneous discourse constructs Rachel as part social worker, part member of the academic community — zigzagging between these two facets of her identity, but not entirely at one with either of them.

In the next extract there is a similar sort of interanimation. It is the place where Rachel's account of what happened after Ms A did not turn up gives place to her analysis of what had happened in terms of social work theory. Rachel interweaves a narrative, casual, story-telling discourse, with an academic discourse of abstract nouns and states of affairs.

Extract 6.23 (lines 153–162)

> *My work with Ms A seemed to stop dead in its tracks. On following up Ms A, checking out whether she wanted any further support from me (she did not). I found an interesting occurrence. Ms A. seemed at ease with the new approach being given to her. There had been a change in intervention, a shift from a child protection model to a medical one. Noticeable, Ms A was being controlled by medication.*

Rachel had added the underlining later, when her friend had suggested that this would highlight her academic analysis. The sentence which contains the underlining has a quite different character to the others, starting with *There* and presenting a list of nominalized social work processes, whereas others have a human actor as subject.

When we discussed this extract, Rachel said

Rachel: That's me, (*pointing to stop dead in its tracks*) and this is me playing the 'I have an elaborated code' syndrome (*pointing to interesting occurrence*). Some of it I'm playing a game — playing a game with words really now .. sometimes it's like the working class person trying to speak posh.
(...)
It's one minute with the dinner jacket on and the next minute with the cleaning outfit. I know that that's what's happening, but I just think 'Oh get on with it, Rachel, get on with it'.

Rachel said 'That's me' when she identified with or owned the language in her essay. For example, she thought *My work with Ms A. stoped dead in its tracks* (lines 153–4) was her own language because it was the sort of thing she would say: metaphorical, slightly exaggerated, jokey, monosyllabic, Anglo-Saxon. By contrast, *I found an interesting occurrence* two lines later, and the sentence with the underlining are more abstract, multisyllabic, Graeco-Latin. These were not the sort of thing she would say, just the sort of thing she had to write. This extract shows Rachel teetering on the edge of an identity as a member of the academic community: more comfortable communicating in spoken language, ambivalent about written language, and shifting between the two. Several similar examples of places where other writers felt they owned writing which had characteristics of spoken language are discussed in Chapter 7.

Rachel's dilemmas over identity

Rachel had a love-hate relationship with the academic community. She identified fully with the values and beliefs of a particular small group of radical feminists she had encountered through Womens' Studies courses, but she had mixed feelings about other groups, departments or disciplines. She wanted to be accepted by them, but only on her own terms. She felt extremely ambivalent about her identity as an apprentice social worker, distancing herself from most aspects of these identities most of the time.

As regards the ways she represented herself in this particular essay, she owned some parts, and disowned others. She felt that she had sincerely presented herself in the last two paragraphs as a serious member of the academic community with a feminist perspective, and as a 'person with a heart', as a person on the ball as regards modern trends, as a person with a feeling for a story and a good sense of humour. Yet she disowned the other two identities which she set up for herself: that of apprentice social worker and that of social work student. She felt she was presenting these identities cynically, in order to get a good mark. This is what she said about disowning the identity of apprentice social-worker:

Rachel: Myself and social work theory don't go at all, but, that's why I
          don't want to be a social worker.
          (...)
          Looking at social work as a job for me, it's like are you changing

the system or are you maintaining it? Are you just maintaining people to fit in or are you trying to change the system that you're working with? And (...) which theory you apply to your practical work will depend on which view you have, and if you don't hold any of them views and you're not quite sure, then you're in a mess like me and thinking what am I doing as a social worker. So (...) I felt like I was playing a game. I felt like I was playing a role, you know, like ..
(...)
What it's made me realize about social work is that people are just playing with people's lives and that's what I don't like.
(...)
I'm not comfortable with that, that's why I felt like I was playing a role, because I didn't feel it was me.

As regards her identity as an Applied Social Science student, she felt she was 'playing a game' of accommodating to conventions. Here she explains how it felt, what she did in order to play the game, and how some good came out of it for her.

Rachel: I felt like I was playing a game. (...) I felt like I was telling a story, and just picked a few quotes out of a book and stuck it in. That's what I did really. But the good thing that came out of it was it did train my thoughts to think well this is what I should be doing, going into a room and having a purpose of working with somebody, and at the end of it we should set the goals for when we meet again. So in that sense it trains your thoughts in knowing what you're doing in that room rather than just arriving there with no plan.

It is interesting that she refers interchangeably to 'playing a game' and 'playing a role': this indicates that the game of words is inseparable from the the question of who you are: discourse and identity are inextricably intertwined. It also captures the way in which the process of accommodating to readers' expectations is central to the discoursal construction of identity, as I discuss further in the next section.

Sincerity and cynicism can follow close on each other. Only 15 lines after the part of the essay which Rachel identified most closely with (lines 197–203, discussed above), Rachel resurrects the *persona* of social-worker-to-be. It is interesting not only because of the change in self-presentation, identifiable in the discourse characteristics, but also because of the complete switch from sincerity to cynicism which accompanies it. This is how she explained her reasons for the switches of identity in her final paragraph

Rachel: I was being extremely optimistic, I suppose, like: 'you come up with something, Rachel, it's not all doom and gloom.' So I kind of put this in here about a challenge to which I hope to succeed. I'm lying really. I feel extremely uncomfortable about it but I just thought I've got to say something positive because you're suppos- ed to be positive, so I just put that in. Like, I mean, I might not even be interested in social work, but I felt like I had to put that in .. in other words playing a role. It's quite easy to play a role and kind of lie .. because I was playing a role I wasn't being myself .. so that's why I felt uncomfortable.

She is making two significant points here. Firstly she gives evidence of what Goffman says: that "affection for one's part is not necessary for it's convincing performance." (1969: 62). This particular sentence was entirely cynical; as far as I know, it was also successfully deceptive. Secondly she explains how a particular *persona*, that of being a social worker, is associated with a particular ethical quality: that of optimism and being positive. In order to convey an impression of being a good social worker, and thereby get a reasonable mark for the essay, she felt she had to project a positive, optimistic *ethos*.

   Rachel often talked about her 'internal wrangles'. By this she meant that she felt as if she was compromising herself by writing in certain ways, but on the other hand she didn't have any options open. She would often have liked to resist the conventions and present a self with which she fully identified, but she didn't have the fluency and flexibility she needed as a writer to be able to do so. She felt particularly dissatisfied that often she was conforming to the conventions not just to 'play the game', but because she didn't know how to do otherwise.

Rachel in relation to her readers

Taking account of readers' values

It is a well-established fact that writers have to consider who is going to read their writing. However, this is not always a simple matter of what is sometimes called 'shared knowledge' or 'common ground'. It is also a question of negotiating an identity in relation to the reader's ideological stance (see Clark and Ivanič 1997). If student writers know that their essay will be read by more than one reader they have a more complicated balancing act to perform. Rachel was the only one of my co-researchers who was aware of a multiple readership. She was expecting two or possibly three different individuals to read her essay, all with different sets of values and beliefs. In this section I discuss in detail the observations she made about the people who would read her assignment, and the discoursal decisions she made on the basis of her assessment of them, their perspectives and values, and their position of power. I focus on extract 6.19, this time from the point of view of the readers' influence over how Rachel represented herself in it.

The actual representation of herself Rachel portrays is always subject to a tension between a desire to appear to be the sort of person her readers expect her to be and will think highly of, and a desire to be true to herself: a tension between accommodating to and resisting the readers' construction of her identity. She knew that two people would be the main readers of her essay: the course tutor whom she knew well, and the external examiner about whom she only knew what the course tutor had said about him. Of the tutor she said:

Rachel: I should imagine Chris would mark on different criteria from the rest of the department. She's new to teaching on social work courses. She's got a more easy-going approach to students.

She knew that there are different perspectives on social work within the academic social work community, but she was not sure where the external examiner stood. For want of more specific information, she assumed that the external examiner would take the more conventional approach to social work, which Rachel summed up as a 'pathological' view of social problems.

In addition she thought while she was drafting the essay that she would be required to give a copy of the essay to her placement supervisor, a social worker at the N.S.P.C.C. called Brian. She only learnt when she had finished the rough draft that this was not necessary. Here are several examples which Rachel and I identified of how she made linguistic choices based on her assessment of the three readers' perspectives and values.

In talking about the end of her essay (lines 197–213, Extract 6.19), she explains how the different readers will have different values, and consequently react differently to this paragraph. She will please the course tutor by including this paragraph, but she is not sure how the external examiner will react.

She thinks he may not value this perspective, and this leads her to decide a) not to elaborate on this particular aspect of the essay and b) to put it at the end rather than the beginning.

Rachel: I put all this stuff in about compulsory heterosexuality by Adrienne Rich, partly because I know the person who's marking it will like this sort of stuff, and I spoke to her and she said that's fine put that in, where if I was giving it to someone else to mark there's no way I would have put that stuff in, because he wouldn't have liked it. It would have been seen as not social work, that personal thing that you shouldn't be talking about sexuality bla bla bla. So I knew I could get away with it, so I put it in there, but I only put it in the end rather than the whole essay being based on it because the external might read it and think I don't like that kind of stuff anyway and they would turn off, where if you put it at the end you know they kind of think this is a nice story and off they go, reading along, thinking she knows a bit of theory .. I might be totally wrong, but trying to think .. you know, if I'd have put that stuff at the beginning, I know I could have got away with it by the person who was marking it, but, maybe the external .. I don't know what the other work is going to be like, and if it's a bit kind of iffy, then every little bit would pull me down, every bit .. irritating thing, especially about Adrienne Rich they wouldn't be too happy with.

Rachel sees this as a compromise in that she's expressing her own perspective in language she identifies with, but she has had to bow to her idea of what one of the readers expects by only writing a small amount on this topic and putting it at the end of the essay.

In addition, she is concerned about how her placement supervisor will react to this perspective. Considering him as an additional reader tips the balance in favour of writing only a short paragraph on these wider social issues, and putting it at the end of the essay. She said:

Rachel: When I had my supervision with Chris and we were talking about this essay I felt that being in a monogamous heterosexual relationship she was locked into that and lost her friends and I asked can I write it's to do with compulsory heterosexuality etc. and she said that's great and I said I don't feel comfortable about writing that at N.S.P.C.C. cos I had to give a copy to Brian — my supervisor.

> And I didn't feel comfortable even talking about that with him. So
> I decided that's what I would do after I'd talked to Chris.

This suggests to me that Rachel was fully aware of the different ideological positions of her multiple readership, and on this basis made decisions about whether to write about the *wider social problem*, where in the essay, and how much about it.

However, her tutor was not aware of the complex considerations which led to these decisions, and was disappointed by the way Rachel handled this aspect of the essay. In discussing this paragraph she said:

Chris: There's a sense in which she could have started there — given an account of the work she did with this family and the analytic work could have started here and she could have expanded that and used examples of the woman's life and circumstances to actually unpack these issues.

Roz: But she knows you know these; these words are symbols for what she shares with you as a member of the social work community.

Chris: So why can't she use shorthand? She also knows that issues like compulsory heterosexuality are not part of the social work mainstream. She knows that I know what these things mean, but she must be certain the external examiner won't have a clue. She knows the audience for this essay is not only me but the external examiner as well. So it's not sufficient from the point of view of the audience. So it needs unpacking.

But it also needs unpacking for me. What I think she means by compulsory heterosexuality or unequal social relations may not be what she actually means by it. So it does need unpacking for me to know really what it is that she's saying. And I mean I probably could predict what she means. That's because I know Rachel quite well: what she thinks about, what she's interested in — the tutor-tutee relationship (on the social work degree) is quite close. If this was for a conventional course the tutor who's marking it wouldn't know her views, so she couldn't rely on shorthand.

But it's not just that. I am actually interested in what she means by it. I want to know. 'Ooo, this looks interesting' and then 'Ohh', so I feel a bit cheated. I think she's not done anything with it, and I feel disappointed, because I wanted to know what she would have done.

Chris feels that Rachel has only touched the tip of the iceberg: it is very common for academic tutors and assessors to indicate that students should have 'unpacked' the issues they have raised. She gives extremely cogent and interesting reasons why Rachel needed to say more, not just for the external examiner or for a tutor on 'a conventional course', but for her too. Chris seems genuinely disappointed that Rachel has not gone into any further detail, and frustrated that she did not give a better account of herself. In spite of her commitment to and understanding of Rachel, however, Chris doesn't seem to be fully aware of the dilemma this multiple readership was posing, or of the delicate juggling act Rachel was attempting to perform in response to it.

Rachel's awareness of the readers' likely reactions affected not only her global discoursal decisions as to what she wrote about, how much, and where in the assignment, but also the exact wording she chose. At line 199–200 she wrote *'compulsory heterosexual relationships (Rich A 1981)*. She said that 'compulsory heterosexuality' would have been a more obvious phrase to use, as that is the actual title of Rich's book which she included in her bibliography. However, to her *compulsory heterosexual relationships* was a less threatening expression — one which perhaps the readers, especially the external examiner, would find more palatable, and therefore they might not feel so irritated at her as they might if she had used the word 'heterosexuality'.

Rachel: It should actually say 'that of compulsory heterosexuality', not
            that of compulsory heterosexual relationships, but I put *that of
            compulsory heterosexual relationships* because I thought it took
            the edge off saying 'compulsory heterosexuality'. But everyone
            who knows Adrienne Rich would know compulsory heterosexual-
            ity is her thing.

When I asked Rachel how *compulsory heterosexual relationships* 'took the edge off saying 'compulsory heterosexuality' she said that 'compulsory heterosexuality' is 'just there .. flashed in front of your eyes .. it's so powerful .. an institution .. because I feel it's making an assumption the person reading it is heterosexual'. Relationships, on the other hand, 'can be good or bad': the reader 'has had time to breathe' and is 'less likely to cut off'.

I think Rachel's intuitions about this can be justified by linguistic analysis of the two expressions. 'Heterosexuality' and 'heterosexual relationships' are different types of nominal group. The first refers to a condition abstracted from individuals and actions; the second refers to a condition which must hold between real people: a relationship. 'Heterosexuality' is a nominalization of the state of being heterosexual: a quality attributed to people or whole social groups. 'Heterosexual relationships' is a nominalization of people relating to each other in a heterosexual way: a plural abstract noun which is easier to trace to particular human stories. However, it could be argued that the more abstract, impersonal form is less threatening, so Rachel's reasoning might not have anticipated the reader's response successfully. I have discussed this example in great detail because I think it shows the subtlety of writers' discourse processes: the careful weighing of linguistic alternatives and selection as a result of balancing how the writer wants to appear against what she assumes about the readers' values and expectations.

Another example of a place where Rachel could point to how her discoursal choices were determined by her assessment of the ideological standpoint of her readers is her treatment of the word *problems* in the following sentence.

> Personally Ms As 'problems' and sense of powerlessness was part of a wider social problem.

She recognized that she was using the word for different types of problem:

(i)   practical difficulties with child care and domestic violence

and

(ii)   prevailing ideologies such as compulsory heterosexuality.

These two meanings of the word 'problem' represented two completely different approaches to social work, meaning (i) focusing on individual, pathological explanations, and meaning (ii) focusing on socio-political explanations. She also recognized that meaning (i) could be used strategically. She said:

Rachel: If I was writing reports I might use *problems* without the do-fers, if it was for a magistrate or something, you'd say this person has really got problems, pulling all the heartstrings, where if you were talking to other more enlightened social workers this person might not necessarily have a problem.

and when I asked whether she could have left Ms A.'s 'problems' without quotation marks acting as 'scare quotes' when writing for her tutor, she replied:

Rachel: I think it would have been a bit patronizing. Because you are actually acknowledging by use of quotes that this woman hasn't got a problem, that it's part of this wider social problem. See on

> problem there (*the last word of the sentence*) it hasn't got a do-fer
> — just here. I mean it would have been, but I wouldn't have felt
> comfortable just writing her problems. I think that Ms A's prob-
> lems without the things on is just painful .. painfully patronizing.
> So the Personally takes the sting out of problem (*last word of sen-
> tence*) and problems has the sting taken out by having the quotes.
> So that's why I put it.

My understanding of this is that

a.   problem in meaning (i) is acceptable to magistrates, but not to the tutor,
      not to enlightened social workers, probably not to the external examiner,
      and definitely not to Rachel;
b.   problem in meaning (ii) is acceptable to Rachel, her tutor, but probably
      not the external examiner.

To remain true to herself, she had to use scare quotes as she did. However, to
ensure that she did not alienate the external examiner, she used the word
Personally to introduce the sentence, indicating that she knows that what
follows is her own interpretation of the situation rather than a universally
accepted interpretation.

   She also distinguishes between her use of scare quotes on the word
'problems' (line 199) and on the word 'natural' (line 203). She thinks that
some readers would agree with her in questioning the use of the word 'problems' in meaning (i) to label Ms A.'s situation, but would not agree with her in
questioning the use of the word 'natural' to describe compulsory heterosexual relationships, the institution of marriage, the family, motherhood and
unequal social relations.

Rachel: In practice working with those two kinds of people — the people
           with the 'problem' and the people with the 'natural', one would
           not necessarily go with the other. One might be enlightened about
           the 'problems' but not about the 'natural'.

Another kind of view she imputed to the external examiner was a view as to
what sort of attitude to social work she should have. This led her to try to
represent herself as optimistic by writing the last sentence of the assignment
(discussed above).

Taking account of readers' knowledge

In addition to considering the views and values of her readers, Rachel had to make an assessment of what they know in order to make judgments about what to write. She made decisions as to what she needed to elaborate on and what she could leave the readers to infer, based on what she thought she could assume they already knew. This was not just a case of depending on shared knowledge in order to achieve clarity and coherence; it was also part of the mainly (but not entirely) subconscious process of constructing an impression of herself as knowledgeable: a highly valued quality in the academic discourse community. In this way considering the reader's knowledge is integrally bound up with self-representation. Rachel gave several insights into how fostering an impression of herself as sharing the required stock of academic knowledge and understanding sometimes involved deceptive practices and sometimes not. I have already mentioned how she depended on her readers' knowledge of the sources of ideas in relation to the way she used quotation marks without a bibliographic entry or a reference in the expression *'goal aimed tasks'* (line 127, in extract 6.13). Here are some other examples.

We were talking about the following, which comes at the end of extract 6.17 (lines 115–117)

> And as change in the family had occured, then the potential for change must be present. (*Davies, M. 1985.*)

Rachel explained that she did not actually know what Davies said about the *potential for change*, but she wanted the readers to invoke this knowledge from their own reading and attribute it to her.

Rachel: I knew from other bits of courses that I'd done that this person says this kind of thing so rather than using a quote from Davies, just use Davies's ideas and then just put (*Davies*) — that's where it's coming from, having the assumption that the person marking it knows Davies and has got the illusion that I've read it. I've learnt that ... I've learnt to do that.

So Rachel uses (*Davies*) as a device for signalling to the reader that she wants them to infer more details of what Davies has to say at this point from their superior knowledge of what Davies wrote, and then give Rachel credit for that knowledge too.

Later she uses the reference to *Rich A 1981* in line 200 (extract 6.19) 'to say where I was coming from'. However, in this case she was giving the impression of being familiar with a body of knowledge which she did in fact share with the tutor. When I asked her why she had included another book by Adrienne Rich: *Of Women Born,* in her bibliography but not in her writing, she said:

Rachel: Right. I just erm put that in to go with motherhood, really. I should have quoted it there, or you know put .. here I should have put both dates, because it's talking about compulsory heterosexual relations, but she also talks about the institution, you know saying there's nothing wrong with motherhood, it's the institution, the way it's controlled and .. women's lives get locked into the institution rather than the actual .. Motherhood's fine, it's just the constraints that are put on you, you know, society .. that make it a problem. So really I should have put that, and I guess I was being a bit lazy, to know that the woman who was marking it would know all this ...

Roz: and know where it's coming on.
            and so having two Adrienne Rich books in the bibliography wasn't a kind of con in any way?

Rachel: Oh no it was definitely, I mean I have read these. I mean I kind of feel I can know what's in them. .. not cover to cover, but I know the bulk of it. So I wasn't conning there, no.

Rachel is expecting the reader (her tutor, if not the external examiner) to infer from the reference in brackets the whole of Adrienne Rich's feminist explanation for social conditions, which is spread over two books. Further, she was expecting the tutor to understand that she, Rachel, knew all of this theory too, which in this case she did. I don't think anyone reading her essay who did not already know Rachel could tell the difference between the impression she created deceptively and the one she created sincerely.

A third place where Rachel depends on readers' knowledge is the sentence:

Extract 6.24 (lines 51–54)

I decided that I would take a task centred approach as opposed to crisis intervention way of working. As Ms A was not in a crisis (.

Rachel intended the use of these terms *task centred (approach)* and *crisis intervention* to conjure up shared knowledge about these social work methodologies in which she could not, in fact, summon enough interest to elaborate on in detail. Her patience with the whole academic game cracked at this point: she did not even check the proper reference for explanations of these terms, as can be seen from the open bracket which was never closed. She said:

Rachel: I just thought: Oh, they'll know what I mean.

That is, she assumed her readers both knew the meanings of these technical terms from social work theory, and knew where they are defined. Had she inserted the reference she would perhaps have succeeded in signalling that she knew the relevant definitions. The terms task centred (work) and crisis intervention appear as chapter headings in the main book Rachel used for writing this assignment: Coulshed (1988) *Social Work Practice: an introduction.* The chapter entitled *Crisis Intervention* starts with a sub-section headed *What do we mean by 'crisis'?* In the chapter entitled *Task-Centred Work* this way of working is highly lexicalized with synonyms and associated terms: task-centred practice, task centred approach, problem solving process, task-centred methods, but the chapter does not contain any section or paragraph devoted to a definition of task-centred work to which she could make an exact page reference, as the conventions of attribution require.

The effect of the unclosed bracket was, in fact, extremely negative. Her tutor did not infer from Rachel's use of the terms that she knew the body of theory to which they referred, as Rachel had rather optimistically hoped. On the contrary, she was irritated with Rachel for being so slap-dash. She wanted Rachel to give a good impression of herself, and felt that she had blown it here.

Rachel elaborated on the way in which she had deceptively set up an identity for herself as someone who had read the theory.

Rachel: Sticking a few quotes in, so that's kind of playing the game.
            (...)
            It's my technique of pretending I've read all these things and I've not. That's me and I've learnt that and I know .. I feel a bit better about doing that, though I've become a bit blasé about it. I just feel it's a game and (...) I can't take it serious (...) It's conveyor belt stuff, it's going through the motions, (...) which isn't me, it's a game. But it is me in the sense I'm learning to *play* the game.

Rachel constructs this identity for herself, not very successfully, in order to gain the necessary grades, but she doesn't take it seriously. An interesting extra dimension is that she does identify with the role of being the sort of person who is pulling this deception off.

Conclusion

The aim of this chapter has been to flesh out and give some coherence to issues of writing and identity around the personal story of a single individual. Rachel's life history gives an example of the sorts of experiences, commitments, allegiances, literacy practices, uncertainties and sense of herself as a writer which a person brings to the act of writing. The particular writing assignment she was engaged in demanded a particular interplay of discourses and associated identities, and Rachel brought to it a richer multiplicity of her own. Yet the identity which is discoursally constructed there is not a whole, or wholly true picture of Rachel: it is an impression born out of the exigencies of the particular interaction, with its inherent power relations and evaluative procedures.

Rachel was caught in a web of sincerity and deception as she attempted to take on social roles and to portray qualities which were valued by her different readers and, wherever possible, to be true to herself. This process was complicated by the fact that Rachel was not a very adept writer: she had difficulty in playing these games and, sadly, even more difficulty in challenging the conventions and presenting herself as she ideally would like to appear. Rachel is an especially interesting case to study because these processes were not entirely sub-conscious and she was able to talk about them, at least in retrospect.

By focusing in depth on a particular individual writing a single assignment I hope to have shown just how complex and sophisticated a set of knowledges and understandings a writer needs to deploy when engaging in academic literacy practices. The fine-tuned sensitivity to the ideological underpinning of different discourses, the anticipation of conflicting reader interpretations and the negotiation of a personal identity within this web of constraints: all this is very different from what many naively refer to as 'study skills' which can be learnt like a simple technology and transferred unproblematically from one assignment to another. If this analysis has gone some way towards alerting tutors to the socially situated diversity of academic literacies, it will have achieved its purpose. I will return to the implications of these insights for academic support for return-to-study and higher education in Chapter 11.

This chapter brings together a number of complementary methodological approaches around a single case-study. In the first section I gave biographical details of Rachel's life, derived from successive and extensive interviews, conversations and meetings. In the central part of the chapter I presented detailed linguistic analyses of the discoursal characteristics of extracts from Rachel's writing using Halliday's Functional Grammar (1994) as my main analytical tool. I discussed these in terms of the way in which Rachel was positioned by her writing, and in terms of origins of this discoursal positioning in her experience, drawing also on extracts from discourse-based interviews with her. In the later sections of the chapter I drew on other parts of the discourse-based interviews to discuss her sense of owning or disowning these discoursally constructed identities, and the role of her anticipation of the readers in her self-representation. I have found these research methodologies and analytical tools to be extremely revealing of the complexities of the discoursal construction of identity, each contributing a different perspective.

In the next four chapters, I move away from the unity and comprehensiveness of the case study in order to focus on four particular aspects of writer identity. In Chapter 7 I focus on the origins of writers' discoursal repertoires in their 'autobiographical selves', with examples from the academic writing of several of my co-researchers, and their comments on it. In Chapter 8 I examine writers' views about the self they want to portray in their writing, and about how their self-representation is shaped by the social relations in which their writing is embedded, drawing extensively on conversations with several writers. Chapters 9 and 10 focus on the 'discoursal selves' which my co-researchers presented in their essays, and are based on linguistic analysis of extracts from the written texts themselves.

Appendix: Rachel's essay

4th yr
social work

<u>Family Case Study</u>

I worked with family c during my second placement with a Child Protection Agency.

<u>Family composition:</u> Ms A (mother)   age 18 yrs
Cohab —   age 22
N (eldest son) age 10 yrs
Twins —   9 months.

There had been two referrals made regarding this family prior to my involvement. One in March 1990 the second July 1990. Both referrals were made via school. The first referral was made because the eldest son (N) had got a large bruise on the inside of his right arm, this was an non accidental injury (NAI) caused by mothers cohab during an incident of domestic violence aimed initially at Ms A. The second referral N reported to teacher that there was increased violence in the home, caused again by cohab. This time the cohab had verbally threatened all three children as well as causing physical harm to N's mother — This had caused N on one occasion to escape from an upstairs bedroom window jumping 30 ft to safety. N then ran through town in the early hours of the morning to contact his natural father.

25 <u>Response to 2nd Referral.</u>
I visited the home
with my supervising officer. My role at this
point was to observe. The child protection
officer dealt with the referral. On being let
30 into the home by MsA, we were asked to go
upstairs so that the Cohabs would not be
aware of our presence. MsA was very shaken
by her past experiences of violence, and on
the one hand wanted to talk to us, but
35 on the other was terrified of the Cohabs
knowing we were there. MsA confirmed that
the Cohabs was no longer living at the
house and had officially left a few days ago.
A decision made not by MsA herself but
40 by her X husband. Otherwise she stood a good
chance of losing Neg Cohabs stayed. On
checking out whether information given by the
School was true (MsA confirmed it was) the Cohabs
became aware of our presence. Things became
45 very heated and in order to defuse the situation
we left leaving MsA our telephone number.

Later that afternoon MsA rang asking for help.
My supervising officer and I discussed my
involvement. I was to befriend, support and build
50 confidence with MsA with a view to protecting
her children in the long term. I decided
that I would take a task centred approach
as a posed to crisis intervention way of working.
As MsA was not in a crisis (
55 As Coulshed defines task centred work as
a "Method of social work in which
clients are helped to carry out
problem – alleviating tasks within
agreed periods of time." (Coulshed 1988:56)
60 This method seemed the best matched to MsA
difficulties and my previous knowledge and
time available. Furthermore, using task centred
work would mean that I was not attempting
to take over MsA life, or imply that I know
65 best. As task centred work takes into account
the persons own views of a problem and ideas
for change, I felt it would aid MsA over —
come some of her powerlessness. Especially as
her life seemed to be being controlled by her
70 Male partner, and the demands of her children's.

child care needs.

My short-term goal was to work with Ms A on over coming her isolation. An identified need that Ms A ~~about~~ discussed with me on the
75 telephone. I started by inviting Ms A and the twins to a drop-in Morning ran by my Agency. I felt that this would, served three perhaps
(i) To get Ms A and the twins out the home.
(ii) Give all three people the opportunity to
80 mix in a different environment.
(iii) A way of Monitoring the home situation.
During our first one to one session Ms A and I drew up a verbally agreed contract. This was done on the bases of how best Ms A
85 could benifit from my intervention. We discussed whether Ms A thought she would benifit from seeing me the same day as the drop-in (weds), or whether another day would be better. Ms A choose to see me on a Monday as she found that
90 weekends were her most stressful. furthermore, that by having contact with our agency twice a week further helped to over come some of the isolation she felt.

I think that the first session with a
95 user, is of great importance to the following
weeks (sessions). The negotiation process that
comes into to play in the first session often
sets the ground rules, this is also worked
with what Coulshed or highlighted as
100 'Asking good questions' (Coulshed 1988 —)

Once we had settled where and when we
should meet, *& for how long*, the second process of negotiation
began to take shape. Both of us coming to the
session with different adgendas meant that
105 we had to prioritize where we were to begin.
(Adair 1976) Ms A's wanted help with coping
with being on her own with the children.
I had to work towards preventing the children
from *being involved in* further acts of violence.
110 I had in my mind the view expressed by
Coulshed that
"focused help given at the right
time is as effective or long term
service" (ibid. 59.)
115 and as a change in the family had occurred,
that the potential for change must be present.
(Davis .M. 1985.)

The immediate task—that was set before
Ms A was to legally protect her self & her children.
120 I felt that my role was to provide Ms A with the
information to do so (assuming she does not already
know this), her task was to carry out this process.
The second task Ms A & I agreed on was that
I would supply her with nursery place addresses
125 and 'drop-ins' and she would follow them up.
[My giving her a reference from the agency if
necessary.] These 'goal aimed tasks' were
arrived at by me as a worker actively
<u>listening</u> to what Ms A had been saying
130 during our 1st long sessions. Thus, I was not
only working within the framework of task centred
approach, but calling on counselling skills
also.

On our fourth session Ms A did not turn up.
135 What was I to do? [Not wanting to seem like
an over enthusiast student] I found it best
to wait—This was difficult for me as all I could
do was think of the worst (that the cohab
had violently returned!)

140 My immediate plan was to wait and see whether Ms A would turn up to the drop-in. There was no contact made then, neither the following Monday. After lengthy discussions with my supervisor I decided to send Ms A a letter,

145 asking her to contact me as soon as possible. Three days later I got a phone call saying that Ms A had been admitted to hospital after taking an over dose.

What happened from this point was that services

150 were put into this family from the hospital. A community psychiatric nurse was appointed the profile of the health visitor and Doctor increased. My work with Ms A seemed to stop dead in its tracks. On following up Ms A, checking

155 over whether she wanted any further support from me (she did not). I found an interesting occurrence. Ms A seemed at ease with the new approval being given to her. There had been a change in intervention, a shift

160 from a <u>child protection model</u> to a <u>Medical one</u>. Noticeable, Ms A was being controlled by medication.

Obviously I felt I had failed (it was my first
'real'case.) I began to think that perhaps MsA
165 was really in a 'crisis' when we first meet
and My assessment of intervention was wrong.
A question I spent Many nights thinking about.
Now writing this case study some months later,
I do not think I choose the wrong
170 intervention. Maybe I could have visited
MsA sooner than I did. I do not think
I could have done more than I did.

I find it interesting how MsA seemed
to have taken well to the <u>treatment</u>
175 <u>Model</u> of medization. How, somehow,
she felt relieved that someone had
found something wrong with her.
Perhaps our task centred work proved far
too challenging for MsA, as It made her
180 realise her position in relation to rest of
society —

On my last visit MsA admitted to me that
she was better off without her Cohab. as. the
fear and threat of violence was reduced.
185 However, during those few weeks when she

Was 'cohab-free'. MsA had been struck
with a greater fear; <u>loniness.</u> Although previously
she had lost most of her friends and all
of her family because of her cohab's violence.
190 She had never felt so alone before.
For better or for worse, she always had her
relationship with he cohab. What stood out
for me, from MsA's fear was, the over
dependance MsA had on her monogamous
195 heterosexual relationship. Secondly how this
had repercussions for her children.
     Personally MsA's 'problems' and sence of
powerlessness was part of a wider social
problem. That of 'compulsory   heterosexual
200 relationships (Rich A 1981), the institution of
marriage, the family, motherhood and inequal
social relations. All of which I think social
work/ers take for granted or 'being so natural'.
The most I could do as a worker, to alerviate
205 the problems of women like MsA   . to place
great emphasis on the importance of keeping
open those links with her female friends;
to offer help, support and provision of information

which will aid women to value
210 their lives more. As opposed to comparing
their lives and seeing themselves in
relation to men.

How I am going to do this is a
much more difficult question to answer.
215 Particularly as the role of a social worker is
so bound with perpetuating the institutions
~~as~~ mentioned previously. However it is
a challenge to which I hope to
succeed.

Bibliography.

Adair   1976   Training for decisions
                        a tutors Manual
                                LONDON. BACIE.

Coulshed V 1988   Social work
                          Practice An
                          Introduction
                               BASW.

Davies M.   1985   The essential Social
                        worker: A guide to
                        positive practice.
                        Aldershot

     Egan   1977.   Exercise in
                        helping skills
                        California Brooks/cole.

     Rich A   of women born.
                            Virago 1978.

     Rich A.   Compulsory heterosexuality
                        and lesbian existence.
                                            1981
                        womens press.

CHAPTER 7

The origins of discoursal identity in writers' experience

Introduction

In this chapter I propose that the discoursal repertoires which writers bring to the act of writing — the 'voices', in Bakhtin's terms — are rooted in their experience, and particularly in their encounters with real people and real texts. I first propose a schematic way of thinking about the identity which a writer brings to an act of writing: the 'autobiographical self', emphasizing the fact that it is, in itself, socially/discoursally constructed, and may be multiple and contradictory. This provides a backdrop against which to focus specifically on 'voices', which are one of many aspects of self which a writer brings to writing. I start by discussing overt instances of writers drawing voices of others into their writing: those places where an actual source is signalled by quotation marks and/or attributed to a specific author. I next discuss the issue of plagiarism, and the way in which some writers stick very closely to source texts as a strategy for acquiring academic discourses as their own voice. In the rest of the chapter I take up the idea that even where the origins of discourses are not signalled they are, for each individual writer, grounded in some initial encounter with, and reaction to, an actual speaking or writing person.

Writing as the product of the writer's life-history

All our writing is influenced by our life-histories. Each word we write represents an encounter, possibly a struggle, between our multiple past experience and the demands of a new context. Writing is not some neutral activity which we just learn like a physical skill, but it implicates every fibre of the writer's multifaceted being. Who we are affects how we write, whatever we are writing, whether it is a letter to a friend or a dissertation.

'Who we are' means, firstly, the subject positions and social relations which are set up for us as a consequence of our social class, ethnicity, gender, physical build, abilities and disabilities, and the way these are constructed in the socio-cultural context in which we live. So, for example, a tall, Deaf woman from an elite Nigerian family background living in North West England is socially constructed and positioned according to the values and beliefs in that social context about people with those characteristics. These values and beliefs will be various, but there will be dominant, taken-for-granted, common-sense constructions of 'people like her' which are likely to have a particularly powerful, though not determining, effect on the 'autobiographical self' which she develops over time. These socially-constructed possibilities for self-hood in turn shape people's life history of experiences, events, encounters and opportunities; hopes, fears and disappointments; values, beliefs and allegiances; self-confidence, anxieties and desires; the tensions and contradictions in their lives, which all bear down on the point of the pen.

Figure 7.1 represents diagrammatically the way in which an act of writing is affected by different aspects of the writer's 'autobiographical self', and how this in turn is shaped by the writer's past experiences. The outer box of the diagram represents the varied and often conflicting values, beliefs and consequent power relations which exist in a person's socio-cultural context, the patterns of privileging among them, and the practices, discourses and genres associated with them, as I discussed in Chapters 2 and 3. These are responsible for shaping the writer's experiences in the way I have just outlined, as represented by arrow (A) in the diagram. The inner box represents the relationship between an individual writer's past and present, in the context of these social elements.

I am suggesting, following Vygotsky's theory of the social nature of cognitive development (see Chapter 2), that a writer's 'autobiographical self' at any moment in time is the product of their past experiences and encounters in all their richness and complexity, shaped as they are by their social opportunities and constraints. As a result of these experiences, these direct and indirect encounters with others, I suggest that writers take forward into the next moment of their lives the elements represented in italics in Figure 7.1: interests (in both senses), ideas, opinions and commitments, 'voices', sense of self-worth, and practices, including literacy practices. By *interests* I mean, mainly, the topics people are interested in, but the word has a second meaning too: what it is in people's interests to be doing. With *ideas, opinions and commitments* I include attitudes, values, and beliefs in relation to a wide range of issues, depending on the writers' experiences and on the other people they have encountered and been influenced by, and the allegiances they have formed as a result. *Voices* can mean the same as 'ideas and opinions', but it has another meaning which is the main focus of this chapter: voices in the sense of ways with words, accents, grammatical, lexical and broader discoursal choices, feeling 'at home' in particular genres and discourses. People's life-experiences also create their *sense of self-worth:* their sense of status in relation to others in a range of social situations. Finally, people bring with them from their past experience a set of familiar *practices, including literacy practices*, on which they will draw during a new act of writing. Although this sketch of the nature of personal identity — the 'autobiographical self' — at a moment in time is simplistic, I believe it captures the essence of social views of human development, and is in harmony with Vygotsky's claim that mental resources originate in the social world (see Chapter 2).

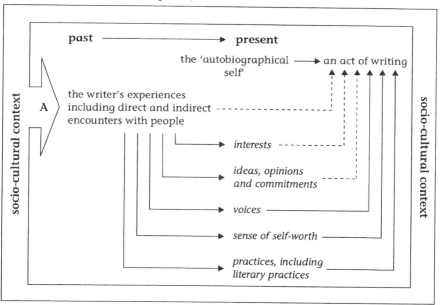

Figure 7.1:   *The effect of past experience on writing*

The arrows between these aspects of people's past and an act of writing represent the way in which people draw on their past as they write. The first three of these arrows in the diagram are dotted, to indicate that these aspects of writers' identity are not necessarily included explicitly or directly in their writing. It depends on the type of writing, and on the context in which it is being done. For example, in some types of writing, writers may draw directly on their experience and write about it. How far this is valued in academic writing varies from discipline to discipline, and is currently a site of discoursal struggle and change in many disciplines. People are sometimes able to write about what interests them, and sometimes not. Taking up the other meaning of 'interests': people are sometimes writing because it is 'in their interests', but sometimes because it is in someone else's interests, and not serving the writer's own interests so much. In some types of writing writers may put forward their own ideas and opinions: this is also a subject of controversy in the academic discourse community. In general, the conventions of academic writing have in the past forbidden students from including their experiences and opinions in their writing, although recently some ideologies of knowledge-making have reversed this convention, for example, personal experience is now valued in anthropology and women's studies. However, I suggest that writers must inevitably draw on the other aspects of their identities whatever type of writing they are engaged in — that is why the arrows from 'voices', 'sense of self-worth' and 'practices' to the act of writing are unbroken. As people write, they have no alternative but to draw on the voices with which they are familiar: to write in ways that they have acquired through their life experience. Some writers have an immense repertoire of voices, of 'styles', from which to choose; some bring to the act of writing a set of contradictory voices: a repertoire shaped by a very varied life.

Sense of self-worth is perhaps the least obvious legacy of a writer's past, yet in my view, one of the most salient. Depending on how self-assured writers feel, they will write relatively authoritatively. People who have been used to being treated with respect are likely to have a sense of themselves as authors, as having something to say. Those who are used to thinking of themselves as inferior to those around them — for whatever reason — are likely to be more diffident, more self-effacing. This is what leads many students to write entirely by appealing to the authority of published 'experts', as I discuss further in Chapter 10.

Writing is not only a text but also a set of practices, and writers bring to any new act of writing the literacy practices into which they have been acculturated through their past experience. In the academic discourse community there are assumptions about the literacy practices associated with undertaking an assignment; for example that it should take a long time, be done in a quiet place, be done on a word-processor, or with a blue or black pen, and that students will treat the process almost with reverence. However, people may bring quite different literacy practices to an academic assignment, and have very different views about its importance to them, as the case study of Rachel in Chapter 6 shows.

In this chapter, I focus mainly on just one of these elements of a writer's past: the origins of some of the *voices* which my co-researchers brought to the act of writing a particular academic essay. Although this may seem to a non-linguist like a narrow focus on only one of many important aspects of the autobiographical self, I suggest that it is in fact a very revealing focus, since these voices are to some extent shaped by all the other elements which I have identified as comprising the 'autobiographical self' of a writer. In discussing the origin of voices I refer frequently to the experiences in which these voices are grounded, and also to the interaction between voices and ideas: in other words, the relationships between the form and content of writing. I also refer to the other elements in Figure 7.1 in Chapter 10: the way in which my co-researchers did or did not incorporate their *experiences* in their writing, the way in which my co-researchers did or did not incorporate their *ideas and opinions* in their writing, and the effect of their *sense of self-worth* on their writing. Two of my co-researchers and I have also written about some of the elements in Figure 7.1 collaboratively (Ivanič, Aitchison and Weldon, 1996).

The intermental/intertextual origins of 'voices'

Bakhtin writes:

> The word's generic expression — and its generic expressive intonation — are impersonal, as speech genres themselves are impersonal. ... But words can enter our speech from others' individual utterances, thereby retaining to a greater or lesser degree the tones and echoes of individual utterances. (1986: 88)

The discourse types on which writers draw have entered their consciousness in some way, through specific spoken or written interactions. I understand these as instances of what Vygotsky means by intermental interactions which provide the scaffolding for expanding intramental resources — specifically, discourse types as resources, as I discussed in Chapter 2. In this chapter I present some examples of places where my co-researchers were able to recall specific voices which gave them access to particular discourses. An aspect of this process which emerges strongly from the data is that in most cases the writers have expressed a desire to identify with the individual from whom they acquired a discourse characteristic. This desire to identify is motivated either by an admiration for something about that individual or, when the individual is their tutor, a desire to please the tutor by appearing to hold the same values and thereby get good marks.

As Bakhtin writes, discourses retain resonances of their origins "to a greater or lesser degree". In quotations and 'plagiarism', the original voice appears to be faithfully reproduced, although it might be considerably shaped by processes of selection and re-contextualization. In paraphrases the original voice may dominate, or the writer may co-opt it to a different, reporting voice. At the other end of the continuum is writing which does not appear either to the reader or to the writer to "retain ... the tones and echoes of individual utterances": they are below the level of consciousness. Nevertheless, some of my co-researchers were able to identify the actual texts or events which were being echoed by some aspects or sections of their writing. I discuss a selection of these in the final sections of the chapter to illustrate how interdiscursivity is rooted in actual intertextuality, and to see some of the diversity of voices from the past, immediate and distant, on which writers may be drawing. These examples illustrate how the actual voices to which writers have had access are one of the factors responsible for their discoursal positioning. In Vygotsky's terms, the intermental encounters people have experienced provide the resources on which they draw for future action — in this case, the action is the writing of an academic essay.

Origins which are signalled

The most explicit instances of actual intertextuality are those places where writers marked a part of their writing as the voice of another by explicitly attributing it, and/or by typographical conventions. These are, by definition, *not* the writer's own voice, yet they are part of the writer's total text, and they interact with the voice in which they are contextualized in various ways. Most of these are simple instances of quotation or paraphrase of other authors, following the normal academic conventions for attribution. I discuss these briefly, focusing on the extent to which the voice of the quoted author does or does not spill over into the voice of the quoting writer. I then discuss places where my co-researchers signalled by some means that the voice they were using belonged to someone else, but did not attribute it. All these instances raise interesting issues about the relationship between the writer's own voice and the voice on which they are explicitly drawing.

Leakage between a quoted voice and the voice of the writer

When writers quote from a source text they bring both the ideas and the discourse style of the original into their writing. The standard definition of paraphrase is that it imports the ideas of the source text, but not its discourse style. In this section I want to show that writers can establish their identity, in terms of both ideas and 'voice', by the way in which they position themselves alongside quoted or paraphrased voices which they attribute to others. The following examples show contrasting ways in which my co-researchers drew on the ideas and discourses of other writers. Cathy[1] positioned herself as disagreeing with the writers she quoted; John held the same opinion as the authority he quoted, but did not allow his voice to be infiltrated by the other writer's voice; Donna aligned herself with both the ideas and voice of the writer she paraphrased.

In Extract 7.1 Cathy constructed her identity through rejection both of the ideas and of some aspects of the voice of the writers of her source text.

Extract 7.1 Cathy — *Educational Studies* (lines 182–194)

> However, this quote from 1976 Rogers and Groombridge takes the treatment of adult education to the extreme by implying that we should be wrapped in cotton wool
>> Adult learners have certain special needs. They are nervous, proud, touchy and humble; anxieties must be soothed, faces saved. They have short-term memory difficulties, must learn at their own pace, and will do better from written than from verbal explanations ...
>
> On the one hand yes, 'second chance' students do need a different kind of help. This is because of the length of time they have been away from education. Many adults as I have said before now have few qualifications due to many things: they may not have got on well at school; they may have missed a lot due to family problems. Nevertheless, it is important that the help given is constructive.

Cathy first passes judgement, based in strongly felt personal experience, on Rogers and Groombridge's position, by saying that they *take the treatment of adult education to the extreme.* Then after the quotation she weighs up the truth of what they say, bringing evidence to support her position. Her very different perspective leads her to use a very different grammar too. Rogers and Groombridge use the present-tense grammar of established facts about characteristics of adult learners: they *have, are, must learn, will do better.* They make adult learners' *anxieties* and *faces* the passive subjects of passive verbs of caring. Cathy, by contrast, refers mainly to adult learners' life experiences — the past-tense possible causes, not the so-called 'truths': they *have been away from, may not have got on well, may have missed a lot.* She acknowledges that help must be given, but without the patronizing use of passive verbs. On the other hand, Cathy does adopt Rogers and Groombridge's use of the categorical present tense in some places: *do need, This is because, it is important that the help given is constructive* perhaps taking on this aspect of their voice to give her views authority. Her own voice is heterogeneous, with aspects of the grammar of the quoted voice leaking into, but not completely taking over the different grammar she is adopting from elsewhere.

In the next extract, John had no argument with the views of the author he was quoting, but he clearly distinguished his own voice from the discourse characteristics of the extract.

Extract 7.2 John — *Medical Ethics* (lines 46–55)

> *For example, if it became known that a patient is H.I.V. positive then it could mean that they are stopped from being able to take out mortgages, insurance and in some cases stopped from working.*
>
> > *"Disclosure by the state that a person has HIV infection can lead to social opprobrium among family and friends and to loss of housing and insurance."* (3)

In this example, the origin of a particular section of John's writing is clearly signalled, following academic conventions of insetting, quotation marks and footnoting, and it is thereby set apart from John's own voice. John does not engage with the author he is quoting in any way: he simply places the quotation in a free-standing position to lend the authority of a published expert to what he has already said in his own way. Although he has no argument with the author he is quoting, he does not allow the discoursal identity in the quoted extract to pollute his own discoursal identity. The quoted extract contains multisyllabic, Latin-origin abstract nouns: *Disclosure* and *social* opprobrium which John prefers not to use himself. Further, the quoted extract is constructed as one long, noun-packed clause with a single main verb, can lead to and an embedded clause that a person has HIV infection. John's own wording of more or less the same content, by contrast, consists of five short clauses, resulting in a high ratio of verbs to nouns. In this way the source of the content of John's writing has not acted as the intertextual origin of the 'voice' John presents as his own.

Donna, by contrast, constructed her identity through assimilation both of the ideas and of the voices of the authors of her source texts. Extract 7.3 is an example.

Extract 7.3 Donna — *Independent Studies: Black women in Western society*
(lines 93–100)

> Furthermore, Black women's construction of their identities in literary and other creative works, challenge the dynamics of power imposed by men and White women, (the 'external forces') [Collins: 1990]. Collins (1990), expresses the view that:
>
> "… self-definition is the key to individual and group empowerment, using an epistemology that cedes power of self-definition to other groups, no matter how well-meaning, in essence perpetuates Black women's subordination." [p. 34].

In the first sentence of this extract Donna makes an assertion and attributes it to Collins. In this way she is claiming it as her own view, as well as acknowledging its source. In the second sentence Donna states Collins' view without claiming it as her own, although I think she implies that she concurs with it. In this way the origins of Donna's ideas and opinions in Collins' book are made explicit.

Further, I suggest that Donna's voice is infiltrated with Collins' voice, or at any rate with the collective voice of the Black feminists such as Collins whom Donna was reading, quoting and paraphrasing for this essay. The first sentence, claiming to be a paraphrase of Collins, has very similar discourse characteristics to the second sentence, which is a direct quotation of Collins. Both contain nominalizations (verbs turned into nouns) and other abstract nouns: *construction, dynamics, self-definition, empowerment, epistemology, subordination*. Both use the metaphor of Argument as War: *challenge, cede*. Both contain noun phrases which are post-modified by prepositional phrases: *construction of their identities in literary and other works, power of self-definition*. Both consist of long, lexically dense clauses (that is, clauses which are packed with meaning-carrying words). Both write the word Black (and Donna the word White too) with an initial capital in order to identify them as political, not colour terms. Of course there are differences, such as the extremely long nominal group as subject (*using ....well meaning*), and standardized subject-verb agreement (*perpetuates*) in Collins' writing. But the similarities seem to me to be enough to claim that the voice which Donna signals as belonging to Collins is leaking into the voice which she claims as her own. She is aligning herself with this African American feminist academic by allowing herself to be appropriated by her discourse style.

Unattributed quotations

Writers sometimes use quotation marks to signal that they are aware of the 'othervoicedness' of the words they are using, even though they did not consider it necessary or appropriate to attribute them. Rachel's expression 'cohab-free' which I discussed in the last chapter is an example of this. In the following two examples the writers intended that the reader(s) should recognize the source of these voices and the allusions they carried with them. In both cases the writers were able to trace the source of the expressions to actual events in their own lives. A further, complicating dimension is that the writers also wanted to distance themselves from these voices, so the quotation marks doubled as scare quotes: I discuss this further in Chapter 8.

In Extract 7.4 Donna put the expression 'Eastern Promise' in quotation marks:

Extract 7.4 Donna — *Independent Studies: Black women in Western society*
(lines 71–78)

Patricia Hill Collins (1990), amongst others, outlines the many images that have been established in Western culture and society that transmit controlling and derogatory images, regarding Black women and their social realities. These images range from the American mammies of the South, the whore, the matriarch, the emasculator, the bitch and the single mother on social security, to the passive totally dominated, full of 'Eastern promise' women of Asia.

Donna's encounter with the words *full of 'Eastern promise'* was a very personal, private one, but one she expected most of her readers to have had too. She described graphically how she had become familiar with this expression:

Donna: Reminds me of the Turkish Delight ad., actually, that's why I used
          it. I thought 'well, how can I put it without having to say the
          Turkish Delight advert?' and I thought *full of 'Eastern promise'*.
          It's a bit of sarcasm actually as well putting it like that.
          (...)
          I think for me putting it in inverted commas emphasized it as
          well.
Roz: Emphasized what?
Donna: You know, full of Eastern .. I mean the image .. I think it made it
          more clear, when people think, you know, the image that's con-
          jured up of Asian women .. it always tends to be barefoot and
          pregnant and totally downtrodden by their menfolk or tradition
          sort of thing and (...) very covered with the veil and whatever and
          sari and you know the very heavily made up eyes, eyeliners and so
          forth which just gives them promise, sexual promise and whatever
          but it's not overly done .. it's made very quietly underneath so I
          thought full of Eastern promise like the chocolate, Turkish
          Delight.
          (...)
          I thought well 'what images of Asian women comes up on the
          TV?' and I thought of different adverts and whatever (.?.) picked
          anything that's Eastern and I thought 'that advert with Turkish
          Delight says it perfectly'. You know where there's all the seduc-
          tion, you know, and there's all this underlying sexuality that goes
          on in that actual advert, and the fact that it's chocolate and then
          you don't expect to taste this sweet taste .. I'd never tasted Turkish
          Delight until after I'd watched the advert, you know, and to see
          this pink jelly stuff! and I tasted it (...) this perfume type tasting
          jelly stuff. It does offer the Eastern promise thing, something you
          wouldn't expect to combine, so you know .. I think it actually says
          it in the advert as well .. 'full of Eastern promise'.
          (...)
          and I think that was why I used it because it was from the actual
          Turkish Delight advert.

In tracing this back in her memory, Donna recounted all the visual images and
allusions she associated with the phrase as a result of hearing it in the Turkish
Delight advert, and the way in which the expression impressed its meaning on
her fully when she ate some Turkish Delight for the first time. The words are

intertextual not just with other words but also with other semiotic media: images, music, and the actual experience of tasting the 'perfume type tasting jelly stuff'. For Donna, the position which these words construct for their user (that is, the particular view of Asian women) was totally dependent on the actual context in which she first heard them. She thought this context was so well-known that she didn't have to mention it explicitly: the Turkish Delight advertizement was among many people's actual intertextual encounters as a result of being broadcast. She expected her reader(s) to be as familiar as she was with the advertizement and to conjure up these images (and, perhaps, the taste of the jelly!) just by reading the words *full of 'Eastern promise'*.

In extract 7.5, Justin is commenting on Larkin's poem *As Bad as a Mile*.

Extract 7.5 Justin — *Aesthetics* (line 93)

Nevertheless, a sense of man fallen from 'grace' is conveyed.

When I asked him whether he identified with the word *'grace'* he said:

Justin: In a sense in that I come from a Roman Catholic background. It's partly a technical term and partly a self-indulgent distancing from my Catholic past, because I'm extremely lapsed.

As he says, *grace* is 'partly a technical term': he is using inverted commas to signal to the reader(s) that he is expecting them to recognize the allusions to the Catholic church. However, this is more than just a discourse-type to Justin. He has a personal relationship with it, as a result of his religious upbringing, and this explains how he came to be re-accenting it the way he did. The whole phrase *man fallen from 'grace'* (line 93) is closely dependent on the context of Justin's own actual encounters with this discourse in his Roman Catholic past. He did not give details, but I imagine him hearing this discourse in sermons, and/or at school. These are personal to him, but also experiences he expects his readers either to share or at least to recognize. The quotation marks signal both that the voice belongs to Catholics, and that Justin does not identify with that voice — aspects of the text which cannot be known from its surface features alone.

The examples in this section originate in actual discoursal encounters which the writers expect their readers to have shared, or at least to know about. Donna and Justin are ventriloquating specific, yet public voices, and so they expect these voices to carry with them certain images and allusions. Communicative competence includes knowing how to do this, and where it falls down.

From plagiarism to ownership

Extract 7.3 from Donna's writing could not possibly attract accusations of plagiarism. She followed the correct conventions for attribution, her paraphrase of Collins was short, and had not been lifted verbatim. Valerie, by contrast, did copy substantial passages from her main source, Berman (1982), without attributing them as clearly as academic conventions require. She acknowledges from time to time that she has been drawing directly on this source, but in many places the actual intertextuality is not conventionally signalled. The following extract is typical of the first 100 lines of her essay.

Extract 7.6 Valerie — *Communication Studies and Sociology* (lines 89–100)

> But Berman points out that the collectivism that seeks to submerge the self in a social role, may be more appealing than marxian synthesis because they are intellectually and emotionally so much easier, and if bourgeoise society is as changable as marx thinks it is how can people even settle on any real self?
>
> Thus the nature of the newly naked modern man may turn out to be just as elusive and misterious as that of the old, clothes one, and maby even more so.

Valerie has clearly acknowledged the source of the content of this part of her essay (Berman points out that), but this phrase suggests that what follows is a paraphrase: that the wording will be her own. In fact it is a patchwork of three extracts selected from the final page of Chapter 3 of Berman (1982), which is reproduced as Figure 7.2 below, with marks to indicate which parts Valerie used. She added words to make it more or less coherent: and (line 94) joins the first two extracts; Thus is added between the first two sections and the third; so allows Valerie to end a sentence which was much longer in Berman. In addition, Valerie has replaced 'volatile' in the original with the word changable which she found by looking up 'volatile' in a thesaurus. The tutor was obviously reading carefully, because he asks 'Who or what are they?' in his marginal comment at line 92. The 'they' in Berman's text refers back to 'individualism ... and collectivism', but Valerie had not copied the part with 'individualism' in it.

I think that this is what university authorities count as plagiarism: patching together extracts longer than a word or two, copied verbatim from published sources, without putting them in quotation marks. Yet from Valerie's perspective it looks very different. She has acknowledged the source, of both. Indeed, the sort of individualism that scorns and fears connections with other people as threats to the self's integrity, and the sort of collectivism that seeks to submerge the self in a social role, may be more appealing than the Marxian synthesis, because they are intellectually and emotionally so much easier.

There is a further problem that might keep the Marxian dialectic from even getting under way. Marx believes that the shocks and upheavals and catastrophes of life in bourgeois society enable moderns, by going through them, as Lear does, to discover who they "really are." But if bourgeois society is as volatile as Marx thinks it is, how can its people ever settle on any real selves? With all the possibilities and necessities that bombard the self and all the desperate drives that propel it, how can anyone define definitively which ones are essential and which merely incidental? The nature of the newly naked modern man may turn out to be just as elusive and mysterious as that of the old, clothed one, maybe even more elusive, because there will no longer be any illusion of a real self underneath the masks. Thus, along with community and society, individuality itself may be melting into the modern air.

Figure 7.2   Valerie's source: part of a page of Chapter 3 of Berman (1983)

and she has made these extracts from it her own by selecting from the source the parts which matter to her, by making her own connections between them, and by making sense of them (via the thesaurus). This could perhaps be seen as a transitional phase as students struggle to make discourses their own, to 'take it to myself', as Valerie put it.

She herself was worried about this, knowing that it was her only way of 'taking to herself' these new ideas, these new discourses, yet wanting to it to be 'her own work'. She asked me how she ought to word and punctuate a section like this, since it is not exactly a quotation, and yet it is drawing directly on the book.

Valerie: That is mixed in there with my words and .. erm .. you know, what I got from the book because (...) sometimes I just turn it round do you know what I mean? and I feel that I should put that [in quotation marks].

Roz: If you .. if you've turned it round would you put the quotation marks on it or not?

Valerie: I do sometimes because I know the words were not invented by
            me.. they were .. they were there (*in the book*).
            (...)
            It's part of not being sure (...) I wasn't taught how to do .. so I'm
            not perfect at these, at how to really do that, you know.
            (...)
            Maybe that's something I need to think about, you know, that I
            should if I turn something round, because I think 'Well, if I've
            turned it round it's still not really my work.' (...) That's what I
            worry about.
Roz: Right, yes.
Valerie: I don't want anybody to think I'm .. I'm cheating, you know what
            I mean?
            (...)
            but like, you see, I wonder sometimes am I taking too much out of
            the book? Am I putting too much in my own words? I think 'God!
            When am I going to find a middle ground?'

I think Valerie's uncertainty here expresses exactly the paradox about originality and, ultimately, the fuzziness of the whole concept of plagiarism. In order
to become a member of a community, to take on its discourse, it is necessary
to try it out in some way, and it is extremely hard to draw the lines between
plagiarism, imitation and acquisition of a new discourse.

A further example of this is Extract 7.7, which is packed with alliteration
(of 'm') and assonance of /æ/and/ɪ/.

Extract 7.7 Frances — *Anthropology* (lines 21–22)

> Before he began his massive analysis of Melanesian life Malinowsky
> had thought ...

By writing in this way Frances gives an impression of herself as someone with
a good feel for the sound of words: a value not usually associated with the
academic community, but one which appealed to her. In a previous draft she
had written:

> Malinowsky's massive analysis of Melanesian life led him to change his
> mind about gifts. He had thought ...

When I asked her about the change she said:

Frances: It's stylistic. When I first wrote 'Malinowsky's massive analysis of
             Melanesian life' I liked all these rolling 'M's, and then after a
             while I thought 'that's all right for a published writer but let's be
             more humble about this and write something a bit ...' Advice to
             budding writers is murder your darling so I murdered it.
             (...)
             I think it's a quote from someone else actually. Quite an old-
             fashioned phrase. Not one you'd readily roll off the lips in the
             1990s. I think it's one of the things which came out of the intro-
             duction to 'Argonauts' or some text I've read that refers to or
             somebody else who refers to it. I recognize that it's not original.
             And it may be that the whole thing is not original. It maybe stuck
             in my mind because it rolls beautifully. Maybe that in the end is
             why I murdered it. But I couldn't tell you where I picked it up
             from. This is another thing about plagiarism. It's very difficult
             after you've read quite a lot to be able to identify every little
             phrase.

Frances seems to me to capture exactly the dilemma students face: they want
to write in ways they have encountered which they admire, yet there is a very
fine line between reprehensible copying and admirable imitation. A further
complication is the issue of what is thought acceptable for a published author
compared with what is thought acceptable for a student author: voice interacts
with self-concept here.

    Sarah was always worried that she was plagiarizing all the time because
she was using the ideas and language she had acquired from her reading and
her tutors. As far as I know, nothing Sarah wrote was 'plagiarism' in the sense
that is so heavily proscribed by university regulations. She did not copy more
than a word or two without attributing it clearly to its source. Yet she was
expressing an idea which is fundamental to the issue of writing and identity:
that all our words and ideas originate in our encounters with the spoken and
written words of others.

    Plagiarism is, as Sarah's worries underline, just a very emotionally
charged manifestation oı a much more pervasive mechanism for becoming
party to new discourses. From the point of view of actual individual writers,
the discourse *types* they have at their disposal all originate in *actual, real*
discourse events and written and spoken texts in their experience. In this way
what Fairclough calls *interdiscursivity* — the process of drawing on abstract
discourse types as we create a new text — is always rooted in *actual intertex-*

tuality. This, it seems to me, takes into account both Fairclough's work on intertextuality and Wertsch's Vygotskyan/Bakhtinian explanation of the acquisition of discourses, as I discussed in Chapter 2. This way of thinking about plagiarism removes it from the province of moral outrage, cheating, regulations and penalties, and treats it as a literacy practice which can be understood in terms of students' struggles to achieve membership of the academic discourse community.

In the rest of this chapter I am focusing on sections of essays which are not in any direct sense quoted or copied, but still resound for the writers with the voice of a person or a written text they remember. Although these origins are diverse, I have divided them into two broad categories for the purposes of presentation: examples of places where my co-researchers can remember first encountering particular words and phrases which they used in their writing, and examples of places where they can remember first encountering discourse features larger than words and phrases. This is an arbitrary distinction, and one which cuts across other possible distinctions among the particular cases, but it does allow certain points to emerge about the way writers adopt voices from their experience and make them their own.

Where do people's words and phrases come from?

John, writing his essay on Medical Ethics, used the word *Aids* as a word in its own right, with only the first letter capitalized, not as an acronym. (This essay was written in summer 1990 when it was still more common to find AIDS as an acronym). He said that he had probably encountered the form *Aids* from reading more recent and more politicized sources than the textbooks read and recommended by his tutor. His spelling of this word had the effect on me of positioning John as highly involved in Aids campaigning, insisting on the spelling which treats the phenomenon wholistically and socially, not just as a medical syndrome. However, John himself was not aware of this significance until I suggested it to him. When I pointed out that he could take a political stand over using this spelling he said

John: I think I will do in future!

This example illustrates the insidiousness of the discoursal construction of identity. People can acquire a particular form subconsciously through intertextual encounters, and then when they use it in their own writing they position themselves (to some readers) in ways of which they are unaware. In this case John was glad about the impression he had given me, but he might not have been, as a later example will show.

John was also able to point to words in his writing which might have become part of his voice through many years of conversation with his ex-partner Richard: *notion, concept, in effect, in one sense.* The chain of events seems to me to be a) John became interested in talking about ideas, causes, effects and meanings as a result of his association with Richard; b) he heard Richard using these words and expressions in their conversations — c) John started to use the words and expressions in the conversations himself: they became part of his discoursal repertoire; d) he drew on this repertoire when writing his essays.

Sometimes my co-researchers were able to point to particular lexical items which they had first encountered in lectures, and then consciously pursued in their reading. When I asked Sarah about her use of the word *deontological* she said:

Sarah: I had to look that up. (...)
Roz:.   Where did you find it in the first place?
Sarah: Oh when we were doing the ethics course we were talking about ontological and deontological theories, meaning the deontologist is the person who adopts fundamental principles.
Roz: And when did you look it up?
Sarah: When I was writing the essay.
Roz: Not when you first encountered it?
Sarah: Oh I did, yes I did actually and then I had to look it up again. I mean in some ways you have to keep looking them up because they just don't go home.

She had heard it during the course, seen it on handouts and in reading associated with the course, and had then checked it in the dictionary to find out its meaning. This shows a very conscious approach to the acquisition of discipline-specific lexis, and the sort of literacy practices and determination involved in the process.

Justin explained how he thought that certain expressions originate in the way philosophers talk — something he has encountered since coming to university but not in his literature classes at Open College. We were discussing the following sentence:

Extract 7.8 Justin — *Aesthetics* (lines 15–16)

> Perhaps the fact that Larkin persisted in his efforts of creativity argues that his pessimism was less overwhelming than the poem seems to suggest.

When I asked him about using the grammatical construction *the fact that ... argues that,* and the verb *seems to suggest,* he said:

Justin: That could simply be I'm used to talking and thinking of people arguing points and stuff now, rather than writing about Shakespearean plays.

This example draws attention to the way in which entering specific disciplinary communities introduces people to new types of mental activity, in this case 'arguing points and stuff', and to the grammatical constructions associated with these activities.

Donna gives a definite reason for acquiring a lexical collocation from her reading. We were discussing the fact that she used the expression *social reality/ies* several times as part of her own discourse — that is, not attributed to any particular author. Of this she said:

Donna: I think I used in my first essay Cohen and (.?.) talk about social reality and I thought 'I like that' and I thought, 'yea that's quite apt' because it's not just an identity it involves much more for me, (.?.) saying 'some of the social realities' .. it's not just identity, it's got their experience there and what's going on and how they live their lives .. so it sort of encompasses everything I wanted to say.

She remembers the exact book from which the expression comes, and she is able to explain exactly why she made it part of her own voice. It was not, as it was for Frances in extract 7.7, the stylistic characteristics of the phrase, but the referential power of the expression that made her adopt it.

Frances liked the way her anthropology tutor had used a term which was invented by a political philosopher, thereby positioning herself as knowledgeable about issues beyond her own field of study. We were discussing the word "warre" in her essay.

Frances: That's Hobbes from Leviathan. I'm getting my own back on .. I don't suppose [my tutor] will ever notice, but she quotes Hobbes a lot in her article.
           (...)

> and I was rather impressed by this, because I thought 'Yes, this is
> bringing in another discipline .. politics, philosophy, history to
> demonstrate a point she's trying to make in an anthropological
> essay' .. and I think this is the same.
> (...)
> Hobbes said the whole purpose of the state was to avoid war .. so
> I haven't made enough of that or I shouldn't have bothered. It's
> neither one thing nor the other.

So she knows that her first encounter with the word *warre*, with this 17th
century, pre-standardization spelling, was in an article written by her tutor and
that it is, in turn, a spelling associated with a political philosopher, Hobbes,
and his theory. However, she doesn't quote either of these sources, expecting
her tutor to recognize the allusion, as her tutor, in turn, had expected her
readers to do. Frances has thereby acquired a particular discourse strategy for
writing anthropology — that of alluding to the work of a philosopher by using
an expression — in this case, just a historical spelling of an everyday word —
from his seminal work. She is mimicking her tutor's way of using the word
spelt in this way: 'getting her own back' on her — as if to say, 'If you can make
these clever allusions which demand a lot from the reader, so can I'. However,
she has a sense that as a student she *cannot* get away with it: students are
required to explain explicitly what they are referring to. This is an issue of
power and status here, not just one of form. This device had positioned her
tutor as knowledgeable and interdisciplinary in her eyes, but when Frances
used the same device she was afraid it would position her as sloppy and vague
in her tutor's eyes.

    When I asked John about the expression *prone to opportune infections*
he had used in his Medical Ethics essay, he laughed, and parodied it by
repeating it in an exaggerated way. I asked him where it had come from and he
said:

John: A medical textbook or a lecture. I wouldn't normally use words as
           'opportune infections'
Roz   You don't put that in inverted commas?
John   No, because it's a part that's filtered in.

John's expression 'filtered in' captures exactly the point about interdiscursivity. He had read these words in a particular textbook and they had
infiltrated his own discourse without him being aware of it and, in this case,
against his will (as I discuss further in the next chapter; for another example

of the same thing, see Clark and others 1990). As a result he was unintentionally positioned as the sort of person who talks about Aids in this clinical, academic way. This is in striking contrast to the way Sarah purposely acquired the word *deontological*, as I described above. It compares and contrasts also with his use of the word *Aids* with only the first letter capitalized, not as an acronym, as discussed above. This had also 'filtered in' subconsciously from his reading of particular campaign literature and media reports and positioned him in a certain way, but this positioning he militantly owned.

Intertextual sources of discourse characteristics larger than words and phrases

Although my co-researchers were more easily able to identify words and phrases which had 'filtered in' from reading, some were also able to identify syntactic characteristics which came from their reading. Sarah told me how she was starting to acquire a 'short sentences' discourse type. We were discussing the fact that she rewrote part of her essay between the first and final draft of the essay, turning them from one long sentence into two shorter sentences. She said:

Sarah: Well it was reading that Mulkay book .. it put a lot of things in perspective for me, and the one thing that struck me even before I read it was his short sentences. And then I read it and found it so easy to understand and it also made sense to me personally, and then I go wielding it round and other people liked it. And I sort of said something to [a tutor]. I actually went to him and said I'm interested in all these things and he said, well, you know, he's very reputable, he's a good person to appreciate
(...)
And when I said I liked integrity in writing, well that really is about being understood isn't it?
(...)
and nobody understands long sentences, do they?

This adds two points. Firstly, acquisition of discourses involves acquiring characteristics of sentence structure as well as lexis. Secondly, Sarah explains how acquisition depends on identifying with, 'appreciating', admiring the person who uses the particular characteristic. In her intermental encounter with Mulkay (through reading his book) she felt that he had virtues which she admired, 'integrity' and reader-friendliness, and so she paid attention to this characteristic of his discourse and adopted it for herself. In Cherry's terms, it was the sort of *ethos* which Mulkay presented (his values as regards what counts as a good person) which Sarah noticed and wanted to adopt.

Justin said that the more direct, conversational, personal style he used was something he had picked up from other writers he admired. He was talking particularly about the way in which he used the pronouns *I* and *you* in his essay.

Justin: There's quite a lot of similarities, not just on that particular point but in other ways as well, with how Ground (*the writer of one of his textbooks*) writes .. his very direct simple language .. something Adrian (*his tutor from Open College*) was very keen on and I agree fundamentally with him about, which I try to achieve here.
(...)
Most of the philosophical or any other — historical for that matter — writing I've come across and really liked has just spoken to me as if you are actually with the person, treating you as an equal without any sense of it being done. It's just very natural and direct.

Donna mentioned another student's essay as the origin of one of the discourse characteristics in hers. I asked her about the way in which she used 'I' in the introduction to her essay.

Donna: She (*a tutor*) 'd given me an essay outline and the introduction that somebody had used and I thought 'well OK I could do that' .. and I tried it.

So in this essay Donna was experimenting with a way with words she had seen in the introduction to another student's essay, which had been judged as 'excellent' [2]. It was as if she had become aware of the possibility of this more subjective view of knowledge-making through her encounter with this other student, but wasn't yet sure whether she wanted to be positioned that way herself. By using *I* in this essay in a limited way, she is trying out this identity to see if she likes it, and can get away with it.

One of the voices which shapes student writing is the discourse in the lectures, seminars and documentation for the course of which the essay forms a part. An example of this is John's opening:

Extract 7.9 John *Medical Ethics* (lines 3–6)

> I will answer this question by splitting the essay into four sections. The first three sections will deal with the problems Aids presents to health practitioners: confidentiality, allocation of resources and nursing and hospital policy.

John said that confidentiality and allocation of resources were lecture titles, and possibly also nursing and hospital policy. The lecture series had shaped what Wertsch (1991) calls the referentially semantic content (131) — that is, John's choices of what to write about. By choosing these items to put in this list and, more significantly, by choosing these topics around which to structure the whole essay, John was ventriloquating his tutor: her course outline, and her lecture series based on it.

The examples in this section so far have illustrated something which is intuitively obvious: that writers draw on discourse characteristics they have encountered during the lectures, seminars, reading, and assignment setting processes which are part of their course, and/or other courses. My co-researchers were also able to give insights into origins of their discourses in intertextual encounters from further afield: in their lives outside, beyond and before higher education.

Angela was able to identify the actual intertextual origin of the discourse of sociology in her essay. She said:

Angela: I can focus on that straight away. The differences between personal problems and social issues .. I read that years ago .. it was in a Raymond Williams book and he kind of separated the two and looked at society and individuals and I think he looked at marriage and said things that happen in marriages .. the breakdown of marriages aren't simply to do with individual personal problems but have to do with social .. he put personal problems in a social context .. so that goes back years ago and had nothing to do with feminism, believe it or not .. or with feminist theory.
(...)
I didn't even think about that while I was writing it, but when you were reading it out I knew exactly where those ideas had come from .. and that must have been when I did Sociology when I was 26 (*9 years earlier*). I bought this paperback of Raymond Williams and just read it and thought: this is brilliant.

Angela is able to identify the actual book which she read nine years before as the prior text for this part of her essay, and recalls the sense of admiration for the 'voice' which seems to accompany so much acquisition of discourses. She identifies the intertextuality of her text with Raymond Williams's in terms of content ('those ideas') rather than form, but in my view these are inseparable. It is not only Williams's ideas, but the sorts of arguments he brings in, his lexis and possibly his syntax which Angela has adopted and adapted. Analysing the text in isolation, I did not 'read' Williams's voice into it; I had only recognized it as critical sociological discourse. I had seen the interdiscursivity, but not the actual intertextuality supporting it.

Frances mentioned a characteristic of discourse in a different department as the origin of resources which helped her with structuring her Anthropology essay. She said:

Frances: I think a lot of this essay has things grouped into threes.
            (...)
            It goes back to Religious Studies last year and everything was discussed in terms of God, human-kind and the universe. And I think that's one of my few ways of encouraging myself to produce some kind of structure: pick out three things.
            (...)
            I think I'm a bit hooked on this attempt to provide some sort of structure.

She had encountered the idea of 'groups of three' in the Part I Religious Studies course, and was using this as scaffolding for the process of structuring this anthropology essay. She wanted to be the sort of person who structures ideas effectively, and found a model for this in the way her Religious Studies tutors had structured their course.

Frances also mentioned how her reading had helped her find out how to structure essays. She talked about the fact that she felt she had not had enough encounters with the discourse of anthropology which she was trying to acquire. She said that she found it very difficult to structure an anthropology essay, whereas she had found it easy to structure a recent literature essay. She said:

Frances: (*about a literature essay*) The essays I've read by Lynne (*her tutor*) gave me a structure to work on. That was a framework — a skeleton .. clothe it here and tie it up at the end. So it was very easy whereas this (*an anthropology essay*) is not.

(...)
> maybe one needs much wider reading in anthropology for that osmotic process of how one does things to penetrate.

Frances had a sense that she needed to read more anthropological discourse to acquire its structuring practices, as she had done for the discourse of literary criticism. She is also drawing attention to the way in which students often read the work of their tutors and that they use these, consciously or subconsciously, as a prop to help them acquire discourse characteristics which the tutors (that is, their assessors) value: an issue I discuss in the next chapter.

John used clear signals to structure his essay, such as these words from Extract 7.9

> *I will answer this question by splitting the essay into four sections. The first three sections will deal with ...*

and these from later in the essay:

Extract 7.10 John — *Medical Ethics* (line 289)

> *In this section I will look at...*

He felt that these had become part of his repertoire only since changing academic direction and starting to study Social Sciences instead of English. However, he did not use sub-headings of any sort but tried to achieve a continuous flow from one topic to another. When I asked whether he would like to be the sort of person who puts headings, he said:

John: I suppose not, because I think it stops the flow, and hopefully ideas carry over and links happen .. and I think it's definitely a big stop sign when one section stops and another starts .. I think there's a bit of a conflict there, between liking them in reference books as something quick and easy to see and another bit which says no they can stop the flow.

I see this as a difference in conventions between different varieties of academic discourse, possibly identifiable along disciplinary lines. I suggest that John's dislike of headings came from the fact that for seven years of his life he was immersed in English Literature as an academic subject, through the influence of his partner at that time who was a university lecturer in an English department, and of the adult education courses he took during that time. Scholarly articles on English literature very rarely use section headings, and aesthetic characteristics like 'flow' are highly valued. His liking for them may well be associated with his more recent experience of social science discourse, where organization and the presentation of research finding under headings is more highly valued. So although John was studying in the broad area of the Social Sciences at the time he wrote his Medical Ethics essay, it seems to me that one at least of the characteristics of his 'voice' can be traced to earlier events and allegiances in his life. In his strategies for the structuring and presentation of his essay he seems to be hovering between membership of the two disciplinary communities, and switching from one to the other.

Justin felt strongly that the whole of the first section of his essay was influenced by Adrian, the tutor he had had in Open College three years previously. The Open College course had been in English Literature. Justin marked three parts as particularly associated with this tutor, underlined here:

Extract 7.11 Justin — *Aesthetics* (lines 7–12)

> "The apple unbitten in the palm" is life unstarted, but already des-
> tined to miss the target. The poem is given a surreal aspect by the
> apple being unbitten and eaten to the core in the same sentence: the
> whole poem is one sentence.
> The direct and simple language of this poem argues a rich and complex idea.

Of this he said:

Justin: I've just noticed bits which pull you right back into the feeling of being in the class with Adrian again: he was very good at saying things very directly and simply and although I don't know how I would have said it differently, it could even be true that I've picked up precisely what he would have said on the same point, but certainly I wouldn't have put it somehow quite that way before working with Adrian. Just the things I've marked — I just feel 'Adriany' about the whole thing. It's partly how Adrian would have or likely did say it and partly how I got better at writing things through the help Adrian gave because, you know, it certainly from my point of view is what Adrian did for me.

Roz: You picked out *surreal aspect* but not *the poem is given a*. Is it as precise as that?

Justin: It's particularly that. It's hard to know because I associate it so I think that is precisely the phrase that Adrian used .. I actually got that from him. I might have been thinking the same thing, I might not, but he actually put the label to it, whereupon I could say yes, that's right.

In this archaeological dig into the sources of his own literary criticism discourse Justin makes several points about the way in which discourses are acquired. Firstly, this is perhaps the best illustration so far of the fact that acquisition of a discourse, and its subsequent use, is often associated with the voice of a particular individual — in this case, Adrian, and that this intermental encounter, in Vygotsky's terms, scaffolds the development of intramental resources. Secondly, spoken interaction can be the intermental/intertextual origin of what later emerge as resources for written language. Thirdly, acquiring the concepts and the labels of a discourse are inseparable (as in the case of *surreal aspect*).

Valerie was able to trace her acquisition of Marxist discourse in years of reading about Marx and Engels. When I asked her when she bought her first book on Marx, she said:

Valerie: Oh God! .. I bought it when I was at the Youth Centre, actually. My first one, I can't remember which one it was now.
(...)
I may have started off with something .. a simplified version of Marx actually, explaining his idea .. something simple like this actually. *(She showed me a book she had bought approximately eight years before, published by the Socialist Workers Party.)* It explains it a bit clearer, you know, and that's what you seem to need to do is go into the more simpler books, and then you go further up.
(...)
[I bought it] just to give me an introduction.

She also showed me more advanced books which had been given to her about four years before by a friend who had dropped out of university. This extract from the interview provides insight into the way someone gradually acquires a discourse, through her successive encounters with it and desire to identify with the ideas it conveys, both through hearing it (when she was introduced to it at the Youth Centre), and through books of various sorts.

Workplace origins are not as obvious in any of the other essays as they are in Rachel's. However, there is a small section of Sarah's essay which she identified as originating in her working life.

Extract 7.12a Sarah — *Environmental Ethics* (lines 29–35)

In this document NIREX proposed three alternative "deep disposal concepts" — basically all involving underground disposal and eventual sealing off after backfilling with suitable grouting material. The

> *important difference between these three concepts is their access arrangements: under land, under the seabed accessed by land or under the seabed and accessed by sea.*

I suggest that this extract constructs Sarah as someone who has worked in this field, and is used to talking and/or writing about such technical matters. Two nominal groups potentially belong to the discourse of those concerned with such operations: *backfilling with suitable grouting material* and *their access arrangements: under land, under the seabed accessed by land or under the seabed and accessed by sea.*

 This becomes particularly significant if compared with the draft version of the same section:

Extract 7.12b

> *In this document NIREX proposed three alternative "deep disposal concepts" — basically all involving underground disposal and backfilling with different access arrangements.*

In this draft version Sarah gave far less detail, assuming shared knowledge as to what backfilling means, and what the different access arrangements might be. When I asked her about the word *backfilling* as she used it in the draft, she said:

Sarah: Well, in the building trade it's used. You backfill. When you've dug a trench and you've finished with it you backfill. So an engineer .. it's a construction engineering term, I suppose. Civil engineers use it.

          (...)

          Maybe it's from the surveyors course, I don't know.

Roz: Do you think it's a term that your tutor is familiar with?

Sarah: Well I don't know. I never even thought about it. It just seemed to be obvious.

          (...)

          It's a word that, as I say I don't have to think about. But you did pick up on that and say well really do you think you ought to explain what it means. Anyway that's more technical so it's less general. I understand. O.K. Point taken.

Roz: But .. I don't know what the answer is, because I don't know your tutor and I don't know the given world of an environmental ethics course.

Sarah: No, I don't think, I think you are right. His given world is the
          given world of philosophy and I'm using this in a special use so I
          need to [explain it].

By *not* supplying the elaboration in the draft, she positioned herself even more
as a member of the community of those who know about these operations so
well that it is not necessary to spell them out. She uses insider familiarity which
originates either in her days of working for the nuclear fuel industry, or in her
days studying to be a surveyor, to supply the elaboration for the final version.

The origins of written argument in a specific conversation

Written language is often grounded in spoken language in a very immediate way.
While we are writing, the "voices of the mind" (Wertsch 1991) are often spoken
voices. This is particularly true of written argument, as Andrews and Mitchell
show (Andrews 1995, Mitchell 1994a, see also Hewlett 1996: 96) An example
of this is extract 7.13, where John is presenting the view that spending money
on Aids patients is a waste of resources, in order later to demolish this view.

Extract 7.13 John — *Medical Ethics* (lines 141–157)

> The main ethical problem that rise out of this huge cost is why is all
> this money being spent on people who are going to die? There are
> very large waiting lists for operations of a very basic kind that make
> life easier and pain free, eg, hip replacements. Why don't we pour the
> money into those? at least the people will live and probably have a
> rewarding life. Even though this could occur with a small percentage
> of the Aids budget it would also be possible to nearly wipe out the
> waiting list for hip replacements. On first consideration this may seem
> to be quite a good idea instead of trying to treat people with HIV why
> don't we let them die pain free and more quickly because after all
> there is no cure and other people could benefit. This idea immediately
> begins to run into problems because ...

John was able to trace the content, and perhaps the form, of the discourse in
his extract. I knew that he was violently opposed to this view and he was only
including it to fulfil the requirement that an academic essay should include
both sides of an argument. When I asked him whether he might voice such
arguments in a discussion, just to play devil's advocate, he said:

John: No! .. I mean my sister did it ..we were talking about Aids and they
              believe people should be sort of sectioned — my reaction was just
              disbelief.

He described a Saturday evening in his sister's living-room, where she and her
husband had been putting forward the homophobic position on Aids. He said
that as he attempted to present this view in his essay, he could hear his sister
speaking. This graphically illustrates the way in which people often draw
intertextually on spoken language when they write.

John explained that he felt under pressure to 'present it in an academic
way', which meant that 'You've got to argue both sides and see things on two
sides'. For him this involved putting into writing things which he could hardly
bring himself to voice: the views he had heard his sister articulating. He said

John: That's an idea I wouldn't entertain .. letting people die pain-free:
              I just wouldn't normally think it's worth mentioning, but because
              it's academic they would want to have such things mentioned.
              It seems such an absurd inconsiderate stupid idea. It goes against
              what I think so much that I wouldn't even entertain thinking
              about it.
              (...)
Roz: Look at the way you've written it.
John: It's different from me, isn't it.
Roz: In what ways?
John: It's almost like a mechanical .. it doesn't flow well. You can almost
              hear me trying to get things out. There's a struggle in there to
              actually say it.
Roz: How do you feel about writing that bit?
John: If I could write essays how I wanted to I suppose it wouldn't be
              (?necessary).
              (...)
Roz: There's masses here that seems to me to fall into the same pattern:
              *on first consideration this may seem ..., This idea immediately
              begins to run into problems because ... ... great implications ...*
John: It's not me .. it's academic waffle, it really is. I've learnt it by
              reading books, being lectured at, getting comments back, writing
              essays. You fall into their trap.

John disowns everything about this section: the whole intellectual activity of
presenting two sides to this issue on which he holds such strong views, the

views he is expressing there, ventriloquating his sister, and the academic lexis and syntax with which he presents what he sees as her side of the story.

The question of voices is extremely complex here. John's sister brought forward the sorts of arguments which John reinvoiced here: he was, so to speak, quoting, or ventriloquating her. Yet he did not put any part of this paragraph in quotation marks, and he did not attribute these questions and views to his sister or to anyone other than himself. Neither did he expect the reader to recognize the voice he was importing. However, this conversation with his sister is certainly not the origin of something which John would now claim to be his own voice — as in some of the previous examples in this chapter. In fact he attempted to disassociate himself from the views he was presenting by various textual devices:

a.   by presenting them as questions,
b.   by the use of expressions which throw doubt on the propositions *On first consideration this may seem to be quite a good idea*, and *This idea immediately begins to run into problems*,
c.   by presenting them as projections from the impersonal nominalization *consideration* and from the impersonal mental process nominal *idea*.

He does not, under any circumstances, want to appear to be even mentioning such arguments himself, yet he feels forced to mention them as part of the conventions of academic writing. No wonder the syntax of this section is so heterogeneous and disjointed!

Conclusion to this chapter

In this chapter I have presented extracts from interviews with co-researchers which throw light on the actual intertextual origins of some portions or aspects of their writing. These were occasions when the writers have heard or read something specific, and from it acquired discursive resources which they have later deployed in their writing. Some of these original encounters were part of events within the course context, others were outside the course context. The examples show how writers pick up a word or two here, a syntactic structure there, an argumentation strategy or a structuring device elsewhere: the sources of the threads with which they weave their discourse are extremely heterogeneous. I suggest that there is a similarly rich history behind every piece of writing, if only every writer had the opportunity to reveal it.

Writers are positioned not in some abstract way by their selection from an 'array of mediational means' which are magically available to all, but this positioning is shaped by their past encounters with these discourses embodied in real individuals, their voices and their texts. I end with some observations on the nature of this interrelationship between actual textual encounters and the more generalized 'interdiscursive' resources which writers have at their disposal at a particular moment for the discoursal construction of their identity.

Firstly, in most cases a reader or an analyst could not possibly recover these origins merely from the words on the page: they belong to the writers' private lives, preferences and practices, and could only be discovered through interviews. In other cases, however, the writer had expected the reader to recognize this source, and had intended this recognition to carry with it additional meaning (as in the example of 'Eastern promise').

Secondly, spoken and written language are inextricably intertwined in the acquisition of discourses. I had originally intended to subdivide this section further into origins in spoken and written discourse, but the examples showed me that it was impossible to do so. One or two — for example, John's conversation with his sister — can be identified as specifically originating in spoken discourse. However, many of the examples of discourse characteristics originating in written discourse involve some form of talking as well.

Thirdly, different aspects of discourse originate in different places: the writers sometimes remember the origin of part or all of the content, sometimes the origin of an organizational device, sometimes the origin of a particular argument, sometimes the origin of a bit of the syntax, and sometimes the origin of a lexical item. Different aspects of a single essay may originate in widely diverse events in the writer's history, both within and beyond the academic discourse community.

Fourthly, noticing and adopting a discourse is often associated with strong feelings of identification with the individuals who use it. People may be roused to such strong feelings by admiration for and desire to identify either with individuals, or with what they stand for, or a mixture of the two. It often involves strong feelings at the moment of encounter — very personal, committed, aesthetic, emotional, and/or sensual, even physical (Donna's Turkish Delight) feelings. It seems to me that encounters with discourses which have evoked such strong feelings are the ones my co-researchers were able to remember and tell me; other discourses may have 'filtered in' less memorably.

In other cases writers have adopted discourses from encounters with individuals whom they have seen as instrumental in their immediate urgent need to please them in order to get good grades for their essays — particularly, their tutors. They recognize the advantage of identifying discoursally with these individuals and with their interests, world views, values and practices, and they feel a mixture of desire and demand to do so.

Fifthly, access to discourses is not random or arbitrary, but socially constrained: all people do not have equal opportunities to hear, read, try out and gradually adopt discourses and their associated identities. Rather, the social worlds in which people move define these opportunities, and consequently restrict the discoursal resources people have available for self-presentation. It is not just a question of accidents of individual biography, but the differential opportunities which are shaped by class, gender and race. For example, John is from a working class background in which he is not likely to have encountered a discourse of examining 'concepts', 'effects' and 'senses': there were social reasons for his lack of access to particular discourses. I suggest that, even if John had of his own accord decided to return to study on an Access course, he may not have acquired this discourse without his acquaintance with Richard. Had he not met and admired Richard, John may never have wanted to try out this discourse for himself. Had he not continued his acquaintance with Richard, he may not have had the opportunity to adopt this discourse gradually, with Richard's voice scaffolding his own, emerging voice. Had it not been for all this, or some similar personal encounter, John might not have had these discoursal resources at his disposal to draw upon when he came to write this essay.

Finally, these examples give a fascinating glimpse into the sorts of intermental encounters which build people's discourse resources, but they do not begin to account for all the writing. That does not mean, however, that it is rare for discourse to originate in actual encounters with individuals face-to-face or through their texts. Vygotsky's theory proposes that all our mental resources, and specifically all our discursive resources, originate in this way. The sorts of in-depth, discourse-based conversations I held with my co-researchers led to some fascinating insights, but they would have been able to give many more if it were possible to probe their memories even more deeply. Most of us are unable to trace these voices of origin: they become subliminal as we begin to use them as our own. Words gradually lose "the tones and echoes of individual utterances" (Bakhtin 1986: 88), and become part of our intramental resources, ready to be "populated with our own intentions":

> ... language, for the individual consciousness, lies on the borderline between oneself and the other. The word in language is half someone else's. It

becomes "one's own" only when the speaker populates it with his own intention, his own accent, when he appropriates the word, adapting it to his own semantic and expressive intention. Prior to this moment of appropriation, the word does not exist in a neutral and impersonal language (it is not, after all, out of a dictionary that the speaker gets his words!), but rather it exists in other people's mouths, in other people's contexts, serving other people's intentions: it is from there that one must take the word, and make it one's own. (Bakhtin 1981: 293–294).

Notes

1.   Cathy is someone I also interviewed during this research. I included this example from her writing here because it illustrates this particular point, but have not referred to her elsewhere in the book.

2.   I am grateful to Romy Clark for the details of what happened in this case.

CHAPTER 8

The sense of self and the role of the reader in the discoursal construction of writer identity

Introduction

In Chapter 7 I wrote about the way in which my co-researchers' writing was rooted in actual texts, experiences and personal encounters in their past histories. In this chapter I move forward in time from the 'autobiographical self' which the writer brings to the act of writing, to focus on the immediate social context in which the writing takes place, particularly the way in which writers' representations of self are shaped, nurtured or constrained by their anticipation of known or imagined reader(s). In the research on which this chapter is based I worked backwards and forwards between Goffman's account of self-representation (1969, as discussed in Chapter 1), and what my co-researchers said, retrospectively, about issues of self-representation. My aim was both to extend Goffman's account and to show how it applies to the social act of writing. The text of the chapter includes many sections in the words of my co-researchers, since many of the insights come directly from them. They give insights into not only which aspects of their discoursally constructed identities they were, temporarily at least, owning and disowning, but also in many cases their reasons for presenting themselves as they did — insights which could not be drawn from linguistic analysis. The degree of sincerity with which an identity is presented and the complex considerations leading to a particular self-representation cannot usually be traced in the linguistic characteristics of the text, and can only be accessed through in-depth interviews with the writers of the sort drawn on here.

In the first part of the chapter I discuss the issue of 'ownership': how far writers identify with the self which they are projecting in their writing. While rejecting the idea of a writer having his or her 'own' voice or language, I find it useful to use the same word 'own' as a verb. In this chapter I talk about discourses which writers 'own' and 'disown': those which they see, at least temporarily, as representing the identities with which they feel comfortable, and those from which they would prefer to distance themselves. This focuses on the fluid processes of identifying, sensitive to the influence of social groups and patterns of privileging, rather than treating identity as a predetermined state of affairs. Similarly, I prefer the verb 'identify' and its nominalization 'identification' to the noun 'identity' as I discussed in Chapter 1.

By paying attention to the authoring voice as well as to its shaping forces I am following Bakhtin's view that all discourse is at least 'double-voiced'. I understand this to mean that *one* of the voices present is that of the current speaker or writer. Individuals have a role in aligning themselves with particular social positions, and accommodating to or resisting the choices which are privileged in the context in which they are writing. The relationship between the voices on which a writer draws and their 'own' voice is that, by choosing another voice to ventriloquate, the writer is giving the impression that s/he espouses the values, beliefs and practices which are associated with that voice. Even if a writer's discourse is explicitly or obviously a tissue of others, the writer has a presence in the decision to write in this way, in the selection and arrangement of these other voices.

I take up the issue that, even though writer identity is constructed discoursally and therefore to some extent out of the writer's control, writers have a sense of the self they would like to convey through their writing: the 'real me'. I discuss the varying degrees to which the writers owned the repre-sentations of themselves in their writing. I examine how conflicting pressures and possibilities led my co-researchers to convey multiple, often contradictory impressions of themselves, and impressions about which they had ambivalent feelings. I end the discussion of self-representation by showing how some of their alignments were long-term, some fleeting, some mere experiments.

I then examine the effect that power relations between the reader and the writer can have on the way writers position themselves. I discuss how the social relations around a particular text contribute to the construction of the social identity of its writer: how the two aspects of Halliday's interpersonal function (social identities and social relations) interact. When making (sub-conscious) decisions about how to represent themselves in their writing, writers have to consider not only their own affiliations but also the expecta-tions of their readers. This is especially true for students writing academic essays, as their readers will also be their assessors. Sometimes the writer's interests, values and beliefs coincide with their reader's: the person they desire to be coincides happily with the person they are demanded to be. However, this is not always so and some of my co-researchers felt constrained to present themselves in ways which, in retrospect, they preferred to disown.

I first discuss accommodation and resistance to the reader's expectations, and the extent to which this amounts also to accommodation and resistance to dominant conventions. Some writers accommodate willingly to their readers' expectations as regards the conventions of academic writing and the identities these set up: a happy coincidence of desire and demand. Some resist the pressure to conform, and are determined to establish what they see as their own identity against the odds. Others are somewhere in between, having a love-hate relationship with academic community membership. I end by discussing in detail a particular issue which arose for Donna in her relationship with her reader: how her ulterior motive of securing a high grade led her to what Goffman calls 'protective practices': strategies for ensuring that her reader didn't lose face in their relationship.

This chapter is concerned with 'the discoursal construction of writer identity' in its more immediate local sense of 'the way in which social interaction affects self-representation in writing', whereas Chapters 9 and 10 are concerned with the ways in which socially available discourses and genres construct identity. In this chapter I show the complex processes of identification which underlie the linguistic features of the text. The writers' perspectives on their writing both contextualize and enrich the discourse analysis of the linguistic features themselves in Chapters 9 and 10.

The sense of 'the real self'

Theoretically the idea of a 'real self' is hard to accept. The self that a writer constructs discoursally is but an echo of actual voices (as discussed in Chapter 7) and of abstract, prototypical voices (to be discussed in Chapters 9 and 10) with which they are familiar. However, my co-researchers had a sense that there is something somewhere which might be called 'the real me' — socially constructed as this sense may be. When I asked John whether succeeding in his course was just a matter of having the knowledge, he replied:

John: No, it's definitely not enough. (...)
Roz: What is the other thing you've got to have?

John: A way of saying things, a way of writing things, a style, just a whole identity, in one sense. (...)
             I would have loved to write an essay for college where I didn't need to take on any identity .. where they could actually see me and my ideas. That would be great and super.

John has an idea that there is somehow a 'real self' which is submerged by the demand that he take on a particular type of academic *persona*, with its set of associated discourse conventions. This idea of a 'real self' seems consistent with John's desire to be totally honest in everything he does. Perhaps John's 'real self' is the self which he associates with discourse types other than academic writing: occasions he is not attempting to give the impression of belonging to a group to which he does not feel himself to belong, and has no desire to belong. He identifies more closely with the impression of himself which he conveys in social contexts such as talking to friends at home.

Angela also talked as if there were a 'real self' to present in writing. I had asked her whether she experienced any difficulties with writing. She replied

Angela: There are other problems like I want this to sound real and genuine. I want me to be there.
             (...)
             [I hope] that people could understand as well me through that piece of work and not get me wrong or not think that I was something that I wasn't.

So the 'real self' is a psychological reality to these student writers. As I will exemplify in the next four sections, they have a clear sense of the discoursally constructed identities which they own and disown.

Owned identities, sincerity and commitment

In order to take account of the sense John and many others have of a 'real me' I present what my co-researchers said about discoursal representations of their identities which they owned, disowned, rejected and aspired to. In this section I present what my co-researchers said about parts of their writing which they owned in some way: the impressions of themselves they wanted to convey — at any rate for the time being.

Owning the content

My co-researchers often thought of 'ownership' in terms of content. Justin owned everything about his essay — even when it got a relatively low mark from his tutor. When I asked him why, his immediate response was that he was pleased with this essay because it presents his own ideas rather than other people's.

Justin: I'm delighted with it.
Roz: Why?
Justin: All sorts of ways. Partly because it's all things that have come from me rather than from anywhere else, although it's based obviously on basic influences it's nothing that I've read. I've just integrated it with my own ideas .. it's all my own ideas based on my own observation.

I interpret this to mean that he is owning the discourse in two ways. Firstly, he has a sense of ownership which can be equated with authorship — owning the propositional content of his writing. Secondly, by choosing to write in this way he is aligning himself with the ideological position of having a relatively subjective view of knowledge, and not highly revering published authorities. I see these two as different but related types of ownership, mapping on to Goffman's (1981) distinction between two aspects of the producer of language: the 'author' — the producer of the ideas in language, and the 'character/ principal' — the self portrayed by language choices.

Valerie also owned the contentious view of Engels she presented in the following extract.

Extract 8.1 Valerie *Communication Studies* (line 155–156)

But Engels was an inadequate observer, because of the way he viewed England from Berlin.

A student cannot take a position like this without either attributing it to a recognized authority, or providing a lot of elaboration and justification. The tutor's marginal comment[1] shows just what a minefield Valerie had stepped into by wanting to express this view. The words in capitals were written quite large, indicating considerable annoyance on the part of the tutor:

INADEQUATE? IN COMPARISON WITH WHAT OR WHOM? Engels' *Condition of the Working Class* (1844) is now regarded as a classic of urban description, after all. (*tutor's comments in the margin of Valerie's essay*)

We discussed this extract after Valerie had seen her tutor's critical response. I am quoting what she said about this at great length, partly because she felt so strongly about it and talked for a long time about it, and partly because what she said raises several interesting and complex issues of ownership of discourse.

Valerie: What I seem to have done is use my twentieth century insight so to speak, but I wasn't aware that I wasn't able .. I wasn't allowed to do that.
(...)
So what to me it seems like, I was using as I say a lot of my own insight.
(...)
So what happened was I sort of got carried away in it and I was putting a lot of my own ideas .. it's my ideas but as I say why can't I be allowed to put it because I am saying the same thing, I just haven't used somebody's book.
(...)
So as far as I'm concerned Engels no matter what he says about Manchester, he has come from a middle class background, right, and he's come from a different country, although he had his factories and so on and he worked for quite a while in Manchester, to me his tone towards the proletariat was condescending.
(...)
So it's like [the tutor] is saying I'm over-critical because of my standpoint. But I mean this is what I felt.
(...)
They are not really thinking about the people really when you come down to it. They were thinking about what they can do for these people. These people are dirty .. now these people don't consider themselves dirty. You're coming from a background where you've had it good all your life, and because there is a difference between how you live and how they live so you come down and say well these people are dirty. It was a kind of contrast between your living area and theirs and it's hard for you to come down, you have to *live* down there to understand, you have to be there.
(...)
So, you know, he looked *at* them .. he describes them as if they were just living in .. there's nothing good about their lives, do you

> know what I mean? They probably wouldn't want to be described
> like that, you know, although they know it's tough, but, you
> know. So that is how I saw that.
> (...)
> Sometimes I feel .. I don't know, I think I may differ (...) but I
> know that I've got insight anyway.

This extract shows just how strongly Valerie owned her critique of Engels. She
felt that her whole history as a poor person had led to her criticism of him. She
was basing her view on insight gained from experience, not just quoting an
eminent academic, which is the only authority she felt her tutor would
recognize. She felt that, by criticizing this position, her tutor was dismissing
these crucial aspects of her identity as irrelevant to intellectual activity.

Several of my co-researchers commented that they owned the ends of
their essays more than the beginnings. They felt that they were representing
themselves towards the end, because they had clarified their own thinking
and/or because they were no longer so dependent on sources for their language.

Valerie: As I got to the end I started to .. it comes more as you get to the
            end and you're getting into it fully.

John liked the end of his essay too, and comments tellingly about why.
Although I asked him about 'style' his answer was mainly in terms of content.
The points I made when discussing Justin's reasons for liking his essay apply
here too: by using 'I' and putting forward their own ideas writers simultaneously position themselves as holding particular views, as having a subjective
view of knowledge, and as being a down-to-earth type of person.

Roz: About style, are there parts you were more pleased with than
         others?
John: Yes, the last part. Sections where I use 'I' a lot better than where I
         try to adopt this academic style. Parts where I feel that I'm putting
         very important beliefs forward.
         (...)
         we're starting very much on my own thoughts, beliefs and feel-
         ings. These are all things I would want to voice and argue about
         and consider, issues that I'd really want to press forward, specially
         things like this: gay men wanting to visit lovers in hospital, I love
         that one.
         (...)

> It's better [than playing the academic game] because it does
> something. If someone reads it hopefully they'll think about what
> I'm writing, they'll think about the ideas. Hopefully if a doctor
> read it who worked in a hospital s/he might think: 'I'd never
> thought about that: how do two gay men comfort each other at
> visiting time?' So hopefully it questions. Whereas if you play
> games it doesn't do that.
> (...)
> [other essays were just] an academic exercise. (...) with 'Aids' there
> was a responsibility there to say things and to make points and to
> get points across. Philosophy's fine (...) but it's more of an indul-
> gence — the world will carry on without that. [whereas] without
> people saying things .. if people stop saying the type of things that
> are in [my Aids essay], (...) then if things like that aren't said and
> people won't argue for them then they won't happen.

John is here drawing attention to an additional point: that writers can identify
with an essay if they see a sense of purpose in it. Yet John sees most academic
writing as 'an exercise', 'an indulgence', something which doesn't construct
the writer as holding a particular position, or even as the sort of person who
holds strong beliefs at all. John feels that relatively impersonal essays represent
him as an uncommitted, uninvolved person, and therefore are not giving the
impression he would want to convey of himself, whereas this essay, and
particularly this part, is closely bound up with his identity as a gay man,
intimately involved in the issue of Aids and contributing to action. It is not an
exercise, it's a statement.

Owning the language

The examples so far have been of the way writers own the identity constructed
by the content of their writing. The next set of examples focus on the way it is
written: on the way in which discoursal choices are positioning writers in
terms of interests, values and beliefs.

Justin, for example, was pleased with the form as well as the content of
his essay.

Justin: I basically like it as a unit, because the whole thing works as a unit
           and the whole idea is that there's a pattern of thought that ties
           together.

(...)

There's the thing about it being as close as it could be, short of being a poem, to the kind of thing going on in my head, which is a separate point, but also I suppose linked to it being readable and understandable.

(...)

What I think I'm doing well is just getting my train of thought down in a way that's nice and accessible and in either case simple, direct language is .. is good, I think, but not necessarily what would be expected in a more formal classical essay style.

In these extracts Justin comments on what he hopes the essay achieved. He is owning the impression he was attempting to convey of someone who can tie ideas together, and someone who is considerate to the reader: that is, the sort of ideology of knowledge-making he is identifying with. (Whether or not he actually conveyed this impression is another matter.)

Valerie was able to identify words which she saw as more a part of her vocabulary than others, for example *contention*.

Valerie: There are some that I'm more .. I've taken to myself a lot more because I've used over a longer period.

(...)

Er, 'contention', I think that's something I would have taken on to myself years ago.

I interpret this to mean that Valerie is willingly accommodating to academic discourse and, when she uses words such as these which she already has in her vocabulary, sincerely presenting herself as a member of the academic community.

Some of the writers were pleased with parts of their writing for stylistic reasons. I see these comments as evidence that they were owning the identities set up by the discourses they are producing, and adding a 'word-smith' dimension to their identity. They are rejecting the view that academic discourse is abstract and dry. Valerie picked out parts of her essay which she felt were her own ideas in 'her own language': in all cases, colourful, metaphorical language (discussed further in Chapter 10).

Donna also enjoyed words and was pleased when she felt that her writing sounded good. Talking about the expression *along with a multitude of other factors* she said:

Donna: Sounds better than saying 'along with other factors' or whatever. I like the way it rang really. It had a nice little flair.

She was positively enjoying academic discourse, both this expression and many other parts of her essay, and did not resist the way in which it positioned her within the community.

Justin, writing his essay for an Aesthetics course, particularly liked his sentence *Prose can describe or explain an emotional experience but poetry can express it.*

Justin: I tried to say what I wanted to say, summing up that paragraph and reinforcing the point, and I noticed as I was saying it that alliteration there: prose and poetry, which is nothing astonishing, but it's there and I think it does help to reinforce the point. (...) I'm pleased with the fact that I think it does the job of concluding that paragraph. ... that sums up what I've said there, restated in a nice concise way and I think also acts as an introduction to what comes next I hope.

What Justin says shows how certain stylistic features (which are probably quite specific to the writing of an Aesthetics essay which spans Philosophy and English Literature) interact with other values. His liking of the alliteration in this sentence is part of his wanting to appear to be the sort of person who ties ideas together well and is reader-friendly.

Aspiring selves

My co-researchers sometimes suggested that they were happy to own an identity which was discoursally constructed in their writing, although they didn't in all honesty feel that this identity was part of them yet. This is, perhaps, what Handel means by the 'prospective self' (1987: 331): the self one might become. Sarah, for example, was aspiring to membership of the philosophy community by using the word *deontological.*

Sarah: 'I threw it in, actually. I thought Hmm'.

I interpret this to mean that she did not yet feel that it was a part of her voice: she was not fluent and at ease with it. But this was not because she resisted this identity: rather, that she was slightly deceptively giving the impression, through the use of this word, of a membership she desired and was in the process of gaining.

Sarah also felt comfortable with the identity constructed for her by the use of the expression *fact directed consequential theories*, an expression she coined herself, even though she felt insecure as to whether she had the knowledge with which to do so. She said

Sarah: It isn't an expression that has appeared in print. It's something that I got together myself, but I feel he ought to know what I mean. You could argue consequential theories aren't all fact directed, but I don't know, you see. We are all still very much beginners as philosophers, I mean, we haven't read enough to know if in fact there are any exceptions to that.

The use of this expression seems to position her firmly within the academic philosophy community, yet she is fully aware that she is only pretending to full membership — unsure whether the expression holds water.

Valerie talked about her desire to 'take to herself' both the ideas and the words she was encountering at university. Although considerable stretches of her essay, particularly the first half, were adapted directly from her source textbook, she did not disown these. She felt they were part of the identity she was struggling to create for herself, rather than an impression of herself which she could as yet sincerely present.

Valerie: So I get this contrast of parts that I want to take to myself and other parts where I haven't, so what I am saying to you now is I want to take everything fully to myself, which I have started doing this year.
            (...)
            I really would like to do so much more with these words. I'd like to take them more on to myself and be more confident in them.

Desired identities

Sometimes writers would like to be presenting themselves in a particular way, but are not doing so, either because of social pressure, embodied in their assessment of their readers' expectations (as I discuss later in this chapter), or because they don't know how to, or a combination of both. These include 'the real self' which John said he would like to project but can't. This aspect of identity is, perhaps what Handel calls the 'desired self' (1987: 331): the self one fears one cannot be. They differ from the projected, but somewhat fraudulent identities discussed in the previous section in that there is no trace of them in the writers' essays: they can only be discovered in what the writers say they wished they had been able to project in the essays.

Valerie was talking about parts of the essay which were important to her, but her tutor had advised her to omit when she wrote on the same topic in the exam.

Valerie: That's the conflict we are torn between when we are in academic
             writing, that you can't do much on your own, you know.
             (...)
             I wish I could have put everything that I thought about but I
             thought 'No, I'd better not.'

She felt that she would like to write in a way which represented her interests and the connections she was making, but couldn't.

Frances talked specifically about the way in which her lack of confidence both affects how she writes and shows in her writing. We were talking about using *I* in the essay, particularly at the beginning.

Roz: You use I as structurer of essay on page 1, and hide it too: *This*
             essay will look at.
Frances: It's not very consistent at all but I would suspect when I carefully
             construct an awkward impersonal it's because I'm not prepared to
             commit myself to the argument.
Roz: Or to the structure?
Frances: Yes. I'm just not convinced that I'm going to get it right. It's not
             deliberate in any way, but I didn't feel comfortable enough with
             it to say 'I will use a framework based on Sahlins and MacCormack
             as well as Mauss to demonstrate what I mean' — what I (*stressed*)
             mean by the rules of gift exchange. I quite see that if I'd allowed
             that to be personal it would have been personal. It would also
             look as if I was more confident of what I was doing.

Frances felt that she would like to give an impression of someone who had her own views and a strong presence in the essay, but she was too unsure of herself to do so.

Sarah talked about the difficulty she had writing in a way that she could feel proud about:

Sarah: It's like looking at lots of furniture and then going away and being
             asked to make some, but you don't know the joins.

This metaphor expresses powerfully how she and others felt about academic writing. She knows all too well from so much reading what she would like to sound like. Her own 'piece of furniture' would be unique, not a copy, but it would still be recognizable as furniture by certain characteristics of the way it is crafted. But she feels she doesn't have control of the craft, and so cannot create the object that would give the sort of account of herself she would like.

Signalling ownership

A reader or analyst might not recognize the writer's intention to signal ownership by the use of inverted commas, since these are more often used as a distancing device (as discussed below). However, writers do sometimes use inverted commas as if to say 'what I might call ....' : to show that they have coined a certain expression and are thereby claiming a very specific type of ownership over it. Rachel's coined expressions *'cohab-free'* and *'goal aimed tasks'* which I discussed in Chapter 7 are examples of this. Here is another example from Sarah's writing.

Sarah first used the metaphor *lock the door and throw away the key* introduced by the words *metaphorically speaking*, and then later in inverted commas. She described how and why she had explicitly signalled that she considered the expression to be her own coinage, and how she felt about the way this expression positioned her.

Sarah: It's mine. I came up with a metaphor and so I put it in inverted commas. I liked it. It was my metaphor. ... I thought 'well that explains to me what I mean. And it's a metaphor so I'll put it in inverted commas.' That's all. I didn't get it from anywhere. And then I used it. I quite like the idea of getting some sort of pattern or a key to understanding, and then using it a couple of times at least.

Sarah is saying 'this is mine, and it's me.' She is owning the choice of metaphor, the discourse strategy of using a metaphor, and the additional discourse strategy of repeating the metaphor. It is not so much the words themselves (which are in fact quite a common, even clichéd, metaphor) as the creative process of using them to explain a point in an academic essay which positions her: she is identifying with people who use metaphors to explain complex ideas.

These writers are claiming these expressions as their own, yet they are not 'single-voiced' discourse: the writers have coined them out of elements which are imbued with associations, even though each new expression is self-consciously unique.

Disowned identities, cynicism and alienation

Writers are positioned by the discourses they subconsciously choose, or are forced in some way to employ. However, writers can in their own minds disassociate themselves from their discourse, stand aloof from that positioning, and disclaim responsibility for it. It is important to recognize that, while writers may feel their 'real self' is protected by the possibility of disowning the discoursal self in their writing, this does nothing to contribute to resistance and struggle for change (see also Street 1996: 133 for this point).

Disowning the language

This section gives examples of the way in which my co-researchers wanted to disassociate themselves from identities they had set up for themselves by their discourse choices.

John disowned the expression *opportune infections*.

Roz: Do you mind using it?
John: No, but I feel slightly embarrassed at using it, because it's not me. In one sense I try to distance myself from [the language of the books I quote], and this has got little bits of it and I don't like that.
           (...)
Roz: But this 'me' that you willingly identify with, doesn't it include being the type of person who can use correct medical ethics terminology?
John: No. Because you don't need to use correct medical ethics terminology. I think the aim of my writing is that anyone could pick up my essay and read it. And if you're going to have things like *opportune infections* it's going to put people off and that's wrong.

John has a strong belief in readability, in language not excluding people. He disowns, or at any rate feels embarrassed by the phrase he used because he sees it as contravening his values. He doesn't want to be the sort of person who uses academic discourse in this exclusive way.

Frances disowned the 'tortured sentences' in her writing which she thought were caused by the fact that she didn't feel fully in control of the content she was writing about. This is rather different from disowning the lexical choice as in the example from John's writing.

Frances: I don't quite like a lot of the writing .. very tortured sentences .. why did I put it like that? It could be much clearer .. but this again is a stronger hold on the content. You can then manipulate it more. You can then say 'I know this better so I can express *myself* more clearly.' But then if I'm struggling to use someone else's words ...

Sarah wanted to disassociate herself from the ecologically unsound views associated with the word *'disposal'* in connection with nuclear waste. In some places she overtly signalled the fact that this word was other-voiced and not one she identified with — by attributing it to NIREX near the beginning, and by discussing its significance at the end of the essay. However, she also used it without any of these overt distancing devices, including two instances at the beginning of the essay before she had attributed it to NIREX. She was concerned that in these places it might be positioning her as the sort of person who believes in the concept.

It is not surprising that John expresses a sense of alienation from his environment as a result of consistently having to project a *persona* with which he does not feel comfortable. For him the member-of-the-academic-community *persona* is entirely a question of demand, and not of desire, and therefore he projects it opportunistically. He said:

John: I felt I was [getting closer to portraying an identity I feel comfortable with in my writing], but this year the more the pressure mounts, and the more I'm asked to do and produce in a certain way, no, I have an overwhelming feeling I'm moving away from it. I think that's one of the reasons I'm getting disheartened.

This sort of alienation can lead to writers doing what Goffman calls fostering an impression cynically, feigning, deceiving their readers, maintaining a show before others in which they did not themselves believe (Goffman 1969: 18 and 209). This is a much more calculated form of deception than that described under the heading 'aspiring selves'. There I was talking about writers somewhat deceptively giving an impression which they did not fully believe they deserved, but sincerely wanted to live up to; here I am talking about writers for entirely ulterior motives giving an impression which they do not aspire to, and know to be false. Writers do this when they feel forced by pressure from their reader(s), which I discuss in further detail in the second part of this chapter. As a result of this cynical self-representation some, especially those in their final year, began to feel a sense of alienation from their writing and the whole environment in which they were 'performing'.

Rejected identities

Some of my co-researchers had clear ideas about how they did not want to appear in their writing, and could recount conscious attempts to resist being positioned in certain ways. This section is about discourse choices they avoided — often in the face of what they saw as considerable pressure to write in a particular way. It seems to me that the choice *not* to do certain things is opting *for* a different identity — a self defined by the affiliations it avoids.

Angela has strong views about impersonal, apparently objective academic discourse, which she expressed by contrasting 'academics' with 'American feminists and poets'.

Roz: Is there anyone you'd like to write like?
Angela: Yes: American feminists and poets.
Roz: Is there anyone you'd hate to write like?
Angela: Yes: academics! Adrienne Rich is one of those people you feel
           she's speaking to you, communicating. Academic writing is cold,
           it seems like hiding things, not thinking. Like [a sociology tutor],
           I read an essay by him which didn't seem to mean anything. They
           seem meaningless, as if you could condense what they say into a
           few paragraphs.
           (...)
           [Being exclusive] is what annoys me about academic text that is
           very mystifying .. uses a lot of jargon, doesn't connect to reality.
           The person doesn't want you to see them. That comes across
           straight away. Using theory and academic knowledge as a barrier
           to stop you getting (.?.).

Angela was also particularly aware of the way a writer is positioned by quoting other writers. In her view, this not only positions writers as someone who reveres established authorities, but also reduces their own authority. She therefore refused to quote, in order to disassociate herself from these positions. She said:

Angela: I think it's obvious that I've read certain things. I didn't feel I needed to prove yet again that I'd read them. Also it feels that you've got to side with that person or argue against them. There's no middle ground. So I've let ideas merge, infiltrate my thinking.
(...)
If you're using a particular idea you must quote, but after a while it becomes yours. It's really important to write your own ideas. I'm against concentrating on texts because there comes a point when you've got to look at your own ideas .. recognize they're as important as anyone else's. If you just look at books your experiences are minimized. Feeling insecure in an environment like this, as an undergraduate, you can be taken over by other people's interpretations. Quoting leads to this.
(...)
I didn't want to [quote] because then it looks as if most of the ideas are from books when the thing is about personal experience not book knowledge.
(...)
Once people know who you've quoted they could disagree with what you're saying because of the view they have of the person you quoted. When I was a child I was never a fan of anyone. I used to look down on people who were great fans. I never identified with that. I thought it stopped you from being critical and thinking for yourself. So if I'd mentioned one or two feminists I'd seem like I was jumping on a bandwagon and identifying myself. A lot of men use Marx like a pop-star — something to latch on to, you don't have to develop your own thinking. I honestly believe they can't think for themselves if they've got to use Marx's ideas to prove or disprove things happening.

She rejected the identity which would have been associated with using a lot of quotation: both the identities set up by her particular choice of references, and the identity of a person appealing to authority as the source of ideas.

Valerie talked about a friend who wrote successful essays by 'just following a book'. She said she would never want to write like that, even though her friend gets very high marks that way. I give further examples of rejected identities when discussing resistance to what my co-researchers saw as the demands of the academic discourse community below.

Signalling distance

Some writers use quotation marks quite prolifically, some not at all. A very common use of them is to signal distance, which has led to such quotation marks being called 'scare quotes'. The desire to distance the self from membership of a particular group is a part of recognizing our own values and beliefs, and signalling this distance is a powerful device of self-presentation. There are several places where my co-researchers were aware that they were using inverted commas partly to signal that words or phrases belonged to others, but partly also that they didn't want their own voice associated with them. These distancing devices are strong, conscious ways in which the writers take up a position. They are explicit statements within the text of rejected identities.

The writer who used this device most prodigiously was Angela. In most cases she was distancing herself from expressions which she saw as part of the discourse of sexism, elitism and a world view which condoned hierarchies and labels. Examples are 'inadequacies', 'intellectuals', 'legitimated', 'students', 'category', 'unknowledgeable', 'unconscious', 'objectivity'. These are words which she felt were used uncritically within the institution of higher education (that is, the academic discourse community), and she was using the scare quotes to show that she didn't want to accept the assumptions behind these words.

There is a particularly interesting place where she is quoting her women informants, but also distancing herself from what she sees as the phony discourse of empowerment which one of them uses. She pointed this out when we were discussing the following extract.

Extract 8.2 Angela *Independent Studies* (lines 229–230)

  Also they found feminist theory 'empowering and liberating' ...

Angela said that these are words she herself would not have used at the time, and that, in this case but not others, signalling that they belonged to the other women doubled with signalling that she did not identify with this way of wording the world.

Justin also used scare quotes. I discussed the way he used them for the word 'grace' in Chapter 7. Here are two more examples.

Extract 8.3 Justin *Aesthetics* (lines 83–84)

  our minds have a different 'language' which involves a symbology that is too 'irrational' for convenient interpersonal communication.

Extract 8.4 Justin *Aesthetics* (lines 110–112)

> The scientific community gives some tacit recognition to the importance of 'unscientific' considerations when it describes its most celebrated theories as 'elegant'.

In extract 8.3 Justin wants to identify himself as the sort of person who would not use the word 'irrational' pejoratively. He commented

Justin: Oh, I say that it's too irrational for convenient interpersonal communication, but that's just a concise way of saying what I want to say. I might use different words, but I prefer to use that word and self-indulgently and otherwise cast doubt on the associations of irrational. It means bad, not so good or whatever, but just as science is supposed to be better, irrational is supposed to be worse.

(...)

Disclaiming some of its connotations, I suppose. I don't know whether that comes across. (...) I know what I wanted it there to do was to disclaim some of its connotations, because it's clear what I mean. I don't know whether it's clear or not that I'm disclaiming the connotations. (...) I suppose what I'm doing is cheating by using a word that I wouldn't use without signalling that I was unhappy with it on one level or another.

Similarly, in extract 8.4 Justin was using the inverted commas to distance himself from the word 'unscientific'. He said 'That's an example of so-called'.

The last two examples are interesting because they come in the same sentences as other words in inverted commas from which Justin is not intending to distance himself. He only uses inverted commas around the word 'language' to signify a special meaning for the word, different from the way he has used it a few lines previously. Similarly, he does not mean to distance himself from 'elegant', just to indicate that he intends a special meaning of that term, as it is used by the scientific community. Justin says 'I don't know whether that comes across': a reader cannot always interpret these signals in exactly the subtle way in which the writer intended them.

In Chapter 7 I discussed how Donna came to use the expression 'Eastern promise' in Extract 7.4. This is what she said about using the quotation marks not only to signal its origin but also to distance herself from it.

Donna: It's a bit of sarcasm actually as well, putting it like that.

She was being 'sarcastic' about that way of describing Asian women in order to establish that she, herself, rejected that way of describing them. The expression is a particularly demeaning and stereotyping way of constructing Asian women. Someone who uses it sincerely — as the speaker in the Turkish Delight advert seems to do — would be positioned as thinking of Asian women simply in terms of their sexuality. Donna distanced herself doubly from this positioning: firstly, she describes such images as *controlling and derogatory* and secondly she puts quotation marks around these particular words.

Two points emerge from these examples. Firstly, using a distancing device is to do with owning the identity which is thereby set up. In all these examples the writers were sincerely positioning themselves against the voice within the quotation marks. There is no deception, cynicism and alienation involved, as discussed in above. Secondly, there is no way of telling from the existence of quotation marks alone that they are intended, and should be interpreted as, distancing devices. In some cases I had misinterpreted them before talking to the writers, for example, I had not realized that Angela had intended to distance herself from the world-view represented by her informants' words *'empowering and liberating'*.

Multiple identities, contradictions and ambivalence

None of the writers except possibly Justin consistently owned the impression they felt they were conveying of themselves. Most of them felt ambivalent about identifying themselves with what they saw as the dominant ideologies of the academic community. All of them wanted to associate themselves with some aspects of academic community membership: for example to present themselves as knowledgeable and thoughtful. But many of them felt that the conventions forced them to dismiss other aspects of their identity, for example, being committed, caring, or funny. They were sometimes ambivalent about the ways they felt they were being positioned by their discourse choices; they sometimes felt that they had given contradictory impressions of themselves; and they sometimes felt they had given multiple but nevertheless coherent impressions of themselves. These heterogeneous and complex self-representations were often jostling alongside each other, often in the same clause, and variously marked linguistically, such as through the use of inverted commas, or of person, in ways not always immediately obvious to the reader.

John explained how he was aware of very subtle distinctions between expressions he had used. We were talking about his conclusion.

Extract 8.5 John *Medical Ethics* (lines 379–382 and 403–415)

> ...It is only by giving people the confidence to be tested (total confidentiality) that testing and then health education in safer-sex can hope to stop the spread of HIV.
>
> (...)
>
> In conclusion I believe Aids has caused problems for health practitioners but I don't believe that these problems are unique to Aids. HIV has done exactly the same to health care practitioners as it did to the gay community and that is to take it by surprise and make them face problems. I think it is fair to say that the problems may seem infinite from what they were but I do not believe it is justified to say that Aids created them. Aids is an opportunity for health care practitioners to be able to demand that the health services be maintained and uplifted instead of run down.

John liked some aspects of the discoursally constructed self in this conclusion and not others.

John: I quite like the ending (...) I don't like the 'being run down'. I should have left it as 'maintained and uplifted'. I should have left that out because that's a bit preaching. And I like the end because I'm stating what I believe and I'm also questioning in one sense the title of the essay.

           (...)

           'It is only' — that's asserting again. There's no question there. 'I believe', 'I think', 'I do not believe'.

John sees this section of his essay setting up contradictory impressions of himself. He is owning the identity of a person who questions and believes, set up by most of what he has written, but not the identity of a person who preaches or asserts, set up by the two expressions *being run down* and *This is only*.

     Sarah felt as if she was on the edge between NIREX and Friends of the Earth, and between an identity as a scientist and as a philosopher. She said:

Sarah: I am viewed as a wishy-washy liberal at the university or even too much one of the scientists, and as a radical by old friends at [the nuclear fuel research institution where I worked]. Now I feel stronger about my role of explaining at the university that scientists are only people.

She was aware that her discourse choices in this essay conveyed this split identity, and that she herself was ambivalent about identifying herself too strongly with either side of the divide (for a more detailed analysis of this see Ivanič 1995, or Clark and Ivanič 1997, Chapter 6).

Frances was sincere, if slightly wary, about the member-of-the-academic-community *persona* she was constructing for herself:

Frances: I've learnt over the year that knowing what it's about isn't enough. You have to present it through the academic hoop. If you're playing the game you've got to play it by the rules and the rules are beginning, middle and end and a continuous argument. And that's what I'm trying to learn. I can see why some people are constrained by this .. perhaps very creative people who want to do things their own way and have a gift for saying things in their own way which isn't necessarily an academic way. I feel I'm prepared to accept this as a discipline, because if I can train myself to do this I can be more systematic within what I see as my more creative stuff.

She had ambivalent feelings about the intrinsic value of academic conventions, but saw them as worth aspiring to, if only as a means to another end of writing ' my more creative stuff' in the future.

John expresses the contradiction he experiences in writing an academic essay. He owns the fact that he is putting forward his own ideas. At the same time, however, he rejects some of the discourse characteristics he feels forced to employ in doing so.

Roz: So what sort of person do you feel you are being when writing this essay?
John: Firstly with all essays I'm always me and I'm always expressing my points and my opinions and that's very important. There is another side that has to jazz things up because they've got to be academically acceptable and they want things like that.
Roz: But what's the 'me' that you are in here?
John: The 'me' is someone talking about their ideas about Aids and in this section about confidentiality, in another about caring .. they're my ideas and what I think about things and that's where the 'me' is.

This quotation brings out the interplay between content and form. Writers are positioned by both what they say and how they say it. John has contradictory feelings about the identity he projects, because he owns the content, but not the form in which he writes.

The examples here show firstly that the writers recognized that they were positioning themselves in different ways in different parts of the essays, or even in different aspects of the same section. This heterogeneity often led to apparent contradictions between positions they were constructing for themselves. They were often able to explain these contradictions in terms of tensions and uncertainty in their own allegiances. Secondly, even when writers were clear about the way they were positioned by the whole, a part or an aspect of their essay, they often had ambivalent feelings about that positioning. Although not all my co-researchers expressed this uncertainty, it seems to me that mature students entering the academic community are likely to have mixed feelings like these about how they want to present themselves in writing. Indeed, this sort of multiplicity and ambivalence may be characteristic of writing for anyone entering any new community.

Identities in a state of flux

Several of my co-researchers mentioned aspects of their discourse which were new, temporary, or something they did not necessarily expect to use again in the future. Sarah talked about 'trying identities on for size'. Some, looking back at their writing after a period of months, were able to identify characteristics which they had felt comfortable to identify with then, but would not feel comfortable with any more: what Handel calls 'retrospective selves' (1987: 331). It is striking to see just how fluid people's sense of themselves is: experience is constantly bombarding people with possibilities for self-hood to the extent that how someone likes to appear one day can have changed by the next. This is perhaps particularly true of certain times in people's lives, of which undergraduate study is one.

Sarah encapsulated the point that discoursally constructed identities are temporary identities when I asked her about the expression *I fear*. This had struck me as an unusual discourse choice for a student, even in philosophy, positioning her as rather self-important. When I asked her about it, Sarah said:

Sarah: I've experimented with lots of styles. This could be an experiment.

Sarah also talked about a less haphazard sort of development in the way she writes. We were discussing the long nominal group *The elimination of the risk of radioactive waste* which she had used in her draft.

Roz: I was wondering whether for you that's something you're comfortable with or uncomfortable with.

Sarah: Well at one time I would have felt quite pleased with myself for getting to the stage where I wrote (?like that). I'm beginning to have enough confidence to feel it doesn't matter.

When I asked John about the word *notion*, he said:

John: Yeah, I like .. I like the idea of it. In [my] Sartre [essay] I've got lots of 'notions'. I just like it as a word. It's a nice word.

Roz: Since when?

John: Quite recently. It's taken over from 'concept' which I used to quite like. I think that's because it does the work of 'concept' and a notion is .. less solid than a concept, so I like to use it because there's a kind of fluidness there. I think it's a very nice word from that point of view.

This shows John changing his discoursal preferences over time: the word *notion* is quite new to his repertoire. It also shows the sort of motivation writers have for change. He has recently added this word to his repertoire because of the precise meaning it captures. I would go so far as to suggest that this is motivated by an increasing critical awareness of different views of knowledge-making. When John says that he likes the 'fluidity' of the word notion it could be that he has identified that 'notions' are held by individuals, in other words, associated with a subjective view of knowledge, whereas 'concepts' are relatively impersonal, objective entities. He is not totally rejecting the identity associated with academic discourses here, but having a well-motivated preference within them.

Donna was also able to recognize two changes in this essay from her discourse practices in previous ones. Firstly, she said that she had never used the word 'I' before this essay. She was trying it out for the first time and said ' I'm not at ease with it.' This discourse strategy was not yet part of her, and may not become part of her. Secondly, when I asked her why she hadn't used an expression like 'In conclusion', she said

Donna: I used to do that with essays, and I thought 'that's a bit 'A' Level'. (...)

> [My friend] pointed out that in a way the person who is reading it
> should actually read it and realize that you are winding up, and I
> thought 'That's a valid point and I'll take that on board.'
> (...)
> All my essays change anyway .. they all change .. there's no essay
> that I can say is the same, not because of the different content, I
> should say, but in the difference in style. The way that I've written
> it every one is different.

She was disassociating herself from a discourse strategy which she felt positioned her as an 'A' level student, and trying out a new way of signalling the
structure of her essay. What she says shows how she was constantly striving
towards a way of writing which would give the sort of impression of her that
she wanted.

Frances pointed out how words which she used didn't belong to her at
the time, but might become her own in the future. We were discussing the
words *primitive analogue* and *exposition* in the following extract

Extract 8.6 Frances *Anthropology* (lines 41–44)

> *Sahlins* in Stone Age Economics suggests that gift giving avoids
> "warre" and that the gift is the primitive analogue of the Social
> Contract. Malinowsky's exposition of the Kula ring shows every
> element of warfare present except the fighting.

Frances talked about the extent to which the two words are part of her own
vocabulary:

Frances: [exposition] is part of university vocabulary .. I'd use it to talk
           about my work here, but not across the garden fence.
Roz: Does it differ from *analogue*?
Frances: Yes, because I know what *exposition* means, quite clearly. It's a
           word which I would be happy with. It's part of my established life.
           Primitive analogue may or may not become established at some
           stage.

She saw *primitive analogue* as a term which at this point belonged to Sahlins,
but in the future might become a part of her own repertoire.

In one of Donna's essays I found the word 'epistemological' in quotation
marks but not attributed to a particular source, just as I have reproduced it
here. In a later essay I found the same word without the quotation marks.

When I asked her about this she said that, in the first essay, she was aware that the word had come from her recent reading: somehow it belonged to others' voices, and so had to be in quotes. By the second essay, however, she was familiar with it, she could use it as her own, and so she no longer needed the quotation marks. This is a vivid illustration of how voices lose their attachment to individuals as they become part of our own resources, as discussed at the end of Chapter 7. Expressions in her current piece of writing such as 'herstories' and 'external forces', which she identified with other authors' voices and signalled as such, may in time become her own, or they may not.

In later interviews several of my co-researchers commented that they wouldn't write something the same way if they had a chance to write the same essay again. Frances said

Frances: If I were to start again I would do it completely differently. And so I've moved on, I've learnt from it, and it's really a bit like not letting go of a painting and taking it out of the frame and adding a bit more, because, you know, you're not actually satisfied with it.

She was able to see a specific way of rewording something which would give a better impression of her grip on the subject. We were discussing Extract 8.7, which is an aside nested within another clause.

Extract 8.7 Frances *Anthropology* (line 156)

— *wives are a very complex part of this pattern not to be discussed here*

Frances explained how she might move on from this discourse choice and the way it positioned her.

Frances: I might be cleverer about it in the future and, say, just mention the details or complexity, and instead of what I said, say 'this is a very complex issue which is not germane to the question' rather than 'not to be discussed here'. There is a difference but I didn't appreciate it then. ... I think the more elegant is something I'm always reaching out for.

This subtle change in wording would convey her understanding of *why* it was inappropriate to discuss wives at this point. The difference in terms of subject-positioning is that she would in this way show herself to be 'more elegant', more aware of the implications of such issues, and hence, perhaps, a more credible member of the anthropology community.

Sarah pointed to a long sentence in her essay and said

Sarah: That isn't me. But it sounded grand. I thought one had to use language like that.

This is relevant to the discussion of identities in a state of flux in two ways. Firstly, a writer in time may no longer identify with the sort of discourse s/he used previously. Secondly, as time goes on a writer may no longer think s/he is under any obligation to conform to a particular discourse type.

Since writing this essay, Angela had moved further along the path of critical awareness about language use. Talking about her essay several months after she had written it, she said:

Angela: If I had to change it now I wouldn't make the sentences so long. Maybe I wouldn't use certain words. Looking at that it sounds fairly academic, but then I don't know another way. I've now learnt another language, and I'd find it difficult to put what I've written there in language that most people communicate in. I'd find it difficult to rewrite *institutional* or *relational practices* or *hierarchical, objectification*. I'd have to really really think about other words for others to understand.

This expresses an important dilemma faced by writers who are critically aware. They recognize that academic lexis is exclusive, and do not want to identify with that exclusive club; on the other hand they see this lexis as a useful short-hand for complex ideas. So Angela had a sense that she no longer identified with some aspects of what she had written, yet did not yet have as part of her repertoire any discourses which would construct an alternative identity.

Finally, Frances described the powerful effect returning to study had had on her life.

Frances: Did I tell you one of my friends — teacher friends — said 'Ach, you can't talk to Frances now, she uses all these big words.' And she was joking. And it's not true. What is true is that I now stand up to her and make her listen to me. It's not that my vocab. has substantially changed, but she's a teacher and she talks a lot and I just used to sit and listen and now I've got so much to say she has to listen to *me*. (...) People I used to talk to I don't find so easy to talk to now. I say I'm using the same words but it's me that's different.

> (...) Perhaps Mary's right: I am using different words, but I'm not
> consciously using different words, just making *her* listen to *me*.

This is a telling example of how people's identities are in a constant state of
flux as a result of participation in new discourses. It is not just a question of a
few new words here and there, but a whole new way of being, not only at the
university but also at home.

So far I have presented quotations from my co-researchers showing how
far they aligned themselves with the positions constructed by their discourse
choices. In the rest of the chapter I discuss why their writing should be such a
mixture between owned and disowned discoursal selves: the effect of social
interaction on self-representation in writing. I consider how the writers
anticipated the response of their readers, and felt pressure as a result to present
themselves in particular ways.

Readers, power relations and the assessment process

Dominant practices, conventions, ideologies don't position writers directly.
The power relationship between readers and writer (in the case of student
essays, a relationship which is set up by the assessment process) mediates the
influence of the wider social context on the individual writer. Unless they
know otherwise, writers assume that their readers' values match what they
perceive to be the dominant values in the social context. What writers assume
about these readers who are in a position of power over them affects, but does
not determine, the way in which they present themselves in their writing. This is
the mechanism through which the dominant ideologies and associated discourses
in the academic community position them (see Fairclough 1989: 24).

In this section I discuss the special nature of the reader-writer relationship
around student essays. There is always a power relationship between writers
and the reader(s) of their writing. This has frequently been considered from
the point of view of the power the writer exerts over the reader. In some forms
of writing, for example, the writing of school textbooks, the power is obviously on the side of the writer. However, in many situations the balance of power
is with the reader(s), and particularly in any situation where the readers are
also assessors, such as the writing of coursework essays.

This is how Valerie summed up her feelings about the pressures which
her readers exerted on her to conform:

Valerie: I'm going to have to learn that I'm going to have to unfortunately
             stick to their boundaries. That's what's so annoying, you know.

I find the phrase 'their boundaries' particularly significant here. Firstly Valerie
sees whatever the pressures are as 'boundaries': something limiting her
freedom to say what she thinks and write 'creatively'. Secondly, I wonder what
the 'their' means. I think it refers both to the individual tutors, whose preferences she thinks she knows, and to 'them' in the more abstract sense: the
institution with authority over her. In the mind of the writer I suggest that the
individual tutors are the representatives of the abstract institution. This is
especially true when they don't know their tutors very well and have no way
of finding out what their personal values really are.

Some of my co-researchers used expressions like 'it's playing their game'.
Here is what John said about the pressure from tutors to position himself as
revering published authorities by including a requisite number of quotations
in his essay. We were talking about a quotation which, we both agreed, added
little to what he had said in his own words.

Roz: Why bother to include Grant Gillett at all?
John: That's academically (?based). [If I didn't use any quotations at all]
          they'd just give you the essays back and say they're not academ-
          ically up to standard. So it's playing their game.

Justin talked about wanting to 'maintain sympathy', to keep the reader thinking
well of him, and he used the conscious strategy of writing in what he considers
is an unpretentious, informal, light-hearted way for this purpose. He said

Justin: (...) obviously it's partly a good thing to do, assuming it doesn't
            get up the nose of your reader, to maintain sympathy, but also just
            to make it readable.

Perhaps all writers who want their work to be read need to 'maintain sympathy': if the writer's style gets 'up the nose' of readers they will just not read
on. However, this is especially important for student writers since they want
their work not only to be read, but also to be judged favourably.

Several of my co-researchers felt that they were under pressure to express
particular views in their writing, whether or not they held them themselves.

Roz: But a lot of what you're learning is other people's thoughts.
Valerie: That is it you know, and it is so annoying so it's not necessarily
             that you'll think that, but this was expected of you, and when you

get your lecture notes are normally .. they give you an idea of what they expect from you, so whether you believe it or not this is what you've got to put and if you start putting things down that you know then you ge .. get told off. Well, you know, you've got to be careful what you put there. Wha .. what do they expect of you? It's very difficult.

What Valerie says here shows the confusion student writers can experience. They know they need to accommodate to their tutor's expectations, and to some extent they know what these are, as Valerie knew that she should include what was mentioned in the lecture rather than what she knew from personal experience. On the other hand they're never quite certain what is expected, and feel they are floundering in the dark.

In this environment of power relations and uncertainty about expectations, student writers set about writing. The result is a discoursal web of subjectivities, partly owned and partly disowned, designed to create a good impression on the reader without compromising the writer's integrity.

Accommodation and resistance

From the point of view of how the writer anticipates the reader's expectations, the discoursal construction of identity becomes a question of accommodation and resistance, as described by Chase (1988) — see Chapter 4, in the section entitled 'Critical approaches to academic discourse'. Chase makes the assumption that there is only one set of norms in the academic community, and student writers accommodate to them, oppose them or resist them. To some extent Chase is right, in that there are some extremely pervasive and powerful conventions, as I show in Chapter 9, which are shaped by and sustain certain privileged ideologies. However, I don't think it is a simple question of accommodation or resistance to a single set of conventions: there are many different norms and constellations of subjectivities open to members of the academic community, depending on differences among fields of study, discourse roles, and ideologies of knowledge-making, as I show in Chapter 10. I suggest that what student writers really try to do is to accommodate to and resist what they perceive to be the expectations of individual reader-assessors. When they know their tutors fairly well they can make an informed judgement as to what will please them; when they don't know their tutors well, or don't know exactly who will assess their work, they then tend to assume they will have the dominant values and expectations, as Rachel assumed about her external examiner (see Chapter 6). In either case they have to decide how far they will be true to themselves in appropriating these values and meeting these expectations, how far they are prepared to accommodate to them for ulterior motives, and how far they are determined to resist them.

The issue of accommodation and resistance is intertwined with the issue of ownership of and distancing from discoursally constructed identities. For some of my co-researchers their desire coincides with what is demanded of them, making it comfortable to accommodate to what they perceive to be their readers' values, beliefs and expectations, but for some it doesn't. Writers sometimes write in ways they prefer to disown (as discussed above) in order to accommodate to what they perceive to be the reader's expectations. Writers are sometimes prepared to resist the readers' expectations because they feel so strongly about rejecting particular identities. In this section I look at these issues from the point of view of anticipating the reader's response and focus particularly on some cases where my co-researchers talked about the tension between accommodating and resisting.

Donna explained how she had found out that her tutor likes things to be 'academic' and values attribution to authority. She talked extremely pragmatically and cynically about accommodating to these values:

Donna: .. and I thought if she wants academic type writing, purely academic she's going to get it so I gave it to her.
(...)
This is what she wants so this is what she'll get. Because I had this feeling that this was what she wanted because there was a book I'd read 'Heart of the Rake' and she'd read it also and she turned round and said 'well I didn't like it very much because it was an OK book but it wasn't very academic.' And I thought 'Fine!' because they didn't use any reference in whatever .. what they did was they used the bibliography at the back but they didn't reference their stuff, which I didn't think there was anything wrong with that.

However, she did not accommodate to the tutor's values in every respect. She used the expression *telling it like it is*, which she identified with 'street talk', well aware that the tutor might be disturbed by it. In spite of her desire to please her supervisor and get a good mark, her reasons for using the expression were too strong for her to change it. This is what she said about her anticipation of the tutor's response:

Roz: Did you have any trouble with using that expression there?
Donna: I didn't, but I thought the tutor might because it's not academic is
            it, really, it's quite basic .. but I liked it how it is.

Angela was quite adamant about rejecting various traditional academic values, as I discussed above. However, in her case, this did not amount to resisting the tutor's values, since she knew that her tutor questioned many of these values too. Knowing that a particular reader does not fall in with dominant conventions can help writers who want to resist them too.

Valerie spoke particularly powerfully about how she wanted to resist but felt that she had to accommodate for the time being. We were talking about how she was going to respond to her tutor's criticisms in preparing for writing an exam answer on the same topic.

Valerie: I was so annoyed by how he criticized my work that I just said 'All
            right, I'll just take that now because I haven't got the confidence
            to be too annoyed about it because' .. you understand, I don't
            know. When I gain the confidence in my writing ability I can say
            'Right, I'm not having that.' But right now .. writing it down is
            when the problem comes. I know what I don't want to do (*just
            follow the books slavishly*), but (.?.) The criticism I feel I'm sensitive
            to: I feel I have to take on what they say.

She seems to be wanting to take up a position as a less conforming, less subservient member of the community, to be the sort of person who speaks her mind on her own terms. However, she feels she has to conform to the requirements of her tutors while she is still struggling so much with academic writing and, I suggest, while she is such a junior member of the academic community.

Some of my co-researchers were prepared to defy what they saw as their readers' expectations in spite of the consequences. John talked in strong terms about discourse practices on which he would not compromise himself. These are all practices which he associates with the academic community and is not willing to adopt. Firstly, about the requirement that a student essay should contain quotations and references to reading:

John: No, I never slot quotations in. I consider that dishonest. ... because
            you're working round someone else's work and ideas, and that's
            not what it's about. It's all about expressing your ideas, and what
            you think, and if someone agrees with you or has had the same

idea before, that's fine: use a quotation, but if you start to work by slotting your ideas round someone else's ideas, then .. it's not you and you may as well ...

Secondly, about his tutor's attempts to suggest the ideal length for quotations:

John: I think it's appalling, I really do. I will never submit to that. I think she can ask me to put quotations in, if these are the rules of the academic game .. I don't like them .. but my quotations are there for a reason. ... the length of the quotation I feel will back up a point and I wouldn't have carried on writing if I didn't feel that it was all appropriate and I will never ever give in to someone telling me to shorten them.

Thirdly, about the way in which academic discourse often puts colloquialisms in inverted commas.

John: I never do it for language, because that's untruthful. If I want the word to be in there, it's in. Sometimes as a compromise I'll change the word, but I never say 'well, you know, here's a word but I know really it shouldn't be in an academic essay.'

Frances talked about resisting the reader's response to a section of her essay. She said

Frances: She's just written 'nonsense' beside that. I still don't agree. Maybe I haven't put it well, and maybe she sees them all as part of the same thing, but I don't.

She is standing up to her tutor's views, although whether she would be prepared to do this in her own writing, say, in an exam question on this topic when she will be assessed on her views, is another matter.

Protective practices towards the reader

Goffman points out that, in any face-to-face social interaction, there will be at least two people putting on performances in front of each other, and in addition to trying to give a flawless impression of oneself, one is also trying to help the other(s) to give good impressions of themselves. Protective practices are strategies aimed at being tactful towards the other(s): helping them to save face, to preserve the impression they want to convey of themselves (see also

Levinson 1983, Brown and Levinson 1987, Scollon 1995 and other work on the pragmatics of face-to-face interaction). These concepts are particularly relevant to face-to-face interaction, and at first sight do not appear to apply to writing. If writing is seen as a social act bounded by the time spent at the word processor or with pen in hand, it cannot involve any protective practices, because the other(s) are not concurrently 'performing' as Goffman calls it. If, however, writing is seen as part of a larger social performance — perhaps all the encounters between tutor and student — then the concept of protective practices becomes relevant. In line with socially situated views of literacy, I think this second way of thinking about academic writing is preferable. I have often heard tutors say that they don't get to know their students until they read something they write, which suggests that the writing should be viewed as part of an ongoing interaction between them. Considering writing as part of the total relationship, a writer can then be seen as employing strategies aimed at protecting the reader's face, although this may be a very cynical view of the practices of the academic community. In the tightly defined power relationship of reader as assessor and writer as assessed, protecting the reader's definition of the situation probably always doubles as a defensive practice. That is, if writers take steps to ensure that the reader does not feel her image has been threatened, they will avoid creating a bad impression of themselves. I illustrate the way in which writers engage in 'protective practices' towards their readers with a detailed discussion of Donna's reasons for presenting herself as she did.

Donna consistently used 'they' to refer to Black women, rather than 'we', she gave no personal anecdotes as evidence for her case, and she was exceptionally liberal with her use of citations. Donna explained that she did this in order to accommodate to what she saw as her supervisor's definition of the situation. Her supervisor was a new, young, white, female member of staff, and perhaps Donna sensed that she was nervous about her role as Donna's supervisor for this project, since Donna is a Black woman, a mature student, and writing about Black women. However, Donna only took this accommodation so far. She felt she should not give an impression of herself as too aggressive in order to avoid offending her reader. Donna writes poetry herself and is extremely committed to the idea of Black women expressing their identity through their writing: indeed, that is the topic of the essay we were discussing. She wanted to convey the fact that she is a fairly militant Black woman as part of the *persona* she portrays in her writing. However, she also wanted to establish credibility as a good student — preferably first class. In the following quotation we see her weighing these two considerations against each other, concerned that the militant Black woman *persona* might jeopardize the good impression she wants to make on the person marking her work. In this long quotation from our discussion, she also points out that she would vary the extent to which she was 'brutally honest' about 'what happens to a Black woman' according to which tutor was going to read it, and according to whether she is writing an academic essay or her 'own writing' (poetry).

Donna: because it's my Independent Study, yes, it has allowed me to be brutally honest .. my tutor may not like it but still .. I don't particularly care, you know, but I .. like .. you know .. I think this one *(pointing to a different essay)* is more brutally honest .. and I was trying to be more diplomatic as well in that essay *(pointing to the one I was asking about)* because it would have been quite easy to have written a lot of stuff but I think I had to remember also who was going to read it. Another Black person who's had the same experience would not feel guilty by reading work that actually stated what happens to a Black woman. For example I lent a book to the girl who lives next door to me and she said *(Donna acts a White voice)* 'it seems that these women are very bitter.' and I said *(Donna acts a patient voice)* 'No, it's not bitter, it's not necessarily angry, it's just telling it like it is.' And I think the telling it like it is might offend other people. I think in that case *(pointing to the essay I was asking about)* I was being diplomatic because some of the images and interpretations of how things came across about Black women would have made people who did not have the same experience feel guilt at first, and offended and probably up tight about reading it so I didn't .. like .. because unless somebody's mind is open to that, and open to deal with that feeling .. in an honest way, then there's no point writing it down .. and in an academic piece of marked work that I knew somebody else is going to mark I didn't see the sense of that . (.?.) and I think, well, I can do that in my own time and in my own writing, put down what is my experience, what is shared experience with a lot of relativity ...
(...) then I think I was being much more diplomatic .. I don't think I needed to be that diplomatic in that essay *(the different one)* as I wasn't going to be hurting anybody's feelings, as such.

In terms of self-presentation, Donna is protecting her tutor from the feelings of guilt she might experience from Donna 'telling it like it is' — she is 'being diplomatic', and thereby preserving a good impression of herself in order to earn a good grade. It is important to recognize that she does not thereby give an impression of herself as a diplomatic person; rather, she avoids giving an impression of herself as an aggressive person. In contradiction to this, however, Donna at the same time wants to present herself as a committed Black woman, and did not altogether hold back from brutal honesty, whatever the tutor might think — as she says at the beginning of this quotation. She does this by quoting many powerful instances of Black women challenging definitions of themselves — but they are always almost clinically academic quotations.

Here is another example of Donna being tactful towards her reader, which involves a specific decision about what content to include in her essay. Donna had wanted to write about several ways in which Black women had redefined their own identity, as she had set out in her original proposal. However, her supervisor had advised her to focus on just one topic: Black motherhood. She was annoyed with her supervisor for 'redefining' her topic, feeling that she, as a Black woman, knew best what needed to be written about, and that it was an insult for her proposal to be changed, and that her own enthusiasm for it was dampened as a result. However, she wanted to please her tutor, and was prepared to compromise her own wishes considerably.

Donna: I was quite peeved at having to do the essay like that and it was totally wrong. (...)
          I look at that and I look at the difference as to what it started out to be and I just thought, you know, that's life ...
          I think if I were to do that essay the way I wanted I wouldn't have concentrated on just motherhood for a start off. I would have looked at other aspects .. there was also I don't know, working women, and different things, different images, I mean like if you look at the entertainment business and O.K., it might not be that different from how white women are portrayed but it's the different way their sexuality is linked up with their singing, which is why I did that second bit (which she omitted) and I think I would have included more to show how Black women have reasserted themselves as not just sexual objects but you know if you listen to the lyrical content of their songs you will hear that there's a

message there that's not the usual la-la wishy-washy you know love song and even if it is a ballad, there's more to it than that. It speaks of their life and what's going on; there's a message within each song. O.K. maybe not everything is political or whatever but a lot of the songs there is a political message and that's an area I would have liked to have gone into and whatever, but I don't think this particular tutor would be ready for that sort of line of thinking so I didn't and I left it out totally.

In order to preserve her supervisor's definition of the situation — that is, the total situation of writing for assessment which she and Donna were engaged in — Donna did indeed make Black motherhood the main topic of her essay and she cut out two pages of her draft in which she addressed the issue of Black women singers and actresses redefining the identity of Black women. She avoided threatening her supervisor's definition of the situation, and thereby avoided portraying herself in a bad light. However, as in the previous example, Donna was only prepared to compromise half way. She felt committed enough to her own views as to what was relevant to the title to include a section on Black lesbians, in spite of advice from her supervisor that this was irrelevant.

Conclusion

Writers cannot portray themselves to readers in a straightforward way. The impression they convey is influenced partly by their own commitments, and partly by what they consider to be their reader's values. People do not always know how they want to present themselves, and it is not always in their best interests to show their colours openly. Consequently writers often create a 'discoursal self' about which they feel ambivalent, owning some aspects of it and disowning others.

Writers must anticipate simultaneously the reader's responses to the content (what Bakhtin calls "addressivity", 1986: 95) *and* the impression the readers will gain of them from the writing. In this chapter I have been drawing attention to the latter, far less frequently discussed, aspect of anticipating the reader's response. When the reader is also going to assess the writing, it is in the writers' interests to give an impression of having values, beliefs and interests in line with the reader's. I showed how student writers feel pressure from their tutor-assessors to take on what they see as the dominant member-of- the-academic-community *persona*. Some desire this identity; others feel it is demanded of them, so they don it reluctantly and subsequently disown it; others again are resistant to it in varying degrees. I discussed the intersection between desire and demand to accommodate to these pressures, and the tensions between accommodation and resistance.

I have done no more than hint at the next stage in the process of positioning: the moment when the reader reads the writing and gains an impression of the writer. On the small amount of evidence I have in this study I am convinced that many of the impressions the readers received of the writers were different from the impressions of themselves which the writers thought they were conveying. Hayes and others (1992) have conducted some preliminary research on this, comparing how students respond to each other's writing with the way tutor-assessors respond to it. They found that the fellow student readers formed very different impressions of the writers from those formed by the tutor-assessor readers. Haswell and Haswell (1995) have studied the way in which readers of different genders construct the 'gendership' of the students who wrote the essays they were reading. Lea and Street (1996 a and b) have begun to investigate the discrepancies between how students think they are presenting themselves in their writing, and the impressions tutors are gaining of them. Further research on these discrepancies would be extremely interesting.

Bakhtin says:

> One can say that any word exists for the speaker in three aspects: as a neutral word of a language, belonging to nobody; as an *other's* word, which belongs to another person and is filled with echoes of the other's utterance; and, finally, as *my* word, for, since I am dealing with it in a particular situation, with a particular speech plan, it is already imbued with my expression. (1986: 88)

In Chapter 7 I discussed what Bakhtin calls "an *other's* word". In this chapter I have been concerned with what Bakhtin calls "*my* word": the characteristics of the situation in which my co-researchers were writing which led them to make particular selections from their discoursal repertoire as they constructed a discoursal self in their writing, and how they felt about it. In Chapters 9 and 10 I move on to discuss what Bakhtin calls (perhaps naively) "a neutral word of a language, belonging to nobody": the 'abstract' discoursal resources my co-researchers were drawing on in order to construct what I am calling their 'discoursal self'.

Notes

1.   Tutors' comments in the margin are an extremely valuable source of data in studying academic literacy, particularly in order to identify the often unstated or unrecognized values, assumptions and expectations which tutors are assessing students' writing. This is becoming increasingly recognized as an object of study by researchers of academic literacy (see, for example Clark 1992, Lea and Street 1997, Street 1996, Joan Turner 1992, 1993a and b).

CHAPTER 9

The discoursal construction of academic community membership

Introduction

Writer identity is 'discoursally constructed' in two ways. In Chapter 8 I focused on one of these: the way in which a writer's discoursal self is shaped by the specific, situated 'discourse' into which s/he enters with one or more actual readers. In this chapter and the next I discuss the second, often neglected, way in which a writer's identity is 'discoursally constructed': by the subject positions — the abstract 'possibilities for selfhood' — which are socially available in the discourse types on which writers draw as they write. Although I exemplify discourse types and associated subject positions through extracts from my co-researchers' writing, my focus is no longer on these specific writers, but rather on the nature of the resources they are drawing on.

In this chapter and the next I examine how the discoursal characteristics of my co-researchers' writing are related to discourse conventions within the wider socio-cultural context in which they are writing, and how these conventions position the writers who draw on them. I do this by detailed analysis of extracts from the essays which I discussed with my co-researchers, as I described in Chapter 5. In this chapter I discuss some of the conventions which conspire to position the writers as members of the academic community: to write with an 'institutional voice'. In the following chapter I discuss variety within and around the edges of this community: the multiplicity of its voices, and of the voices my co-researchers drew into it.

As an introduction to the topic of this chapter, look at these two ways of starting a sentence:

a. *It is with great regret that I inform you that ..*

b. *Despite the feminist critiques of masculinist 'objectivity' v 'subjectivity'*

I think that it is intuitively obvious, even on the basis of such minimal samples, that the person writing these two sentences is participating in very different events with very different purposes in very different domains of social life. In this chapter I explore the bases for this intuition, identifying some of the linguistic characteristics of written academic discourse, as in (b), which set it apart from other written discourses. My aim is to show how people participating in the discourses of the academic community take on themselves interests, values, beliefs and knowledge-making practices which are specific to higher education as an institution.

This chapter develops and illustrates the discussion in Chapter 2 about a) the relationship between ideologies and discourses, and b) the relationship between conventions and actualities. Institutional interests, values and practices shape discourse conventions, and they construct the identities of the actual writers who draw on these discourse conventions. It is worth considering whether people are positioned directly by institutional values beliefs and relations of power, and their discourse choices and practices are an inevitable outcome of that positioning, or whether they take on the discourse conventions and practices of an institution and as a result unwittingly buy into its values, beliefs and relations of power. It seems reasonable to suppose that both these processes are happening simultaneously, and interacting with each other. For example, an individual might have an objective view of knowledge, and their discourses and practices would reflect that choice. Or s/he might take on the categorical, third person present tense discourse of objectivity without having chosen this particular view of knowledge. In this chapter I am not attempting to distinguish these processes from each other, but assuming that one or both might be responsible for the positioning processes which I am discussing.

In Chapter 10 I will be showing that the academic community is not homogeneous or monolithic: that there are multiple and competing discoursal resources which can be deployed even within the single genre of the academic essay, offering individuals a wide range of possible positions within the academic community. In this chapter, however, I focus on the commonalities which position all the writers I studied within a single discourse community. I first use extracts of approximately 50 words each from the mid-point of each of the eight essays. I discuss how the minute detail of grammatical and lexical choice positions writers as sharing the interests, values, beliefs and practices of the academic community. I then consider briefly how far larger scale characteristics of discourse organization position writers as members of the academic community, and what aspects of the values and practices of the community they are thereby identifying themselves with.

Institutional identity in lexical and grammatical choices

As the example with which I began this chapter illustrates, it is often possible to recognize a discourse type from a sample just a few words in length. In this section I show how this is possible, by taking very short extracts from eight writers' essays and identifying the linguistic features which characterize them as 'academic discourse'. I suggest that these discoursal characteristics are a function of the interests, values and practices of the academic community, and that by participating in these discourse practices the writers I studied are identifying with those interests, values and practices.

In order to show that all eight writers to some extent adopted an institutional voice, I have taken a more or less random extract from one essay by each of them (see Chapter 5 for a brief explanation of how these essays were chosen, and when and under what circumstances they were written). I found the exact mid-point of each essay and, starting with that sentence, selected approximately 50 words. Some extracts are slightly more or slightly less than 50 words long, as I did not break off in mid-sentence. I only shifted from the mid-point if it contained a substantial direct quotation from another writer. My reason for selecting such a short extract was that I wanted to show that just a few words can position a writer within the academic community. There are also some quite striking contrasts among the extracts, but in this chapter I will be concentrating on characteristics they share. The extracts are presented in Figure 9.1.

Extract 9.1 John — *Medical Ethics* (lines 205–214)

> The argument that this would be encouraging people to take drugs is strongly out wayed by the fact that if we don't give people the chance to come into the health service without chastising them in some way Aids will just carry on to spread. If health carers actually had to think about funding for supplying users with drugs as well as needles they might actually start to make some progress in the fight against Aids in the drug user community.

Extract 9.2 Rachel — *Social Work* (lines 103–109)

> Both of us coming to the session with different adgendas ment that we had to prioritize where we were to begin. (Adair 1976) Ms A's wanted help with coping with being on her own with the children. I had to work towards preventing the children from being involved in future acts of violence.

Extract 9.3 Angela — *Independent Studies: Mature women undergraduates* (lines 242–246)

> Despite the feminist critiques of masculinist 'objectivity' v 'subjectivity' in academic discourses, for the undergraduate woman student, her overall academic training, continues to 'teach' her to silence her subjective knowledge, and hide or disassociate herself from her multidimensional and knowledgeable 'I'.

Extract 9.4 Frances — *Anthropology* (lines 141–145)

> So while the "hau" embodies the ideas of return of something of the gift, Parry (Man. 461) points out that Hindu gifts, especially those to priests are completely different, they are permanently given. That gift is not a loan or a pledge. It extinguishes the donors rights in favour of the recipient.

Extract 9.5 Justin — *Aesthetics* (lines 78–84)

> Control of language cannot achieve control of our ideas because language is a device for expressing ideas to others and our minds have a different 'language' which involves a symbology that is too 'irrational' for convenient interpersonal communication.

Extract 9.6 Sarah — *Environmental Ethics* (lines 236–241)

> If the method for selecting the ideal geological criteria is based on compuer modelling the computer input must be reliable.
> These are just a few areas of concern I identified. But they serve to illustrate the fact that there are many areas of uncertainty to prevent a reasonable consequential analysis of this method for disposal of radioactive waste.

Extract 9.7 Donna — *Independent Studies: Black women in Western society* (lines 228–234)

> In fact, Alice Walker's 'Sophia' in the "Colour Purple" (1982), resorts to a similar form of impulse to protect her children with no thought for

herself. [*see also*: Braxton: 1990]. So Black women by depicting their experiences in creative forms are able to demonstrate their nurturing as mothers and challenge various forms of oppression used to control and pathologise their lives [Walker: 1984; Collins: 1990].

Extract 9.8 Valerie — *Communication Studies* (lines 162–165)

He saw in Manchester the possibility that the bourgeoisie would mend their ways: if they did not, they would (Engels predicted) be caught up in revolution.

For Engels, Manchester resindets (largely alienated from each other by class) maintained mutually exclusive sectors of existence. Politically and economically, they were poles apart.

Figure 9.1   A sample of approximately 50 words from an essay by each writer

In what follows I take five linguistic features, explain them in a way which will, I hope, make sense to a wider social scientific community, and apply them to the samples in Figure 9.1. My aim is to show that a linguistic analysis can support more intuitive analyses of the ways in which discourses construct identities. I discuss similarities among these eight extracts in terms of these five linguistic features:

1.   Clause structure
2.   Verbs (Process types)
3.   Nouns, nominalization and nominal groups
4.   Tense, mood and modality
5.   Lexis

The characteristics on which I focus are all, I suggest, associated with particular values, beliefs and practices which are part of the institutional identity of the academic community.

I originally examined these features using the analytical tool of Halliday's Functional Grammar (Halliday 1994). In the discussion which follows, however, I have not assumed that readers know his terminology or techniques. In some places I have replaced his terms with more widely known linguistic terminology, usually keeping the Hallidayan terminology in brackets; in others I have explained the significance of particular categories or distinctions. Readers who know Halliday's grammar will, I hope, be able to retrace my steps and retrieve the original Hallidayan concepts I used. While I have adopted Halliday's Functional Grammar as an analytical tool, I am not adopting along with it his view that particular contexts of situation determine or prescribe particular linguistic features. Rather, I want to show in this chapter that some discourse practices, with their associated values and beliefs, are extremely pervasive in the academic community, and in Chapter 10 that there is, nevertheless, variation in these practices, and that they are open to contestation and change.

1. Clause structure

Language varies in the way in which its clauses are structured. One aspect of this variation is how much information is packed into clauses: different types of clause structure make meaning in different ways. Halliday (1989) uses metaphors to compare meaning-making in spoken and written language:

> The complexity of the written language is its density of substance, solid like that of a diamond formed under pressure. By contrast, the complexity of spoken language is its intricacy of movement, liquid like that of a rapidly running river. (87)

These metaphors graphically represent differences which are connected with the social, physical and mental practices of meaning-making. I suggest that the academic community privileges solitary, premeditated, compacted, product-oriented meaning-making practices, that all my co-researchers to some extent entered into these practices, and that participating in them had consequences for their identities. The linguistic evidence on which this turns is the density of the clauses in their writing.

This aspect of clause structure can be analysed using the technique of calculating 'lexical density'. Lexical density is a measure first developed by Ure (1971) and subsequently refined by Halliday (1989). In this section I use Halliday's definition of lexical density as the average number of lexical words per clause. This involves counting (a) the number of 'lexical words' in an extract, and (b) the number of clauses in it, then dividing (a) by (b). An average of 5 or above counts as high lexical density, as one might expect to find in many academic and bureaucratic texts. An average of 2 or below counts as low lexical density, as one might expect to find in informal chat. There are difficulties in applying this measure, as the analyst has to decide what to count as 'a lexical word', and what not, and to decide what to count as a 'clause'. However, provided these decisions are made according to some clearly defined and consistent criteria, lexical density can provide a useful way of describing this particular aspect of clause structure.

The measure was originally intended by both Ure and Halliday as a way of making comparisons between texts of at least 100 words in length. It was designed to calculate an average, and it is not statistically meaningful for shorter stretches of text. However, I have found that calculating the lexical density of individual clauses and short stretches of text is extremely useful as a way of probing the fine detail of discoursal heterogeneity. I am not claiming any statistical significance for the lexical density figures I am presenting. Rather, I am using them to show how the writers I studied were all to some extent structuring their clauses according to the practices associated with academic and bureaucratic written discourse.

To calculate the lexical density of my samples I used Halliday's guidelines, as set out in *Spoken and Written Language* (1989). In deciding what to count as a clause, Halliday counts all what he calls paratactic (coordinate) and hypotactic (subordinate) clauses as separate clauses. In counting clauses, in any dubious case I veered on the side of recognizing more clauses rather than fewer. For example, in extract 9.7 I counted *by depicting their experiences in creative forms* as a separate, non-finite clause, although someone might argue that it is not a complete clause, and therefore should not be counted separately.

Halliday distinguishes embedded clauses from others. Embedded clauses are those which are an integral part of the meaning of another clause. For example, in Extract 9.8, the words

(i) *the bourgeoisie would mend their ways*

contain a finite verb — *would mend* — and so they are a clause. But the clause is part of the meaning of *the possibility* in the larger clause:

He saw in Manchester the possibility that the bourgeoisie would mend their ways

So (i) is an embedded clause, not an independent clause. Halliday does not count embedded clauses like (i) as separate clauses in calculations such as these. However he calls the 'that'-clauses of reported speech 'projected clauses', and he does count them as full clauses rather than embedded clauses in calculations of lexical density.

By the term 'lexical word', Halliday means a 'meaning-carrying word' such as *mend, Manchester*, as opposed to a grammatical or functional word such as *the, would*. Halliday does not give any firm guidelines on what to count as a lexical word. In cases of doubt, I have veered towards counting fewer lexical words rather than more. For example, in extract 9.1 I counted health *service* as a single lexical item, and in extract 9.7 I have counted *"Colour Purple"* as a single lexical item, although each of these appears orthographically as two lexical words. I also disregarded attributions in brackets, such as (Man. 461). As a result of these decisions, my calculations always underestimate the lexical density rather than vice versa. Figure 9.2 shows the number of clauses, the number of lexical words, and the resulting calculation of lexical density for each extract.

All these samples have a lexical density of more than 3 lexical words per clause. Five out of the eight extracts have a lexical density of over 7 lexical words per clause: indicating that these extracts are highly compacted with lexical content. The extract from John's writing is exceptionally lexically dense, compared both with the other extracts and with some other parts of his essay. This is accounted for by the fact that, in the first sentence, there are three long clauses embedded within the clause as a whole. This results from John's highly skilled use of the nouns 'argument' and 'fact', as discussed under the heading 'nouns, nominalizations and nominal groups' below.

The extracts are too short to base any generalizations on, but that is not my aim. My aim here is to show that, even in a short, randomly selected extract, it is possible to see that all eight writers have, by the time of writing in their second year at university, taken on a voice which positions them within the academic community — a voice which is shaped by academic community practices, and implicates its users in these practices. By writing in a way which is towards the top end of the lexical density scale, all the writers are to a greater or lesser extent engaging in a practice which is associated with the academic community. They are premeditating and slowly formulating ideas, compacting them into relatively lexically dense clauses, and committing them to paper. This is a practice associated with all continuous written prose, not just academic, but it is one of the practices which people are obliged to take on when they become members of the academic community, whether or not they have engaged in it previously. It involves sitting alone for extended periods and formulating ideas into words, without the sort of prompting and feedback from interlocutors which they would get in conversation. But for most of my co-researchers this was an extremely unfamiliar practice: one which jarred with their whole way of being before they decided to return to study in their mid-twenties or later. They were used to pursuing knowledge and understanding through interaction, in the style of the "rapidly running river". The practice of having to compact meanings into lexically dense written prose, in the style of the "diamond formed under pressure", was alien to all of them except Angela:

Extract and Writer	No. of lexical items (a)	No. of clauses (b)	lexical density (a/b)
9.1 John	36	3	12
9.2 Rachel	21	3	7
9.3 Angela	23	3	7.7
9.4 Frances	24	6	4
9.5 Justin	19	4	4.8
9.6 Sarah	28	4	7
9.7 Donna	29	4	7.3
9.8 Valerie	26	7	3.7

Figure 9.2   Lexical density of the extracts in Figure 9.1

a way of being and communicating which constituted a threat to their identity. Yet the evidence above shows that they were all accommodating to this practice, and renegotiating their identities in a quite fundamental, physical way in the process.

2.   Verbs (Process types)

Another significant characteristic of these extracts is that they are about relationships between abstract entities and about people's mental activities, rather than about human actions. This positions the writers as being concerned with ideas and mental activities: the business of the academic community. It also positions them as believing that intellectual activity involves explicit mention of relationships between ideas and of who thinks or writes what, rather than the understandings which are implicit in accounts of actual experiences. This characteristic shows itself in the choices of verbs.

The verbs in the main and subordinate clauses of the extracts are:

John	is outweighed by, had to think about, might start to make
Rachel	meant, wanted, had to work
Angela	continues to 'teach', silence, hide, disassociate
Frances	embodies, points out, are, are, is, extinguishes
Justin	cannot achieve, is, have, involves

Sarah   *is based on, must be, are, serve to illustrate*
Donna   *depicting, resorts to, are able to demonstrate, challenge,*
Valerie   *saw, did not (mend), would be caught, maintained, were*

Many of these are verbs which express states of affairs ('relational processes' as defined by Halliday 1994, pages 119–138). These are the verbs which I would categorize directly in this way:

> *meant, disassociate, are, is, embodies, ?cannot achieve, have, involves, is based on, must be, maintained, were*

One of these verbs, *is based*, can only function metaphorically as a relational process because it is in the passive with no mention of an actor: if it were active a human actor would have to be mentioned, and the literal, material meaning of the verb would be foregrounded (see Joan Turner 1993a and b for discussion of this type of metaphor for relationships between ideas in Western academic culture). I have included *cannot achieve* in this list because it carries a meaning of 'having' as well as the meaning of 'getting'. All of these are categorical in modality (that is, they are not accompanied by modal verbs such as 'might'), and all except *meant* and *maintained* are in the present tense. This preponderance of present tense, categorical 'relational process' verbs positions the writers as interested in general truths, states of affairs and relationships among entities (in most cases, abstract entities, as I show in the next section).

The verbs *points out that* in extract 9.4, and *saw* in extract 9.8 are both used for the intellectual activities of academics. The verb *meant* in extract 9.2 can also be interpreted as a mental process of cognition, although it doesn't say who was doing the meaning. Another mental process verb worth mentioning is *(I) identified* in extract 9.5. It is in an embedded clause, so not part of my original list, but it is further evidence of the focus on mental activity. These references to verbal and mental processes reinforce the dominant ideational meaning of these extracts as within the semantic field of knowledge-making, and position the writers as interested in what people think and what things mean.

There are several verbs which suggest action (what Halliday calls 'material processes'), but are not referring to the physical actions of people or objects. They are used metaphorically, with abstract actors and/or goals instead of human or concrete ones. These are the verbs and verb complexes which I categorize in this way:

John	is outweighed, might start to make,
Angela	continues to teach, silence, hide,
Frances	extinguishes,
Sarah	is based, serve to illustrate,
Donna	resorts to, are able to demonstrate, challenge

I have already discussed *is based* as a material process verb functioning metaphorically to represent a relational process. Two of these verbs, (a) *illustrate* and (b) *demonstrate*, belong to a group which is particularly hard to classify. They imply that a human is 'seeing' something, but that human is rarely mentioned. What is seen is usually a fact or state of affairs, expressed in some form of nominalization (see the next section).

Extremely few of the verbs in the main clauses of these extracts are concerned with the physical actions, mental processes or feelings of people in the world, rather than academics. The only ones I would classify in this way are:

John	if health carers actually had to think
Rachel	Ms A. wanted and I had to work
Donna	depicting their experiences in creative forms

Of these, *think* and *wanted* represent mental processes; *work* and *depicting* represent physical actions (material processes). Such verbs are greatly outnumbered by the other types.

Again, the extracts are too few and too short to draw any statistically valid conclusions about the way these writers use verbs, but that is not my intention. Rather, I want to show that, even in a randomly chosen tiny extract, their choice of verbs is identifying them with the academic community's interest in the relationships among entities and ideas, and in intellectual activity. Although these interests may be based in the lived reality of people's day-to-day lives and actions, they are abstracted away from them, and expressed in terms of states of affairs and universal truths.

3. Nouns, nominalization and nominal groups

The types of verbs identified in the previous section are even more interesting when considered in conjunction with their associated nouns. Here I list the nouns which act as 'head nouns': the main subject or object of the verbs identified above.

John	argument, fact, health carers, funding, they (= health carers), progress
Rachel	coming, Ms A., help, I, preventing
Angela	critiques, student, training, her, knowledge, herself, 'I'
Frances	"hau", ideas, Parry, gifts, they (= gifts), gift, loan, pledge, It (= gift), rights
Justin	control, control, language, device, minds, 'language', symbology
Sarah	method, modelling, input, areas, they (= areas), fact,
Donna	'Sophia', form, thought, women, depicting, nurturing, forms
Valerie	He, possibility, they (= the bourgeoisie), they, Engels, revolution, Engels, residents, sectors, they (= residents)

The majority of these nouns are inanimate. Of the animate nouns, all are human, but only Rachel's refer people in her experience: herself and Ms A., the woman she was writing about. A second group of human nouns consists of people the writers have met through reading: a published academic writer (*Parry*), a character in a published novel ('*Sophia*'), and a published political philosopher (*Engels*). A third group consists of types of people rather than actual people: health carers, student, women, people, the bourgeoisie, residents. (Angela's '*I*' is a concept, not a person.) This adds up to a preponderance of abstract nouns as participants, and where there are human participants, they are almost all writers, book characters and types of person rather than real individuals. This gives the writing (apart from Rachel's) its character of being about abstract, generalized content, one or more steps removed from actual events in people's lives.

Considering all the nouns in the extracts as a whole, not only those which are acting as subject or object of the main verbs, I note that many are nominalizations, general nouns and carrier nouns. All eight extracts contain nominalizations — 'nouny' ways of expressing an idea where a 'verby' way would be possible:

John	argument, chastising, funding, supplying, progress, fight, user
Rachel	coming, coping, being, preventing, being involved, acts, violence
Angela	critiques, training, knowledge
Frances	return, gift
Justin	control, expressing, communication

Sarah	*selecting, modelling, input, concern, uncertainty, analysis, disposal*
Donna	*impulse, thought, depicting, experiences, nurturing, oppression*
Valerie	*possibility, revolution, existence*

In addition, there are several general nouns — that is, nouns which have an extremely general meaning which is likely to need substantiation (Halliday and Hasan 1976: 274–275): *method, criteria, areas, device, sectors,* and carrier nouns — that is, nouns which refer to mental or verbal processes, and need propositions to substantiate them (as described in Ivanič 1991): *fact, ideas, ways, argument, experiences, possibility* (the last three are also nominalizations). Nominalization, general nouns and carrier nouns are all devices which allow the writer to cram ideas together, to pack them into each other:

> Nominality means freedom of movement. When processes, qualities, states, relations, or attributes are 'objectified', they take on potentialities otherwise reserved for persons and objects. (Halliday, 1967: 24)

> The quality of the noun is that it captures a concept on the wing and holds it still for inspection. (Bolinger, 1980: 27)

By using nouns of this sort, the writers identify themselves with those who engage in such knowledge-compacting, objectifying, and capturing practices.

Another discourse characteristic which is associated with knowledge-compacting is long nominal groups. Nominal groups are groups of words which function as subject or object, consisting of a 'head' noun (as discussed above) and all its associated words: the adjectives, prepositional phrases and, in some cases, embedded clauses which modify it. I have already discussed these in passing while discussing clause structure, as long nominal groups lead to long and often lexically dense clauses. Here I focus on the way in which all writers are compacting their meanings into nominal groups. Halliday's definition of a nominal group is the head noun and everything modifying it, including any embedded clauses. In these short data extracts, each writer uses between one and four nominal groups of six words or longer. Here is the longest nominal group (so defined) in each writer's extract, with the number of words in it and the proportion of lexical words to total words.

John's longest nominal group (29 words; 41% lexical words)

> the fact that if we don't give people the chance to come into the health service without chastising them in some way Aids will just carry on to spread.

Rachel's longest nominal group (11 words; 55% lexical words)

> preventing the children being involved in future acts of violence

Angela's longest nominal group (11 words; 64% lexical words)

> the feminist critiques of masculinist 'objectivity' v 'subjectivity' in academic discourses

Frances's longest nominal group (9 words; 44% lexical words)

> the ideas of return of something of the gift

Justin's longest nominal group (10 words; 50% lexical words)

> a symbology that is too 'irrational' for convenient interpersonal communication

Sarah's longest nominal group (23 words; 48% lexical words)

> the fact that there are many areas of uncertainty to prevent a reasonable consequential analysis of this method for disposal of radioactive waste

Donna's longest nominal group (11 words; 64% lexical words)

> various forms of oppression used to control and pathologise their lives

Valerie's longest nominal group (9 words; 44% lexical words)

> the possibility that the bourgeoisie would mend their ways

The writers' longest nominal groups vary from 9 to 29 words in length, ranging from 64% to 41% lexical words. Most of these longest nominal groups include embedded clauses, which increase the length but reduce the lexical density. This is particularly true of the sample nominal groups from John's, Sarah's and Valerie's writing. Long nominal groups, embedded clauses, and a high proportion of lexical words characterize language in which ideas are compacted, often as a result of slow, premeditated composition practices. These characteristics position the writers among those familiar with written text, and used to compacting ideas, rather than stringing them out more loosely. These practices characterize academic discourse, although they are not exclusive to it. The fact that all eight of my co-researchers are, to some extent, engaging in these phsical and mental practices positions them as apprentices to, if not members of the academic community. The sample nominal groups from Angela's and Donna's writing having a much higher proportion of lexical words than the others, positioning them as more comfortable with the practice of compacting ideas in writing: this perhaps reflects the fact that they are the most confident writers of my eight co-researchers, although in the same year of study as the others.

4. *Tense, Mood and Modality*

The characteristics of the verbs and nouns in the extracts are complemented by patterns of tense, mood and modality. The tenses of all the verbs in Angela's, Frances's, Sarah's, Justin's and Donna's extracts are present and so is the main verb of the first, long clause in John's extract. These present tenses function to express timeless truths, and position their writers as interested in such truths.

All the extracts are in exclusively declarative mood. They contain no interrogatives or imperatives. This positions the writers as presenters of information, attempting to influence their interlocutors' knowledge and beliefs, rather than seeking for information or attempting to influence their interlocutors' actions. However, this is not representative of the essays as a whole: they contain 26 questions in total, (but no imperatives); I discuss this further as an aspect of local discourse organization later in this chapter.

As I mentioned when discussing verbs above, the modality in the extracts is predominantly categorical. The following are the only modalized verbs in the extracts:

John	*would be encouraging, might actually start to make some progress*
Rachel	*had to prioritize, had to work*
Justin	*cannot achieve*
Sarah	*must be reliable*
Donna	*are able to demonstrate*
Valerie	*would mend their ways, would be caught up*

Valerie's hypothetical modals are predicted by Engels, not her, and John's *would be encouraging* is not his own voice, but that of the unnamed person or people who put forward this argument. Three others are associated with a categorical stance: *cannot, are able to* and *must be*. John's *might* is the only modal representing the writer's own tentativeness, suggesting uncertainty and speculation rather than being in control of facts and truths. I conclude that, in these extracts at least, the patterns of modality are positioning the writers as relatively certain and knowledgeable. I suggest that this is a fairly pervasive characteristic of members of the academic community, or at any rate a characteristic which new members of the community think they should be displaying. This is often, however, a site of misunderstanding between students and tutors, since tutors often expect more provisionality in student writing, but do not make this requirement explicit.

5. Lexis

My co-researchers had a strong feeling that belonging to the academic community was a question of using particular words. They felt that becoming a member of the community involved acquiring vocabulary and 'dressing their ideas up' in words which they may not have used before. As I discussed in Chapter 8, they felt ambivalent about this, unsure whether the new words are actually tools for intellectual activity which would be impossible without them, or an exclusive veneer to make ideas seem grand when they could just as easily have been expressed in more familiar words.

Lexis which identifies language with the academic community includes Graeco-Latin words (Corson 1985), certain prepositions and conjunctives (Hartnett 1986), nominalizations and carrier nouns, discussed already, and lexical items (often more than a single word) which are used metaphorically to convey abstract meanings, some of which have been discussed in the section on verbs (process types). The writers vary in the extent to which they use lexis which is characteristic of the academic community. Here are lexical items, most of them Graeco-Latin words, in the extracts which, I suggest, contribute towards positioning their users as members of the academic community.

John: *argument, fact, chastising, progress*
Rachel: *session, agendas, prioritize, preventing, acts, violence*
Angela: *Despite, feminist, critiques, masculinist, objectivity, v, subjectivity, academic, discourses, subjective, disassociate, multidimensional, knowledgeable*
Frances: *embodies, permanently, extinguishes, recipient*
Justin: *device, symbology, irrational, interpersonal, communication*

Sarah: *selecting, ideal, geological, criteria, identified, illustrate, fact, areas, uncertainty, reasonable, consequentialist, analysis, disposal*

Donna: *resorts to, impulse, depicting, experiences, creative, demonstrate, nurturing, challenge, oppression, pathologise*

Valerie: *possibility, bourgeoisie, predicted, revolution, alienated, mutually, exclusive, sectors, existence, politically, economically*

Some of these are technical in the sense that they belong to particular disciplines, for example *masculinist, discourses, consequential, symbology, pathologise* (as I discuss further in Chapter 10). The majority, however, are the more general vocabulary of the academic community, or somewhat more specifically, of the social sciences. Most have been discussed in previous sections. It is worth summarizing, however, the way in which lexis of this sort positions its users, bringing together some observations across word classes.

Firstly, I suggest that using words of this sort positions writers as being involved with particular intellectual processes. Many of the words are associated with argumentation: *argument, despite, critiques, v, ideal, analysis, demonstrate, possibility*. Others are associated with defining, evaluating and/or classifying: *feminist, masculinist, subjective, multidimensional, criteria, reasonable, irrational, sectors*. Others are associated with abstracting and generalizing: *fact, progress, violence, disposal, communication, experiences, oppression*.

Secondly, when writers use words of this sort they convey an impression that they know what they mean, and that they belong to the community of those who use them comfortably. I suggest that people often feel comfortable with, or can give the impression of feeling comfortable with words in writing which they would hesitate and stumble over when talking. In fact several of my co-researchers stumbled when reading parts of their writing out loud, although they gave the impression of having written them fluently. Good examples of words from the extracts which, I suggest, not everyone would know the meaning of or feel comfortable to speak aloud are *prioritize, subjectivity, recipient, criteria, interpersonal, oppression, bourgeoisie*. By using these a person can get a sense of being an insider to 'the long word club', but at the same time contribute to excluding others (Gardener 1992).

I am not suggesting that using any one of these, on its own, positions the writer as a member of the academic community, nor that it would be impossible to find these lexical items in other discourses. Rather, it is the density of such lexis which positions these writers as members of the academic commun-

ity. Most of these lexical items could be found in other discourses too: as I
have said before, discourses are not hermetically sealed, but leak into each
other. A discourse which uses any of these lexical items shares something with
academic discourse, and vice versa. For instance, the word *challenge* also
belongs to media discourses of politics and of sports such as tennis and
football. When somebody uses it in any of these settings they invoke for the
readers/ hearers a little of the other discourses too. It is a particular case of a
word being 'populated with other people's intentions', to adopt Bakhtin's way
of putting it. In using such a word the writer/ speaker takes for herself as a part
of her identity the power of movement between the various discourses
invoked. Donna, by using the word *challenge*, projects an image of herself not
only as a member of the academic discourse community but also as someone
familiar with its many resonances.

6. *Other*

These extracts also contain other lexico-syntactic characteristics which are
associated with academic community discourse practices, and position their
users as participants in those practices. Angela, Frances and Justin use quotation marks to draw attention to particular lexical items. This practice is
restricted to academic discourse and a few other types of writing where self-
consciousness about language is valued. The extracts written by Rachel,
Frances and Donna include citation of published authors. This practice is
highly specific to academic discourse, associated with valuing accumulated
knowledge and wisdom. Those writers who include attribution to sources in
their writing are positioning themselves as sharing this value. However it is not
an essential defining feature of academic discourse, and indeed it is a practice
contested by some members of the community, as I discuss in Chapter 10.

   There are no second person pronouns, and few first person pronouns in
the extracts. Rachel and Sarah use 'I', Rachel to describe her own actions as an
apprentice social worker: *I had to work towards preventing*, Sarah to write
about her own intellectual activity: *I identified*. Three writers use first person
plural pronouns and determiners: Rachel to refer specifically to herself and Ms
A.; John and Justin to refer to people in general. The fact that first person
pronouns and determiners are rare is, I suggest, associated with the traditional
belief that intellectual work is an impersonal activity. This avoidance of the
first person positions the writers (other than Rachel) as having a relatively
objective view of knowledge-making and not being personally involved either

in what they are writing about or in their relationship with their readers. This is particularly noticeable in Angela's and Donna's writing where the topics they are writing about directly include their own experience. I expand on the ways in which the eight writers use first and second person pronouns and determiners throughout their essays in section 10, when discussing alternative ideologies of knowledge-making.

Conclusion to this section

It seems to me significant that, by analyzing small samples, I am able to demonstrate these points, suggesting that it might be possible to take *any* extract of 50 words from any of the writers, and show them to be positioned as members of the academic community by some aspects it. A cursory analysis of the whole essays shows this to be true of all but Rachel. There are parts of her essay longer than 50 words (for example, lines 1–51, 163–172) which, if extracted from the whole, might not be immediately identified as positioning her within the academic community. I conclude that all these writers are positioned within the academic discourse community by lexico-grammatical choices such as the ones detailed above in some parts of their essays, but not homogeneously throughout. Further, I suggest that the lexico-grammatical conventions are themselves associated with particular interests, values, beliefs, and practices, although I am only able to use my intuitions to suggest these associations. My claim in relation to writing and identity is that the writers are, by appropriating the conventions, willingly or unintentionally becoming party to these interests, values, beliefs and practices.

Finally, although I am suggesting that all eight writers are positioned as members of the academic community by these short extracts, their discourse, and hence the way they are positioned is not uniform. For example, John, while writing lexically dense clauses with long nominal groups containing nominalizations and carrier nouns, does not use a high proportion of Graeco-Latin lexis and he employs a range of types of modality, not restricted to categorical. Angela, by contrast, identifies herself within the academic community by all the criteria mentioned here, except for her resistance to the use of citation in this extract and in her whole essay. Frances identifies herself as writing within the academic community by using a citation, and by the metaphorical use of material processes. However, her clauses are not lexically dense, her nominal groups are not long and she does not use a lot of typically academic lexis in this extract. These differences in discoursal characteristics carry with them consequences for exactly which interests, values, beliefs and practices they construct for the writers, as discussed throughout this section. Some of the reasons for these differences are differences in disciplines, differences in what I am calling ideologies of knowledge-making, differences in the nature of the task, differences in writing practices and experience, as I discuss Chapter 10, and differences in access to discourses, as I discussed in Chapter 8.

Discourse organization as an aspect of the institutional voice

By 'discourse organization' I mean characteristics of the texts which involve analysis of units larger than the clause (Halliday's 'textual function' of language). In talking of 'organization' rather than 'structure' I am following Hoey (1983, 1986, 1988). He identifies patterns of clause relations in texts which are evidence that language users do organize language above the level of the clause, but he is sceptical about attempts to specify predictable 'structures' for texts, as linguists do for clauses. In this section I am proposing that the way in which the writers chose to organize their meanings above clause level is a function of the interests, values, beliefs and practices of the institution of higher education. I look briefly at the eight essays from the point of view of their discourse organization, both relatively global organization of the whole essay and relatively local organization of relations among clauses and sentences. Doing this requires me to break down the traditional linguistic distinction between 'form' and 'content' even more than in discussing lexico-grammatical features. In order to comment on the organization of text, it is necessary to specify what is written about in what order, rather than talking in abstract terms about categories such as 'verbs' and 'subjects'. Here, even more than when discussing features of the clause, 'discourse' is a matter of both the form and the content of language (This is one of the five principles of a socio-cognitive theory of genre articulated by Berkenkotter and Huckin 1995: 4).

Global discourse organization

All the essays were recognizable as academic essays by a combination of characteristics of their title, layout, length, and/or by having a particular form of introduction, middle and conclusion. All began with a title and/or a statement of the task assigned and range in length from six to seventeen pages.

These characteristics alone do not position the writers within the academic community, but they contribute towards that positioning. For Rachel, for example, who had not written more than a brief postcard before the age of 24, identifying with these practices was a big step. By organizing their work in this way the writers positioned themselves as sharing the goals of other members of the academic community: goals of setting themselves an intellectual project in their title, in their assignment specification and/or in their introduction, addressing it through extended exposition and argument in middle sections which are organized and signposted to a greater or lesser degree, and reaching closure on the task at the end. The only essay to differ in this respect is Rachel's: it begins as a professional social work report (as described in Chapter 6), but introduces elements of the academic essay is it progresses.

Local discourse organization

It is the exact elements, or 'moves' (as Swales, 1990, calls them), which make an introduction characteristic of academic discourse, rather than the mere existence of an introduction. In this section I mention briefly some of the characteristics of the more local relationships between clauses and sentences which identify them as academic discourse. Each of the issues I mention here could have a whole book devoted to it. I merely want to indicate the range of aspects of local discourse organization which can be identified with the aims and activities of the academic community, and show that, by organizing their discourse in this way, the writers were affiliating themselves with these aims and activities.

Most of the writers indicated clearly how the middles of their essays are divided into sub-topics, either by headings (Rachel, Angela and Sarah) or by signposts of various sorts (John, Justin and Valerie). Rachel only used headings within the first third of her essay: _Response to 2nd referal_ and _Child care needs._ However, from then on she had no further headings, as if the headings belong to the social-work report part of the essay, but not to the academic discussion. Apart from Rachel's, paragraphs were not related chronologically, but by moving from one topic to another, and/or according to the development of an argument. In my view this characteristic positions the writers as interested in abstract issues and in sustaining arguments: the practices of the academic community.

Many parts of the essays are organized according to the problem-solution pattern discussed by Hoey (1983 and elsewhere). One way in which this manifests itself is in the use of a question and answer format. There are 27 questions in the eight essays as a whole. Some of these are expressed as indirect questions and all are rhetorical in the sense that they are subsequently answered by the writer. Here is an example.

Extract 9.9 John — *Medical Ethics* (lines 312–319)

> For example, does, the prostitute (male or female) who has V.D not get treatment because they may also have the HIV infection. As soon as the health carer [takes] this step in allowing people to say wether they do or do not want to look after someone this means that the obligation of treating all people is immediately removed.

In addition John's assignment was presented in the form of two questions: *'Why is Aids seen as an illness presenting problems for health care practitioners? To what extent is this belief justified?'*, and he opens his essay with the words:

Extract 9.10 John — *Medical Ethics* (lines 1–2)

> I will answer this question by splitting the essay into four sections.

The preponderance of declaratives with a smattering of interrogatives seems to me to be a function of the activity of the academic community: setting out to make statements which are explicitly or implicitly presented as extended answers to questions. This mood pattern positions the writers as participating in these question-answering, problem-solving practices, which are very different from, say, the short question-and-answer sequences of secondary school classrooms.

Most of the middle sections of the essays are devoted to the presentation of an 'argument': that is, the presentation of the writer's position on a topic, or of the writer's proposed 'solution' to a 'problem'. There is a growing body of theory and research about argument in academic writing (see, for example, Mitchell 1994 a and b, Andrews 1995, contributions to Costello and Mitchell (eds.) 1995), and a complete analysis of the nature of argument in these essays would be long and complex. Here I can do no more than mention the fact that these writers all engaged in a variety of argumentation strategies. These involve relating one assertion to the next in non-chronological ways which build up to a connected whole. Here are two examples:

a.   general or broad statement followed by elaboration of detail

Extract 9.11 Valerie — *Communication Studies* (lines 108–114)
> Both Engels and Moses were agents in the shaping and reshaping of cities. Engels was the overseas visitor (to Manchester) with a bourgeois background, Moses the New York practitioner under fierce scrutiny from Berman, the author who had personal experience of the Bronx.

In Extract 9.11, the first sentence makes a generalization and the second (containing two main clauses separated by a comma) explains in detail how the generalization is true of each individual.

b.   cause and effect

Extract 9.12 Sarah — *Environmental Ethics* (lines 137–143)
> So that although it is a fact that artificially produced radiation constitutes a very small proportion of all radiation in the atmosphere, any additional amount, however small, could alter a delicate balance in nature which has evolved between organisms and naturally occurring radiation over vast amounts of time. The task of eliminating the risk of radioactive waste would, therefore, be extremely complex.

In this extract the long first sentence is presented as a cause of the fact, mentioned in the second sentence, that the task would be extremely complex.

In developing an argument, a writer has to decide what needs defining, explaining, elaborating or supporting, how, and what doesn't need it. The need to do this is, I suggest, common to the 'umbrella' academic discourse I have been discussing in this chapter. But what needs to be stated explicitly and what can be left implicit, what sort of evidence or authority can and should be called upon and in what circumstances differs quite significantly from subject area to subject area, as I discuss in the next chapter (see also Street 1996), and how much elaboration is required differs from culture to culture (see Turner and Hiragara 1996). Engaging in these decisions progressively entrenches people in their membership of the academic discourse community. Students have to become increasingly adept at judging what these decisions entail, and learn how to respond differently from one course to another.

Extended writing also requires the writer to maintain coherence across stretches of texts by deploying cohesive devices, manipulating given and new information into the best positions in clauses, and packing information which

has already been spelt out in detail earlier into nouns when it is needed later
(see Halliday 1988). The need to do this is, I suggest, common to most if not
all academic discourses. But again, exactly how to do it differs from subject
area to subject area. Here is an extract which allows me to illustrate these
aspects of discourse organization.

Extract 9.13 Frances — *Anthropology* (lines 54–62)

> Thus the social and economic needs of both sides are met and peace
> maintained. Continuation is assured because the visitors leave with
> kula gifts which they must return at a later stage both for the continu-
> ation of the symbolic relationship and the opportunity to continue the
> gimwali.

> The pressure to maintain reciprocity comes from the tension between
> prestige, solidarity, and materiality which all parties want from the
> system.

The last sentence in this extract was, in Frances's mind, a pivot for her whole
argument. In order for the full force of her claim to be comprehended, she
needed the reader to be able to treat *The pressure to maintain reciprocity* as
'Given' — as already established in the previous paragraph. She assumed that
her reader, as an anthropologist, would infer the connection between what she
had written in the previous paragraph and the words *maintain reciprocity* in
this key sentence. She could therefore bundle the idea into an abstract noun
phrase, and introduce it with the cohesive definite article *The* to indicate that
it is something the reader should already know about. She could then place it
at the beginning of the sentence as a launching-pad for her main claim, that it
comes from the tension between prestige, solidarity and materiality.

However, not being an anthropologist, I missed the significance of this
crucial sentence the first time I read it. I did not see the connection between
The pressure to maintain reciprocity and the details in the previous paragraph. The coherence depended on the writer's and the reader's identities as
anthropologists, not on some neutral linguistic features. This example shows
the complexity of what student writers have to learn to do in order to maintain coherence in local discourse organization, and how easy it can be for
them to slip up. Such an example shows that it is impossible to separate form
and content, and highlights the inadequacy of generalized prescriptions about
the form of academic writing. To make decisions about how to maintain
coherence the writer has to know a great deal about the content of the subject
area, and has to take on the perspective of a member not just of the academic

community, but of a particular sub-community within it. Attempting to do so is an act of identification, one which is so intellectually demanding that it may be very elusive.

Conclusion to this chapter

In this chapter I have discussed discourse characteristics in the eight writers' essays which lead me to identify them as academic discourse, and to see the writers positioned within the academic community, more specifically within the social science sub-community. I first showed these identification processes in relation to linguistic choices within clauses in short, randomly chosen extracts from my co-researchers' essays, and the types of positioning associated with them. I then discussed how similar identification processes were at work in local discourse organization beyond the confines of clauses, showing that, while membership of the academic community as a whole involves participating in such discourse practices as problem-solving, generalization, argumentation, elaboration and the maintenance of coherence, the exact ways of doing this are specific to different fields of study, as I discuss in Chapter 10.

In terms of the dimensions of writer identity which I introduced in Chapter 1, I am claiming that one aspect of each of these writers' 'discoursal self' was academic community membership. By participating in these particular discourse practices, the writers took on the *persona* of a member of the academic community. I have also suggested that these discourse practices are associated with particular interests, goals, values, beliefs and knowledge-making practices which are common to members of the academic community. These include beliefs concerning what Cherry (1988) would call *ethos*: beliefs about what constitutes a 'good person', such as being knowledgeable, being organized, having a position, and being able to talk in abstract, general terms. When writers participate in the discourse practices I have identified in this chapter they are thereby becoming party to the interests, goals, values, beliefs and knowledge-making practices of the academic community.

However, academic discourse is not monolithic. The next chapter is about variation and contestation within academic discourse, showing that the eight writers were positioned differently within and beyond the academic community: both differently from each other, and differently by different parts of their essays.

CHAPTER 10

Multiple possibilities for self-hood in the academic discourse community

Introduction

As I said at the end of the last chapter, academic discourse is not monolithic. Rather, the academic order of discourse represents a site of struggle in terms of ideologies of knowledge-making and relations of power within the academic community. There are many academic discourses, some of them co-existing relatively comfortably, some of the competing for dominance. My eight co-researchers positioned themselves differently from each other, and each of them constructed multiple, sometimes conflicting, subjectivities in their writing through the way they drew on these discourses and the subject positions inscribed in them. I have already illustrated the multiple voices of an individual writer, shaped by her personal history of opportunities, constraints and allegiances, through the case-study of Rachel in Chapter 6. In this chapter I provide an overview of the dimensions on which writers can differ while still positioned within the academic community: the subtle differences between discourses available within it. My concern here is primarily with multiplicity in the available discoursal resources for self-representation, although by illustrating these with examples from my co-researchers' writing, I also show how individual writers are multiply positioned by their creative recombinations of these resources.

In contrast to Chapter 9, I am not suggesting that the extracts discussed in this chapter are representative of the essays as a whole. On the contrary, in many cases I am suggesting that a few words — perhaps only part of an extract — position the writer momentarily in a specific way. Snatches of different discourses can be patched together, and this is what leads to the shifts and contradictions in the discoursal self which I discussed in Chapter 8.

I first discuss variation within academic discourse of three sorts: variation by discipline, department, course, and/or tutor, variation by role within the academic community, and variation by ideological stance towards the nature of academic endeavour. I then discuss the way in which writers draw on discourse conventions which are not exclusive to the academic community: public domain discourses, more conversational discourse types, and discourse characteristics associated with literary and journalistic writing.

Aspects of identity related to fields of study

People writing within the academic community are positioned by their discourse choices as members of, or as familiar with one or more particular disciplines, departments and/or courses. I prefer to use the more fuzzy term 'fields of study' rather than the term 'disciplines' because the characteristics I am discussing may not be generalizable beyond my co-researcher's particular courses, departments and experiences, and because in many institutions of higher education the 'discipline' might not be the salient unit within which writing is defined. Particular fields of study have particular 'knowledge-making principles': particular objects of study, bodies of knowledge, values, beliefs and practices.

There is no typology of discipline-specific discourse characteristics against which to match data such as mine. Several researchers have studied academic discourse from the point of view of its discipline-specific characteristics, but this research has been conducted, like mine, on small samples of data. These studies tell us something about the particular articles they studied, but cannot be taken as representative of disciplines as a whole. Bazerman (1981), Lovejoy (1991) and Macdonald (1992) each compared three specific articles from different disciplines. Young (1990) compared selections from lectures and textbooks from engineering, sociology and economics. Others took small samples from particular fields: Faigley and Hansen (1985) and Hansen (1988) — the social sciences; Macdonald (1989) and Fahnestock and Secor (1991) — literary criticism; Vande Kopple (1992) — scientific writing; Myers (for example, 1985, 1989, 1990) — writing in biology; contributors to Bazerman and Paradis (eds.) (1991), Jolliffe (ed.) (1988) and Nash (ed.) (1990) — various. Many of these researchers focused on a single linguistic aspect of their data; so, for example, we know from Vande Kopple's study something about the characteristics of noun phrases in scientific writing, but not about other aspects of scientific writing.

As I said in Chapter 2, it is theoretically unsound to attempt to specify such a typology, since discourses and genres are always open to contestation and change, and in reality all samples of discourse are relatively heterogeneous, recombining generic and discoursal resources creatively, rather than simply adhering to a template. However, the paradox of this more dynamic, post-modern view of genre is that it is not possible to talk about hybridity without being able to describe the resources which are creatively recombined. In what follows I do not claim that certain characteristics are discipline-specific in any fixed way, but suggest that particular discourse characteristics might be shaped by particular aspects of particular fields of study, and so position the writers as participating in the interests, values, beliefs and practices of that field of study.

Taking the view that there is no typology of discourse types means that it is, in theory, impossible to give examples of them. The only way of talking about 'abstract' discourse types is to infer their characteristics from the interdiscursive evidence of them in samples of actual language in use. This is the approach I take in this chapter. While my aim is to indicate the multiplicity of available discoursal resources, I am only able to do so through a discussion of how my co-researchers drew on them in these specific instances: these are 'telling cases', if not 'representative' ones. This case study approach has the advantage that it grounds the discussion of multiplicity in the experience of actual people writing actual essays, but it cannot claim to be generalizable.

In addition to there being no established typology of discipline-specific discourse characteristics, there is no tried and tested range of analytic tools for this purpose. However, the sociologists of scientific knowledge, linguists, educationists and rhetoricians mentioned above, along with some others, have suggested several features which are particularly worth attending to, providing a preliminary set of analytic tools for such work. Bazerman (1981) suggested paying attention to the author's perceptions of the object under study, the literature of the field, the audience, and the author's *persona*. Swales (1990) and others following his lead have identified discipline-specific variations in the move structure of introductions in professional research articles. Barnes (1969) pointed out the way in which lexis distinguished subjects across the secondary curriculum. More recently researchers have been concerned to develop analytic tools for comparing syntactic characteristics of writing in different disciplines. Lovejoy (1991) compared cohesion and information strategies in the introductory section of one scholarly article from each of three disciplines. Macdonald (1992) used a seven-way distinction to classify types of head noun acting as grammatical subject. Vande Kopple, as already mentioned, focused on noun phrases. Young's study was closest to mine in that she used Halliday's Functional Grammar as her analytic tool. The analytic tools these researchers used seem to me to be more useful than the typologies or templates which are implicit in their findings — comforting as these might seem in the pipe-dreams of the researcher!

Macdonald (1992 and 1994) makes the crucial point that researchers can and should make connections between the linguistic characteristics which distinguish disciplines and the epistemology of the discipline: what she calls its 'knowledge-making principles' (1992: 535). Macdonald writes:

> [My study] suggests that text-level differences can be found among the disciplines in relations between the particular and the abstract and in whether scholarly work is treated as cumulative. If disciplinary sub-fields differ in their assumptions about whether and how knowledge can be built within a field and whether they have common problems to address and common contributions to refer to, we should expect to find disciplinary differences relevant to knowledge making at both the sentence level and the text level. Our methods of analyzing sentence-level practices need to be adapted to the kinds of differences we have reason to believe may be involved in knowledge making. (1992: 535)

She says that assumptions about "whether and how knowledge can be built" include assumptions about what sorts of things count as objects of study, as claims, grounds (evidence) and warrants; what has to be elaborated and what can be taken for granted as shared knowledge; what has to be substantiated and how — an elaboration of the ideational aspects of Bazerman's (1981) list. It seems to me that what she says makes the connection between the ethnographic approaches of sociologists of scientific knowledge and more linguistic approaches. MacDonald is saying that we should be trying to interpret textual detail in terms of the interests, values, beliefs and practices which shape it. In terms of Fairclough's diagram (my Figure 2.1) we should be seeing how layers 2 and 3 shape layer 1. Sociologists of scientific knowledge go straight for layers 2 and 3; linguists focus on layer 1.

Myers (1990), MacDonald (1994) and Berkenkotter and Huckin (1995) contribute to this project by theorizing and providing detailed case-studies of the historical development, objects of study, epistemologies, goals, methodologies, norms, practices, values and beliefs of academic disciplines, and of the processes of acculturation into them. I am attempting to build on this work by making connections between specific lexico-syntactic features and the 'knowl-edge-making principles' of different fields of study in order to suggest that these discourse characteristics have consequences for the identity of writers who adopt them.

In the analysis on which this chapter is based I have concentrated mainly on lexico-syntactic features at clause level, partly to avoid the need to provide extended extracts by way of illustration, and partly because I wanted to point out the significant differences which can be observed even within the structure of clauses. However, fields of study differ in respect of many factors which have consequences for identity spanning both content and form above the level of the clause, factors such as types of generalization, types of abstraction, modes of argumentation, the nature of explanation, the extent and nature of elaboration, the nature of data, the relationship between theory and data, the role of theory in argument. Recent research on rhetoric and literacy (for example, Mitchell 1994a, Street 1996, Lea and Street 1996a and b, 1997) points to these sorts of differences between fields of study, and the task of analyzing such factors systematically poses a challenging research agenda for linguists (a point I take up in Chapter 11).

In the following three sub-sections I take three fields of study which were represented in my co-researchers' writing, identify lexico-syntactic differences among them, and discuss how they position their writers differently within the academic community. I have chosen three sharply contrasting fields of study: sociology, literary and related studies, and natural sciences because my main purpose is to illustrate the point that the discourses associated with different fields of study position those who participate in them differently in terms of their objects of study, their views of knowledge and knowledge-making practices.

Sociology

Parts of John's, Angela's, Donna's and Valerie's essays position them as 'sociologists' — as people who have read sociology books, and who identify in some way with the interests, values, beliefs and practices of sociologists. Here are two extracts from the writing of each which seem to be positioning their writers in this way.

Extract 10.1 John — *Medical Ethics* (lines 24–25)

> One, the virus is transmitted mainly (at the moment) by activity that is seen to deviate from a societal norm.

Extract 10.2 John — *Medical Ethics* (lines 109–111)

This section of the essay examine how the health care practitioner/ N.H.S. will deal with the allocation of resources.

Extract 10.3 Angela — *Independent Studies* (lines 80–82)

All the women in this study are white, English women whose ages range from 26 to 34. Most of us are from a variety of working class backgrounds and have a variety of former occupations and educational experiences.

Extract 10.4 Angela — *Independent Studies* (lines 376–384)

I think also it has been made clear from the responses of the women, that these are not simply individual problems and contradictions, but problem that occur commonly enough, to view them as fundamentally related to institutional and relational practises, and the ideology of British higher education. These commonly experienced contradictions and problems I think, arise from two main premises. (1) the hierarchical definition, nature and objectification and reification of academic 'knowledge' within and outside the institution; and (2) the hierarchical nature of relations between academic teaching staff and students.

Extract 10.5 Donna — *Independent Studies* (lines 134–138)

In Western society the ideology of motherhood is centred on the notion of women remaining in the private sphere. However, Black women, due to socio-economic factors and racism are unable to remain purely in the realms of the domestic/private sphere [Bryan et al: 1985; Davis: 1990].

Extract 10.6 Donna — *Independent Studies* (lines 146–154)

In addition, studies carried out in the past, like the '1965 Moynihan Report' has treated Black motherhood as a pathological, and inferior, which perpetuates negative perceptions held about 'Black motherhood' [Phoenix: 1988; Collins: 1990]. Moynihan (1965), quotes high rates of divorce, single mothers, illegitimate births, and female-headed units to substantiate his claims that Black families operate through a matriarchal system that has caused the instability of the Black family [Davis: 1982; Zhana: 1988; Collins: 1990].

Extract 10.7 Valerie — *Communication Studies* (lines 4–8)

> The second part examines notions of the city, and modernity, by contrasting Engel's view of Manchester in the mid C19 with Moses's work in New York over a period of one hundred years later.

Extract 10.8 Valerie — *Communication Studies* (lines 137–145)

> Engels described Manchester as would a man burdened with a dialectic and struggling for an ideology. In Manchester Engels saw serious exploitation of the working class: squalid industrial conditions and squalid housing. In fact he saw a sharp and distinctive devide between the working class quarters and the upper classes preserve.

I suggest that these extracts, in addition to positioning their writers as members of the academic community in ways which I identified in Chapter 9, position them as involved in the sorts of intellectual projects which are typical of sociologists, and that these intellectual projects shape the lexico-syntactic characteristics of their writing.

Part of John's intellectual project, as put forward in Extract 10.2, is to examine how a particular social group (health care practitioners) will deal with a particular socio-economic matter (the allocation of resources). Angela's intellectual project is to collect data from a particular social group (described in Extract 10.3), and to discuss their experience in terms of sociological concepts (as in Extract 10.4). Donna's intellectual project is to discuss how a particular social group, Black women, are represented in literature. Part of this project is sociological: identifying how the group is sociologically defined, as she does in examples 10.5 and 10.6. Part of Valerie's intellectual project, as described in Extract 10.7, is different in that its defining concept is not a social group, but a socio-cultural artefact: the city. The project is to identify what sorts of social theories are represented by different notions of 'the city'. By undertaking these projects, as a part or the whole of the function of their essays, these writers are positioned within a broadly defined community of sociologists: those interested in social groups and in developing theories of culture and social relations.

These intellectual projects, I suggest, shape the lexico-syntactic characteristics of the discourse of these extracts, as summarized in Figure 10.1. The aspects of the extracts picked out here are more specific than 'academic discourse', and characterize a more specialized discourse which positions its users as interested in the objects of study and knowledge-making activities of sociologists.

Lexico-syntactic characteristics of sociological discourse	Examples in Extracts 10.1–10.8
a. (i) social policy-makers and (ii) social theorists participate in mental and verbal processes	*(i)* Moynihan quotes *(ii)* Engels saw
b. referring to social groups	the health care practitioner/N.H.S., academic teaching staff, students, Black women, single mothers, female-headed units, Black families, the working class, the upper classes
c. referring to social processes, states and relationships	working class backgrounds, racism, the realms of the domestic/private sphere, Black motherhood, inferior, divorce, instability, exploitation, industrial conditions
d. referring to sociological constructs: (i) verbs used metaphorically and (ii) abstract nouns	*(i)* deviate, perpetuate, *(ii)* societal norm, institutional and relational practises, the ideology of British higher education, the hierarchical definition, nature and object-ification and reification of academic 'knowledge', Western society, socio-economic factors, matriarchal system, notions of the city, modernity
e. citing sociologists and sociological reports as authorities	(In the extracts from Donna's essay)

Figure 10.1   Some lexico-syntactic characteristics associated with sociology

Characteristics a(i), (b) and (c) are the objects of study of sociologists: they are topics, and, hence, words, which would not be likely to appear in the discourse of fields of study outside the social sciences. These words would not be used by many psychologists, and they represent the concerns of only some courses and fields of study within education, anthropology and linguistics. Characteristics (d) and (e) are associated with the intellectual project of theorizing about social groups and the social states, processes and relationships which affect them. These characteristics position their writers as sharing in this intellectual project which is typical of many fields of study within the social sciences. There are other members of the academic community who are ideologically averse to engaging in such projects and/or do not value them, and would not be likely to use such expressions in their discourse. Here, then, is evidence of a set of discoursal resources which belong to a specific sub-group of academic discourse, with particular consequences for subjectivity in terms of interests, values and practices.

Literary and cultural studies

Being a 'sociologist' contrasts with the intellectual activity of studying a work of art: 'literature' and a wide range of other cultural creations, including film, architecture, street theatre and television series. The intellectual project in these fields of study is, I suggest, to attend in detail to the plots, characters, images and forms of these works, identifying their significance in terms of their cultural context, considering them in the light of critical theories, and/or analyzing ways in which their form relates to their content. These are what Macdonald (1989) calls conceptually-driven rather than data-driven fields of study in which interpretive skill is highly valued; in addition, knowledge of critical theory is valued by some, but not others. Another characteristic of these fields of study is, I suggest, that they value aesthetic qualities in academic text more than other academic communities do.

Parts of John's, Justin's, Donna's, and Valerie's essays position them as sharing some of the values and practices of these fields of study. None of the essays was specifically set in an English Literature department, but Justin chose to analyse a poem for part (a) of his essay. Valerie's task had an object of cultural study in central focus: the city, and the task which Donna set herself involved the study of cultural works written in English. John's assignment did not relate to either of these disciplines, but he used discoursal strategies drawn from his familiarity with the study of English literature (see Chapter 7 for discussion of the origins of this discourse in his literacy history).

There are two global structural characteristics which I would associate with the study of English Literature. Firstly, John began his essay with a quotation from a play — something which is, I suggest, not typical of sociological discourse. Rather, it identifies him with the values and practices of the 'literary/cultural studies community' both by choosing this way of opening his essay, and by valuing a work of literature. Secondly, none of these writers used section headings. Section headings are common in much sociological writing, being seen as signals of ordered thinking and reader-friendliness. By contrast, in writing about literature the ability to create a seamless flow between paragraphs is highly valued, and section headings are viewed as a crude intrusion on this flow.

These more global discourse features are accompanied by particular lexico-syntactic discourse characteristics in Justin's, Donna's and Valerie's essays which associate them with the objects of study of the literary and cultural studies academic community, and the interpretive intellectual project of literary and cultural criticism. Here are some specific extracts.

Extract 10.9 Justin — *Aesthetics* (lines 1–15)

> "As Bad as a Mile" is a striking example of Larkin expressing pessimism in his poetry. This six lines of verse in two stanzas uses the everyday experience of throwing an apple core at a bin and missing, to discuss his view of flawed humanity. The failure is not mischance but an inbuilt fault felt "spreading back up the arm".
>
> The apple links human fallibility to the Original Sin of the Bible story and so represents life. "The apple unbitten in the palm" is life un-started, but already destined to miss the target. The poem is given a surreal aspect by the apple being unbitten and eaten to the core in the same sentence: the whole poem is one sentence.
>
> The direct and simple language of this poem argues a rich and complex idea. We may dispute Larkin's conclusion but the experience described is a common one, and many of us will have felt a similar reaction to missing our targets be they trivial, the bin, or important, fulfilment in life.

Extract 10.10 Donna — *Independent Studies* (lines 214–218)

> In Morrison's "Song of Solomon" (1989), Pilate-Reba's mother, comes to Reba's defence, when her daughter is in danger. The outraged mother of old is resurrected, just as those in folklore, [for example: 'Nanny the Maroon' in African-Caribbean folklore; see also: Braxton: 1990; Dadzie: 1991)

Extract 10.11 Donna — *Independent Studies* (lines 340-346)

> In the 'Untitled Story' (1988), the story tells of the reunion of Shirley with her daughter Evenlyn from Barbados. Untitled Story demonstrates the deep relationship they have and the bond between them, also it tackles the issue of Evenlyn's rape by her stepfather, and the feelings of betrayal, hurt, revenge and near insanity that are experienced by the mother and Evenlyn.

Extract 10.12 Valerie — *Communication Studies* (lines 65-66)

> Now at the climactic moment of the play, Lear tears off his royal robes ...

Extract 10.13 Valerie — *Communication Studies* (lines 216-222)

> But I suspect that Tom Wolfe's fictional write-off of New York (in 'Bonfire of the Vanities) could as well have been sited in Moses's time as twenty or so years later. To some impartial observers, New York is among the most heartless and disillusioning of urban sprawls.

Extract 10.14 Valerie — *Communication Studies* (lines 239-244)

> So Moses (in Berman's view) appeals to all residents of New York (without regret for ther pattern of living) to trust the integrity of the urban planner and the urban architect.
>
> Both Engles and Moses leave acres of room for calamity and despair.

These extracts contain the discourse characteristics summarized in Figure 10.2. Characteristics (a), (b) and (e) are associated with the objects of study in these fields: the fact that they are studying texts and creative work. Characteristics (c) and (d) relate to the intellectual project of attending in detail to what happens in those texts. Characteristics (d) (where the feelings of respondents are concerned), (e), (f) and (g), are associated with the intellectual project of interpretation: of relating the object of study to its cultural context and to generalized concepts, being what Macdonald (1989) calls a 'conceptually driven discipline'. Through the use of these discourse characteristics these four writers position themselves as associated with the interests, values and practices of these fields of study. Donna's essay contains many more similar examples; the other three do not.

In addition, Valerie is concerned with her own style of expression, using vivid metaphors and descriptions frequently in her essay like, for example, *leave acres of room for calamity and despair* in extract 10.14. Valuing colourful language is, I suggest, also associated with literary and related fields

Lexico-syntactic characteristics of the discourse of literary and related studies	Examples in extracts 10.9–10.14
a. names of specific texts, their authors, and/or other 'creators' (i.e. a town planner) as the first element in a clause (Theme)	*"As Bad as a Mile", In Morrison's "Song of Solomon", 'Nanny the Maroon', In the "Untitled Story", Untitled Story, Tom Wolfe's ..('Bonfire of the Vanities), Moses*
b. lexis specific to discussing text and genres, often as the first element in a clause	*poetry, This six lines of verse in two stanzas, The poem, sentence, The direct and simple language, at the climactic moment of the play, fictional write-off*
c. names of specific people, places, objects and actions, often in the information-carrying, later part of the clause (Rheme)	*the everyday experience of throwing an apple core at a bin and missing, The apple, Pilate-Reba's mother, the reunion of Shirley with her daughter Evenlyn, Evenlyn's rape by her stepfather, Lear tears off his robes, New York*
d. verbs for and nominalizations of the feelings of characters and of respondents to the work	*will have felt, outraged, feelings betrayal, hurt, revenge and near insanity, to trust, calamity and despair*
e. present tense verbal and mental processes of the writer and of literary authors, literal and metaphorical	*expressing, discuss his view of, argues, dispute, described, tells, is resurrected, demonstrates, tackles, suspect, appeals*
f. abstract nouns, nominalizations, and nouns referring to general psychological categories (valued in interpretive approaches, but not in critical theory approaches)	*flawed humanity, the failure, human fallibility, life, life unstarted, fulfilment, the outraged mother of old*
g. literary theory as source	**Braxton: 1990**

Figure 10.2   Some lexico-syntactic characteristics associated with literary and related studies

of study and also with activities outside the academic community: professional writing and journalism. It is part of Valerie's sense of herself as 'creative' and 'artistic': personal qualities (*ethos*) which she wanted to convey in her writing, as I discussed in Chapter 8.

Natural Sciences

A striking contrast to the discourses of the social sciences and of literary and related studies is the discourse of the natural sciences. It has very different lexico-syntactic characteristics associated with very different objects of study and knowledge-making practices. This voice carries with it a subjectivity quite different from the other two. An example of this is one short section of Sarah's essay. The dominant disciplinary discourse in her essay is the discourse of philosophy, but she includes a section (Extract 10.15) on the technical scientific aspects of nuclear waste. In this section she presents scientific detail in a way which, I suggest, positions her as also familiar with, comfortable with, and competent in the objects of study and knowledge-making practices of natural scientists.

Extract 10.15 Sarah — *Environmental Ethics* (lines 121–135)

> The hazards of Radioactive waste
>   The main problem with all categories of radioactive waste is its potential hazard to the health of humans and other organisms. The characteristics of the waste which determine this hazard are the types of radiation emitted (alpha, beta or gamma) and its "half life", that is the time for the activity to have decreased by one half. The rate of decay varies widely from Argon 41, which has a half life of 100 minutes to Uranium 238 (the most common form of uranium in nature) which has a half-life of 4500 million years. It has been shown that a greater than average incidence of cancer and leukemia has been detected in some people exposed to very high levels of radiation (100 times the background dose). But no certain evidence has been discovered of the hazards of small doses of radiation although many suspect that malignancies and genetic defects can be caused by even very small cumulative doses. (9).

This section of Sarah's writing contains the lexico-syntactic characteristics summarized in Figure 10.3.

I suggest that characteristics (a), (b), (c) and (d) are associated with the interest

Lexico-syntactic characteristics of the discourse of the natural sciences	Examples in extract 10.15
a. use of numbers	*100 minutes, Uranium 238, 4500 million years*
b. other expressions of quantity	*rate of decay, very high levels of radiation, very small cumulative doses, decreased by one half*
c. specialized lexis for (i) physical objects and (ii) physical processes	*(i) organisms, malignancies and genetic defects, (ii) emitted, incidence*
d. clauses representing states of affairs concerning physical objects	*The characteristics of the waste which determine this hazard are the types of radiation emitted*
e. passive mental processes with no mention of humans doing the thinking	*But no certain evidence has been discovered of the hazards of small doses of radiation*
f. present and present perfect tense categorical modality —	*is, are, determine, varies, has been detected*
g. explicit objective modality	*It has been shown that*

Figure 10.3   Some lexico-syntactic characteristics associated with the natural sciences

of natural scientists in physical objects and quantification, and that characteristics (e), (f) and (g) are a function of the belief among many natural scientists that they are presenting objective fact in which the scientist has no role. By writing in this way Sarah is, in this section of her essay, identifying herself with these interests and beliefs.

Conclusion to this section

I have given examples of discourses associated with three fields of study and shown how they position their users quite differently. They represent one dimension on which a range of alternatives exist within the academic community. By adopting a voice associated with a particular field of study, a writer is aligning herself or himself with its objects of study and knowledge-making practices.

However, the idea of 'multiple identities' is not simply a matter of different writers in different fields of study being positioned differently from each other: individual writers often shift identity within a single piece of writing. I showed this in my case study of Rachel Dean (Chapter 6) and it emerges indirectly from the analysis above, in that John, Valerie and Donna are drawing on both the discourse of sociology and the discourse of literary and cultural studies (see also Clark and Ivanič 1997, Chapter 6, and Ivanič, Aitchison and Weldon 1996 for analyses of shifting disciplinary identities in Sarah's writing). Positioning in relation to a particular field of study may be *relatively consistent* throughout a piece of writing (for example, Angela associated herself with the knowledge-making practices of critical sociology throughout her essay, as exemplified in Extracts 10.3 and 10.4); *confined to a single section* (for example, Sarah only associated herself with the knowledge-making practices of the natural sciences in the section quoted in Extract 10.15); or just in a few words *embedded in a different discourse* (for example, Donna shifted from a 'literary studies' identity to a 'sociology' identity with the words *forms of oppression used to control and pathologise their lives* in Extract 9.7).

Writers also have to shift their positioning in this respect from one writing assignment to another. For example, John pointed out that the *personae* associated with different fields of study position him as having different personal qualities. Discussing the difference between writing an essay about Aids for a Medical Ethics course and another he wrote soon after for a philosophy course, he said:

John   There are two John's. In the Aids essay there's a kind of hopefully
            socially aware John, and in the philosophy essay there's the
            person who is good at playing with ideas and in one sense forget
            the social side. The nice thing about philosophy is that it involves
            philosophical thinking .. you can say 'well, if people die ...' and
            it's just an idea. Or play Aristotle and his tiers of class and it's just,
            I mean, in a socially aware essay I would be appalled by it, but in
            a philosophy essay I can say well it's just an idea. So I think they
            are two different people, but I feel I am both of them and that's
            very important.

He is drawing attention to the way in which each *persona* has its own associated *ethos*. John presented himself differently in the two different course contexts, in this case, for the same reader. The difference in subject-positioning stems mainly from what he was writing about: writing about ethical considerations positions him as a member of the sociology community with a 'sociology *persona*', and as a person with a 'socially aware' *ethos*; writing about hypothetical situations positions him as a member of the philosophy community with a 'philosophy *persona*', and as a person with a 'good at playing with ideas' *ethos*.

Aspects of identity related to role in the academic community

Identification with the objects of study and knowledge-making practices of fields of study is not the only dimension on which alternatives exist. Some members of the academic community are students, apprentices, novices within the community, 'readers' of their subjects; others are established, professional members of the same community: tutors, lecturers, researchers and theorists whose tasks are to teach and to contribute to the community's knowledge-making projects. However, this is not a clear-cut distinction. I suggest that, in order to achieve a good degree, a student has to skilfully combine some characteristics of being an established member with those of being an apprentice. As Bartholomae wrote:

> I think that all writers, in order to write, must imagine for themselves the privilege of being 'insiders' — that is, the privilege both of being inside an established and powerful discourse and of being granted a special right to speak. (1985: 143)

In this section I present examples of discourse characteristics which seem to position writers more as novices in the academic community, without "the privilege of being 'insiders' ", and those in which they have assumed that privilege.

Differences on this dimension are caused not by what is being written about, but by the nature of the social relations surrounding the event in which the writers are participating. In terms of Kress and Fairclough's distinction between 'genre' and 'discourse' (as outlined in Chapter 2), this is a difference in 'genre', and associated more with Halliday's Interpersonal function of language. It is concerned with differences between the social relations surrounding different types of writing (different 'genres'). I suggest that there is a continuum between types of writing in which the writer has higher status and therefore more power than the reader, and types of writing in which the power relations are reversed. To illustrate this, I draw a broad working distinction between two types of writing in the academic community at opposite ends of this continuum: *an essay for assessment*, in which the role of the writer is to be a student, an apprentice, still on the margins of community membership, and *an article for publication*, in which the role of the writer is to be an insider with the "special right to speak": to contribute to the knowledge-making projects of the community. This is not a watertight distinction: the evidence here shows the two genres leaking into each other in the writing of second year undergraduates, and reveals contradictions between the two writer-roles they set up.

A 'student' role

The task of writing an essay which has been assigned and will be assessed by a tutor positions writers as students rather than as contributors. Although there were short sections in which several of them tried on the role of contributor, the overall project they undertook was one of a student. A particularly interesting example of this is Frances's task. It is:

"There is no such thing as a free gift" Discuss.

The wording of this task is a familiar format for eliciting a display of knowledge on which tutors or examiners intend to judge students. Such wording would never appear as the title of an academic article, but frequently appears, as in Frances's essay, as the title of student work. Frances responded to this by interpreting her task to be to outline the arguments put forward by well established anthropologists for and against this position, to examine other anthropological studies to see whether their evidence supports the position or not, and on the basis of this analysis to draw a conclusion. Such a project would not be considered worthy of publication, as it makes no original contribution to theory or research. But this task interpretation was not highly valued by the tutors marking the essay — they gave it a medium to low grade. When I asked one of the tutors why, she said that high marks were achieved by those students who made a small anthropological study of their own in a community to which they had access, and evaluated the statement in relation to the practices of that community. In other words, those who took on the social roles of contributors were more highly rewarded than those who took on the roles of students. This case is particularly poignant and telling because of the following extract from Frances's essay:

Extract 10.16 Frances — *Anthropology* (lines 228–232)

> A similar picture could be built up if English people from close mining communities like the Weardale of my childhood was studied, for many of the reciprocal rights and obligations differed from but were as apparent as those in the Pakistani communities of today.

Frances could have taken on the role of 'contributor'. She would have liked to study the Weardale of her childhood, and build up a picture of the reciprocal rights and obligations there from her memories and her family connections in the area. However, she had assumed from the wording of the assignment that she should be adopting the 'student' role, and that her global task was to show her familiarity with established theory and research.

This opportunity lost is reflected in the linguistic characteristics of extract 10.16. Firstly her potential contribution to the anthropology community remains buried in the passive verbs *could be built up* and *was studied*. Secondly, the community which she knew so much about, the *Weardale of my childhood*, the details of which would have made an extremely original contribution, is buried in a long noun phrase at the beginning of a clause, so that it carries no communicative significance to the reader whatsoever.

Here are some extracts which illustrate specific discourse characteristics associated with the social purposes of student essays.

Extract 10.17 Frances — *Anthropology* (lines 111–115)

> Balanced reciprocity as Sahlins sees it, characterises reciprocity that it prompt and equal, usually between people of the same generation.

Extract 10.18 Frances — *Anthropology* (lines 277–280: i.e. the end)

> I hope that by looking at these examples to have illustrated the truth of Professor Douglas's statement that "the whole idea of a free gift is based on a misunderstanding, there should not be any free gifts."

Extract 10.19 Sarah — *Environmental Ethics* (lines 284–288)

> In terms of moral theory, consequentialism is based on the general premis that only the consequences of an act are important — and is therefore a system which is built around the notion of some goal that is to be obtained — the greatest good. In particular, utilitarianism aims

to promote the greatest happiness for the greatest number of people. This is a theory which adopts a single basic principle, as opposed to deontological theories which appeal to fundamental principles of what is right.

Extract 10.20 Donna — *Independent Studies* (lines 420–422)

The sexuality of Black women is a complicated aspect of their multidimensional lives and experiences, that has yet to be fully expressed in the literary and mass media. [Collins: 1990].

These extracts illustrate some discoursal features which, I suggest, position their writers as students of, rather than as contributors to, knowledge. Firstly, there are present tense statements of universal truth in categorical modality which are authorized by being attributed to published writers (examples 10.17 and 10.20). It is not the presence of attribution which distinguishes student essay writing from academic articles. Rather, it is that attribution is just as common in the middle and end of the essay as it is at the beginning. It is not functioning to establish the extent of existing knowledge before adding to it, but rather laying out existing knowledge has become the purpose of the whole enterprise. It is also interesting to note that Frances refers to an authority as 'Professor Douglas'. By mentioning Douglas's superior position in the academic hierarchy Frances draws attention to her own role as 'student'. The more conventional attribution 'Douglas' would, I suggest, have treated her as an academic of more equal standing.

Secondly, student essays consist mainly of assertions which are already taken as given within the field of study, as Sarah observed when she described the way she wrote Extract 10.19 as 'like a teacher'. She pointed out that an established philosopher writing an academic article would not need to define consequentialism, utilitarianism and deontological theories in the way she does in this extract. A philosopher writing a textbook may have to, and a lecturer giving a lecture may have to. She continued:

Sarah   I know he knows this but I'll tell .. I'm putting it down. I don't need it for my essay. It doesn't help the essay in any way. But it's .. (...) I'm marking the .. laying out the theory very basically, so .. well, because he said I ought to, and because I then realized well, perhaps if you're going to talk about consequential theories you ought to explain what they are.

This local discourse function of defining what are fundamental terms in the discipline the way a teacher would seems to me to position the writer as student, being assessed on command of existing knowledge, rather than as contributor to the development of the discipline.

A 'contributor' role

The social purpose of an academic article is quite different. Broadly, it is to make a contribution to knowledge, although the nature of this contribution differs from one field of study to another, as discussed earlier in this chapter. In this section I show how Angela and Justin positioned themselves in the role of contributor, and how others seemed to be moving sporadically and/or temporarily into this role.

Angela's first sentence is:

Extract 10.21 Angela — *Independent Studies* (lines 1–4)

> This piece of research (1), which is a small scale study of the experiences of mature women undergraduates in higher education, arose from a number of questions relating to my contradictory and problematic experiences, which I had been thinking about over the past three years.

This sentence sets out the sort of project which might appear in a research article. Some of the more local lexico-syntactic characteristics of Angela's writing are shaped by this project. Here are two examples.

Extract 10.22 Angela — *Independent Studies* (lines 39–42)

> Of crucial importance, however, is that I found the differences in the women's responses lay in some of the rich details of their explanations, rather than in their overall, general experiences of higher education as a whole.

Extract 10.23 Angela — *Independent Studies* (lines 149–150)

> A comparison of the women's overall positive and negative experiences of higher education reveals a number of contradictions.

In these extracts Angela herself is uncovering new knowledge, as represented by the words *I found*, *reveals*. In the case of *reveals*, the actor responsible for this is *comparison*, a nominalization of a mental process which is about to be carried out by Angela in the rest of the section. She uses categorical, present tense modality authoritatively for theoretical statements without attributing them to other authors, as in the verb *lay*.

I associate four characteristics with what Bartholomae calls "being insiders, ... granted a special right to speak". These were prevalent in Justin's and Angela's essays; Frances, Sarah, Donna and Valerie also experimented occasionally with taking on the *persona* of fully fledged membership of the academic community, particularly towards the ends of their essays. The four characteristics were as follows.

Use of the first person
Justin uses the inclusive *we/our/us* confidently to refer to himself along with other analysts engaged in the task of interpreting literature, evaluating philosophical theory, and pursuing the intellectual projects of philosophy. Others from time to time used the first person, but on the whole in association with less weighty intellectual tasks. I discuss this in more detail later in this chapter.

Unattributed assertions
Like Angela, Justin used categorical, present tense modality for interpretations, philosophical claims and observations about philosophical theories, indicating either that they were his own, or that he was an authoritative member of the community who did not need to provide the grounds for stating them. I suggest that it is a generic characteristic of academic articles to use categorical modality for definitions, evaluations and statements of fact which are not attributed to other authors. This characteristic is relatively rare in these writers' essays, apart from Angela's and Justin's.

Presupposed shared knowledge
Another difference between the student essay genre and the academic article genre is the extent to which the writer can treat some things as shared knowledge. As Sarah said, students writing essays have to be a bit like teachers, explaining every term they use in order to show that they know what it means, but experts writing academic articles can use discipline-specific terms without needing to explain them. In stark contrast to Sarah, Justin used technical terminology of philosophy such as *utilitarianism* without defining it. Valerie does the same in Extract 10.24: she uses the term *managed capitalism* without explaining it.

Extract 10.24 Valerie — *Communication Studies* (lines 302–305)

> In Britain now there are few if any ideologies left to nurse, as we proceed in fits and starts in the era of managed capitalism.

Justin used presupposition in Extract 10.9. The expression

> is a striking example of Larkin expressing pessimism in his poetry

presupposes that Larkin expresses pessimism in his poetry; and

> to discuss his view of flawed humanity

presupposes that Larkin has a view of flawed humanity. These give the impression of someone thoroughly familiar, at any rate with Larkin's work, if not with the whole body of knowledge of the English Literature community.

Making claims
This characteristic of the academic article genre is associated with the first two: the use of the first person, and assertions which are not buttressed by appeals to authority. However, it deserves special attention, since claims are essential to argumentative writing. Here are four examples.

Extract 10.25 Frances — *Anthropology* (lines 265–268)

> Within a modern market economy a gift system which provides brides, goods, services, social relationships and prestige functions as powerfully as the system of total prestation that Mauss elaborated in The Gift.

Extract 10.26 Justin — *Aesthetics* (lines 73–75)

> I also want to claim that the perception of this truth is at least part of what we mean by the aesthetic experience.

Extract 10.27 Sarah — *Environemntal Ethics* (lines 364–367)

> I have already, I think made the point that a technical solution seems to be an ever receeding goal, that research has increased the number of ways in which we know we are uncertain, so reversibility I fear is the only principle to adopt for the present.

Extract 10.28 Sarah — *Environemntal Ethics* (lines 472–475, i.e. last sentence)

> The main thrust of my argument has been to show that neither fact directed consequential theories nor fundamental principles provide the answer to the moral issues involved in this case.

In Extract 10.25 Frances is experimenting very tentatively with making a claim within the overall framework of what is predominantly a student essay. Indeed it is scarcely recognizable as a claim at all. It is only the fact that a *modern market economy* has not been mentioned elsewhere in the essay, and that this assertion is followed by argument with examples, that identifies this as a claim at all. In stark contrast, Justin and Sarah mark their claims with metadiscoursal markers: *I want to claim, I have already made the point that* and *the main thrust of my argument*.

In examples 10.27 and 10.28 Sarah seemed to be writing more as a fully-fledged philosopher than as a student. Perhaps the most startling feature in these extracts is the nested clause *I fear* in Extract 10.27. This is more than subjective modality: it is a mental process not of cognition or perception, but of emotional response. I suggest that such an expression is not unusual in academic philosophy articles, in which philosophers are frequently emotionally stirred by their deductions, whereas it sounds a little odd in a student essay.

All the writers except for Angela and Justin seemed on the whole to be discoursally positioned as students, as members of the community who do not yet have the privilege of "being granted a special right to speak". Angela and Justin made discoursal choices which assumed this privilege, Angela successfully, and Justin less so. Others flirted with this identity, unsure whether and how to assume it: momentarily "taking on the role — the voice, the *persona* — of an authority whose authority is rooted in scholarship, analysis or research" as Bartholomae (1985: 136) puts it. While discoursally positioning themselves predominantly as students, these writers are occasionally trying on the clothes of the expert.

Aspects of identity related to ideologies of knowledge-making

In this section I discuss a third type of discoursal positioning which interacts both with positioning in relation to fields of study and with positioning in relation to role within the community. I suggest that particular discourse choices support particular ideologies ("representational perspectives" as Wertsch (1991) calls them) of intellectual activity, of knowledge and of knowledge-making.

In Figure 10.4 I list ideological positions in relation to knowledge-making which I or other researchers have identified (for example, Caywood and Overing 1987, Lamb 1991, Lea 1994). These are in principle independent of

each other, although those on the right may cluster together as relatively normative, and those on the left are likely to cluster together as relatively oppositional.

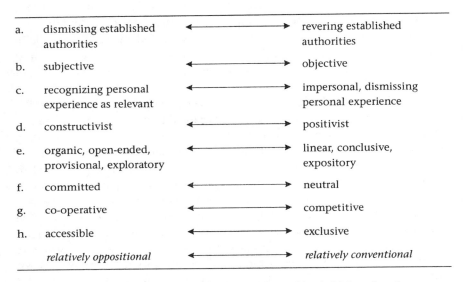

a. dismissing established ←————————→ revering established
    authorities   authorities

b. subjective   ←————————→ objective

c. recognizing personal   ←————————→ impersonal, dismissing
    experience as relevant   personal experience

d. constructivist   ←————————→ positivist

e. organic, open-ended,   ←————————→ linear, conclusive,
    provisional, exploratory   expository

f. committed   ←————————→ neutral

g. co-operative   ←————————→ competitive

h. accessible   ←————————→ exclusive

    relatively oppositional   ←————————→ *relatively conventional*

Figure 10.4   Some alternative ideologies of knowledge-making in higher education

Caywood and Overing (1987: xii) argue that ideologies of knowledge-
making such as those I have listed on the right of Figure 10.4 are privileged,
more highly valued in most contexts in higher education in the U.S., and they
argue on feminist grounds for the alternative ideologies on the left; Lamb
supports their view (1991: 13), and evidence in the work of Lea (1994) and
Clark (1992), studying higher education in the U.K., leads to the same conclusion. In general I think members of the academic community stereotype
each other along lines such as these: some feminist academics defining the
qualities on the left hand side as positive and feminine, some scientists
defining the qualities on the right hand side as positive and scientific. In this
section I am concerned to identify discoursal features which are associated
with such beliefs about the nature of the academic endeavour and so position
writers as having particular ideological stances towards knowledge-making. In
what follows I discuss dimensions (a) and (b) in some detail, and the others
more briefly, merely suggesting ways in which they might be discoursally
constructed.

a.   Respect for authority

One striking difference between my eight co-researchers was the extent to which they showed respect for authority by citing published authors. Figure 10.5 summarizes the different sources of knowledge to which the writers referred explicitly in their essays (See endnote 1 for an explanation of what I counted as attributions when compiling this table). The figures are raw numbers, not taking account of the different lengths of the writers' essays. Nevertheless I think the table brings out particular preferences on the part of the writers which position them as valuing particular sources of knowledge.

Writer	Rachel	John	Angela	Frances	Justin	Sarah	Donna	Valerie
Field of Study	Social work	Medical ethics	Indep. Studies	Anthropology	Philosophy	Environ. Ethics	Indep. Studies	Sociology
Items in the bibliography	6	22	0	6	1	8	43	6
attribution to named authors	7	11	0	35	1	19	79	38
attribution to summarized, unnamed published writers	0	0	0	0	3	6	3	0
attribution to women co-researchers	0	0	43	0	0	0	0	0
attribution to self	7	9	20	6	18	28	7	5

Figure 10.5   Attributions of knowledge-making activity, knowledge or belief to different sources

The table shows that Donna and John are outstanding in including many items in their bibliographies, giving the impression that they hold published authorities in high esteem, and showing themselves to be well-read: a personal quality highly valued in the academic community. Frances, Sarah, Donna and

Valerie use relatively high numbers of attributions of knowledge and ideas to published sources in their texts, positioning them as valuing texts as sources of knowledge. John, contradicting the impression given by his large bibliography, has relatively few textual attributions. Angela and Justin, by contrast, make a strong statement of opposition to this value by having no textual references to published sources (Justin's one reference being a work of literature rather than an academic reference). They position themselves as defying the value placed on published texts, and opposing the convention which requires members of the academic community, particularly students, to provide evidence that they have read the relevant literature in the field. This opposition may put them at risk in the assessment process, but may contribute to a gradual re-evaluation of this requirement.

The table brings out broad contrasts between the attribution practices of the eight writers, but it does not go into detail about the specific ways in which they make reference to published authors. In a more detailed study of this particular aspect of discoursal positioning it would be illuminating to distinguish between the numbers of citations to hegemonic rather than oppositional sources, and between agreeing or disagreeing with established authorities as opposed to merely quoting them.

Attributing ideas to published authors shows respect for authority, but it connects to other values too, and hence defies a simplistic categorization as conventional/oppositional. When writers make clear the source of their knowledge and understandings, they are showing that these are not objects, separated from people, but made through a process of research and/or thinking and communicating. People who oppose an objective view of knowledge might want to associate themselves with this practice. Attribution also acknowledges the property rights of others over their contributions to knowledge. Such acknowledgement is highly valued in the academic community. Writers who deliberately refuse to attribute ideas to published authors pose a challenge to these values, perhaps suggesting an alternative ideology that everyone has equal rights to authoritativeness, and that knowledge is common property.

Figure 10.5 also shows how often the writers explicitly attribute what they have written to themselves. Using relatively more attributions to self also positions the writer as opposing the view that published authorities are the appropriate sources of knowledge. I discuss the issue of attribution to self further in the next section.

b. Subjectivity vs objectivity

Although 'subjectivity' is usually associated with the use of the first person, I suggest that it is also associated with careful attribution to other sources, as discussed in the previous section. Further, the use of the first person is not a straightforward measure. There is a continuum from not using 'I' at all, through using 'I' with verbs associated with the process of structuring the writing, to using 'I' in association with the research process, and finally to using 'I' with verbs associated with cognitive acts. Not using 'I' at all gives the impression that the writer is withdrawing from all responsibility for the academic essay. None of my co-researchers do this. Using 'I' in association with the process of structuring the essay still leaves room for its content being presented as if it were objective and factual. Donna is an example of this. She uses the word 'I' only in paragraph 2 of her essay and one other place, and only as the agent of cognitive/verbal/material processes related to the construction of the essay:

Set of extracts 10.29: Donna — *Independent Studies* (lines 12–25, and line 266)

> I intend to demonstrate briefly
> I would then like to examine
> I would like to focus mainly on .... to assess
> I also wish to examine
> I intend to indicate
> Earlier I mentioned that

A vivid illustration of the way in which discoursal choices are associated with ideological stance towards knowledge-making is a change Sarah made between her penultimate and final draft:

Extract 10.30a Sarah — *Environmental Ethics* (line 238), draft version

> These were just a few areas of concern which were identified,

Extract 10.30b — *the same,* final version

> These are just a few areas of concern I identified.

At the time of writing this essay, Sarah was developing consciousness about objectivity and subjectivity, reading books in the sociology of scientific knowledge. She said that she wanted to align herself with a subjective view of knowledge, and changing the passive which were identified to the active I identified, stating explicitly that she herself had done the identifying, was a direct result of this changing stance towards academic work.

Using 'I' in association with at least some of the knowledge claims and beliefs acknowledges the writer's responsibility for them and property rights over them. Many people argue that it is unnecessary to state subjectivity explicitly, as any categorical assertion will be taken to be the result of the writer's cognitive act. I would suggest that those writers who choose to make their role in knowledge-making explicit are taking a different ideological stance from those who don't. For example, Donna does not do this at all, whereas John does so eight times, six of which are in the final section and in his concluding paragraph. This is associated to some extent with the distinction discussed in the previous section between student essay genre and academic article genre. Writers who present themselves as knowledge-makers are also positioning themselves as having property rights, as contributors to the field.

c.   personal experience is relevant — irrelevant
Recognizing personal experience as relevant concerns what sort of evidence the writer draws on in order to support an assertion, rather than the source of that assertion. Angela makes it clear from her opening sentence (Extract 10.21) that she sees personal experience as integral to intellectual work, saying that her research *arose from a number of questions relating to my contradictory and problematic experiences, which I had been thinking about over the past three years*. She includes herself as one of the sources of her research findings. She refers to her own experiences in commentary parts of her essay. She also uses *we, us,* and *our* to include her own experiences alongside those of the women she studied as part of the basis for her argument. For example:

Extract 10.31 Angela — *Independent Studies* (lines 439–442)

> As mature undergraduate women, most of us nearing the end of our time in higher education, with great effort and determination we have managed to struggle through, survive, and to some extent resist institutional pressures to 'conform'.

Donna, by contrast, although writing about Black women, does not refer to her own experience at all, and never uses first person plural in order to identify herself with the experience of which she is talking in the third person. An instance of this silence is

Extract 10.32 Donna — *Independent Studies* (lines 81–84)

> Despite of such imagery, Black women have resisted these externally defined images of their social realities, that portray them as worthless, insignificant and inferior [Zhana: 1988; Bryan et al: 1985; Braxton et al: 1990; Collins: 1990].

Donna could have replaced the words Black women, their and them by we, our and us to include herself as part of the experience to which she is referring, but she didn't. By adopting this particular hegemonic convention of academic discourse in her writing, Donna is positioned as not considering personal experience relevant to her argument, although it is quite clear from my conversations with her that she does (as I discussed in Chapter 8).

d.   constructivist — positivist
This is a well recognized and highly significant continuum on which members of the academic community differ in terms of their ideologies of knowledge-making. It is so important that it is related to several others on the list, and thus is hard to exemplify independently. The constructivist end of the continuum represents the belief that reality is socially constructed, contingent and local: that reality can only be known in relation to its social context. A constructivist ideology of knowledge-making might lead to writing which consists of many examples from real life, narratives of lived experience, references to real people, objects and social settings, and 'participants perspectives': representations of reality by people who are experiencing it. By contrast, a positivist ideology of knowledge-making is the belief that there are objective, generalizable, universal truths which can separated from their immediate context, and can be uncovered by the analytic processes of scientists. This ideology might lead to writing which consists of many abstractions, categorical statements of definition and categorization, and (in some cases) statistical proofs. These ideologies might be further characterized by the absence of features associated with the opposite end of the continuum. On careful consideration of my co-researchers' writing, I do not think that they were aware of this distinction. Even though several of them were writing about social constructionist theories, I suggest that the way they did it tended towards the positivist end of the continuum. Apart from Angela's (as exemplified above), most of their writing contained a preponderance of abstractions and uses of categorical modality (as indicated in Chapter 9), and relatively few attributions, most of them to established authorities (as suggested by Figure 10.5).

e.   organic — linear

Caywood and Overing (1987) mention this distinction as one which is significant for feminist academic writing. Neither they nor, as far as I know, anyone else, have identified exactly what this distinction might mean. It is easy enough to see how it applies to the process of writing: these are two very different ways of setting about writing which might end up with similar products. The terms have a certain psychological reality: in research on both gender differences and cultural differences the terms are used quite liberally. One way of applying the distinction to the texts themselves is to think about how far they are open-ended, provisional and exploratory or neatly boxed and conclusive. Of this Sarah said:

Sarah: Did I tell you about a friend of mine was telling me that in my essays I never really kicked the ball into the net? dribbling down the football pitch and kicking the ball and everyone going hooray, it's there .. sort of thing.

Here is Sarah's penultimate paragraph which seems to me both to reach closure and to contain exploratory, speculative elements.

Extract 10.33 Sarah — *Environmental Ethics* (lines 461–465)

> Given the supposition that the best possible action would be taken, rather than inaction, Goodin's principles do provide a good foundation for policy decisions. I feel that Hare would accept these principles as the "best at the time" but with the proviso that we leave options open for continual re-evaluation. That would involve more second-level thinking, listening to arguments, reconsidering evidence as consequences show themselves, and constantly adapting our principles.

In this extract Sarah does 'kick the ball into the net' by writing *Goodin's principles do provide a good foundation for policy decisions.*
But she also speculates on what she *feel(s)* that Hare would accept, and what that *would involve*. There is a sense here that, for her, the possible ways of thinking about this problem are endless, and too complex to deal with in one conclusive statement.

f.   committed — neutral

Within the social sciences there are many topics on which people have very strong feelings and views, and there are competing ideologies as to whether it is appropriate to show one's commitment or not in academic writing on these topics. This is tied up with competing views about the social role of the academic: to describe the world or to change it.[2] Some members of the academic community believe that the role of the academic is to preserve detached neutrality; others value commitment. John, Rachel, Angela, Sarah, Donna and Valerie were all writing about topics on which they had strong personal political views. Their commitment showed in several places in their essays. For example, John felt extremely strongly about the topic of his essay, which was Aids. He tried to fall in with what he saw as the dominant ideology of taking a neutral stance, as I discussed in Chapter 7. However, he did not keep this up. In Extract 10.34 he came out quite clearly with his own view and, although he presented a supporting argument for it, he did not consider an opposite point of view.

Extract 10.34 John — *Medical Ethics* (lines 299–306)

> The problem that then arises should a health carer be able to refuse to nurse or treat someone with Aids? The simple answer is no, if some- one has put themselves into the medical profession they know that there is a very strong possibility that they could be looking after people with seriously contagious infections.

John slipped between neutral and committed stances towards knowledge- making: in some places he tried to keep his own views out of his writing; in others he let his colours show.

g.   *co-operative — competitive*

This dimension applies to the process of writing rather than to the product. By a co-operative ideology of knowledge-making I mean the belief that knowledge is not the property of an individual, and that intellectual pursuits will be the richer for being undertaken in groups. By a competitive ideology of knowl- edge-making I mean the belief that individuals can own knowledge. I suggest that this ideology underpins many practices of higher education such as assessment on the basis of individual assignments and promotion on the basis of single-authored work.

Both Angela and Justin gave the impression that they held a co-operative or collaborative view of knowledge-making, though with very different ideas of the participants in the collaboration. Angela set up her research project as a collaborative venture between herself and four other women. Her use of 'we' in association with mental and verbal processes supports a collaborative rather than competitive approach. Justin also uses 'we' in association with mental acts, presenting the intellectual project of philosophy as a collaborative venture between equal members of the philosophy community. By contrast, the way the other assignments are set up forces the writers into taking an isolated, competitive approach to knowledge-making, appearing from the discoursal evidence to have worked on these essays without any form of co-operation. They are positioned by their discoursal choices as single authors, as independently responsible for the contents of their writing. In fact this belies the actual collaborative practices in which some of them engaged, as I illustrated in the case study of Rachel Dean (Chapter 6).

h.   accessible — exclusive

Several of my co-researchers mentioned a commitment to making their writing accessible and reader-friendly, and to avoiding the sort of language which they felt excludes people from the academic community. The discourse characteristics which they felt were associated with this value were those more associated with 'spoken language'. No-one would explicitly identify themselves with the opposite value, exclusiveness, but members of the academic community are in danger of positioning themselves as an elite by the very fact of using the sorts of discourse characteristics I described in Chapter 9, whether they intend to or not.

In the next section I discuss how my co-researchers drew on discourse characteristics which aligned them with interests, values and practices which are not dependent on or specific to the academic community.

Aspects of identity which are not dependent on the academic community

The distinction between 'academic' and 'non-academic' discourse types has a certain psychological reality. My co-researchers expressed a strong feeling that there are ways with words required of them in the university which are significantly different from the language they are used to elsewhere. Many researchers take the distinction for granted (for example, Swales 1990, Odell and Goswami 1985). While it seems useful to draw this crude distinction between discourse types inside and outside the academic community for analytic purposes, it is important to recognize that it is not a water-tight divide in reality. Discourse types which I have identified as originating in the academic community can be found outside it too, and the 'non-academic' discourse types which I identify here can be found in the academic community too, as this data demonstrates. As the academic community becomes more heterogeneous in its interests, values, beliefs and practices, so the array of discourse conventions within the community diversifies, and the patterns of privileging among them shifts. A secondary agenda for this section is to discuss ways in which these discourses which are not primarily associated with the intellectual projects of the academic community interface with and leak into those which are. In many places different discourses are closely interwoven, sometimes within the same clause; in others they are separated by headings or other signals.

It is not possible to give a comprehensive list of subject positions outside the academic community which people might draw into their academic writing. My aim here is to give some examples from my co-researchers' essays of how aspects of writers' autobiographical selves which are not dependent on being students also shape their discoursal selves in their academic writing.

Positioning as a feminist

Gender is socially constructed, not biologically determined, and so the way a woman feels and behaves (including how she writes) depends on the views of women's roles and characteristics which exist in her cultural context and on her positioning of herself consciously or subconsciously among these positions. I am therefore not suggesting that any of the writers was discoursally positioned as a woman. However, some of them politicized their identity as women, and this is a different matter. Three women were discoursally positioned as feminists. The campaigning aspects of feminist discourse straddle both academic and non-academic settings. The two discourses, if they can be separated at all, seem to feed off each other: Women's Studies as an academic discipline draws on the discourse of the feminist movement at large; the feminist movement at large uses the discourse which is developed and published by feminist social scientists. Through discourse choices which construct them as members of the Women's Studies academic discipline, Rachel, Angela and Donna are also identifying with the wider political grouping of people aware of feminist issues and/or actively engaged in feminist action. Here is one example to illustrate this point:

Extract 10.35 Angela — *Independent Studies* (lines 362–368)

> *Enabled by the conventional one-way academic teaching processes, our valuable experiential knowledge, within the institution, we find, has been generally invalidated.*

> *Within higher education, we have been forced to deny whole dimen-*
> *sions of ourselves, from which our personal knowledge is partically,*
> *but primarily rooted in our real and valuable experiences of social life.*

Firstly words to do with power and struggle, such as *invalidated* and *forced*, while quite acceptable in academic communities such as Women's Studies, are also part of the discourse of the feminist movement as a whole. Secondly Angela foregrounds issues which are central concerns in feminism as a whole, as well as the academic community of Women's Studies, through the express- ions *valuable experiential knowledge, our personal knowledge, our real and valuable experiences of social life,* and *deny whole dimensions of ourselves.* Thirdly, the way Angela uses *we, our* and *ourselves* referring to herself and other women, which I suggested above is associated with an alternative ideology of knowledge-making, conveys the impression that she is committed to her socio-political identity as a woman.

Positioning as a Black feminist

Concerning both gender and race, Valerie said

Valerie: the thing about me is I cannot just write as an ordinary person, I have to have .. to say, look this person when you read it you've got to know that I'm a Black woman

However, neither she, nor I, nor any independent analysts to whom I have shown her essay have been able to pinpoint any aspects of content or form which do tell the reader that she is a Black woman, either biologically or socio- politically.

Donna, however, affiliates herself with a political stance which recognizes the double oppression of 'Black women', and fights to resist it. In her essay Donna distinguished between 'black' as a biological state and 'Black' as a political issue. Of course, those who identify with this political issue are likely to be, biologically, black women, but the two are not in principle the same thing. Donna identifies herself with Black feminist issues by the very fact that she chose to write on the topic she did:

CRITICALLY ASSESS THE WAYS IN WHICH BLACK PEOPLE HAVE REDEFINED THEIR OWN IDENTITY IN LITERATURE AND MASS MEDIA

Her essay is full of discourse which she could have encountered in Black feminist publications and events rather than academic sources, and which positions her as active on this political issue, rather than as a detached academic observer. In addition, she consciously and intentionally uses the 'street talk' expression *telling it like it is* which discoursally constructs her as Black (as discussed also in Chapter 8, and later in this chapter).

Positioning as a gay activist

As with gender and race, writers' biological sexuality does not shape their writing directly. However, being homosexual, bisexual or heterosexual is a socio-political as well as physical identity. John chose to write about Aids from a range of alternatives: an issue which is of special concern to gay people. Being gay himself, he found it hard to remain neutral on the subject, although he attempted to do so, as I have discussed elsewhere. Further, the way in which he wrote about it drew on particular discourse characteristics which I associate with Aids campaigning, positioning him as a provider of information and a campaigner for particular responses. Here are three examples

Extract 10.36 John — *Medical Ethics* (lines 18–19)

> Even though Aids is a devastating illness that we don't have a cure for, it does not present any new problems in terms of confidentiality.

Extract 10.37 John — *Medical Ethics* (lines 88–100)

> Doctors/Nurses may be sympathetic and understanding about the virus but society has shown that they can be both unsympathetic, unkind and ignorant. HIV must be fought through perceptions and affirmative attitudes. It is essential that patients know what is actually being done to them, that the specialist they see will keep all material confidential and that if the patient refuses consent for information to be given then that decision will be respected.

Extract 10.38 John — *Medical Ethics* (lines 362–366)

> If gay men are having to visit lovers in hospital how will the hospital adapt to men wanting to show affection to each other after all the main weapon we have against Aids at the moment is support and understanding.

These extracts exemplify the way John used 'we' either to refer to people in general, or possibly to refer to the writer and the particular group with which he identifies, not including the reader. They contain highly emotive and evaluative words: *devastating, unsympathetic, unkind and ignorant, essential, illness that we don't have a cure for, it does not present any new problems,* and statements of what must be done: *must be fought, the main weapon we have.* These characteristics are independent of content, and might be associated with public or media spoken or written discussion of any of a wide range of socially salient and controversial issues. Two other characteristics seem to me to be specific to the discourse of Aids campaigning; lexical collocations associated with *Aids* awareness, exemplified in these extracts by *perceptions and affirmative attitudes,* and the spelling of *Aids* as a word rather than capitalized as an acronym.

These discourse characteristics construct John as someone extremely familiar with the current Aids debate: as someone personally involved in the issues, as someone who is in command of the facts, and as someone with a clear position on the issues. However this does not necessarily position him as gay. Although it is likely that a man affiliating himself so strongly with the Aids campaign is also gay, it is his political commitment to the issue and not his sexuality which is determining his discourse choices.

Other political allegiances

Some discourse characteristics position writers as holding particular beliefs and having particular values, affiliations and allegiances associated with public institutions and/or political movements. As I discussed above, there is a powerful ideology within the academic community that its members should not show their political commitments but should write in a so-called 'neutral', 'objective' way. I do not believe this is possible, whether or not it is desirable. Even when my co-researchers were trying to be balanced and objective, their allegiance to particular groups outside the university came through in their writing, if not in what they wrote, then in their lexico-syntactic choices. Examples of this are the identities as feminist, Black feminist and Aids campaigner which I discussed above. Another example, which is not associated with gender, race or sexuality, but purely with political affiliation is the way in which Sarah wrote about nuclear waste. She showed her allegiance to the Friends of the Earth position by using their discourse comfortably when presenting their views, and she signalled her dismissal of the NIREX position by putting some of their discourse in quotation marks to distance herself from it. In spite of her desire to distance herself from the NIREX position, however, some of their discourse did leak into hers in ways which she later disowned. I discuss this in detail in Ivanič (1995) and Clark and Ivanič (1997), Chapter 6.

Marxian discourses, like feminist discourses, straddle the academic community and certain groups outside the academic community: the academic and political discourses feed each other. When a student uses Marxian discourse in her academic essay she is, to some extent, aligning herself with a political position associated with some form of Marxism, unless she explicitly disowns it. This issue arises in Valerie's essay. It is of particular interest since Valerie is Black, working class and, as I discussed in Chapter 7, had encountered Marxism outside the academic community. Affiliation with a Marxist position is not, in principle, something which is dependent on the academic community, nor is it specific to any field of study, although it is an important issue within the social sciences and humanities in general. Interest in Marxian ideas can either lead to or stem from higher education.

One part of her essay which is particularly interesting from the point of view of whether she aligns herself with Marxism or not is where she was describing Engels' view of Manchester, the beginning of which is given in Extract 10.8. This extract contains a great deal of lexis, lexical collocation and propositional content which in my view belongs to Marxian discourses: *burdened, dialectic, struggling, ideology, serious exploitation of the working class, squalid industrial conditions, squalid housing, sharp and distinctive devide between the working class quarters and the upper classes preserve.* In the last two sentences these Marxist interpretations are introduced by *Engels saw.* So is Valerie detachedly reporting Engels' view here, or is she reporting a state of affairs as she, too, would view it, and adding the information that Engels saw it too? Is this account fact or the fabrication of Engels' mind? The expression *Engels saw* does not necessarily detach Valerie from the view which follows it.

This discussion has raised two more general issues in relation to the discoursal construction of identity. Firstly, I have questioned the idea that, by reporting the discourse of another, writers disassociate themselves from the positioning inherent in that discourse. As Voloshinov (1973) theorized, discourse is characteristically double-voiced, and even direct quotation is populated by the reporting voice through the way it is selected and contextualized. Secondly, this particular example has emphasized the point that form and content are inextricably interwoven in the discoursal construction of identity. Valerie's ventriloquation of both the form and content of Engels' and Marx's political writing in this example and elsewhere positions her implicitly as aligning herself with their views. Later in the essay, however, Valerie contradicts this implicit positioning by explicitly criticizing Engels' analysis (see Extract 8.1).

Positioning in terms of power and status

As I discussed under the heading 'Aspects of identity related to role in the academic community', my co-researchers differed in the extent to which they presented themselves discoursally as 'a student' or as 'a contributor' in the academic community. I suggest that the tentativeness and lack of authoritativeness which I discussed there may be a product of a socially constructed view of the self which is not specific to the academic community. Rather, I suggest that it may be associated with the ways in which gender, race and nationality, sexuality, class and geographical origin are socially constructed in the wider cultural context of the U.K, where many ideological messages privilege men, White people, Western European nationalities, heterosexuals and those from the middle-to-upper classes. My co-researchers' predominant adoption of the 'student' role may, I suggest, have been associated with the fact that six of them were women, that two of these were Black women, that three were homosexual, and that seven were the first members of their families to pursue a higher education. These aspects of their autobiographical selves may have led them to feel a sense of powerlessness, and to view themselves as people who have no rights. Fortunately, however, this view of the self is not socially determined, but open to contestation and change. For example, Angela — a lesbian woman of Italian/Ukrainian nationality from a working-class background — while still experiencing oppression on these grounds, had resisted and challenged the social construction of her self as inferior, and had taken on the identity of a person with the right to speak.

Being a creative writer

These final two sections of this chapter are not about the discoursal construction of world views or social relations, but about the discoursal construction of the practice of writing itself. Here is a selection of extracts which draw on conventions more closely associated with creative writing, story-telling and journalism than with academic writing.

Extract 10.39 Sarah — *Environmental Ethics* (412–414)

> — under that sort of threat they might be well advised to, metaphori-
> cally speaking, lock the door and throw away the key.

Extract 10.40 Valerie — *Communication Studies* (lines 33–35)

> For Marx the clothes are ripped off, the veil's are torn away. The
> stripping process is violent and brutal.

Extract 10.41 Valerie — *Communication Studies* (lines 166–169)

> Moses (in Berman's interpretation) rampaged through New York as an
> environmental tyrant gathering funds from all points of the compass
> to impose his plan upon — the city.

Extract 10.42 Valerie — *Communication Studies* (lines 285–295)

> In conclusion, Engles's study of Manchester was flawed because
> of the historical thesis he carried in his hand-luggage.
> Manchester's proletariat may have suffered in the mould
> described by Engels but they lacked the capacity to wear a revolution-
> ary mantle. If the city is a stage for dramatic preformance, with
> backcloth, lighting equipment and the semblance of a plot, then
> Engels had marshalled a number of characters who did not know their
> lines.

In extract 10.39 Sarah self-consciously draws attention to the metaphor she is
using with the words *metaphorically speaking*. By using the metaphor she
shows herself to have a creative way of expressing things; by using the
metadiscourse she shows herself to be aware that a metaphorical expression
like this needs to be announced in academic discourse, although it would not
need to be in other types of writing.

Valerie's writing is full of metaphor and colourful language, explaining
through vivid pictures of events rather than abstract exposition about them.
Extract 10.40 is copied almost word-for-word from Berman: it is the fact that
she chose it that discoursally positions her as a person who dramatizes, paints,
sees things in metaphors, is 'imaginative'. Valerie said that using the metaphorical expression *wear a revolutionary mantle* in Extract 10.42 was part of
her identity, and she was disappointed by her tutor's advice to write the more
literal *realise a revolution* in the exam. In her view, her use of metaphors and
vivid descriptions like the ones in these extracts is a part of her 'mixture of
artistic flair coming out', and this artistic flair is something she associates with

being a Black woman — something it is important for her to convey in her writing (see the quotation above).

I suggest that these extracts and others like them, particularly in Rachel's and Valerie's writing, position their writers as wanting to entertain and give aesthetic pleasure to their readers as well as to inform and/or persuade them. This positioning is not tied to a particular workplace identity or political stance. It is associated rather with a particular view about what counts as good writing. Good story-telling, jokes and colourful language are valued in journalism and literary writing, but not given high priority by the majority of the academic community, except possibly in writing about English literature.

Bringing talking into writing

When people talk spontaneously, for example in a casual conversation, they are processing ideas into language 'on-line'. This is very different from the slow process of crafting ideas into writing, which often involves long periods of thought between words and frequent reformulations and reorderings to get the wording right. These two conditions of language production — the spontaneous and the painstakingly planned — lead to very different discourse characteristics (as I discussed in Chapter 9; see also Halliday 1989). My co-researchers' writing did not uniformly display the characteristics of the prototypical discourse type of academic essays which I described in Chapter 9. In some places some of them used syntax which I would suggest is associated more with the 'rapidly running river' of spontaneous, unplanned language use. I did not find these discourse characteristics consistently in continuous stretches of writing, usually just in a few words.

In Chapter 7 I discussed the way in which John could trace one part of his essay (Extract 7.13) to a conversation he had had with his sister. I pointed out the way in which that part contained questions and other characteristics which are more common in face-to-face conversation than in academic essays. There were several other places where John seemed to be writing 'as he would talk', using shorter than average clauses and noun phrases, embedded questions and looser, more complex patterns of coordination and subordination. An interesting example is Extract 9.1 which I analysed in Chapter 9 as containing many characteristics of prototypical academic discourse. It contains the very long phrase *the fact that if we don't give people the chance to come into the health service without chastising them in some way Aids will just carry on* to spread. Yet one of the very reasons why this noun phrase is so long is that it contains a subordinate 'if'-clause with looser syntax within it. Here are two more examples of these characteristics of 'talking' embedded in John's writing.

Extract 10.43 John — *Medical Ethics* (lines 174–177)

> *This whole notion of experimenting rases ethical issues in that should people who are likely to die become guinea-pigs and should they be given straws to clutch at?*

Extract 10.44 John — *Medical Ethics* (lines 275–278)

> *This does not mean to say because they do this that medical resources should be denied them or that funding to help prevent infection, e.g., health education should be stoped.*

A particularly interesting example of 'bringing talking into writing' is the way in which Donna used what she called 'street talk', as discussed in Chapter 8. Extract 10.45 shows how she used the words *'like it is'* as if they were part of the expression 'telling it like it is'. Yet she embedded these words in a very different kind of syntax and combined them with the much more 'academic' expression from sociological/Black feminist discourse: *asserting their social realities.*(This example is discussed in more detail in Ivanič 1994b.)

Extract 10.45 Donna — *Independent Studies* (lines 85–88)

> *Black women have challenged these external definitions of their lives, by have sought to construct their own 'herstories' and by asserting their social realities like it is. [Collins: 1990].*

Conclusion to this chapter and Part Two

In this chapter I have discussed positioning within the academic community to a greater degree of delicacy than I did in Chapter 9. I identified three aspects of academic discourse which can position writers differently. I first presented ways in which the writers identify themselves with particular fields of study through their discourse choices. I then suggested that, simultaneously, particular linguistic characteristics position their users as having a particular role within the community. I suggested that a third dimension interacts, also simultaneously, with the other two, having to do with the writers' ideologies of knowledge-making. Finally I identified aspects of the discoursal self which originate in, or are shared by non-academic contexts. I suggested that the use of these discourse types positions the writers who use them as people familiar with particular ways of viewing the world, sometimes aligning themselves with them, sometimes distancing themselves from them; as people familiar with, or trying on different social roles, and ways of writing. I have attempted to show exactly which discoursal characteristics I am using to identify discourse types, rather than claiming their existence intuitively.

I have also discussed some of the ways in which these discourses and identities interface with each other, and with the more overarching discoursal identity associated with the academic community, discussed in Chapter 9. Throughout I have emphasized the multiple and often contradictory nature of positioning. Writing potentially attributes to writers multiple, jostling subject-ivities. Writers are simultaneously positioning themselves discoursally as participating in particular fields of study, having a particular role in the academic community, and having a particular stance towards knowledge-making. Further, these positions and affiliations are not fixed or consistent, but jostle against each other in a constant process of negotiation from section to section, even from clause to clause.

Throughout Part Two I have been developing the idea that it is useful to think of four types of voice in the text: the voices of individuals from the past (Chapter 7); the unique, often heterogeneous, authoring voice of the present writer (Chapter 8); the power-wielding voice(s) of the real or imaginary future reader(s) (Chapter 8); and the abstract voice types of socially ratified discourses (Chapters 9 and 10). These four types of voice interplay in complex ways which I have, I hope, brought out in cross-referencing between the chapters in Part Two.

Notes

1.   In compiling Figure 10.5 I considered all mentions of verbal and mental processes in the writing, and all mentions of the source of content. I included

      a. *direct and reported discourse, with or without reporting verbs, for example:*

      Extract 10.46 Angela — *Independent Studies* (lines 270–271)

            Lou stated that 'Our own experiences and knowledge are undervalued in academic life and that academic knowledge and language are overvalued'.

      Extract 10.47 Frances — *Anthropology* (lines 111–113)

> Balanced reciprocity as Sahlins sees it, characterises reciprocity that is prompt and equal, usually between people of the same generation.

b. *non-integral attribution, for example:*

Extract 10.48 Donna — *Independent Studies* (lines 49–52)

> They have defined themselves as 'Black' following their shared experiences of British colonialism and their marginal positions in Britain [Amos et al: 1984; Bryan et al: 1985; Smartt et al: 1986; McLaughlin; 1990]

c. *nominalizations of verbal and mental processes, for example:*

Extract 10.49 Valerie — *Communication Studies* (lines 227–229)

> the notion is always tinged with promise, both for individuals and groups.

d. *explicit objective and subjective modality, for example:*

Extract 10.50 Justin — *Aesthetics* (lines 22–23)

> I think that truth can be an aesthetic principle as well as an aesthetic quality in art.

Extract 10.51 Justin — *Aesthetics* (lines 66–67)

> Both could be said to be less than wholly truthful.

e. *mentions of texts or authors, for example:*

Extract 10.52 Frances — *Anthropology* (lines 18–20)

> To illustrate this argument I will look at; Gift Relationship by Richard Titmuss, Pakistanis in Britain by Muhammad Anwar and A Pakistani Community in Britain by Alison Shaw.

There are also places where one or more of these features are combined. These textual features are not normally brought together either in discussions of writing from sources or in discussions of discourse representation. However, in this section I am treating them all as ways of indicating explicitly the sources of content. Focusing on any one of these linguistic categories would be easier to quantify, but would miss the richness and complexity of intertextual reference and attribution of authority.

2.   I am grateful to Romy Clark for pointing this out.

CONCLUSION

CHAPTER 11

Writer identity on the agenda in theory and in practice

Introduction

In this book I have been developing the claim that the writer's identity is an important and under-theorized dimension of the act of writing. My central focus has been what I have been calling the 'discoursal self': the portrayal of self which writers construct through their deployment of discoursal resources in their own written texts. In Part One of the book I discussed how existing research on language, literacy and academic writing contribute to an understanding of the concept of 'the discoursal self'. In Part Two I elaborated and expanded on the concept of 'the discoursal self' through analysis of writing by mature students in higher education.

In this final chapter I address the question: 'So what?' Why is 'writer identity', and more specifically, 'the discoursal self' of interest in the study of language, literacy and writing? Perhaps more important: How might an understanding of 'the discoursal self' contribute to the improvement of teaching and learning about writing in higher education? These questions are related to an issue I raised in Chapter 1: the role of theory and research findings in practice. I emphasize that the improvement of teaching and learning about writing is a question not just for those who are responsible for providing extra help with academic writing (so-called 'study skills teachers' or 'academic support tutors'), but also for the academic community as a whole. I propose that particular ways of thinking about writing and identity can be of use, even have a liberatory power, for all of us as we write in institutional settings.

Putting identity on the agenda in theorizing writing

I have responded to Cherry's (1988) plea for writing researchers to address the issue of self-representation in writing which has not previously been fore-grounded other than in Cherry's own article. Many of the insights resulting from my study of mature students writing academic essays can, I believe, be generalized to apply to the discoursal construction of identity in other types of writing and spoken language use. Here I explain what I think the study has contributed towards this understanding and make some suggestions as to what remains to be further investigated.

The contribution of this study

I began the book by introducing four ways of thinking about writer identity: a writer's autobiographical self, a writer's discoursal self, the self as author, and socially available possibilities for self-hood / subject positions. In each of Chapters 7–10 I make specific claims about the nature of 'the discoursal self', and how it is connected with the other three aspects of writer identity, which I summarize here:

Chapter 7:
– Writers bring their autobiographical self to the act of writing, and with it many resources from their life-history, specifically:
 experiences, including direct and indirect encounters with people
 interests
 ideas, opinions and commitments
 a personal repertoire of 'voices' (discourses and genres)
 a sense of self-worth
 a personal repertoire of practices, including literacy practices
– The discoursal resources out of which writers construct their discoursal self are the product of actual intertextual (in Vygotsky's terms, 'inter-mental') encounters in the writer's life-history.

Chapter 8
– Writers have a sense of owning and disowning aspects of the discoursal self they present in their writing.
– The construction of a writer's discoursal self is mediated by social interaction. That is, the actual writer-reader relationship in which an act of writing is embedded influences how writers portray themselves through their discoursal choices

Chapters 9 and 10
- A writer's discoursal self is constructed by the socially available possibilities for self-hood to which s/he has access, and the patterns of privileging among them.

Chapter 9
- Particular characteristics of academic discourse pervade student writing, and particular identities — in terms of objects of study, view of knowledge, and knowledge-making practices — are inscribed in these discourse characteristics.

BUT

Chapter 10
- Academic discourse is not monolithic, and hence there are not one but many socially available possibilities for self-hood within the academic community, some of which exist in peaceful co-existence, others are hotly contested and compete for dominance.
- Writers creatively recombine the discoursal resources at their disposal in order to construct the unique discoursal self which they present in their writing. These creative re-combinations contribute towards discoursal change and hence new possibilities for self-hood in the future.

The distinctions I have drawn between four ways of thinking about identity (at the end of Chapter 1) and these findings about the discoursal self can, I believe, inform and enrich writing theory and research. In the rest of this section I revisit some of the research I outlined in Chapter 4 and discuss how my study complements and extends it.

It is important to bring the writer into the picture in relation to other elements in a social view of writing. As I argued at the end of Chapter 4, considerable attention has been paid to the context, the reader, the task, goals and purposes, and processes, but researchers other than Cherry have neglected the writer, perhaps for fear of seeming overly romantic and 'a-social' by discussing the individual who produces the writing. I hope that my approach restores the various aspects of 'the writer' to their place as a legitimate object of interest in a social view of writing.

The idea of '(discoursal) identity' is part and parcel of the idea of '(discourse) community': a community only really exists by common acts of identification by individual members. By showing (in Chapter 9) exactly how student writers claimed academic discourse community membership through their discourse choices in their writing, I have, I believe, both confirmed and enriched the concept of 'academic discourse community'. My study (particularly Chapters 6, 8 and 10) also revealed the sorts of tensions, discontinuities and contradictions which have been said to characterize discourse communities, clothing with detailed personal examples the generalizations made by Harris, Bizzell and Swales (see Chapter 4 for references).

Writing researchers referring to such concepts as intertextuality and appropriation are, I think, making fundamentally the same claim as I am: that writers construct a discoursal self from socially available discoursal resources which have particular subject positions inscribed in them. The particular contribution of my research has been to provide specific linguistic detail and insights from the writers themselves to substantiate this claim. In so doing, I believe I have increased our understanding of the complexity of these processes. I have also forged the connection between work on 'intertextuality' and 'appropriation', and that on 'imitation', by showing how writers do not encounter discourses and their associated subject-positions in some abstract way, but gain access to them through actual encounters in their life histories (in Chapter 7). This connection can be understood in terms of the interplay between the autobiographical self, socially available possibilities for self-hood and the discoursal self.

The idea of the discoursal construction of identity also provides a useful angle on student writers' tendency to plagiarize. Instead of viewing this as a crime prompting moral outrage one should, perhaps, view student writers' practices of lifting phrases wholesale from their reading as one of the consequences of their desire to identify with the academic discourse community. Copied words are not, to them, an infringement of intellectual property, but a means whereby they can construct the discoursal self which they understand to be required (as discussed in Chapters 7 and 8).

While I have not made any new contribution to theory and research on authorship, authority and authorial presence, I have, I think, set this work within a wider framework for thinking about writer identity. Firstly I have argued that the self as author is only one out of four ways of thinking about the identity of the writer (as presented at the end of Chapter 1). Secondly I have discussed how authoritativeness is one out of many characteristics of the self which are constructed by the writer's discourse choices (as shown in Chapter 10).

Overlapping with the study of authority in writing is the study of the writer's 'voice'. There is a temptation to treat the writer's 'own voice' as a valid and unitary concept. The distinctions I have drawn and the research reported in Part Two confirm Hashimoto's view (1987, see Chapter 4) that the writer's 'own voice' is an articulation of socially available possibilities for self-hood, the fabric of which is highly dependent on the writer's 'autobiographical self'. Secondly, the distinction between 'the self as author' and 'the discoursal self' generates two definitions of the writer's 'voice': (i) what the writer wants to present, including how authoritatively to say it, and (ii) the sorts of words the writer feels comfortable using. There is an interaction between these two meanings of 'voice', but in my view it is useful for analytical purposes to distinguish them from each other.

I have taken account of Cherry's distinction between 'ethos' and 'persona' as different aspects of the self which a writer represents in writing. I found it hard to identify specific linguistic features to associate with the discoursal construction of 'ethos': what type of human being a writer is. I think nearly all my examples illustrated the discoursal construction of 'persona': which discourse community/ies writers are identifying with, which roles within it/them, and which interests, values, beliefs and practices they are aligning themselves with. There were some exceptions: certain personal qualities such as 'having a heart' (Chapter 6), being 'creative', and being modest (Chapter 10), seemed to have discoursal correlates, mainly in what Halliday calls the Inter-personal aspects of grammar — that is, in the markers of mood and modality, but I did not find many examples which I could classify in this way. Maybe 'ethos' as Cherry defines it can be conveyed by behaviour and can be talked or written about — as John talked about wanting to seem 'socially aware' (see Chapter 10), but cannot be traced to specific textual features. Maybe discourse cannot construct credibility directly, but only indirectly by identifying the writer with interests, values, beliefs and practices which a specific discourse community recognizes as the insignia of 'a good person'. I conclude that the distinction may well be a useful one, but that 'ethos' in the sense of 'personal qualities' is hard to pin down to the linguistic features of a text. The distinction between 'ethos' and 'persona' aside, the main aim of my research has been to develop and elaborate the general concept of self-representation in writing which Cherry first put forward.

The idea of the discoursal construction of identity is fundamental to critical approaches to academic writing. Critical theorists such as Bizzell, and basic writing theorists such as Shaughnessy and Rose have drawn attention to the qualities which non-traditional entrants to higher education bring to the academic community, and the challenges they pose to its whole edifice of values and practices. I think this position is greatly enhanced by viewing writing as a site of struggle in which writers are negotiating an identity. This perspective foregrounds the autobiographical self which writers bring with them to the act of writing, and throws into question which subject positions they might want to occupy, and which they might choose to resist. Writers may not be willing to compromise their identity by becoming party to the dominant practices of the community. Non-standard syntax can be understood not so much as a failure to conform to conventions as a signal that the writer may be drawing uncomfortably on contradictory, possibly jarring voices in the construction of a discoursal self. There is no such thing as 'impersonal writing'; rather, every written text is, among other things, a statement of the identity of the writer, and hence in itself a form of social action. Through the discoursal construction of self in writing, students can assert or negate particular versions of self (in addition to asserting or negating particular representations of the world), thereby contributing to the reproduction or contestation of patterns of privileging among subject-positions within the academic community.

In this section I have discussed the contribution my research makes to theory and research on academic writing. However, many of the findings can be extended to apply to the study of all types of writing, of literacy and of discourse in general; in other words, to the fields of study I introduced in Chapters 1–3. Particularly, the focus on identity and processes of identification seems to me to help to explain the link between specific texts, events and individuals on the one hand, and large-scale discoursal and social change on the other. The aim of critical discourse analysis is to show how and why language changes over time. The aim of this book is to set the experience of individual writers, struggling to shape their ideas and their selves, against the background of discoursal and social change. But it also contributes to an understanding of discoursal and social change by suggesting how person-by-person processes of alignment with particular subject positions contribute to collective action. Although each person's configuration of alignments is unique, people are not isolated individuals: it is remarkable how many people with very different life-stories are all making their contribution towards resisting, say, the privileged convention of presenting understandings as categorical truths. So what seem like individual acts of identification can build up gradually to large scale social change in, for example, views of knowledge or representations of gender.

In the next section I identify some important aspects of writer identity which were missing from my study, and I suggest aspects of the discoursal construction of identity in general, and writer identity in particular which I think would be worth researching in the future.

Suggestions for future research

The discoursal construction of identity is a relatively new research focus, providing a challenging, multidisciplinary project for the future. There are still many theoretical questions about the social construction of identity in general which need to be pursued. Further research might clarify the distinctions and relationships among the terms 'self', 'person', 'role', 'identity', 'ethos', 'persona', 'subject', 'subjectivity', and 'voice'. Further research is needed in order to give us a more principled way of talking about the issue of authenticity: how can we account for the psychological reality of 'the real self', and incorporate this less apologetically in our understanding of social identity? More studies need to focus on the way in which social interaction mediates social construction in a wide range of settings. These issues need to be addressed in general and also tied specifically to linguistic evidence — linguistics has tools to offer for this analysis which should not be ignored. More studies like mine in a wide range of settings would contribute to a better understanding of the way in which specific textual features become imbued with social meanings and have the potential to position their users.

As research on the discoursal construction of identities in general progresses it will be possible to carry out more informed research on ways in which this affects writing. Even while more general aspects of the discoursal construction of identities are being worked on, however, writing researchers can take up the focus on writer identity, both to advance understanding about the writing process and to contribute to the more general research agenda. Researchers might use discourse-based interviews like mine about issues of identity with populations other than mature students in higher education: learner writers of different ages, in different school systems and in a variety of cultural settings; people writing in a variety of genres other than academic assignments. In my view the guiding questions I was asking are worth pursuing with different groups: what versions of self are these writers constructing for themselves discoursally, which do they own and disown, and why?

For those interested in issues of identity in academic writing there is plenty of scope for further research. This was an issue-raising study, showing the richness and complexity of what is involved in the discoursal construction of identity, but it paid only cursory attention to some issues. For example,

Chapter 10 included a brief section on the way in which different possibilities for self-hood are inscribed in the discourses of different fields of study. In this respect there is a need for more sophisticated and systematic analyses of aspects of discourse above the level of the clause, such as discipline-specific conventions governing generalization, elaboration, explicitness, attribution and modes of argumentation. In the same chapter I suggested that there may be a relationship between writers' life histories, their sense of self-worth, the way in which they are discoursally positioned by their writing, and ideologies of authorship in the academic community. This suggestion would be worth further investigation. A particularly valuable complement to this study would be further research on readers' impressions of the writers whose texts they have read. Do readers construct the same impressions as the writers thought they conveyed? Hayes and others (1992) and Haswell and Haswell (1995) have started to pursue this research issue, although their work is not accompanied by linguistic analysis of the particular discourse features which are conveying particular impressions.

It may be possible to follow up some aspects of this study either in more detail, or with larger numbers, to see whether generalizations can be based on insights and speculations presented here. For example, it would be interesting to focus only on the use of graphic and metadiscoursal markers such as scare quotes to discover which sorts of things students distance themselves from consciously — possibly over a wide range of subject areas. To take a different type of example, it would be interesting to take up the question of how students position themselves discoursally in relation to environmental issues: a topic raised by my study of Sarah. By studying several students on the same course, or on a set of related courses on environmental issues, it would be possible either to clothe this topic with more detail, or to arrive at some generalizations about it. Yet another perspective would be to take one or a small number of discourse features which look interesting from the point of view of positioning and focus on how a larger number of students use them and how they feel positioned by them. For example, the word 'problem' was extremely interesting from this point of view in Rachel's writing; another focus might be the use of long noun phrases.

Literacy researchers need to achieve a more satisfactory convergence between the study of texts and the study of practices. Studying practices involves understanding how literacy is embedded in people's lives and the differing ways in which they go about similar tasks involving literacy (as explained in Barton 1991, 1994). Such practices around writing play their own role in socially constructing writer identity (as I argued in Chapter 3) and they also affect and relate to the discoursal construction of identity. Although I have made a step in the direction of this convergence by focusing on writers' feelings and intentions, and by briefly describing Rachel's literacy practices in Chapter 6, I did not make three-way links between practices, issues of identity and texts. It seems to me that this is something future researchers need to aim for.

Another complementary line of research which would be worth pursuing would be to look at how the same person constitutes their identity differently in different settings, both through their writing and through other semiotic means. This would be particularly interesting because it would put academic literacy into perspective: a person's identity is bound to prove much more diverse on such evidence, and it would be possible to trace interplay between different aspects of their lives. This seems to me to be an important dimension which is missing from my research: it was something I was aware of, but did not collect sufficient evidence of and did not have space to address.

In short, there are many avenues for further study within the broad field of the social construction of identity, in the more specifically linguistic field of the way in which textual features manifest identity, and in the particular field in which I am interested: the discoursal construction of writer identity for students in higher education.

Putting writer identity on the agenda in the teaching and learning of academic writing

In Chapter 1 I said that my personal motivation for studying something to do with writing came from my work as a teacher of writing, particularly in further education with adult students. More recently, working with John Simpson and Denise Roach had convinced me that writer identity was an important issue in writing and learning to write, particularly for mature students returning to study. In this section I suggest some implications of this study for the teaching of writing within support systems in higher education, return to study programmes, and more generally.

The role of theory and research findings in practice

Theory and research are only as good as their practical value. Theory and research ought be a resource to help people to understand their experience and their environment. In her chapter entitled 'Theory as liberatory practice' hooks (1994) says that theory should serve transformatory and liberatory ends: 'I saw in theory a location for healing' (p. 59). Since my interest in writing and identity grew out of a desire to help people to achieve liberation and fulfilment, I have a commitment to ensuring that my theory and research is useful in practice and, if possible, also has liberatory potential. I suggest three criteria which theory and research findings need to meet in order to be of use in practice: relevance, explanatory power, and accessibility, and a fourth which needs to be met in order to achieve the ends set out by hooks: emancipatory power.

As I said above, my claim to relevance is based on the fact that studying the relationship between writing and identity grew out of issues raised by student writers themselves. After concentrating on this area for many years, I remain convinced that identity is of central importance in thinking about writing. I have often had the experience myself of not being able to find the right words for what I want to write, and then realizing that it is not so much a problem of the meaning I want to convey as a problem of what impression of myself I want to convey. I have come to see every act of academic writing as, among other things, the writer's struggle to create a discoursal self which resolves the tension between their autobiographical self and the possibilities for self-hood available in the academic community.

By 'explanatory power' I mean the power to provide understandings and explanations which really do illuminate the issues which are being discussed. With some types of research there are recognized tests of 'robustness' for theory and 'reliability' and 'validity' for research findings. The type of exploratory research I have presented here cannot be subjected to such tests. It is more a question of whether the arguments and examples I have presented are convincing, provide ways of understanding phenomena which were previously less understood, and stand the test of application to practice. My co-researchers assured me of the value to them of our jointly produced understandings, and join me in hoping they will be similarly useful to others.

As regards accessibility, I have tried to write this book in ways which make it readable to many types of readers, but I realize that it may be too detailed to be of interest to many who want to use its ideas in practice. I have therefore published some of the ideas here in a shorter form (Ivanič 1995, and a revised version as Chapter 6 in Clark and Ivanič 1997), and two of my co-researchers and I wrote an article which presents many of the issues from their own perspectives and in their own words (Ivanič, Aitchison and Weldon 1996). (See also Lea and Street 1996a and b for examples of publications by researchers committed to this principle.)

By 'emancipatory power' I mean the power to help people change the social conditions which affect their lives so as to improve their opportunities. To achieve the ends mentioned by hooks it is essential for theory and research findings to fulfil this criterion along with the others. In my view the theory and research findings in this book do have the potential to contribute towards social transformation and liberation. By recognizing that writing is a social act in which, among other things, we make a statement about ourselves, we can use it actively to affirm those values, beliefs and practices which we want to sustain, and to resist those values, beliefs and practices which we see as harmful. Writing contributes towards shaping future possibilities for self-hood for others (see also Clark and Ivanič 1997).

But whether or not theory and research findings are of any use in practice depends not only on these criteria, but also on the pedagogical principles which guide the insertion of theory into practice. The traditional relationship between theory and practice in academic support is one in which teachers as 'knowers' translate theory into prescriptions about the characteristics of academic writing and practical tips on how to do it, which they 'transmit' to learners. In my view this may lead to some short-term benefit for learners, but will not have the emancipatory value which hooks proposes.

In order for theory to have this effect, learners themselves need to be able to engage directly with it, and to have opportunities to discover for themselves what use it may be in helping them to understand their experience. In order to achieve this I recommend classes with titles such as 'Critical Approaches to Academic Discourse', in which students read, among other things, the article by Mavis Aitchison, Sue Weldon and me which I mentioned above, or Chapter 6 of this book: the case study of Rachel Dean, or the part of Chapter 1 where I spell out four meanings of 'writer identity', or other selections. Students can then compare the examples with their own experiences, tasks and drafts, discuss whether the theoretical distinctions are of any use for reflecting on their experience, and if so, make use of them for this purpose. Taking a step further, theory can provide students with tools for critically evaluating the social context in which they are learning, for identifying ways in which it restricts their opportunities and/or the opportunities of others, and ultimately for envisaging more inclusive alternatives, and fighting for them. Such a pedagogy is founded on a view of learners as intellectuals, as researchers and as active participants in social struggles, not just passively receiving knowledge and advice, but searching for understandings which will be of direct use to them, which will open up new fields of vision and new perspectives, and provide a basis for their own emancipatory and transformatory action.

This principle — that theory and research findings are not just for theorists or for teachers-as-mediators, but are directly relevant to students — underlies the recommendations in the next section.

Implications of this research for academic support provision[1]

In this section I suggest some specific implications of this research for the learning and teaching of academic writing. The sorts of students I have in mind are adult return-to-study students, or students on an academic support programme, but I think what I am suggesting can apply to learners of any age in any setting. I am referring to 'learner writers' and 'student writers', meaning primarily people who are in pedagogical settings designed for improving their writing, and those who write as part of their studies. However, we are all learner writers all the time, and I think these suggestions can be of use to everyone.

The overarching implication is that writer identity should be included in any programme of study concerned with academic writing. Not only is it a significant factor in any act of writing in the ways I have shown in this book, but it also connects a particular act of writing to the bigger picture: discussing the writer's identity places an act of writing in the context of the writer's past history, of their position in relation to their social context, and of their role in possible futures. Bringing identity explicitly onto the agenda in the learning and teaching of writing transforms it from a local 'fix-this-essay' undertaking into a much more broadly conceived project.

An adequate approach to the teaching of writing should pay attention to all four meanings of writer identity, as I set out at the end of Chapter 1: the autobiographical self, the discoursal self, the self as author, and possibilities for self-hood/subject positions. In my view it is useful both to distinguish between these four aspects of writer identity, and to discuss the ways in which they are interrelated. For example, a discussion of subject positioning would focus on socially available possibilities for self-hood, but would also include attention to the writer's sense of who s/he is and where s/he is coming from, (autobiographical self), of being positioned as relatively authoritative or lacking in authority, and of the discoursal self which each individual writer is constructing in their own writing. (See also Ivanič 1994b for other ways of thinking about the pedagogical implications of different aspects of writer identity.)

Issues of identity cannot be addressed in writing exercises. In order to help people learn how to negotiate their identities through writing it is necessary to build the teaching of writing around writing tasks with real communicative purposes for real readers. This can include writing for teachers, but it must be writing which will be read and, if necessary, assessed, on the grounds of content, not just accuracy. Just as this research was based around essays which were part of coursework in higher education, rather than tasks which were set up specifically for the purpose of the research, so the teaching of writing needs to be socially situated (see Clark 1992).

Most of the suggestions which follow can be summarized as raising learners' critical awareness of the nature of writer identity, so as to give them maximum control over this important aspect of writing. I mentioned Critical Language Awareness (C.L.A.) in Chapter 5 as a research methodology; here I am recommending it as a pedagogy. C.L.A. focuses on the critical discussion of discourses, discourse practices and the way in which they position language users. In relation to writing it means recognizing that writing in a particular way means appearing to be a certain type of person, as discussed in Part Two of this book; that is, it involves raising awareness of the discoursal self and gaining control over it. C.L.A. also involves action as a result of awareness. It is based on a view of language in which discourses do not mechanistically determine what people say and write, but are open to contestation and change. Learners are encouraged to make choices as they write which will align them with social values, beliefs and practices to which they are committed, if necessary opposing the privileged conventions for the genre and thereby contributing to discoursal, and thus social, change. (For more detailed discussion of Critical Language Awareness as a goal in language education, see Clark and others 1990, 1991, Ivanič 1990, Fairclough 1992d, Janks and Ivanič 1992, Clark and Ivanič 1997, and forthcoming.)

Learner writers need to be aware that writing is an extremely complex social act, and it is not their weakness which causes them to get stuck with it. Not just people who are construed as 'learners', but everyone has to face the difficult task of deciding how to present themselves in writing: which discourse types and associated identities to accept, and which to reject.

Students need to develop a critical awareness of their own life-histories, and the sorts of social constraints which may be responsible for any difficulties they have with acquiring particular discourse-types. If someone is able to blame the inequities of society for the fact that a certain discourse doesn't come easily to them, and recognize the political implications of this inequity, they are likely to stop taking the blame on their own shoulders for the difficulties they face. This might be a lot more enabling than thinking that they must just try harder. As I suggested in Chapter 10, part of the autobiographical identity which women, older people, Black people, homosexual and bisexual people, and working class people might bring with them to their studies is a sense that they do not have the right to a voice in the academic community. Tutors should be aware of this possibility, and find ways of critically examining the source of such feelings. Discussion of what writers are bringing with them to the act of writing might also focus on what aspects of their autobiographical selves they want to ensure they do not relinquish in the face of institutional pressure to reposition themselves.

Rather than learning just the characteristics of powerful discourse types and attempting to reproduce them, students should explore the way in which different discourse types position them, and discuss the personal and political consequences of participating in them. Such discussion should include an understanding of the fact that discourse types are not fixed, but are in a constant state of flux and struggle as to what is valued in a particular social context. This type of critical awareness of relationships between writing and identity gives students a sense that there are alternatives available, that they have a degree of freedom in this respect, that their writing is part of a wider struggle between competing subject-positions within the academic community as a whole, and that by their choices they might eventually contribute in some small way to social change.

Students need to discuss the writer-reader relationship explicitly from the point of view of self-representation. All too often an understanding of 'the reader' is limited to issues of background knowledge, expectations and/or considerate use of signposting. The issue of what impression the reader is going to receive of the writer as a person remains covert, yet this may be exactly what is subconsciously bothering the writer. It is worth both mentioning this as an element in the writing process, and focusing on it during writing conferences and tutorials.

There has been a tendency in some recent approaches to the teaching of writing to champion the writer's 'voice' in a rather uncritical way. Writing teachers often use the term 'voice' without recognizing that there are two dimensions to it, as I explained above. It would, in my view, be more profitable to treat the two aspects of voice separately. In relation to the writer's 'voice' in the sense of *form* — the discoursal self — it would be useful to pay attention to the socially available possibilities for self-hood, and the constraints on them which I have referred to frequently throughout this book. The writer's 'voice' in the sense of *content* — ideas and beliefs — can then be given separate attention, as I discuss next.

Having disentangled 'voice' in the sense of authorship from the other meaning of voice', I think it has a special set of implications for the teaching of writing. I would go so far as to say, if writing isn't equated with authorship, why bother to learn to write at all? This idea is at the heart of a good deal of existing theory and research on the learning and teaching of writing. Book titles in this tradition capture the principle: *Writing with Power* (Elbow 1991), *Writing with Reason: The emergence of authorship in young children* (Hall 1989). Having a driving purpose for writing, having a burning desire to convey a message, a story, some ideas or strongly held views are the whole point of writing, and must be central to writing pedagogy. We should be teaching that writing something always means having the power to make decisions (except when copying), and that the point of writing is to say something that matters to the writer. We should be providing opportunities for learners to develop a sense of purpose and authorship. At least in writing classes, everyone should encounter powerful reasons for writing, should experience what it means to be an 'author' and should have the right to be authoritative on topics which matter to them. Developing a sense of authorship is a guiding principle for good practice in the teaching of writing on Return to Study courses and in Adult Literacy provision (see Gardener 1992, Mace 1992, and contributions to Barton and Ivanič (eds.) 1991), and particularly in community publishing initiatives (see the contributions to Mace 1995).

Issues of authorship, authoritativeness and authorial presence also need to be discussed and problematized. All of us, as writers and learner-writers, need to recognize the way in which authority is contested: Who has the right to author particular types of writing? Who has the right to be authoritative on particular topics? Which types of writing conventionally foreground the author, how, and why? Which types of writing conventionally obscure the author, how, and why? In the light of this discussion, learner-writers need to critically assess how far, and in what ways, they want to establish their authorial presence in particular tasks. It is important to pay attention to cultural differences in such discussions: members of different cultural groups feel differently about how authoritatively they are willing to present themselves, depending on religious beliefs and social customs.

Critical awareness of issues of identity as a writer can be the first step towards collective action. By discussing ways in which they are positioned by the discourse conventions available to them, groups of students can identify points of convergence in their reactions to these positionings. Such discussions can lead to collective decisions to affirm some values, beliefs and practices, and to challenge others. In this way, students might begin to see writing as a political act in which, through their individual discoursal alignments, they are contributing to the reproduction or re-shaping of the ideological landscape.

Finally, learner writers can profitably engage in mini-versions of this research for themselves. One dimension of this is to conduct their own ethnographies of the academic discourse communities they are newly members of, finding out (among other things) what the possibilities for self-hood are in these specific social contexts, and what positions they, as students, are expected to occupy in their academic writing. Sources of evidence for such studies would be the spoken and written instructions they receive for writing their assignments, feedback they, and other students receive on their assignments, their text-books and recommended reading, and the way in which social relations are conducted in their departments. Writer identity is one of many aspects of academic discourse practices which can be investigated in this way.

Another way in which learners can become researchers is by critically reflecting on their own experience of grappling with academic writing. Our experience as co-researchers on this project was that the sorts of discussions we held for research purposes were also very useful learning opportunities for everyone involved. If tutors talk to students about their dilemmas over self-presentation, and their reasons for wanting to write in one way rather than another, it helps the students recognize these dilemmas and figure out how to face them. Exactly the same sorts of questions as I asked my co-researchers would in my view be useful in pedagogical situations. Learner writers can make explicit for themselves the way in which their identity is constructed in their writing by answering the questions 'What impressions do you think you are giving of yourself in your writing in general?' 'Which parts of the writing construct these impressions?' The question 'Which of these impressions are you happy to be giving of yourself? Why?' can lead into discussing issues of ownership, accommodation and resistance. Further questions such as 'Where do you see yourself in this? and where not?' can raise learners' consciousness about the fact that writing can present, conceal, and give a false impression of aspects of our identities. A question sequence like ' Did you feel under pressure to write any of it in a particular way? Which parts? Where was this pressure coming from?' can help learner writers to recognize the way in which they are responding to privileged conventions and to the expectations of their readers. The questions 'Is there any way you would hate to write?' and 'Is there anyone whose work you have read that you would hate to write like?' can help learner-writers to see the possibility of resistance, and their own small contribution to struggle and change in conventions.

Discussions of this sort also help tutors to understand these dilemmas from the students' perspectives, and take them into account both in future planning and in the way they assess students' writing. In the next section I discuss how tutors and the academic community as a whole might reconsider their practice in the light of the theory and research findings presented in this book.

Implications of this research for the academic community as a whole

Institutions of higher education are full of complaints about student writing. The mismatch between students' writing and institutional expectations is frequently attributed to a literacy deficit on the part of the students. The most common response is to set up some sort of 'fix-it' study skills provision with the aim of remedying this irritating literacy deficit as quickly and cheaply as possible. My research has led me to see this mismatch in a quite different light, and to propose that academic institutions, in addition to providing the sort of support recommended in the previous section, ought themselves to be examining and remedying their own practices.

Firstly, the quotations in Chapters 6, 7 and 8 contain many insights into students' experience of writing. They show how there are often subtle and valid explanations for what students have written, and they reveal the extent of thought and strategy that students have put into their writing. Complex negotiations of identity lie beneath the surface of what may appear at first glance to be 'inadequate' academic writing. The implication of this is that tutors should learn to view students' writing as the product of their developing sense of what it means to be a member of a specific academic community, of who they are and how they want to appear to be. Wherever possible tutors should themselves be listening to students' own understandings of what is going on, not making assumptions on the basis of surface evidence. They might then be less inclined to jump to damning judgements of student writing, and might instead be able to help students come to a more conscious understanding of these processes, in the way my co-researchers did through participation in this research.

Secondly, Chapters 6, 8, 9 and 10 show that meeting institutional expectations is not just a question of 'literacy', but more a question of identity. Writing a good student essay which will be highly valued requires complex insider knowledge. The values and practices which need to be demonstrated in academic writing differ from department to department, even from tutor to tutor. The sorts of guidelines students receive often contain detailed instructions on such things as layout and margin width, and give little, if any guidance on what will actually constitute good writing. When there is any attempt to specify this, it amounts to little more than exhortations that the writing be 'well structured', or that arguments be 'supported with evidence'. Yet when students attempt to follow these sorts of instructions, they quickly find that they need a great deal of insider knowledge in order to know exactly what counts as acceptable essay structure, argumentation, proof, or clarity in that community: exactly what needs defining, what needs elaborating, what needs supporting, and how. It is not just a question of knowing how to produce a decontextualized generic form, but it depends on context- and content-specific details, as I illustrated at the end of Chapter 9 (see also Turner 1994, Hewlett 1996 and Street 1996 for discussion of this issue). In other words, students need to know what is involved in taking on an identity as member of a specific discourse community. In my view, it is the responsibility of the academic community as a whole to turn its highly developed intellectual abilities to the task of identifying its own values, beliefs and practices, and subjecting them to critique. Tutors should clarify to themselves what they are asking students to do, and why. They would then be in a position to share their insider knowledge more democratically, making membership of the academic discourse community less exclusive, more accessible, and more open to contestation.

Finally, the mismatch between students' writing and institutional expectations points up the way in which academic discourses position and co-opt students. Chapter 9 of this book examines how particular values, beliefs and practices are inscribed in the characteristics of academic discourse which students feel under pressure to adopt. Students often face a crisis of identity, feeling that they have to become a different sort of person in order to participate in these context-specific and culture-specific knowledge-making practices of academic institutions. As Chapters 6, 7 and 8 show, many students bring with them to the act of writing autobiographical selves which may be ignored by the academic community. In my view it is the responsibility of the academic community to subject their values, beliefs and practices to critical scrutiny, and to recognize alternatives and possibilities for change The discourses of the academic community do not need to be mystifying, oppressive or exclusive. Institutions of higher education need to recognize and place value on the full diversity of knowledges, wisdoms, ways of learning and ways with words which new members could bring to them. The increasing presence of students from a wide variety of backgrounds and non-traditional study routes exerts urgent pressure on the academic community to take up this challenge.

Writing and identity beyond pedagogy

The aim of this series of studies in written language and literacy is to advance insight into the multifaceted character of written language. This book in the series has concentrated on just one of these facets: the capacity of written language to construct the identity of the writer. Studying writer identity has led me to bring discourse analysis of written texts together with insights drawn from in-depth conversations with the writers of the texts, and to relate these to theory and research in linguistics, education, social sciences and literacy studies. Although the book focuses on the experience of mature students writing in academic contexts, the issues it raises are relevant to writing in other contexts too.

Writing is not a neutral 'skill', but a socio-political act of identification in which people are constructed by the discoursal resources on which they are drawing, construct their own 'discoursal identity' in relation to their immediate social context, and contribute to constructing a new configuration of discoursal resources for the future. While language can, to some extent, be donned and discarded like a set of clothing, it also has deeply personal consequences, going right to the heart of our being, defining our social selves. For these reasons, I suggest that issues of identity are not an 'optional extra' for literacy theorists, but are central to a social view of writing.

I suggest that all of us can gain control over our writing by recognizing that it is communicating not only some subject matter but also an impression of ourselves. The fact that we are putting ourselves on the line in a relatively non-negotiable way is one of the things that makes writing difficult. When we are not happy with what we have written it may be that we need to change the way it positions us, rather than just the subject-matter — although these two are intertwined. The recognition that writing is 'personal' in this way can be rather daunting, but it can also be reassuring, even liberating to understand the source of difficulty. I hope that as you read this book you have found some of what it says illuminating in relation to your own experience of writing, not only within the academic community but in the rest of your lives as well.

Notes

1.   This section is a reworking of part of an article entitled "Writer Identity" originally published in *Prospect: The Australian Journal of TESOL 10.1.* (Ivanič 1995). I am grateful to the editor for permission to use it in its revised form here.

References

Abrams, D. and M. Hogg (eds.). 1990. *Social Identity Theory.* London: Harvester Wheatsheaf.

Aitchison, M. 1994. "Academic Gifts". Unpublished typescript, Lancaster University.

Andrews, R. (ed.). 1989. *Narrative and Argument.* Milton Keynes: Open University Press.

Andrews, R. 1995. *Teaching and Learning Argument.* London: Cassell Education.

Arrington, P. 1988. "A Dramatistic Approach to Understanding and Teaching the Paraphrase". *College Composition and Communication* 39: 185–197.

Baker, D., J. Clay and C. Fox (eds.). 1996. *Challenging Ways of Knowing: In English, Mathematics and Science.* London: The Falmer Press.

Bakhtin, M.M. 1973. *Problems of Dostoevsky's Poetics.* Trans. by R.W. Rotsel. Ann Arbor, MI: Ardis.

Bakhtin, M.M. 1981. "Discourse in the Novel". (First published in 1929) In M. Holquist, (ed.), *The Dialogic Imagination.* Trans. by C. Emerson and M. Holquist. Austin: University of Texas Press.

Bakhtin, M.M. 1986. "The Problem of Speech Genres", and "The Problem of the Text in Linguistics, Philology, and the Human Sciences: An experiment in philosophical analysis". In C. Emerson, C. and M. Holquist (eds.), *Bakhtin: Speech Genres and Other Late Essays.* Trans. V. McGee. Austin: University of Texas Press.

Barnes, D. 1969. "Language in the Secondary Classroom". In D. Barnes, J. Britton and H. Rosen, *Language, the Learner and the School.* Harmondsworth: Penguin.

Bartholomae, D. 1985. "Inventing the University". In M. Rose (ed.), *When a Writer Can't Write.* New York: Guilford.

Barton, D. 1991. "The Social Nature of Writing". In Barton and Ivanič (eds.).

Barton, D. 1994. *Literacy: An Introduction to the Ecology of Written Communication.* Oxford: Blackwell.

348

Barton, D. and M. Hamilton. 1998. *Local Literacies*. London: Routledge.

Barton, D. and S. Padmore. 1991. " Roles, Networks and Values in Everyday Writing". In Barton and Ivanič (eds.).

Barton, D. and R. Ivanič (eds.). 1991. *Writing in the Community.* Newbury Park, CA.: Sage Publications.

Baumeister, R. F. 1986. *Identity: Cultural Change and the Struggle for the Self.* New York: Oxford University Press.

Baynham, M. 1995. *Literacy Practices: Investigating literacy in social contexts.* London: Longman.

Bazerman, C. 1980. "A Relationship between Reading and Writing: the Conversational Model". *College English* 41: 656–661.

Bazerman, C. 1981. *The Informed Writer: Using sources in the disciplines.* Boston: Houghton Mifflin.

Bazerman, C. 1981. "What Written Knowledge Does: Three examples of academic discourse". *Philosophy of the Social Sciences* 11: 361–87.

Bazerman, C. 1988. *Shaping Written Knowledge: Essays in the growth, form, function, and implications of the scientific article.* Madison: University of Wisconsin Press.

Bazerman, C. and J. Paradis (eds.). 1991. *Textual Dynamics of the Professions: Historical and contemporary studies of writing in professional communities.* Madison: University of Wisconsin Press.

Benson, N., S. Gurney, J. Harrison and R. Rimmershaw. 1994. "The Place of Academic Literacy in Whole Life Literacy: Three case studies". In Hamilton, Barton, and Ivanič (eds.).

Berkenkotter, C. and Huckin, T. 1995. *Genre Knowledge in Disciplinary Communication: Cognition/culture/power.* Hillsdale, N.J.: Lawrence Erlbaum.

Berman, M. 1983. *All that is Solid Melts into Air: The experience of modernity (Second edition).* London: Verso. (First edition: New York: Simon and Schuster, 1982.)

Besnier, N. 1989. "Literacy and Feelings: The encoding of affect in Nukulaelae letters". *Text* 9: 69–92. (Reprinted in B. Street (ed.) 1993b).

Besnier, N. 1990. "Language and Affect". *Annual Review of Anthropology* 19: 419–451.

Besnier, N. 1991. "Literacy and the Notion of Person on Nukulaelae Atoll". *American Anthropologist* 93: 570–587.

Besnier, N. 1995. *Literacy, Emotion and Authority: Reading and writing on a Polynesian atoll (= Studies in the Social and Cultural Foundations of Language 17).* Cambridge: Cambridge University Press.

Biff. 1993. The Plagiarism Cartoon. First printed in *The Guardian Weekend*, September 1993.

Billig, M. 1987. *Arguing and Thinking: A rhetorical approach to social psychology.* Cambridge: Cambridge University Press.

Bizzell, P. 1982. "Cognition, Convention and Certainty: What we need to know about writing". *PRE/TEXT* 3: 213–243.

Bizzell, P. 1986. "Foundationalism and Anti-foundationalism in Composition Studies". *PRE/TEXT* 7: 37–56.

Bizzell, P. 1987. "What is a Discourse Community?" *Penn State Conference on Rhetoric and Composition.* University Park, University of Pennsylvania.

Bizzell, P. 1989. "Cultural Criticism: A social approach to studying writing". *Rhetoric Review* 7: 224–230.

Bizzell, P. 1992. *Academic Discourse and Critical Consciousness.* Pittsburgh, PA: University of Pittsburgh Press.

Bolinger, D. 1980. *Language: The loaded weapon.* London: Longman.

Bourdieu, P. 1977. *Outline of a Theory of Practice.* Cambridge: Cambridge University Press.

Brodkey, L. 1987. *Academic Writing as a Social Practice.* Philadelphia, PA: Temple University Press.

Brooke, R. 1988. "Modeling a Writer's Identity: Reading and imitation in the writing classroom". *College Composition and Communication* 39: 24–41.

Brown, P. and S. Levinson. 1987. *Politeness: Some universals in language usage (= Studies in International Sociolinguistics 4).* Cambridge: Cambridge University Press. (Originally published in E. Goody (ed.), *Questions and Politeness.* Cambridge: Cambridge University Press, 1978)

Bruffee, K. A. 1986. "Social Construction, Language, and the Authority of Knowledge: A bibliographical essay". *College English* 48: 773–790.

Burkitt, I. 1991. *Social Selves: Theories of the social formation of personality.* London: Sage Publications.

Campbell, C. 1990. "Writing with Others' Words: Using background reading text in academic compositions". In B. Kroll (ed.), *Second Language Writing.* Cambridge: Cambridge University Press.

Caywood, C. and G. Overing. 1987. Introduction. *Teaching Writing: Pedagogy, gender, and equity.* Albany: State University of New York Press.

Chafe, W. 1982. "Integration and Involvement in Speaking, Writing, and Oral Literature". In D. Tannen (ed.), *Spoken and Written Language.* Norwood, N.J.: Ablex.

Chase, G. 1988. "Accommodation, Resistance and the Politics of Student Writing". *College Composition and Communication* 39: 13–22.

350

Cherry, R. 1988. *"Ethos* versus Persona: Self-Representation in Written Discourse". *Written Communication* 5: 251–276.

Clark, R. 1992. "Principles and Practice of C.L.A. in the Classroom". In Fairclough (ed.), 1992d.

Clark, R. and R. Ivanič. 1991. Consciousness-Raising about the Writing Process. In Garrett, P. and James, C. (eds.) *Language Awareness in the Classroom.* London: Longman.

Clark, R. and R. Ivanič. 1997. *The Politics of Writing.* London: Routledge.

Clark, R. and R. Ivanič. (forthcoming) "Critical Discourse Analysis and Educational Change". In L. van Lier (ed.), *Encyclopedia of Language and Education, Volume 6: Knowledge about Language.* Dordrecht: Kluwer.

Clark, R., C. Constantinou, A. Cottey and Yeoh, O. C. 1990. "Rights and Obligations in Student Writing". In Clark and others (eds.).

Clark, R., N. Fairclough, R. Ivanič, and M. Martin-Jones. 1990. "Critical Language Awareness Part I: A critical review of three current approaches to language awareness". *Language and Education* 4: 249–260.

Clark, R., N. Fairclough, R. Ivanič, and M. Martin-Jones. 1991. "Critical Language Awareness Part II: Towards critical alternatives". *Language and Education* 5: 41–54.

Clark, R., N. Fairclough, R. Ivanič, N. Mcleod, J. Thomas, and P. Meara (eds.). 1990. *Language and Power. Selected proceedings of the BAAL Annual Meeting, September 1989 (= British Studies in Applied Linguistics 4).* London: Centre for Information on Language Teaching and Research.

Cooper, M.M. 1989. "Why are we Talking about Discourse Communities?" In M.M. Cooper and M. Holzman, *Writing as Social Action.* Portsmouth, NH: Boynton/Cook Publishers.

Connolly, W. 1991. *Identity \ Difference.* Ithaca, N.Y.: Cornell University Press.

Corson, D. 1985. *The Lexical Bar.* Oxford: Pergamon Press.

Costello, P and S. Mitchell (eds.). 1995. *Competing and Consensual Voices: The theory and practice of argument.* Clevedon: Multilingual Matters.

Currie, P. 1990. "Argument and Evaluation in Organizational Behaviour: Student writing in an introductory course". In S. Anivan (ed.), *Language teaching methodology for the nineties.* Singapore: Regional Language Centre.

Currie, P. 1991. Entering a Disciplinary Community: Expectations for and evaluation of student academic writing in one introductory course in organisational behaviour. Unpublished Ph.D. dissertation: Department of Linguistics and Modern English Language, Lancaster University.

Dudley-Evans, T. and W. Henderson (eds.). 1990. *The Language of Economics: The analysis of economics discourse.* London: Modern English Publications and The British Council.

Ede, L. 1984. "Audience: An introduction to research". *College Composition and Communication* 35: 140–154.

Ede, L. and A. Lunsford. 1990. *Singular Texts/Plural Authors: Perspectives on collaborative writing.* Carbondale and Edwardsville: Southern Illinois University Press.

Eggins, S., J.R. Martin, and P. Wignell. 1987. Writing Project Report. *Working Papers in Linguistics No 5.* Linguistics Department, University of Sydney.

Elbow, P. 1981. *Writing with Power.* New York: Oxford University Press.

Elleray, J. and R. Rimmershaw. 1995. "The Interaction of Academic and Non-Academic Literacies: A case study". Paper presented at the British Educational Research Association Conference, Bath.

Emig, J. 1971. *The Composing Processes of Twelfth Graders.* NCTE Research Report No. 13. Urbana, IL: NCTE.

Fahnestock, J. and Secor, M. 1991. "The Rhetoric of Literary Criticism". In C. Bazerman, and J. Paradis (eds.).

Faigley, L. 1986. "Competing Theories of Process: A critique and a proposal". *College English* 48: 527–542.

Faigley, L. and Hansen, K. 1985. "Learning to Write in the Social Sciences". *College Composition and Communication* 36:140–49.

Fairclough, N. 1988. "Register, Power and Socio-Semantic Change". In D. Birch and M. O'Toole (eds.) *Functions of Style.* London: Pinter Publications.

Fairclough, N.1989. *Language and Power.* London: Longman.

Fairclough, N. 1992a. *Discourse and Social Change.* Cambridge: Polity Press.

Fairclough, N. 1992b. "Discourse and Text: Linguistic and intertextual analysis within discourse analysis". *Discourse and Society 3.2.* (pp. 193–217).

Fairclough, N. 1992c. "The Appropriacy of 'Appropriateness' ". In Fairclough (ed.) 1992d.

Fairclough, N. (ed.). 1992d. *Critical Language Awareness.* London: Longman.

Fairclough, N. 1995. *Critical Discourse Analysis.* Longman: London.

Fairclough, N. 1996. "Discourse Across Disciplines: Critical Discourse Analysis in the study of social change". Paper delivered as the keynote address to Eleventh World Congress of the Association Internationale de Linguistique Appliquée, Jvaskyla, Finland, August 1996.

Fish, S. 1980. *Is There a Text in this Class?* Cambridge: Harvard U.P.

Flower, L. 1989. "Cognition, Context and Theory Building". *College Composition and Communication* 40 : 282–311.

Flower, L. 1994. *The Construction of Negotiated Meaning: A social cognitive theory of writing.* Carbondale and Edwardsville: Southern Illinois University Press.

Flower, L., V. Stein, J. Ackerman, M. Kantz, K. McCormick, and W. Peck. 1990. *Reading to Write: Exploring a social and cognitive process.* New York: Oxford University Press

Flower, L. and Hayes, J. 1980. "The Cognition of Discovery: Defining a rhetorical problem". *College Composition and Communication* 31: 21–32.

Foucault, M. 1988. "Technologies of the Self". In Martin, Gutman and Hutton (eds.)

Freed, R. C. and G. J. Broadhead. 1987. "Discourse Communities, Sacred Texts, and Institutional Norms". *College Composition and Communication* 38:154–165.

Gardener, S. S. 1992. *The Long Word Club.* Lancaster: Research and Practice in Adult Literacy Publications. (Originally published as *The Development of Written Language within Adult Fresh Start and Return to Learning Programmes.* London: ILEA Language and Literacy Unit, 1985).

Gecas, V. and Mortimer, J. 1987. "Stability and Change in the Self-Concept from Adolescence to Adulthood". In Honess and Yardley (eds.)

Gee, J. 1990. *Social Linguistics and Literacies: Ideology in discourses.* Basingstoke: Falmer Press.

Gergen, K. 1991. *The Saturated Self.* New York: Basic Books.

Gergen, K. and K. Davis (eds.). 1985. *The Social Construction of the Person.* New York: Springer Verlag.

Giddens, A. 1991. *Modernity and Self-Identity.* Cambridge: Polity Press.

Gilbert, N. and M. Mulkay. 1984. *Opening Pandora's Box: A sociological analysis of scientists' discourse.* Cambridge: C.U.P.

Goffman, E. 1969. *The Presentation of Self in Everyday Life (Second edition).* London: Allen Lane, The Penguin Press. (First edition: 1959.)

Goffman, E. 1981. *Forms of Talk.* Oxford: Blackwell.

Graddol, D. and O. Boyd-Barrett (eds.). 1994. *Media Texts: Authors and readers.* Clevedon: Multilingual Matters in association with The Open University.

Graves, D. 1983. *Writing: Teachers and children at work.* Portsmouth, N.J.: Heinemann.

Greene, S. 1990. "Toward a Dialectical Theory of Composing". *Centre for the Study of Writing Occasional Paper No 17.* Berkeley, C.A.: U.C.L.A.

Greene, S. 1991. "Writing from Sources: Authority in text and task". *Centre for the Study of Writing Technical Report No 55.* Berkeley, C.A.: U.C.L.A.

Gumperz, J. and Cook-Gumperz, J. 1982. "Introduction: Language and the Communication of Social Identity". In J. Gumperz (ed.) *Language and Social Identity.* Cambridge: Cambridge University Press.

Hall, N. (ed.). 1989. *Writing with Reason: The emergence of authorship in young children.* London: Hodder and Stoughton.

Halliday, M.A.K. 1967. *Language, Society and the Noun.* London: University College.

Halliday, M. A. K. 1978. *Language as Social Semiotic: The social interpretation of language and meaning.* London: Edward Arnold.

Halliday, M. A. K. 1988. "On the Language of Physical Science". In M. Ghadessy (ed.), *Registers of Written English: Situational factors and linguistic features.* London: Frances Pinter.

Halliday, M. A. K. 1989. *Spoken and Written Language (Second edition).* Oxford: Oxford University Press. (First edition: Victoria: Deakin University Press, 1985.)

Halliday, M. A. K. 1993. "New Ways of Meaning: A challenge to applied linguistics". Paper delivered as the keynote address to the Ninth World Congress of the Association Internationale de Linguistique Appliquée, Thessaloniki, Halkidiki, 1990. In M. A. K. Halliday, *Language in a Changing World.* Melbourne: Applied Linguistics Association of Australia.

Halliday, M.A.K. 1994. *Introduction to Functional Grammar (Second edition).* London: Edward Arnold. (First edition: 1985.)

Halliday, M.A.K. and R. Hasan. 1976. *Cohesion in English.* London: Longman.

Halliday, M.A.K. and R. Hasan. 1989. *Language, Context and Text: Aspects of language in a social-semiotic perspective (Second edition).* Oxford: Oxford University Press. (First edition: Victoria: Deakin University Press, 1985.)

Hamilton, M., D. Barton and R. Ivanič (eds.). 1994. *Worlds of Literacy.* Clevedon: Multilingual Matters.

Hamilton, M., R. Ivanič and D. Barton. 1992. "Knowing Where We Are: Participatory research in adult literacy". In J.P. Hautecoeur (ed.), *ALPHA92: Current Research in Literacy: Literacy strategies in the community movement.* Hamburg: Unesco Institute of Education.

Handel, A. 1987. "Perceived Change of Self among Adults: A conspectus". In Honess and Yardley (eds.)

Hansen, K. 1988. "Rhetoric and Epistemology in the Social Sciences: A contrast of two representative texts". In Jolliffe (ed.).

Harré, R. 1979. *Social Being: A theory for social psychology.* Oxford: Blackwell.

Harris, J. 1989. "The Idea of Community in the Study of Writing". *College Composition and Communication 40*: 11–22.

Hart, D., J. Maloney and W. Damon. 1987. "The Meaning and Development of Identity". In Honess and Yardley (eds.)

Hartnett, C. 1986. "Static and Dynamic Cohesion: Signals of thinking in writing". In B. Couture (ed.), *Functional Approaches to Writing: Research perspectives.* London: Frances Pinter.

Hashimoto, I. 1987. "Voice as Juice: Some reservations about evangelic composition." *College Composition and Communication 38*: 70–80.

Haswell, J. and R. Haswell. 1995. "Gendership and the Miswriting of Students". *College Composition and Communication 46*: 223–254.

Haswell, R. 1988. "Dark Shadows: The fate of writers at the bottom". *College Composition and Communication 39*: 303–315.

Hayes, J. and L. Flower. 1980. "Identifying the Organization of Writing Processes: An interdisciplinary approach". In L. Gregg and E. Steinberg (eds.), *Cognitive Processes in Writing.* Hillsdale, N.J.: Lawrence Erlbaum.

Hayes, J., K. Schriver, C. Hill, and J. Hatch. 1992. "Assessing the Message and the Messenger". *The Quarterly of the National Writing Project and the Center for the Study of Writing and Literacy 14*: 15–17.

Heath, S. B. 1983. *Ways with Words.* Cambridge: Cambridge University Press.

Hebborn, E. 1991. *Drawn to Trouble: The forging of an artist.* Edinburgh: Mainstream Publishing.

Herrington, A. J. 1985. "Writing in Academic Settings: A study of the contexts for writing in two college chemical engineering courses". *Research in the Teaching of English 19*: 331–359.

Hewlett, L. 1996. "How can you 'Discuss' Alone?: Academic literacy in a South African context". In Baker, Clay and Fox (eds.).

Hockey, J. 1987. "On Borrowed Time: Some mature students' experience of a university education". Unpublished manuscript: School of Independent Studies, Lancaster University.

Hodge, R. and G. Kress. 1988. *Social Semiotics.* Cambridge: Polity Press.

Hoey, M. 1983. *On the Surface of Discourse.* London: Allen and Unwin.

Hoey, M. 1986. "Overlapping Patterns of Discourse Organization and their Implications for Clause Relational Analysis in Problem-Solution Texts". In C. R. Cooper and S. Greenbaum (eds.). *Studying Writing: Linguistic approaches.* Beverly Hills, CA: Sage Publications.

Hoey, M. 1988. "Writing to Meet the Reader's Needs: Text patterning and reading strategies". *Trondheim Papers in Applied Linguistics 4*: 51–73.

Hogg, M. and C. McGarty. 1990. "Self-Categorization and Social Identity". In Abrams and Hogg (eds.).

Honess, T. and K. Yardley (eds.). 1987. *Self and Identity: Perspectives across the lifespan.* London: Routledge and Kegan Paul.

hooks, B. 1994. *Teaching to Transgress: Education as the practice of freedom.* New York: Routledge.

Hounsell, D. 1984a. "Learning and Essay-Writing". In F. Marton, D. Hounsell and N. Entwistle (eds.), *The Experience of Learning.* Edinburgh: Scottish Academic Press.

Hounsell, D. 1984b. "Essay Planning and Essay-Writing". *Higher Education Research and Development 3*: 13–31.

Hymes, D. 1974. *Foundations in Sociolinguistics: An ethnographic approach.* Philadelphia: University of Pennsylvania Press.

Ivanič, R. 1990. "Critical Language Awareness in Action". In R. Carter (ed.). *Knowledge about Language in the Curriculum: The LINC reader.* London: Hodder and Stoughton . (Originally published in *Language Issues 2*: 2–7, 1988.)

Ivanič, R. 1991. Nouns in Search of a Context. *I.R.A.L. XXIX* : 93–114.

Ivanič, R. 1994a. "Characterizations of Context for Describing Spoken and Written Discourse". In S. Čmejrková, F. Daneš and E. Havlová (eds.) *Writing vs. Speaking: Language, Text, Discourse, Communication.* Tübingen: Gunter Narr Verlag.

Ivanič, R. 1994b. "I is for Interpersonal: Discoursal construction of writer identities and the teaching of writing". *Linguistics and Education.* 6: 3–15.

Ivanič, R. 1995. "Writer Identity". *Prospect: The Australian Journal of TESOL* 10: 1–31.

Ivanič, R. and W. Moss. 1991. "Bringing Community Writing Practices into Education". In Barton and Ivanič (eds.).

Ivanič, R. and D. Roach. 1990. "Academic Writing, Power and Disguise". In Clark and others (eds.).

Ivanič, R. and Simpson, J. 1988. "Clearing away the Debris: Learning and researching academic writing". *Research and Practice in Adult Literacy Bulletin* 6: 6–7.

Ivanič, R. and J. Simpson. 1992. "Who's Who in Academic Writing?" In Fairclough (ed.) 1992d.

Ivanič, R., M. Aitchison and S. Weldon. 1996. "Bringing Ourselves into our Writing". *Research and Practice in Adult Literacy Bulletin* 28/29: 2–8.

Janks, H. and R. Ivanič. 1992. "Critical Language Awareness and Emancipatory Discourse". In Fairclough (ed.) 1992d.

Jolliffe, D. (ed.). 1988. *Writing in Academic Disciplines (= Advances in Writing Research 2)*. Norwood, N.J.: Ablex.

Karach, A. 1992. "The Politics of Dislocation: Some mature undergraduate women's experiences of higher education". *Women's Studies International Forum* 15: 309–317.

Karach, A. and D. Roach. 1994. "Collaborative Writing, Consciousness-Raising and Practical Feminist Ethics". In Hamilton, Barton and Ivanič (eds.).

Kaufer, D. and C. Geisler. 1989. "Novelty in Academic Writing". *Written Communication* 6: 286–311.

Kirsch, G. and D. H. Roen. 1990. *A Sense of Audience in Written Communication*. Newbury Park, CA.: Sage Publications.

Klassen, C. 1991. Bilingual Written Language Use by Low-Education Latin American Newcomers. In Barton and Ivanič (eds.)

Kreitler, S. and H. Kreitler. 1987. "The Psychosemantic Aspects of the Self". In Honess and Yardley (eds.)

Kress, G. 1989. *Linguistic Processes in Sociocultural Practice (Second edition)*. Oxford: Oxford University Press. (First edition: Victoria: Deakin University Press, 1985.)

Kress, G. 1994. *Learning To Write (Second edition)*. London: Routledge. (First edition: 1982.)

Kress, G. 1996. "Writing and Learning to Write". In D. Olson and N. Torrance (eds.), *The Handbook of Education and Human Development: New models of learning, teaching and schooling*. Cambridge, Mass: Blackwell.

Kress, G. and T. van Leeuwen. 1996. *Reading Images: The Grammar of Visual Design*. London: Routledge.

Kress, G. and T. Threadgold. 1988. "Towards a Social Theory of Genre". *Southern Review* 21: 215–243.

Kristeva, J. 1986. *The Kristeva Reader*. Edited by T. Moi. Oxford: Basil Blackwell.

Labov, W. 1963. "The Social Motivation of Sound Change". *Word* 19: 273–309.

Laclau, E. 1994. *The Making of Political Identities*. London: Verso.

Lamb, C. 1991. "Beyond Argument in Feminist Composition". *College Composition and Communication* 42: 11–24.

Latour, B. and S. Woolgar. 1986. *The Social Construction of Scientific Facts (Second edition)*. Princeton: Princeton University Press. (First edition: Beverly Hills and London: Sage, 1979.)

Lea, M. 1994. " 'I Thought I Could Write Until I Came Here': Student writing in Higher Education". In G. Gibbs (ed.), *Improving Student Learning: Theory and practice*. Oxford: Oxford Centre for Staff Development.

Lea, M. and B. Street. 1996a. "Academic Literacies". *Learning Matters* 3: 2–4. Brighton: University of Sussex Enterprise Unit.

Lea, M. and B. Street. 1996b. "Perspectives on Academic Literacies". *ExChanges* 2: 4–5. London: Centre for Higher Education Access and Development, University of North London.

Lea, M. and B. Street. 1997. "Tutor feedback on student writing: Report on an ESRC research project". Unpublished paper.

Levinson, S. 1983. *Pragmatics*. Cambridge: Cambridge University Press.

MacDonald, S. P. 1989. "Data-Driven and Conceptually Driven Academic Discourse". *Written Communication* 6: 411–435.

MacDonald, S. P. 1992. "A Method for Analyzing Sentence-Level Differences in Disciplinary Knowledge Making". *Written Communication* 9: 533–569.

MacDonald, S. P. 1994. *Professional Academic Writing in the Humanities and Social Sciences*. Carbondale and Edwardsville: Southern Illinois University Press.

Mace, J. 1992. *Talking about Literacy: Principles and practice of adult literacy education*. London: Routledge.

Mace, J. (ed.). 1995. *Literacy, Language and Community Publishing: Essays in adult education*. Clevedon: Multilingual matters.

Maimon, E.P., G.L. Belcher, G.W. Hearn, B.G. Nodine, and F.W. O'Connor. 1981. *Writing in the Arts and Sciences*. Boston: Little, Brown and Co.

Martin, J.R. 1989. *Factual Writing: Exploring and challenging social reality (Second edition)*. Oxford: Oxford University Press. (First edition: Victoria: Deakin University Press, 1985.)

Martin, L.H., H. Gutman and P. H. Hutton (eds.). 1988. *Technologies of the Self: A seminar with Michel Foucault*. London: Tavistock Publications.

Matsuhashi, A. 1982. "Explorations in the Real-Time Production of Written Discourse". In M. Nystrand (ed.), *What Writers Know: The language, process and structure of written discourse*. New York: Academic Press.

Milroy, L. 1980. *Language and Social Networks*. Oxford: Basil Blackwell.

358

Mitchell, S. 1994a. The Teaching and Learning of Argument in Sixth Forms and Higher Education: Final Report to the Leverhulme Trust. Hull: University of Hull.

Mitchell, S. 1994b. "A Level and Beyond: A case study". *English in Education* 28: 36–47.

Moss, W. 1987. *Breaking the Barriers.* London: Access to Learning for Adults (ALFA).

Murray, D. 1978. "Internal Revision: A process of discovery". In C. Cooper and L. Odell (eds.), *Research on Composing.* Urbana, Ill.: National Council of Teachers of English.

Myers, G. 1985. "The Social Construction of Two Biologists' Proposals". *Written Communication* 2: 219–245.

Myers, G. 1989. "The Pragmatics of Politeness in Scientific Articles". *Applied Linguistics* 10: 1–35.

Myers, G. 1990. *Writing Biology: Texts in the social construction of scientific knowledge.* Madison: University of Wisconsin Press.

Nash W. (ed.). 1990. *The Writing Scholar.* Newbury Park, CA.: Sage Publications.

Nelson, J. and J.R. Hayes. 1988. "How the Writing Context Shapes College Students' Strategies for Writing from Sources". *Centre for the Study of Writing Technical Report No 16.* Berkeley, C.A.: U.C.L.A.

Nystrand, M. 1982. "Rhetoric's 'Audience' and Linguistics' 'Speech Community': Implications for understanding writing, reading and text". In M. Nystrand (ed.), *What Writers Know: The language, process, and structure of written discourse.* London: Academic Press.

Nystrand, M. 1986. *The Structure of Written Communication: Studies in reciprocity between writers and readers.* Orlando and London: Academic Press.

Nystrand, M. 1989. "A Social-Interactive Model of Writing". *Written Communication* 6: 66–85.

Nystrand, M. 1990. "Sharing Words: The effects of readers on developing writers". *Written Communication 7.1.* (pp. 3–24)

Odell, L. and D. Goswami. 1985. *Writing in Non-Academic Settings.* New York: Methuen.

Olson, D. 1977. "From Utterance to Text: the bias of language in speech and writing". *Harvard Educational Review* 47: 257–281.

Ong, W. 1982. *Orality and Literacy: The technologising of the word.* London: Methuen.

Parker, I. 1989. "Discourse and Power". In Shotter and Gergen (eds.)

Pennycook, A. 1993. "Plagiarism: A research report". *Hongkong Papers in Linguistics and Language Teaching.* 16: 123–124.

Porter, J.E. 1986. "Intertextuality and the Discourse Community". *Rhetoric Review* 5: 34–47.

Progressive Literacy Group. 1986. *Writing on Our Side.* Vancouver, B.C.: Progressive Literacy Group.

Rabinow, P. and H.L. Dreyfus. 1983. "How We Behave: Interview with Michel Foucault". *Vanity Fair* (November 1983).

Recchio, T. 1991. "A Bakhtinian Reading of Student Writing". *College Composition and Communication* 42: 446–454.

Ritchie, J. 1989. "Beginning Writers: Diverse voices and individual identity". *College Composition and Communication* 40:152–187.

Roach, D. 1990. "Marathon". (Illustrated by Sarah Padmore.) *Research and Practice in Adult Literacy Bulletin* 11: 5–7.

Rorty, R. 1979. *Philosophy and the Mirror of Nature.* Princeton, N.J.: Princeton University Press.

Rose, M. 1988. "Narrowing the Mind and the Page: Remedial writers and cognitive reductionism". *College Composition and Communication* 39: 267–302.

Rose, M. 1989. *Lives on the Boundary.* New York: Penguin.

Rossan, S. 1987. "Identity and its Development in Adulthood". In Honess and Yardley (eds.).

Roth, R. G. 1987. "The Evolving Audience: Alternatives to audience accommodation". *College Composition and Communication* 38: 47–55.

Royster, J. Jones. 1996. "When the First Voice You Hear is Not Your Own". *College Composition and Communication* 47: 29–40.

Rutherford, J. (ed.). 1990. *Identity: Community, culture, difference.* London: Lawrence and Wishart.

Scollon, R. 1994. "As a Matter of Fact: The changing ideology of authorship and responsibility in discourse". *World Englishes* 13: 33–46.

Scollon, R. 1995. "Plagiarism and Ideology: Identity in intercultural discourse." *Language in Society* 24: 1–28.

Scribner, S. and M. Cole. 1981. *The Psychology of Literacy.* Cambridge: Harvard University Press.

Shatzman, L. and A. Strauss. 1973. *Field Research.* Englewood Cliffs, N.J. : Prentice-Hall.

Shaughnessy, M. 1977. *Errors and Expectations.* New York: Oxford University Press.

Shotter, J. and K.J. Gergen (eds.). 1989. *Texts of Identity*. Newbury Park, CA.: Sage.

Slugoski, B.R. and G.P. Ginsburg. 1989. "Ego Identity and Explanatory Speech". In Shotter and Gergen (eds.)

Stein, M. 1986. "Teaching Plagiarism". Paper presented at the Annual meeting of the Conference on College Composition and Communication, New Orleans, available from ERIC, ref: ED 298 482.

Sterling, G. 1991. "Plagiarism and the Worms of Accountability". *Reading Improvement* 28: 138–140.

Street, B. 1984. *Literacy in Theory and Practice*. Cambridge: Cambridge University Press.

Street, B. 1988. "Comparative Perspectives on Literacy Research". In Street, B. and McCaffery, J. (eds.) *Literacy Research in the U.K.: Adult and school perspectives*. Lancaster: Research and Practice in Adult Literacy Publications.

Street, B. 1993a. "The New Literacy Studies: Implications for education and pedagogy". *Changing English* 1: 113–126. (Keynote address at the *Domains of Literacy Conference*, University of London Institute of Education, September 1992).

Street, B. (ed.) 1993b. *Cross-Cultural Approaches to Literacy*. Cambridge: Cambridge University Press.

Street, B. 1993c. "Culture as a Verb: Anthropological aspects of language and cultural process". In D. Graddol, L. Thompson and M. Byram (eds.) *Language and Culture (= British Studies in Applied Linguistics 7)*. Clevedon: British Association for Applied Linguistics in association with Multilingual Matters.

Street, B. 1994. "Struggles over the Meaning(s) of Literacy". In Hamilton, Barton and Ivanič (eds.)

Street, B. 1995. *Social Literacies: Critical approaches to literacy in development, ethnography and education*. London: Longman.

Street, B. 1996. "Academic literacies". In Baker, Clay and Fox (eds.).

Swales, J. 1990. *Genre Analysis: English in research and academic settings*. Cambridge: Cambridge University Press.

Swales, J. 1993. "Genre and Engagement". *Revue Belge de Philologie et d'Histoire* 71: 687–698.

Tajfel, H. (ed.) 1982. *Social Identity and Intergroup Relations*. Cambridge: Cambridge University Press.

Tannen, D. 1985. "Relative Focus on Involvement in Spoken and Written Discourse". In D. Olson, N. Torrance and A. Hildyard (eds.), *Literacy, Language and Learning*. Cambridge: Cambridge University Press.

Thompson, G. and Ye Y. 1991. "Evaluation in the Reporting Verbs Used in Academic Papers". *Applied Linguistics* 12: 365–382.

Turner, John. 1985. "Social Categorization and Self-Concept: A Social-Cognitive Theory of Group Behaviour". In E. Lawler (ed.) *Advances in Group Processes: Studies in the social psychology of intergroup relations*. London: Academic Press.

Turner, John. 1991. *Social Influence*. Milton Keynes: Open University Press.

Turner, Joan. 1992. "Focusing on Values and the Value of Focus in Academic Writing". In D. Baker (ed.), *International Association of Teachers of English as a Foreign Language Annual Conference Report, 1992*. Whitstable: IATEFL Publications.

Turner, Joan. 1993a. "Falling into Place: Conceptual metaphor and western academic culture" *Journal of Intercultural Communication Studies,* III: 49–62.

Turner, Joan. 1993b. "Turns of Phrase and Cultural Understanding: Metaphor and language teaching". Paper given at *10th World Congress of Applied Linguistics*, Amsterdam, August 1993.

Turner, Joan. 1994. Conceptualising Academic Literacy: Beyond skills". In W. Scott and S. Mulhaus (eds.), *Languages for Specific Purposes*. London: CILT (Centre for Information on Language Teaching) in association with Kingston University School of Languages.

Turner, Joan and M. K. Hiragara. 1996. "Elaborating Elaboration in Academic Tutorials: Changing cultural assumptions". In H. Coleman and L. Cameron (eds.), *Change and Language (= British Studies in Applied Linguistics 10)*. Clevedon: British Association for Applied Linguistics in association with Multilingual Matters.

Ure, J. 1971. "Lexical Density and Register Differentiation". In G. Perren and J. Trim (eds.), *Applications of Linguistics: Selected papers of the Second International Congress of Applied Linguistics*. Cambridge, Cambridge University Press.

Vande Kopple, W. 1992. "Noun Phrases and the Style of Scientific Discourse". In S.P. Witte, N. Nakadate and R.D. Cherry (eds.), *A Rhetoric of Doing: Essays on written discourse in honor of James Kinneavy*. Carbondale, Il: Southern Illinois University Press.

Voloshinov, V. 1973. *Marxism and the Philosophy of Language.* Trans. by L. Matejka and I.R. Titunik. New York: Seminar Press.

Weldon, S. 1994. "From patchwork prose to personal style". Unpublished typescript, Lancaster University.

Wertsch, J. 1991. *Voices of the Mind.* Hemel Hempstead: Harvester Wheatsheaf.

Young, L. 1990. *Language as Behaviour, Language as Code: A study of academic English.* Amsterdam: John Benjamins.

Index

exclusiveness 27, 31, 71, 228–30,
241, 259, 269–71, 282, 304,
312, 344–5
exposition 136–7, 239, 304, 319
external examiner (effect of)
159–66, 245

F
face 7, 34, 60, 99, 103, 110, 115,
196, 213, 217, 230, 235, 247–8,
320, 339–44
face-to-face encounters 59–60
Fairclough 5, 10–1, 18, 16, 37,
40–51, 53–7, 61–4, 92, 97–8,
117–8, 196–7, 242, 284, 296,
339
feminist issues 126, 313–4
fine art 2–4
first person 134, 202, 226, 272,
301–2, 307–8
forgery 3–4
form and content 27, 39, 185, 204,
278, 317–8
formulaic 135, 140
Foucault 10, 13, 18
front 99, 142, 162, 247
functional grammar 31, 39–40, 44,
132, 169, 259, 284
future tense 30

G
Gee 50, 58–9, 67–73
general noun -s 266–7
generalization 58, 65, 81, 96, 110,
113, 145, 212, 262, 266, 271,
277–9, 282, 285, 291, 309,
328–30

genre 43–9, 54, 79–81, 114, 131–3,
138–42, 148, 182–5, 217, 256,
274, 283, 292, 296–7, 301–2,
308, 328, 333, 339
theory 45–6
theorists 79–81
Giroux 92
given information 138
Goffman 12, 19–25, 42, 55, 94–5,
98–104, 158, 215–9, 229, 247–8
Graeco-Latin (see Latin)
grammar 31, 37–40, 44, 72, 132–8,
148, 153, 169, 188, 259, 284,
331
grammatical subjects 135, 138
grapheme 62

H
habitus 24
Halliday 37–45, 55, 61, 64, 77,
118, 132–3, 151, 169, 216,
259–61, 264, 267, 274, 278,
284, 296, 320, 331
handwriting 100
head noun 136, 265–7, 284
heterogeneity 44–5, 131, 237, 261
historical context 15
human
actions 20, 100, 153, 263
actor 136, 155, 264
agents 54, 134–8
participants 135, 146, 153, 266
hybridity 10, 150, 135, 283

I
ideational meaning 40–1, 264
identities in a state of flux 237, 241

literacy (*continued*)
  history 115, 119, 125, 289
  studies 55, 109, 345
  (see also practices, literacy)
long word club 271

M
marginal comment 193, 219
Martha's Vineyard 38
mature students 4–9, 13–8, 67–8,
  106–7, 111, 126, 237, 327–8,
  333–5, 345
meaning-making 69, 86, 260
media 15–8, 44, 49–55, 58, 70, 82,
  99, 125, 145, 192, 201, 242,
  272, 299, 314–6, 328, 333, 338
mediated action 51–4
mediation 15–7, 39, 53–5, 99, 145,
  212, 242, 328, 333, 338, 345
mental
  activities 263
  processes 67, 211, 264–5, 295,
    300, 313, 322–3
metadiscoursal markers 303, 334
metaphorical language 30, 223
methodology 19, 24, 85, 115–8,
  129, 144–5, 166–9, 284, 339
modality 139, 259, 264, 269–70,
  273, 294, 299–303, 309, 323,
  331
modalization 118, 145
monolithic 13, 22, 68, 73, 79–80,
  92, 106, 256, 279–81, 329
mood 151, 259, 269, 276, 331
move structure 283
multiple identity 11, 68
multisyllabic 156, 188

N
narrative 15–6, 134–8, 145, 155,
  309
nominal group(s) 135, 162, 190,
  208, 259, 262, 265–9, 273
nominalization 11, 136, 153,
  162–3, 189, 211, 216, 259, 262,
  265–7, 270, 273, 292, 300, 323
non-finite clause(s) 148, 261
nouns 11, 30, 50, 134, 155, 188–9,
  202, 259, 262, 265–73, 278,
  288, 292, 309
novelty 89

O
object(s) of study 75, 253, 282–96,
  329
objectivity 232, 255–8, 268–70,
  307
objective view of knowledge 256,
  272, 306
obligation 139, 241, 276, 298
opposition 90–3, 304–6
order of discourse 93
outlining 133–4
ownership 4, 30, 34, 55, 79, 102,
  131, 141, 148, 156, 169, 188,
  193, 201, 215–6, 219, 222–3,
  227–9, 234–5, 242–5, 251, 317,
  328, 342

P
paraphrasing 89, 189
passive 188–90, 264, 294, 298, 307
Pecket Well College 70
pedagogic practice 115, 123

In the STUDIES IN WRITTEN LANGUAGE AND LITERACY the following titles have been published thus far:

1. VERHOEVEN, Ludo (ed.): *Functional Literacy: Theoretical issues and educational implications.* 1995
2. KAPITZKE, Cushla: *Literacy and Religion: The textual politics and practice of Seventh-day Adventism.* 1995.
3. TAYLOR, Insup, and M. Martin Taylor: *Writing and literacy in Chinese, Korean, and Japanese.* 1995.
4. PRINSLOO, Mastin and Mignonne BREIER (eds): *The Social Uses of Literacy. Theory and Practice in Contemporary South Africa.* 1996.
5. IVANIČ, Roz: *Writing and Identity. The discoursal construction of identity in academic writing.* 1998.
6. PONTECORVO, Clotilde (ed.): *Writing Development. An interdisciplinary view.* 1997.